Soviet Policy in East Asia

A COUNCIL ON FOREIGN RELATIONS BOOK

210
200
100
400
100
―――
1000

COUNCIL ON FOREIGN RELATIONS BOOKS

SOVIET POLICY IN EAST ASIA

Edited by Donald S. Zagoria

Yale University Press   New Haven and London

Designed by Nancy Ovedovitz and set in Linotron 202 type. Printed in the
United States of America by Vail-Ballou Press, Binghamton, N.Y.

Library of Congress Cataloging in Publication Data
Main entry under title:

Soviet policy in East Asia.
  "A Council on Foreign Relations book"—Half title.
  Includes index.
   1. East Asia—Foreign relations—Soviet Union.
2. Soviet Union—Foreign relations—East Asia.
I. Zagoria, Donald S.   II. Council on Foreign Relations.
DS518.7.S68   327.4705   82-50445
ISBN 0-300-02738-9   AACR2

10   9   8   7   6   5   4   3   2   1

To my son Adam and his generation; may they live in peace

Contents

Preface ix

Acknowledgments xiii

1: The Strategic Environment in East Asia 1
Donald S. Zagoria

2: Asia in the Soviet Conception 29
John J. Stephan

3: The Political Influence of the USSR in Asia 57
Robert A. Scalapino

4: The Sino–Soviet Conflict: The Soviet Dimension 93
Seweryn Bialer

5: The Northern Territories: 130 Years of Japanese
Talks with Czarist Russia and the Soviet Union 121
Fuji Kamiya

6: Soviet Policy in Southeast Asia 153
Donald S. Zagoria and Sheldon W. Simon

7: The Soviet Union and the Two Koreas 175
Ralph N. Clough

8: The Soviet Union's Economic Relations in Asia 201
Ed. A. Hewett and Herbert S. Levine

9: Prospects for Siberian Economic Development 229
Robert W. Campbell

10: Soviet Military Power in Asia 255
Paul F. Langer

11: Coalition Building or Condominium? The Soviet
Presence in Asia and American Policy Alternatives 283
Richard H. Solomon

Contributors 329

Index 333

Preface

Although it has become increasingly fashionable to speak of a multi-polar world, the relationship between the two superpowers, the Soviet Union and the United States, will remain at the center of international relations in the 1980s and probably well into the twenty-first century. Both superpowers, moreover, will be drawn increasingly into the Asian–Pacific region. The United States already conducts more of its trade with the Pacific than it does with all of Western Europe. And the region is of increasing strategic importance to the United States because of its alliance with Japan, its growing ties to noncommunist Southeast Asia or the Association of Southeast Asian Nations (ASEAN), its new links to China, and its growing concerns about the Indian Ocean. For the Soviet Union, East Asia is a priority second only to Europe. Three-fourths of the Soviet Union lies in Asia; one-third of Asia lies within the USSR; 80 million people, or approximately one-third of the Soviet population, live in Asiatic regions of the USSR; and 50 million Soviet citizens, about 20 percent of the population, are of Asian nationalities. The region is of mounting strategic importance to the Soviet Union because of Moscow's bitter conflict with China, the world's most populous country; Moscow's strained relations with Japan, the world's second largest industrial state; and Moscow's deteriorating relations with the United States, the other superpower.

This is why the Council on Foreign Relations asked me to put together a volume on Soviet policy in East Asia. This book is the result.

There are nine factors that will shape the future of Soviet–American relations in Asia. All of these are dealt with in one or more chapters of this volume.

Perhaps the most important element in shaping future Soviet–American relations in Asia will be the overall nature of Soviet–American relations during the coming decade. Are the two superpowers now entering into a new cold war? Or will they, after a sharp deterioration in relations following the Soviet invasion of Afghanistan, find enough common ground to resume a modified détente? Part of the answer to this question will emerge from the new round of theater nuclear arms control discussions that have recently begun in Geneva. Another part will emerge from the new strategic arms negotiations between the two superpowers projected to begin in 1982. Will these nuclear arms talks lead to some real reductions in nuclear forces on both sides or will they become bogged down and break up in mutual frustration? What will be the outcome of the continuing crisis in Poland? These are the kinds of questions that could not be answered with any certainty as this book went to press early in 1982. But there can be no doubt that the future of Soviet–American relations in Asia will be shaped to a crucial extent by the overall direction of Soviet–American relations. Some of the issues relating to that global competition are discussed in my introductory chapter and in the chapters by Robert Scalapino (3), Seweryn Bialer (4), and Richard Solomon (11).

A second element of importance in shaping Soviet–American relations in Asia is the Soviet–American–Chinese triangle. Will China continue on its present course of seeking an anti-Soviet united front with the United States, Japan, and NATO? Or will the Chinese eventually decide that their national interests are better served by some accommodation with Moscow and a more evenhanded balancing act between the two superpowers? This issue is discussed in several chapters, but it is the central focus of the chapter by Seweryn Bialer.

Third, there is the growing role of Japan in the Soviet–American–Japanese triangle. Will Japan continue on its present course of alliance with the United States and its tilt toward China? Or will Japan eventually seek to pursue a more independent and more evenhanded policy involving some accommodation with Moscow at the expense of its relations with the United States? Defense issues and chronic trade problems have raised storm clouds over the Japanese–American relationship. Will these clouds darken or is the Japanese–American alliance made of firmer stuff? The Soviet relationship with Japan is the subject of the chapter by Fuji Kamiya (5), but several other chapters in this volume also touch on it.

The military balance of power between the two superpowers in Asia will also shape the future of Soviet–American relations in the region. Now that the Soviet Union has achieved strategic nuclear parity with the United States, regional military balances will become increasingly important in the risk calculations of both great powers. This issue is analyzed by Paul Langer (chap. 10); it is also dealt with by Richard Solomon.

The bitter conflict between Vietnam and China is yet another critical factor in the Far Eastern power equation. The dynamics of this equation, and its relationship to the two superpowers, are explored in the chapter by Donald Zagoria and Sheldon Simon (6).

Another regional conflict with the capacity to involve the major powers is that between the two halves of still-divided Korea. These complex issues are analyzed in the chapter by Ralph Clough (7).

Not the least important element in Soviet policy in Asia is the Soviet perception of Asia and Asians. Russian experience in Asia during the past several hundred years has been one of almost permanent war, invasion, or conquest. Russia occupies the heartland of Eurasia. As George Vernadsky has pointed out, this means that it has been placed by nature between East and West, constantly subject to pressure from both sides and itself capable of exerting pressure in either direction or both. The long and bloody Russian historical experience in Asia has left a deep imprint on Russian national psychology. This and other aspects of the Russian view of Asia are analyzed by John Stephan (chap. 2).

So far, with the exception of a few selected countries such as Vietnam and North Korea, the Soviets do not have a very large economic presence in the region. The prospects for Soviet trade with East Asia are analyzed by Ed. Hewett and Herbert Levine (chap. 8).

There is also the intriguing question of how fast the Russians will seek to develop Siberia and the Soviet Far East and what impact this might have on future Soviet policy in the region. Robert Campbell discusses the economic aspects of Siberian development (chap. 9).

Finally, Soviet worldwide expansion, the Soviet military buildup in Asia, and the evident Soviet dissatisfaction with the present balance of power in the region virtually guarantee that the Russians will not rest content with the existing status quo in East Asia. This challenge poses a number of complex issues for American policymakers. Richard Solomon's concluding chapter presents the most comprehensive discussion of these policy issues, but they are discussed in several other chapters as well.

Naturally the authors in this volume are not always in agreement on these complicated questions. But we are hopeful that, by identifying the key policy questions and addressing them in a variety of ways, this volume may be of use to government officials as well as to academics, journalists, and others interested in this increasingly important region of the world.

Acknowledgments

This volume is a collective endeavor, and I want to express my appreciation to those who made it possible. First, it could not have been produced without the assistance of the Council on Foreign Relations, whose president, Winston Lord, took an active interest in the project from the very start. Robert Legvold, director of the Council's Soviet project, provided enormous substantive and organizational help. Andrea Zwiebel contributed invaluable technical assistance in the preparation of the manuscript. My wife, Janet D. Zagoria, edited and rewrote portions of several of the chapters.

I wish, too, to thank each of the authors. In the course of writing these chapters, we met twice to review and to critique each other's work. As a result of these sessions and the written comments that flowed from them, we all enriched our own perspectives and substantially revised our original chapters. There was a spirit of good-natured collegiality throughout this process. I also want to thank Allen S. Whiting and Stephen S. Kaplan for their contributions to the study group that led to this volume.

The Rockefeller Foundation provided the principal financial support for the volume, for which we are most grateful.

Finally, I want to express my gratitude to the staff of the Yale University Press, and in particular to Marian Ash, for their patient support and encouragement.

1

The Strategic Environment in East Asia

DONALD S. ZAGORIA

As the 1980s began, a new cold war between the Soviet Union and the West, supported by China, was looming on the horizon. Although the Western powers disagreed on how to meet the Soviet challenge, there was a growing consensus on the global nature of that challenge.

• The Soviet Union is a power with global ambitions. Soviet Foreign Minister Andrei Gromyko has stated that no problem in the world can be resolved without Soviet participation, a statement indicating that Moscow has a rather broad conception of its own security concerns. Soviet military power has grown substantially in the past fifteen years and the Soviet Union is now perceived by many nations to be at least the equal of the United States and perhaps stronger in certain categories of military power. The Soviets have signed friendship treaties with a dozen or so countries in Asia, Africa, and the Middle East, all of which imply a considerable degree of commitment to the security of those far-flung countries.

• Soviet ambitions are still on the rise. In many regions of the world, including the Asian–Pacific region, the Soviets believe that the existing balance of power is unfavorable to them, and they are determined to increase their own influence and power there.

• During the past decade the Soviets have increasingly resorted to armed force in order to spread their power and influence. Since 1975, seven pro-Soviet communist parties have seized power or territory in Africa and Asia with armed force. (The countries are South Vietnam, Laos, Angola, Ethiopia, Afghanistan, South Yemen, and Cambodia.) Although the events leading up to communist victories in each of these cases were complex, involved a variety of indigenous forces, and certainly cannot be attributed only to Soviet manipulation, the Russians were active players in each instance. They were not simply bystanders. Moreover, when indigenous anticommunist forces threatened communist rule in Afghanistan in 1979, the Soviets invaded that country in order to crush the rebellion. Finally, after threatening to invade Poland in order to crush a popular, grass-roots workers' movement that was challenging the dominant role in Poland of the Polish communist party, the Soviets in late 1981 encouraged the Polish military and security forces to undertake a brutal repression, a course of action that led to American economic sanctions against the Russians. It was this disturbing pattern of Soviet behavior that contributed to the breakdown of détente and to the emergence of a loose coalition among the United States, Western Europe, Japan, and China, a coalition that has as its major goal the containment of further Soviet expansion by military means.

• The Soviet Union has an imbalance of foreign policy resources. The attractiveness of its ideology to other parties and states is receding as the structural weaknesses of communist systems become increasingly apparent. Because the Soviet Union has only limited trade with a few select countries, its economic influence in the world economy is small. Culturally, too, the Soviets are handicapped. In Europe the Russians are regarded as semi-Asiatics; in Asia they are regarded as European interlopers. Thus, the most important card that the Soviets possess for expanding their power is the military card—the shipment of weapons, advisers, and even Cuban combat troops to intervene in local conflicts.

• Although determined to expand their power throughout the world, the Soviets continue, at least under the Brezhnev regime, to be low-risk, cautious expansionists. They are not "high rollers" comparable to Hitler's Germany. Their preferred pattern of expansion is to exploit internal instability in the Third World—civil wars, regional conflicts, and so forth—rather than to intervene directly with their own military forces. By inserting themselves into local conflicts, often with heavy shipments of arms supplies, advisers, and offers of "friendship treaties," the Soviets have succeeded in establishing considerable influence in many of the troubled regions of the Third World.

In sum, the Soviets intend to try to convert their growing military power into greater political influence throughout the world. As one of two superpowers, the Soviet Union has a sense of "entitlement" to a greater role in world affairs, and it is determined to bring that power to bear in all the regions of the world. Moreover, as long as the Third World remains unstable, the Soviets will be able to exploit a variety of opportunities that arise there to change existing regional balances of power in their favor.

In the Asian–Pacific region the Soviets have a variety of incentives for wanting to increase their power and influence. First, the United States, Moscow's principal adversary, has a powerful coalition of allies and friends in East Asia, a coalition stretching from Japan to Australia. The Soviets seek to counter that American alliance system and to develop a countercoalition of states friendly to themselves. Second, Moscow seeks to isolate and to encircle China in an effort to keep China weak. Should China become a great power, the Soviets know that, in the long run, it will almost certainly become Moscow's most dangerous adversary. The Soviets do not fear China by itself, at least not in the near future. What they fear is an industrialized China, armed by the West and increasingly tied to the West. Third, particularly now that Japan has overtaken the Soviet Union economically as the second largest industrial power in the world, the Soviets are determined to discourage Japan from becoming a strong military power, and they are anxious to cut Japanese–American military ties as well as to obstruct the further growth of Japanese–Chinese relations. In Southeast Asia the Soviets are out to consolidate their ties to the new group of Indochinese communist states (Vietnam, Laos, and Cambodia), to weaken American and Chinese influence among the Association of Southeast Asian Nations (ASEAN) countries, and to prevent ASEAN from joining an anti-Soviet Pacific coalition.

Finally, the Soviets are intent upon increasing their naval and maritime power in the key waterways of East and West Asia: the Western Pacific, the South China Sea, and the Indian Ocean. They have been steadily increasing the size of their Pacific Fleet for many years and now that that fleet has regular access to Vietnamese ports, Moscow's ability to project its naval power throughout Asian waters will be greatly enhanced.

The Soviets not only have powerful incentives for expanding their power in Asia; regional conflicts often provide them with opportunities to insert themselves into a position of influence. By supporting India against Pakistan and Vietnam against China, the Soviets expanded their influence in both South and Southeast Asia. By supporting Ethiopia against Somalia, and South Yemen against North Yemen, the Soviets strengthened their position in the Indian Ocean. By supporting Syria and other "rejectionist" Arab states against Israel, the Soviets have established a strong position in the Middle East.

Thus, the Soviet Union has both strong incentives and frequent opportunities for expanding its power in the Third World and it now has a great variety of military means at its disposal to help accomplish that goal. One of the main questions I wish to address in this chapter is: What are the prospects for further Soviet expansion in Asia, particularly in the Asian–Pacific region?

THE NEW EQUILIBRIUM IN EAST ASIA

As the world enters the 1980s, and only five years after the fall of Saigon, East Asia is distinguished from many other developing regions of the world by a relatively stable, pro-Western balance of power. Most of the region, with the exception of Vietnam, Laos, and Cambodia, is tied into a Western alliance system in one way or another. Japan is a firm and an increasingly cooperative U.S. ally. The Japanese have increased their financial support for the maintenance of U.S. troops in Japan, participated for the first time in joint naval exercises with the American and Australian fleets, and begun to engage in joint planning with American military forces. The U.S.–Japan Mutual Security Treaty, which in earlier years was a subject of considerable acrimony in Japan, is now more broadly accepted by Japanese public opinion than at any time in the past three decades. China has entered into a new strategic and economic rapprochement with the United States and become a quasi-ally of the West—primarily out of fear of Soviet expansion.

American relations with its South Korean ally, shaken by the Carter administration's misguided decision to withdraw American combat troops from South Korea, have been restored by the Reagan administration. Taiwan has weathered the withdrawal of American recognition and is domestically more stable and militarily safer than at any time before the U.S. recognition of China.

In Southeast Asia the Philippines provides the United States with key air and naval bases; Thailand is tied to the United States by the Manila Pact; both Malaysia and Singapore are members of a five power pact, which includes Great Britain, New Zealand, and Australia. All the ASEAN countries, including Indonesia, rely on the United States or other Western countries for their arms supplies. Finally, Australia and New Zealand are tied to the United States by the ANZUS Pact.

Ideologically, too, pro-Soviet, Marxist forces in East Asia are increasingly on the defensive. The strength of indigenous communist and Marxist forces in East Asia is considerably less today than at any time since the end of World War II. The Japanese Socialist party has suffered a substantial decline in popular votes throughout most of the 1970s. Following the death of Mao Zedong, the new Chinese leaders have adopted a bold new pragmatic course of economic development that includes many "capitalist" devices for stimulating production and they themselves have called into question the viability of the Soviet model of development. In Indonesia, Thailand, and Malaysia, where a decade or two ago communist parties were serious contenders for power, they are no longer so.

This relatively stable, pro-Western strategic environment in East Asia explains why the Soviet Union, despite its considerable buildup of naval and air power in the Pacific, has not yet been able to translate its military power into political influence in East Asia as it has done in more unstable regions of the world. And it explains too why the United States is more satisfied with the situation in East Asia than in many other regions of the world.

I want to ask two important questions: What factors are at the root of this pro-Western, strategic setting? And what are the prospects for a Soviet "comeback" in Asia?

The main ingredients of the favorable strategic setting in East Asia are: (1) the new cold war between the communist states; (2) China's dramatic turn to the West; (3) the gradual reassertion of Japan; (4) the end of the period of American drift; (5) the development of ASEAN; (6) the Korean standoff; and (7) the dynamic economic growth in the region that could lead to a new Asian–Pacific trading community.

The New Cold War between Communist States

In Asia today, with the sole exception of the Korean peninsula, which still remains divided along East–West lines, the most serious and bitterest confrontations are those between contiguous communist states: Russia against China, China against Vietnam, and Vietnam against communist insurgents supported by China in Cambodia. All the Asian communist states (and I include Russia, three-fourths of whose territory lies in Asia) are finding that their most active and dangerous adversaries are not faraway Western powers but neighboring communist states with whom they share disputed and heavily armed borders and a historical record of conflict going back several centuries—a record undiminished by a supposedly common ideology. Thus, in Asia geography has proved to be a more constant element in international relations than ideology.

Moreover, these East–East conflicts are not mere transient elements in the international relations of East Asia. They are likely to last throughout the 1980s and even further into the future. They have deep historical roots. Indeed, viewed in historical perspective rather than through the prism of the cold war, what is happening now can be explained more easily. Asia is entering a postcolonial period in which historic power rivalries that were temporarily diminished by the common struggle against colonialism are being revived. In the colonial period indigenous communism, nationalism, and Soviet imperialism were often allied for the specific purpose of ejecting the West from Asia. But the end of Western colonialism and the retreat of American power from Asia following the U.S. defeat in Vietnam have demonstrated that this anticolonial alliance was ephemeral. Russia and China, brought together initially by a common threat from the United States as well as by ideology, have returned to a historical geopolitical rivalry that began in the seventeenth century when czarist Russia began its eastward expansion at the expense of the Manchu empire. And both Vietnam and China, and Vietnam and Cambodia, have resumed ethnic and geopolitical rivalries that go back nine or ten centuries, long before the arrival of the West.

Paradoxically, communist ideology will feed these national rivalries because, for all its internationalist pretensions, communism has turned out to be one of the most nationalistic of all modern ideologies. Indeed, red nationalism is even more intense, more xenophobic than the common garden varieties of nationalism found everywhere.

The combination of East–West and East–East conflicts in Asia means that all three communist states are now encircled by a combination of old and new adversaries. Russia is surrounded by NATO on the west and China, Japan, and the United States on the east. China is surrounded by Russia on the north and Russia's new ally, Vietnam, on the south. Vietnam is surrounded by China on the north and ASEAN, supported by the United States and Japan, on the east and west. This is a strategic nightmare that all three communist states want to dissolve.

For the noncommunist states of the region, however, this new situation provides an enormous strategic benefit. None of the communist states will be able to apply excessive pressure on any of the noncommunist states and they may even be forced into accommodation with them. Both Russia and China, for example, are wooing ASEAN. Moreover, to the extent that the communist states of Asia fear one another more than they fear the West, each of them will prefer a Western presence in key strategic areas of Asia to the presence of a communist adversary. China, for example, has already asserted its interest in a continuing U.S.– Japanese alliance. Both Russia and China would also undoubtedly prefer the continuation of the American presence in South Korea to the presence of each other. Furthermore, both Russia and China will now be ambivalent about the advance of communism in Asia. The victory of indigenous communist parties in Thailand, Malaysia, or the Philippines is no longer clearly in the Soviet or the Chinese interest. It now depends on which side of the Sino–Soviet conflict that indigenous communist movement is likely to position itself. Both Moscow and Beijing, for example, would almost certainly prefer a conservative, but friendly, government in Thailand to a hostile communist government.

Provided these internecine communist conflicts can be contained and do not erupt into a wider conflagration, the new East–East conflict should thus contribute to a new balance of power in East Asia that is more favorable to the West, and stabler, than anyone could have imagined in the mid-1970s.

China's Turn to the West

The second recent trend in Asia that contributes to the new equilibrium of power in that region is the stunning transformation in Chinese domestic and foreign policy since the death of Mao Zedong. Since 1976 there has been a series of Chinese actions that, taken together, constitute a revolution in the global strategic chessboard. Let me briefly list them:

• China has established full diplomatic relations with the United States and called upon the United States to play a much stronger and more active role in containing Soviet power and influence.

• China has signed a peace treaty with Japan and urged the Japanese to strengthen their security ties with the United States.

• China has announced its support for NATO and has increased its contacts with that Western defense alliance.

• China has given its support to ASEAN against Vietnam and has taken military action against Vietnam, a country that it accuses of having become a Soviet puppet.

• Chinese leaders have visited Romania and Yugoslavia in an effort to support those countries' independence from Moscow.

• China has stepped up its efforts in the Third World to encourage resistance to Soviet expansion. During the Shaba crisis of 1978, for example, the Chinese foreign minister flew to Kinshasa to demonstrate Chinese support for General Mobutu's government against the Cuban-trained invaders from Angola.

• Perhaps most significantly of all, China has formulated plans for a vast program of modernization that will involve a huge influx of Western technology, credit, and trade. China has also joined the International Monetary Fund (IMF) and the World Bank. Thus, China's economy is increasingly linked to the West.

In sum, because of its overriding interests in containing Soviet power and building a modern economy, China has discovered many parallel interests with the West. Although a limited accommodation between China and the Soviet Union cannot be ruled out sometime in the 1980s, it is difficult to imagine any fundamental change in the situation—one that would remove the worst fears of each side about the other—and there are formidable obstacles to even a limited détente.

The strategic implications of this Sino–Western partnership would be difficult to exaggerate. China, along with the United States and Japan, now represents a massive barrier to the further expansion of Soviet and Vietnamese influence in East Asia.

The Cautious Reassertion of Japan

In recent years the outside world has voiced two apparently contradictory fears about the future role of Japan in international relations. On the one hand the Russians and some Asians warn that Japan is bound to attempt to convert its newly acquired great economic strength into military power and that this will destabilize Asia. On the other hand there are repeated charges in the United States and within Japan itself that Japan has no foreign or defense policy and that Japan continues to behave according to an outmoded notion of pacifism born out of the traumas associated with Nagasaki and Hiroshima.

I do not believe that either the image of Japanese remilitarization or the image of Japanese passivity is accurate. On the contrary, the preponderance of evidence suggests that Japan is cautiously moving to find a role for itself in the world. There is a new defense dialogue going on within Japan and an increasing willingness on the part of the Japanese press and of high-ranking Japanese bureaucrats and politicians to discuss Japanese security problems. Although Japan's defense budget is still relatively low in terms of GNP ratios, it is, in absolute terms, the eighth largest defense budget in the world, and by the late 1980s Japan could have the fourth or fifth largest defense budget in the world.

The Japanese are also moving into more active security cooperation with the United States. There is declining opposition among all the Japanese political parties to the U.S.–Japan Mutual Security Treaty, and a joint U.S.–Japan Consultative Committee has for the first time laid down guidelines for defense cooperation and joint planning. The Japanese have also for the first time allocated several hundred million dollars to help defray the cost of American troops stationed in Japan. More recently, the Japanese have for the first time participated in joint naval exercises with the American and Australian fleets.

At the same time, the Japanese have, against vehement Soviet opposition, signed a peace treaty with China, greatly increased their economic and political contacts with the Chinese, and taken a strong line against the continued Soviet occupation and militarization of the four Kurile islands that have been in dispute between the two countries since the end of World War II. After the Soviet invasion of Afghanistan and the Vietnamese invasion of Cambodia, the Japanese imposed rather stiff sanctions on both the Russians and the Vietnamese.

In Southeast Asia the Japanese have greatly expanded their economic and political ties to ASEAN. Japan is now the first or second largest investor and trade partner of each noncommunist country in the region. Japan has established regular ministerial contacts with the ASEAN governments and it has greatly expanded cultural exchange programs in the entire region.

Although Japanese–South Korean relations have had some bumpy periods during the past decade and despite the fact that the Koreans have an ambivalent feeling about their former colonial masters, the long-term trend on the Korean peninsula is toward a substantial improvement in relations between the two countries.

Finally, the Japanese are also beginning to play a key role in economic diplomacy. They have greatly expanded their economic assistance to Pakistan, Thailand, and Turkey, three countries of vital importance to the West.

In sum, the trend is neither toward mindless militarism nor toward an abnegation of Japanese responsibility. Japan is treading an extremely cautious but purposeful path in the world arena and, in the decade ahead, it is likely to begin to define a more comprehensive role for itself in Asia. Fears about Japanese militarism are misplaced. But a somewhat more assertive Japan is likely to be an additional force for stability in Asia for a variety of reasons.

First, Japanese defense expenditures and security arrangements are oriented now and for the foreseeable future to the defense of the home islands. It is extremely unlikely that the Japanese will develop an offensive military capability, including nuclear weapons, unless there is a radical shift in the existing Asian balance of power.

Second, although Japan's security will continue to be served by an alliance with the United States, its interests will not be served by gratuitously provoking the Soviet Union. Over the longer run Japan may even have an increased interest in helping Russia to develop Siberia in an effort to gain access to Siberian energy resources. By balancing its trade and investment between China and Russia and by using economic leverage, Japan could hope to extract the maximum political, strategic, and economic benefit.

Finally, Japan's interests as a great but vulnerable economic power (highly dependent on importing energy and raw materials) require it to wield its influence in strengthening the existing economic and political system in the region rather than undermining it. Only if the present international system proves hostile to Japan's economic interests, or if the Japanese feel themselves much more threatened than they do at present, will Japan become an anti-status quo power.

The End of American Drift

Following the U.S. defeat in Vietnam and the Carter administration's proposals to withdraw American combat troops from South Korea, American credibility in East Asia fell to a new low. Throughout the region Asian leaders began to question the reliability of their American friends and allies and to search for new ways to safeguard their security.

Although these fears have not yet been completely allayed, the period of U.S. drift in East Asia now appears to be coming to an end. After the Reagan administration took power, a new American buildup in the Indian Ocean got under way, there were plans for expansion of the hard-pressed American navy, and the new administration canceled the U.S.

withdrawal from South Korea. At the same time, the new administration stepped up military and economic assistance to key Asian allies such as Thailand and Pakistan.

The Success of Asean

Another important factor in the stability of East Asia is the extraordinary development of ASEAN, the first successful regional organization in the history of Southeast Asia. The five ASEAN countries—Indonesia, the Philippines, Singapore, Malaysia, and Thailand—have adopted a common front against the Vietnamese invasion of Cambodia and they have played a major role in the United Nations and other world forums in keeping this issue at the forefront of world attention. As a result of common concern over communist subversion in the region the ASEAN countries have also taken cooperative steps to counter such threats. The five have also adopted a common front in such international agencies as UNCTAD and GATT, they have developed joint strategies to deal with the industrial countries, and they have taken cooperative steps to defuse territorial disputes and to discourage the growth of secessionist movements within their borders.

At a Bali summit in 1976 the heads of state of the five countries signed the ASEAN Concord and the Treaty of Amity and Cooperation. The treaty is the first binding agreement among Southeast Asian countries. It covers current problems and anticipates future contingencies. The member nations agreed to set up the machinery for settling disputes.

Since the Bali summit the five ASEAN countries have held annual foreign ministers' meetings and there have been frequent bilateral exchanges of visits between heads of state. In the military-security area, although ASEAN refrains from calling itself a military alliance, there is growing arms standardization and frequent bilateral and trilateral security cooperation. Underlying ASEAN's concern for regional unity is the realization that regional tensions facilitate exploitation by external powers. Since the fall of Saigon the ASEAN countries are increasingly aware that they must sink or swim collectively and that if they want to keep predatory external powers out, they must achieve some degree of regional cooperation.

The Korean Standoff

Although the heavily armed border between North and South Korea remains one of the potential flash points in Asia, there are substantial reasons to believe that the precarious peace on the Korean peninsula that has lasted since 1953 will remain.

Perhaps the principal key to peace on the Korean peninsula remains

the presence of American forces in South Korea and the continuation of
the American commitment to defend South Korea against any attack
from Pyongyang. As long as this commitment remains firm and credible,
neither Pyongyang nor Moscow is likely to want to risk stirring the pot in
Korea.

Under present circumstances both Moscow and Beijing have compelling reasons to avoid a new Korean war. The Russians, for their part,
could not afford to let North Korea win or lose such a war. A North
Korean loss in a new Korean war would have profound political and
psychological consequences on the Soviet Union's other allies and treaty
partners. But there could be no North Korean victory over South Korea
without Moscow's running the risk of a Soviet–American military confrontation. Moreover, even if North Korea could somehow come to
dominate South Korea, a unified communist Korea might eventually
gravitate toward China and severely complicate security problems on
Moscow's southern flank. At the very least, if Korea were to be unified
by the North, Soviet leverage on North Korea would be greatly reduced.
Thus, there are no compelling reasons for Moscow to support North
Korean efforts to unify all of Korea, much less to risk a war in the
process.

The Chinese have equally compelling reasons to avoid a new Korean
war. As long as Beijing is preoccupied with the threat from Russia and
Vietnam it has no desire to involve itself in a war with the United States
in Korea. On the contrary, Beijing's interests are best served by a gradual rapprochement between North and South Korea and between North
Korea and the West.

Economic Dynamism

Yet another element that contributes to a new equilibrium in East Asia is
the extraordinary rate of economic growth in the region. To be sure,
rapid economic growth can have destabilizing consequences—as recent
events in Iran demonstrate—and, at the very least, this growth will pose
new problems to all the countries of the region. Still, properly managed
and distributed in a reasonably equitable manner, rapid economic growth
also contributes to stability.

The noncommunist East Asian countries are the fastest growing countries in the world and they are likely to remain so during the 1980s.
Japan is by all odds the most successful of the industrial democracies. It
has overcome two oil crises, dealt with stagflation, increased labor productivity, and resumed a 5–6 percent annual rate of growth. By the late
1970s Japan overtook the Soviet Union as the world's second largest
industrial power and, sometime in the mid-1980s, it is likely to overtake

the United States in per capita income. South Korea, Singapore, Taiwan, and Hong Kong, the so-called Gang of Four, have averaged close to 10 percent increases in GNP during the past fifteen years and the ASEAN countries have not been far behind. All the developing East Asian countries are well on the road toward industrialization and much higher living standards. One recent visitor to the region, an economist, concluded that most of the region will attain present Japanese and European living standards by the end of the lifetimes of most Asians being born today. This means that by the year 2000, the biggest upsurge in production and living standards that the world has yet seen will take place in this region.

Another recent visitor to Southeast Asia, Henry Kamm of the *New York Times,* a journalist who has spent most of the last twelve years in the region, concludes that there is a "continuing rise, however uneven in many aspects, of the standard of living and the state of peace in the countries of the region that reject Communism, while the three Communist countries are mired in war, social upheaval and economic stagnation or decline." Kamm notes that rising economic prosperity for the noncommunist countries of the region has trickled down. "There is ample proof that the floor has risen for the many while the ceiling has gone higher for the few."

One of the most important consequences of this rapid growth is that the countries in the region are beginning to develop a sense of regional community and shared interest. Already the United States trades more with the Pacific than with any other part of the world including Western Europe, and U.S. trade with ASEAN is growing faster than U.S. trade with most other parts of the world. Trade ties are also growing between Canada and the Pacific, between Australia and ASEAN, between South Korea and ASEAN, and so on. As China industrializes, it too is bound to increase its trade with other Pacific countries. Already in the past few years Chinese trade with both the United States and Japan has increased by substantial amounts. It is this development that lurks behind much of the recent talk about the need for a Pacific Community. Precisely what form such a community is likely to take in the decade ahead remains unclear. But there is little doubt that such an organization is likely to emerge sometime in the 1980s.

If all the above factors are taken into account, it seems possible to conclude that, to a far greater degree than in other Third World areas, the Soviets are faced in the Asian–Pacific region with countervailing military power, regional cohesion, and socioeconomic resilience of a kind that thwarts their ambitions. The combination of these various obstacles to Soviet advance suggests that the Soviet approach in East Asia during the 1980s is more likely to be a holding policy than an ambitious

and adventurous effort to spread Soviet power. The main Soviet in-
terests in the region are likely to remain essentially conservative ones.
Moscow's principal goal will be to prevent the emergence of an anti-
Soviet coalition in the region.

THE POSSIBILITIES FOR A SOVIET COMEBACK
IN ASIA IN THE 1980S

The 1970s have generally seen a serious failure of Soviet policy in East
Asia. The major exception to this failure has been Vietnam, where the
Soviets have now gained access to important air and naval facilities from
which they can project their growing military power into the Pacific and
Indian oceans. However, the two main Soviet efforts, of containing
China and keeping it weak, and of weakening the American alliance
system in East Asia, have both failed. China has moved into alignment
with the United States and Japan and is at the beginning of a modernization program that, by the year 2000, could significantly increase China's
power and ability to oppose the Soviets. America's relations with East
Asia have not been better in the twentieth century. For the first time, the
United States does not need to choose between China and Japan. It is on
friendly terms with both major powers. By contrast, Moscow's relations
with the countries of East Asia are almost universally poor.

There are two basic reasons for this Soviet political failure in East Asia.
First, the Soviet military buildup and expansion by military means have
brought about a loose anti-Soviet coalition of virtually all the noncommunist countries in East Asia plus China. In short, the same considerations that led to the breakdown of détente with the United States have
also led to the deterioration of Soviet relations with the countries of East
Asia. Second, the conditions in East Asia itself, conditions I have just
described, mean that there are fewer opportunities for the Soviets to
exploit in East Asia than there are in many other more unstable regions
of the world.

Moscow's failure in East Asia in the 1970s, however, raises the question of whether there are possibilities for a Soviet comeback in the region
during the 1980s. There are five possible scenarios for such a comeback:
(1) instability in the region; (2) further shifts in the military balance in
Moscow's favor; (3) the unraveling of U.S. relations with China, Japan,
or ASEAN; (4) a Soviet breakthrough with Japan; and (5) a successful
Soviet reconciliation with China. I will discuss each of these in turn.

Instability in East Asia

The Soviet Union is a relentlessly opportunistic power. It seeks to expand its influence with minimal risks by exploiting opportunities that

arise in unstable areas. Any number of such opportunities might arise in East Asia in the 1980s. In this respect, China and the Philippines are two of the big question marks.

In recent years China has embarked on a vast new program of rapid modernization at home while adopting a vehement anti-Soviet line in its foreign policy. To promote these two goals of rapid modernization and deterrence of Soviet expansion, China has moved into an entente with the United States and Japan. Both for economic and strategic reasons, then, China should have a continuing interest in a close relationship with the West.

There are, however, a number of uncertainties in the Chinese domestic scene that make it difficult to predict future Chinese policy with any degree of confidence. In the first months of 1981 the new Chinese leadership coalition led by Deng Xiaoping was challenged on a number of significant issues by other groups within the Chinese leadership. The trial of the Gang of Four, the issue of demaofication, and the pace of economic reform all seemed to involve considerable strife among Chinese leaders. On foreign policy a very sharp Chinese reaction to the Reagan administration's initial views on upgrading relations with Taiwan suggested that some hardliners within the Chinese leadership were not satisfied with the terms that Deng extracted from the Americans on that issue. And, from time to time, there were articles in the Chinese media indicating that some groups within the Chinese leadership advocated improving relations with the Soviet Union in order to balance more effectively between Washington and Moscow rather than tilting so one-sidedly to the United States, as Deng advocated.

Thus, a critical and an inherently unpredictable variable in China is the question of Deng's longevity. The early demise of the 76-year-old leader could lead to a new and bitter struggle for power within the top ranks of the party and army elite before there is general agreement on China's new course in domestic and foreign policy.

The struggle for power within the elite is bound to be exacerbated by growing socioeconomic problems that are certain to plague China for the remainder of the twentieth century. There are at least 20 million unemployed. Many of the unemployed are educated and disgruntled youth for whom it is virtually impossible for the Chinese to find jobs. Most Chinese factories and plants are already overstaffed and technologically backward. To modernize these plants will mean substituting machines for manual labor. This process will worsen China's unemployment problem. Rising inflation is still another problem; in 1981 it was running at 7–8 percent per year and probably higher in the cities. There was also a huge budget deficit for 1980 of about $12 billion. The inflation and deficits were products of economic reform.

China also has a serious energy crunch. Oil, to which many Chinese had looked as the key to future development, is giving the leaders more problems than were expected. Vice-Premier Gu Mu recently told a Japanese delegation that the Gang of Four had exaggerated China's oil potential. Only 8.3 million of the contracted 9.5 million tons of oil due to be shipped to Japan in 1981 actually went there. In 1982 the figure may decline still further to 8.1 million tons against the promised 15 million tons.

China also faces an extremely serious food problem. Deng himself said in 1979 that the most important problem confronting the Chinese "is to have enough to eat." The Chinese have officially conceded that between 1957 and 1977 there was a decline in the per capita production of grain. That the condition of life in the Chinese countryside is far from satisfactory was dramatically confirmed in the winter of 1978–79, when tens of thousands of peasants trudged to Beijing and camped outside the official residence of the party leaders to protest their poverty. According to eyewitness reports by foreign correspondents, many of the peasants were sick, dressed in rags, and wretchedly poverty-stricken. Some tried to sell their children because they could not feed them. One of America's leading experts on the Chinese economy, Jan Prybyla, estimates that the food supply is barely adequate. Moreover, if food production is to improve, China will have to modernize its agriculture. The old strategy of "extensive" rural development—relying on increased inputs of labor, land, and capital—has reached the point of diminishing returns. To break out of this traditional trap China needs qualitative changes in technology and basic changes in the social relations in the countryside.

Yet another serious problem in China is the growing gap between city and countryside, a gap that is bound to be widened by modernization programs that favor the urban areas. Over time this could produce a rebellious peasantry.

Finally, there is the problem of rising expectations that are bound to be disappointed. The death of Mao and the rise of the Deng coalition brought new hopes to the Chinese people that their long-depressed standard of living would improve. Yet the accumulating social and economic problems are leading the new Chinese leaders to a much slower and more cautious pace of economic advance than they had originally intended. A relatively slow growth rate means that even by the turn of the century China will still be at the level of the poorest countries in the world.

These accumulating socioeconomic tensions could produce periodic explosions. Already there are well-documented reports of strikes and unrest. New dissident voices are being heard both in the universities, where there are demands for greater freedom, and in some factories, where there are demands for independent unions on the Polish model. There is also a growing crisis of popular confidence in the Communist party.

This combination of leadership differences and social tension could lead to a protracted post-Deng succession struggle. The major domestic issue in such a struggle will be how to deal with China's mounting domestic problems—greater reform and liberalization or increasing repression and centralization. A related issue will be the question of whether to continue the economic opening to the West or to pursue a more autarchic economic strategy. If China were to adopt a more repressive, centralized, and autarchic economic system (a neo-Stalinist-type system) and to abandon its efforts for economic reform, it might also turn inward. At the same time, a post-Deng leadership struggle is bound to raise some of the basic issues of Chinese foreign policy—particularly whether China should continue to tilt so one-sidedly toward the West or to strive for a more balanced policy of maneuvering between Moscow and Washington.

Another country in the region where political stability during the 1980s may be in doubt is the Philippines. Political and social forces are increasingly polarized between pro- and anti-Marcos forces. Although they are not all working together, the anti-Marcos side includes a still small but growing communist guerrilla movement, a continuing Islamic rebellion on the island of Mindanao, and substantial opposition to Marcos from among some students and intellectuals, some sections of the labor movement, and some of the opposition politicians. Benigno Aquino, one of the leading dissidents and a potential successor to Marcos, has warned of a "terrible gathering storm that may well turn the Philippines into the next flash point in Southeast Asia." One of the most thoughtful American observers of the Philippines, Professor Carl Lande of the University of Kansas, has recently concluded that "the longer the restoration of democracy is delayed, the greater the possibility becomes that the present authoritarian system will be replaced not by a democratic but by a totalitarian—and bitterly anti-American—government." Were such a development to take place sometime in the 1980s, the strategic consequences for the American position in Asia would be grim. The American navy and air force are critically dependent on naval and air bases at Subic Bay and Clark Field.

Elsewhere in the region there are a variety of economic, social, and political problems that could, particularly in combination, threaten political stability. Many of the countries, especially Indonesia, desperately need to provide employment for a rapidly growing population and to distribute the proceeds of growth more equitably. Some, such as South Korea, will have to find ways of incorporating into the nation's political life a large labor movement, a growing middle class, and a better-educated student population aware of modern political ideologies such as democracy. Throughout much of Southeast Asia there are strong anti-Chinese feelings. In Indonesia, during 1980, anti-Chinese riots swept some of the cities of Central Java. In Thailand the several great economic families of Chinese origin are the object of growing resentment. Because the Chinese are the middlemen in the economies of many of the countries of Southeast Asia, they are a convenient scapegoat for frustrations that are endemic to rapid economic growth.

Perhaps the most alarming problem in the region is the general lack of institutionalization of many political systems. In several of these countries the military is ruling, either directly or indirectly. In many of them the whole political system rests on one man or on a narrow oligarchy. There are few institutionalized procedures for passing power from one leader to another or from one group or faction within the army to another. The assassination of South Korea's president, Chung Hee Park, in 1979 led to a year of very grave political and social instability in South Korea. Political authority in the Philippines rests heavily on the shoulders of one man, President Ferdinand Marcos, and his demise or overthrow would very likely produce a major struggle for power within the army and the other groups within the elite. Thailand has seen more than ten coups in the past three decades. In these cases, and in China too, the demise or overthrow of the principal leader could easily produce crises of transition that are bound to hamper economic progress and also to raise doubts about the future course of foreign policy.

To be sure, it is possible to exaggerate these internal problems and, particularly, the impact they will have on foreign policy. Through all its recent coups Thailand has remained firmly in the Western camp. Now that it is confronted with a Vietnamese adversary supported by the Soviet Union, it will have additional reasons for remaining there under whatever leadership comes to the fore. Similar considerations apply to the other East Asian countries. Confronted with powerful Soviet and Vietnamese adversaries, China and the ASEAN countries will have good reasons for continuing their alignment with the West. In the face of its challenge from North Korea, so will South Korea.

Still, the problems I have identified are serious. Any one of them, or some combination, could lead to setbacks for the Western alliance system in the region and to opportunities that the Soviets could exploit.

The Soviet Military Buildup

Yet another threat to the existing balance of power in East Asia is the steady but substantial Soviet military buildup in that region of the world.

(See Langer's chapter 10 for the details.) Now that the Soviet Union has achieved strategic nuclear parity with the United States, regional military balances will become increasingly important in the risk calculations of both great powers. In recent years the Soviets have developed an impressive array of forces capable of being directed against the Far East. These include: central strategic nuclear forces that can reach any point in Asia; a specifically Asia-oriented nuclear theater force that includes SS-20s and Backfire bombers; a modernized China-oriented ground force of about 51 divisions; growing forces near Japan, including new and permanent military bases on some of the disputed Kurile Islands near Japan's northernmost island of Hokkaido; some 2,000 combat planes; and, finally, a rapidly growing Pacific Fleet with an enlarged base complex in Vladivostok and Petropavlovsk, now supplemented by Soviet naval and air facilities in Vietnam, South Yemen, and Ethiopia, facilities that will significantly expand the scope of Soviet power projection in the Pacific and Indian oceans.

In the past fifteen years the Soviet Pacific Fleet has more than doubled its tonnage to 1.5 million tons while that of the United States Seventh Fleet has been reduced by one-third to about 650,000 tons. Between 1977 and 1980 alone, the Soviets added some 270,000 tons of new ships to their Pacific Fleet, more than one-third the total tonnage of the American Seventh Fleet. The Soviet Pacific Fleet is now the largest of the four Soviet fleets. All this should be measured against the fact that the American navy is increasingly reaching a point of overextension.

Although the Soviets are enhancing their naval capacities in the region, the American Seventh Fleet still retains a substantial qualitative edge. Moreover, the United States has a large Third Fleet of about 2 million tons in the Eastern Pacific and the Japanese navy has about 200,000 tons of shipping.

Still, the trends are worrisome. If these adverse trends were to continue, and if the Soviet Union were one day to achieve military superiority in the Pacific, the political and psychological impact on the region would be considerable.

The Unraveling of American Relations with Japan, China, or ASEAN

Yet another means by which the Soviets might make a comeback in East Asia is by exploiting any unraveling of American relations with key allies and friends in the region. In the case of the relationship between the United States and Japan, the early 1980s witnessed a steady increase of frictions between the two Pacific partners over trade relations and the question of defense burden sharing. There were many signs of a rising

tide of protectionism in the United States and Europe over Japanese
auto exports:
• In France, customs authorities were delaying Japanese cars at French
ports and the French industry minister condemned growing Japanese
auto exports. This prompted a protest from the Japanese government.
• In Washington, two senators prepared a bill aimed at curbing auto
imports and several top U.S. officials claimed that the United States has
a "right" to expect lower car imports from Japan.
• In Brussels, the European Economic Community (EEC) was preparing a report on "inconclusive" talks with Japanese automakers and Bene-
lux countries were considering imposing import controls on Japanese
cars.
• The EEC's Council of Ministers had approved a proposal for monitoring imports of Japanese passenger cars, televisions, and machine tools.
This decision to monitor imports was intended as a warning to Japanese
firms.

Thus, free trade was under mounting pressure in some of the key
industrial democracies on which Japan depends for its vital export markets. Rising unemployment, slower growth, and other economic difficulties in both Europe and the United States were likely to keep the trade
problem alive. The continuing U.S. hectoring of the Japanese on trade
issues, unless it is controlled, is bound to leave deep scars on the
Japanese–U.S. alliance.

Alongside the trade issue between the two countries there is an equally
dangerous issue of burden-sharing. For several years the United States
has been urging the Japanese to increase their defense spending. Former Secretary of Defense Harold Brown said during a visit to Tokyo
before leaving office that the Japanese choice was not between guns and
butter but between guns and caviar. He added that a nation that spent
only $10 billion on defense and $40 billion on welfare had its priorities
wrong. These statements reflect a growing feeling in the United States
that the Japanese need to carry a fairer share of the defense burden now
borne by the United States in defending the western Pacific.

Unless the United States and Japan handle these economic and defense issues with great care and sensitivity, they have a potential for
escalation. Americans could come to the conclusion that the Japanese
are unfair economic competitors who are unwilling to bear their proper
share of the Western defense effort; Japanese could come to the conclusion that the Americans are taking unfair action against Japanese exports because of their own economic inefficiency and, at the same time,
are insisting on unreasonable increases in Japanese defense spending.

There is an equally serious threat to the unity of ASEAN. Indonesia
and Malaysia, more suspicious than the other members of China's long-

range intentions in the region, are eager to reach an accommodation with Vietnam in order to use Vietnam as a counterweight to China and to help Vietnam reduce its dependence on the Soviet Union. Other ASEAN states, particularly Thailand and Singapore, believe that the immediate threat to the region is not China but Vietnam supported by the Soviet Union. They are, therefore, less willing to reach an accommodation with Vietnam and more inclined to tilt toward China in an effort to bleed the Vietnamese in Cambodia. These divergent perspectives could over time lead to increasingly serious divisions within ASEAN that could be exploited by the Soviet Union and Vietnam.

Finally, American relations with China were coming under considerable strain in late 1981 because of China's insistence that the United States must "soon" end all arms sales to Taiwan. An immediate crisis in American–Chinese relations was averted when President Reagan decided not to sell advanced fighter planes to Taiwan while going ahead with replacement sales for fighter planes that the Taiwanese already have. But the Chinese registered strong disapproval even of this action, and in late 1981 they began to take a somewhat harder line toward the United States. For example, they have become more critical of certain aspects of American foreign policy, especially in the Third World; they have begun again to condemn the United States along with the Soviet Union as a "hegemonic" superpower; and they have made subtle suggestions that they might yet renew the discussions with the Soviet Union that were terminated after the Soviet invasion of Afghanistan.

Did all this represent merely China's effort to strengthen its hand on the Taiwan issue? Or was China signaling the United States that it had other options?

In either case, the issue of Taiwan is a potentially critical barrier to the further consolidation of American–Chinese relations. Handled skillfully and with prudence on both sides, the issue might be deferred. But if it is not handled with skill, it could, sooner or later, lead to a serious crisis in American–Chinese relations.

A Soviet Breakthrough with Japan

One of the most important strategic developments in the early 1980s has been the growing disarray in the NATO alliance. By exploiting the growing antinuclear and neutralist sentiment in Germany, the Soviets hope to break up NATO. These recent trends in Europe are likely to strengthen the Soviet belief that, by applying a judicious mixture of carrots and sticks, Moscow can also pry Japan away from the United States. Toward this end, the Russians will probably step up their efforts to separate the economic and territorial issues in their relations with

Japan. While refusing to offer any concessions on the disputed territorial issue, Moscow will try to lure Japan deeper into Siberian development. (See chapters 5 and 9 by Kamiya and Campbell.)

Still, the obstacles to any substantial improvement in Soviet–Japanese relations remain formidable. Regaining Japan's "lost territories" is, as Kamiya makes clear, increasingly popular in Japan, and no Japanese government could compromise on this issue without serious political fallout. At the same time, the Russians are unlikely to offer any concessions on the territorial issue because the disputed Kurile Islands are increasingly important to Moscow's military buildup in the Sea of Okhotsk. There are also deep mutual suspicions between Moscow and Tokyo, suspicions reinforced by four wars during the past century. Nevertheless, an accumulation of serious strains in the U.S.–Japan alliance could eventually drive Japan into an accommodation with Moscow.

A Sino–Soviet Reconciliation

As Bialer points out in chapter 4, perhaps the most significant scenario for a Soviet comeback in Asia during the 1980s would be a Soviet reconciliation with China. Bialer suggests three big incentives for Moscow's wanting to reach such an accommodation with China in the 1980s. First, there is the prospect of Moscow's deteriorating relations with the United States. Second, the succession struggle after Brezhnev may well throw up a new Soviet leadership anxious to reduce tensions with China. Finally, the acute economic problems that the Russians face in the 1980s should incline them toward wanting some breathing space with the Chinese.

Bialer suggests, also, that the key factor in this scenario will be the behavior of the United States. China's main interest in the United States lies in the American ability and resolve to resist successfully Soviet worldwide expansion. If, in the 1980s, the Chinese become convinced that the balance of world power is shifting further in the Soviet direction, China may become more amenable to a partial reconciliation with the Kremlin.

For a number of reasons, however, the prospects of such a reconciliation between Russia and China remain small. As Bialer indicates, deep negative feelings toward China on the part of the Soviets make it unlikely that the Soviets will go far enough in offers of reconciliation. There are powerful nationalistic and racial feelings on both sides. Moreover, the Chinese know that if they respond positively to Soviet overtures, this will endanger their American connection. Then, too, the Chinese leaders know the Soviets too well to believe that they can negotiate with the Russians successfully from a position of weakness. And China is now almost completely encircled by Moscow. Finally, the Russian and

Chinese empires extend along thousands of miles of common borders without any buffer zones between them. This situation alone makes compromise difficult.

In sum, there are a variety of ways in which the Soviets might make a comeback in Asia during the 1980s. None of them is likely. But much depends on the wisdom and resolve of American policy in the region. That is the final issue to which I now turn.

UNITED STATES POLICY IN EAST ASIA IN THE 1980S

Perhaps the basic issue confronting American policymakers in East Asia during the 1980s will be how to manage relations with allies and friends in an era of erosion of alliances.

There is a consensus within the United States that the foremost American ally in East Asia will remain Japan. Yet the United States--Japan relationship requires careful tending in at least three areas: security relations, economic relations, and trade with the Soviet Union. In the security realm, as Solomon points out in chapter 11, the United States has to define more carefully the role it wants Japan to play in a division of labor. At the same time, the Japanese must come to assume greater security responsibilities commensurate with their growing economic power. On the economic issues, bolder steps will have to be taken both in Tokyo and in Washington to prevent a rising tide of anti-Japanese sentiment in the United States due to mounting trade imbalances with Japan. Finally, the United States will have to coordinate carefully with Japan the alliance's policy on economic relations with the Soviets. Otherwise, the Russians will be able to play the two allies off against each other.

Although there is a consensus within the United States on the need for a strong alliance with Japan, there are great and as yet unresolved divisions on how the United States should move to develop ties with China. At one extreme, some say that the United States is so weak relative to Russia that it has no alternative but to enter into an alliance with the People's Republic of China (PRC) against the Soviet Union. At the other extreme, others say China will doublecross the United States once it becomes stronger, that totalitarian countries can turn on a dime, and so forth. There are many positions in between.

In the concluding chapter of this volume, Solomon stakes out a position midway between "evenhandedness" toward Russia and China on the one hand—a policy made impractical by the disparity in power between the two—and an alliance with China on the other. He calls for building the *first* steps of a "stairway" toward a fully developed security relationship with China while communicating to Moscow that *its* actions will, in some substantial measure, influence the pace and direction in which those American–Chinese security relations grow.

Of course, there are difficulties in implementing such a policy. Can the United States convince the Soviets that American policy toward China will be conditioned in some part by Soviet behavior? Does not the United States offend China by linking the development of American relations with the PRC to Soviet behavior? How does the United States go down the security staircase with China once it has gone up? Will not many Asians see a building up of China's military power as a long-term threat to their own interests? Finally, at what point does the United States, by going up the staircase with China, close off important options in dealing with Moscow on such critical issues as stabilizing the nuclear arms race and reducing tensions between the two superpowers? The contributors to this volume were unable to reach any complete agreement on these complex issues.

Speaking only for myself, I would like to see the United States move in the general direction of developing a solid, stable, and institutionalized relationship with the PRC. Although the development of such a relationship is likely to include the sale of some carefully selected defensive weapons to China (something Secretary of State Haig has already promised), American efforts to build a stable relationship with China should concentrate more on the economic, political, and cultural areas of the relationship rather than on the military. There are a number of reasons for this.

• Likely American military sales to China will not appreciably alter the present balance of power between China and Russia.

• The Chinese leaders themselves have placed military modernization fourth, behind other modernization priorities.

• The cost of modernizing China's armed forces will be astronomic, and China cannot afford to buy expensive foreign arms at a time when it is facing serious problems of economic readjustment and budget cutting at home.

• The best PRC defense against Soviet attack or intimidation for the foreseeable future is the Chinese strategy of a "people's war." What deters the Soviet Union from invading China is not the high level of Chinese military development but rather China's "strategic indigestibility." As Field Marshal Montgomery once said: There are two rules of war. The first is not to invade Russia. The second is not to invade China.

• As Bialer points out, China is interested in the American connection primarily for the ability of the United States to deter further Soviet expansion. China's primary interest in the United States is not in the acquisition of arms.

• There is no substitute for American military power. If the Pacific balance of power is turning against the United States, the response should be to increase American power in the region, not that of China.
• Finally, virtually all the American allies in the Pacific would be worried by any significant American effort to increase China's military power.

But if there is a strong case not to press ahead quickly on military sales to China, there is an equally strong case to develop stable ties to China, ties that are substantial enough to withstand inevitable strains in the relationship. First, as long as the Russians are preoccupied with a threat on two fronts, they are more likely to be restrained in challenging either Chinese or American interests. I recognize that there is the contrary argument that the closer the United States moves to China, the more this is likely to provoke rather than to deter Moscow. But the Russians are well aware how weak China is militarily and how weak it is likely to remain in the foreseeable future. They will probably be provoked only by massive American arms or technology transfers to China, particularly technology that would aid China's nuclear capacities. And such transfers will almost certainly not be made by any American administration under any contingencies now foreseeable. In sum, a policy of keeping up a two-front deterrent threat against the Kremlin does not require any particular level of American arms sales to China, much less a military alliance with China against Russia. It *does* require a stable United States–China relationship.

The Soviets are extremely well aware of their geopolitical vulnerabilities. In World War II, Russia was fortunate to have neutralized Japan in 1941 because of the Japanese preoccupation first with China and then, after December 1941, with the United States. In 1943, Stalingrad was the decisive battle of the war because, if the Russians had lost, Japan would almost certainly have entered the war on the German side and doomed Russia to defeat. As it was, the Soviets waited until the war in Europe was over before they committed themselves to the Far Eastern theater. And throughout the course of the war, they kept close to a million troops on their Siberian border for fear of having to fight on two fronts.

Now the Russians once again face a two-front problem. As long as this situation persists and as long as U.S.–China relations are stable, Moscow will have a very strong incentive for behaving with some restraint, for avoiding risks of war, and for avoiding a frontal challenge either to China or to the United States.

In addition to contributing to deterrence of the Russians, a solid American relationship with China is important for two other reasons. It eases the U.S. defense burden—a burden that would almost certainly grow if there were a Sino–Soviet accommodation, and it improves the prospects for peace and stability in Asia. There are four main trouble spots in East Asia: Korea, Taiwan, Indochina, and the Sino–Soviet border. As long as there is a stable U.S.–PRC relationship, China has an interest in restraining North Korea, in avoiding any confrontation with Taiwan, and in opposing further Vietnamese expansion in Indochina—against the Thais, for example. Moreover, a stable U.S.–PRC relationship makes it less rather than more likely that the Soviets will seek a solution to their China problem through war.

Important as the U.S.–PRC entente is in containing the additional expansion of Soviet power, it would be wise to recognize that there are several realistic limits to the further development of the Chinese–American relationship. The issue of Taiwan is bound to be a continuing stumbling block. The United States will continue to have an interest in Taiwan's stability and security. This interest will conflict with the PRC's equally strong interest in reunifying China. Also, both the United States and China have allies who are uneasy about the growing connection between the two powers. The South Koreans, for example, fear that the United States will attach greater priority to China than to small allies such as South Korea, and they especially fear that any modern U.S. arms that go to China may wind up in the hands of the North Koreans, South Korea's most dangerous adversary. North Korea fears that the U.S.–Chinese entente will come at the expense of China's support for North Korea against the United States, and it is therefore trying—so far without success—to warm up its relations with the Soviet Union, a development that must be of considerable concern to China.

In Southeast Asia the United States will be inhibited from too close an identification with the Chinese because the Chinese are regarded with great suspicion by most of the ASEAN countries, particularly Indonesia and Malaysia. Most of the noncommunist Southeast Asian countries have large Chinese minorities who are more prosperous than the indigenous population and are therefore the source of great envy and resentment. Many of the ASEAN governments, especially some of the military leaders in the ASEAN countries, look upon these Chinese minorities as a potential fifth column. All the ASEAN governments have fought indigenous communist movements that have drawn on the support of local Chinese minorities. These communist movements have in the past been supported by the PRC.

These Southeast Asian fears of China may be diminished in the years ahead as China tones down its support of revolutionary movements in the region and seeks to improve its relations with the governments there. To some extent this is already occurring. But most of the ASEAN countries will continue to harbor fears about China's long-range intentions and they will not welcome too close an identification between the United

States and the People's Republic of China, especially one that leads to swift growth in China's military power.

Yet another limit on the U.S.–PRC entente is likely to be differences in attitude toward arms control negotiations with the Soviet Union. Although the Reagan administration is clearly not so enthusiastic about arms control as the Carter administration was, it has committed itself to the arms control process. Any American administration will have an interest in seeking to stabilize the strategic arms competition with Moscow. Moreover, the Reagan administration will be pushed in this direction by its European allies.

The Chinese came to regard U.S.–Soviet arms control talks in the early 1970s with great suspicion. For the PRC those talks seemed to suggest that the West was eager to relieve its own security burdens on Moscow's western front while allowing the Soviets to increase their pressure on China.

Finally, there are limits on the degree of U.S.–PRC cooperation that result from their different systems and their different ideologies. In the United States there will always be a fear that the PRC will want to make an accommodation with the Soviet Union and that such an accommodation, if it comes, will be not merely tactical but one that is reenforced by a common ideology. These fears have already been strengthened by an ongoing debate within China over whether the Soviet Union is still a "socialist" country. The fact that such a debate continues suggests that there are some Chinese leaders who would give an affirmative answer to that question.

In the human rights area, too, there are likely to be differences between the two countries. Although the Reagan administration is putting that issue on the back burner, the United States is a democracy and public opinion will not allow human rights issues to be placed on the back burner indefinitely. If there is growing repression in China and a return to a type of neo-Stalinist economic model, as seems possible during the coming decade, these developments are bound to have some impact on the United States.

Also, there is a growing recognition in the United States that China is still quite weak both economically and militarily. Although this is a source of relief to many Americans, it also sets limits on the plans of the most enthusiastic "China card" players, who have to recognize that although the China card is useful in containing Soviet expansion, it is not a trump card.

Undoubtedly there are similar reservations within China about the nature of the U.S. system. From time to time there are clear indications in the Chinese media of the existence of a school of thought that would like to pursue a policy of equidistance between Moscow and Washington.

For such reasons Americans should not delude themselves into believing that the U.S.–PRC relationship will, in the foreseeable future, be as close as the U.S. relationship with its democratic allies in Europe and Japan.

Nevertheless, if the United States is realistic in its aspirations, there is no reason why the U.S.–PRC relationship, which has already developed quite rapidly during recent years, should not continue to grow and become deeper during the 1980s.

Finally, after strengthening its alliance with Japan and consolidating its relations with China, the United States needs to expand its relations with ASEAN. Both economically and strategically, noncommunist Southeast Asia is bound to be of growing importance to the United States in the 1980s. Together the five ASEAN countries account for about one-quarter of total U.S. trade with the Pacific. And because these countries are likely to continue to grow rapidly in the decade ahead, their trade with the United States should continue to expand. Strategically, a unified ASEAN serves as a barrier to the further expansion of Soviet influence in the region. Moreover, of the many countries in the Southeast Asian region, only two—Vietnam and Indonesia—have the size and potential to be the dominant powers there. As long as Vietnam remains an ally of the Soviet Union, the United States has a big stake in a friendly Indonesia. Also, as the Indian Ocean becomes an arena of growing strategic importance, the waterways of Southeast Asia that link the Western Pacific and the Indian Ocean will assume growing significance. In the recent past several American administrations have tended to take this region for granted as they concentrated on relations with the major powers. The Reagan administration seems to have reversed this unhealthy trend. But a great deal of work remains to be done to convince the region that the United States is a reliable, long-term ally, that it is not going to "farm out" the region to Japanese or Chinese protection, and that it seeks a genuine partnership.

In sum, as the 1980s begin, the position in which the Soviets find themselves in East Asia is not an enviable one. But the other side of the coin is that the Western position in East Asia also contains a vast array of hazards and challenges, the solutions to which will be neither quick nor easy.

2

Asia in the Soviet Conception

JOHN J. STEPHAN

As an approach to understanding Soviet perspectives on Asia, this chapter proposes to: (1) identify the salient geographic and historic factors shaping Russian and Soviet attitudes toward Asia, (2) assess the changing role of Asia in Moscow's global priorities, (3) examine Soviet perceptions of current trends, and (4) suggest some of the opportunities that might attract Soviet initiatives in the region.

The escalation of Soviet activities in Asia in general and in Afghanistan in particular has prompted widespread commentary. A good deal of this commentary is oversimplified, creating a misleading impression of certitude that such a complex and elusive subject does not possess. A few cautionary remarks are therefore in order.

Ascertaining Soviet perceptions of Asia is a chastening exercise for anyone seeking to go beyond superficial generalizations. Any expectations of uncovering a coherent conception, let alone a blueprint for action, quickly founder on the shoals of inaccessible data and contradictory evidence. To be sure, one can impose a spurious logic on the subject by taking Moscow's public pronouncements at face value. This approach has the disadvantage of overlooking what a prominent Soviet commentator candidly acknowledged: that expressions of policy can conceal as well as reflect real interests and intentions.[1] Moreover, recent studies have suggested that international affairs and area specialists in the USSR have since the early 1960s relied less on ideology as a guide to analysis.[2] Conversely, one can discount Marxism-Leninism as rhetoric and instead explain Soviet perceptions under the rubric of Russian nationalism, geopolitics, group psychology, or some combination thereof. Yet as Alexander Dallin warns, ignoring the role of Marxism-Leninism in shaping Soviet views is as dangerous as overemphasizing its importance.[3]

1. Aleksandr Bovin, quoted in Morton Schwartz, *Soviet Perceptions of the United States* (Berkeley: University of California Press, 1978), p. 6.

2. William Zimmerman, *Soviet Perspectives on International Relations* (Princeton: Princeton University Press, 1969), pp. 282–90.

3. Alexander Dallin, "Introduction," in Donald Treadgold, ed., *Soviet and Chinese Communism* (Seattle: University of Washington Press, 1967), p. 368.

At a minimum, Marxism-Leninism molds Soviet perceptions of Asia by providing the conceptual categories and vocabulary with which these perceptions are expressed. To be sure, Marxism-Leninism is consciously wielded as a supple forensic instrument to legitimize Soviet interests in Asia, justify the behavior of allies, appeal to Third World nations, identify "reactionary" and "progressive" elements within capitalist countries, discredit the policies of rivals, and project an image of the USSR being in the vanguard of irresistible historical forces. At the same time, Marxism-Leninism deeply influences patterns of conceptualization and analysis, as can be seen in a widespread tendency of Soviet commentators (privately as well as publicly) to adopt holistic approaches to problems and to explain trends in terms of dialectical processes. The interaction of ideology as a conscious tool and ideology as an unconscious prism is a subtle one that invests Soviet views with an irreducible kernel of ambiguity. This ambiguity is compounded by deceptive appearances. Although wrapped in Marxist-Leninist trappings, some views of Asia in fact antedate the October Revolution. Other views are of recent origin, despite their being depicted as having deep roots in Russia's past.

Another obstacle to generalization is the heterogeneity inherent in the terms *Asia* and *Soviet*. Asia encompasses a kaleidoscopic range of nations and cultures, a range only marginally reduced in this chapter by focusing the inquiry on East and Southeast Asia. Sophisticated Soviet observers know that Asia has no cultural, economic, political, or ideological coherence. Consequently, there is no Soviet view of "Asia" except at the level of rudimentary slogans and stereotypes. Rather, there is a multiplicity of views on individual Asian countries or on subregions within Asia.

Asia's diversity is matched by that of the USSR. It would be misleading to assume that Soviet views are unified or even consistent. Displays of monolithic solidarity at party congresses and habitual use of the first person plural by Soviet spokesmen should not lead one to conclude that there are identical views on Asia within the party or government. If a wider sampling of Soviet society is considered, regional, ethnic, educational, and occupational factors enhance the variety of concepts of Asia.

Finally, the manner in which Soviet perspectives on Asia bear upon foreign policy can only be impressionistically inferred from fragmentary evidence. A considerable number of professional specialists on East and Southeast Asia conduct research at institutes in Moscow and on a smaller scale in Leningrad, Novosibirsk, and Vladivostok. Some of these institutes are heavily engaged in providing background studies for party and government organs. The Institute of World Economy and International Relations is said to maintain especially close ties with the party *apparat*. The Institute of the Far East reportedly has a similar relationship with the

Foreign Ministry. The Foreign Ministry, in turn, has its own research and training programs on Asia in the Institute of International Relations. Asian specialists attached to the Institute of the USA and Canada are tapped by party and government alike for their expertise. The formal administrative structure of these institutions is often transcended by personal friendships and unofficial bureaucratic alliances.

The direct influence of Asian experts on policy formulation is probably marginal although one senior Soviet analyst privately opined that it was growing. Sinologist Mikhail Kapitsa is said to have made significant inputs within the Foreign Ministry at certain junctures. Ivan Kovalenko, a section chief in the party's International Department, has been identified as the "commander-in-chief" of the USSR's Japan policy.[4] Kovalenko does publish articles on Japan and China in *Pravda* and in professional journals under the penname I. I. Ivkov. "Ivkov's" pronouncements are said to carry weight because they allegedly represent the views of the Politburo. But it remains an open question to what extent Kovalenko influences, as opposed to reflects, leadership thinking on Asia.

GEOGRAPHIC AND HISTORIC INFLUENCES

Geography has exerted a pervasive influence on Russian and Soviet perceptions of Asia. Russia and Asia are not contiguous, as the term *Sino-Russian frontier* implies, but overlap spatially and ethnically. Three-quarters of the Soviet Union lies in Asia. One-third of Asia lies within the USSR. Eighty million people (approximately 30% of the Soviet population) live in Asiatic regions of the USSR. Fifty million Soviet citizens (about 20% of the population) are of Asian nationalities.

Asia's spatial interpenetration with the Soviet Union is symbolized by the vast Eurasian plain, which stretches from the Urals to Mongolia. In the absence of major barriers, waves of migrations have moved across the plain for centuries, displacing or absorbing earlier inhabitants. The Russians are but the most recent wave. An awareness of the plain's historic permeability and ethnic evanescence leaves many Russians with a half-formed sense of territorial insecurity that manifests itself not only in the predilection for strong central authority but in what amounts to a national fixation on frontier defense.[5]

---

4. Matsui Shigeru, *Soren no tai-Nichi senryaku* (Soviet Strategy toward Japan) (Tokyo: PHP, 1979), p. 10.

5. Books and articles about frontier defense form a minor literary genre whose current state was manifested at a 1978 conference on "Literature, Art, and the Defense of Sacred Boundaries of the Motherland," S. Tsvigun, "Khudozhnik i granitsa," *Literaturnaya Gazeta*, Jan. 17, 1979.

The search for natural frontiers, for security, helped propel Russians across Siberia and Central Asia.[6] A similar admixture of anxiety and will to power underlie what Chinese, Japanese, and American observers perceive as Soviet expansionist pressures in Asia and the Pacific today. A metaphorical Eurasian plain with attendant insecurities and outward impulses is still very much alive. Moreover, with the maritime deployment of strategic weapons, the "plain" now extends well into the Indian and Pacific oceans.[7]

History has also left a deep imprint upon Russian views of Asia, particularly selected historical episodes that the regime uses to mobilize and channel public consciousness. Images of the Mongol conquest ("the most traumatic historical experience of the Russian people")[8] are triggered by shrewdly worded propaganda about the territorial appetites of "Great Han chauvinism." Japanese claims in the Kurile Islands are portrayed as following a tradition of predatory designs on the Russian Far East from the Siberian Intervention (1918–22) to the miniwars around the Manchurian perimeter in 1937–39. Ominous motives are ascribed to nineteenth-century American commercial interests in the Amur region, to American involvement in the Siberian Intervention, and to Washington's wartime plans to occupy the Kurile Islands. Ubiquitously present in school curricula, books, and museums, these tinted images of the past pervade the Soviet environment and shape the collective historical consciousness.

The cumulative weight of geography and history manifests itself both implicitly and explicitly in Soviet articulations about Asia. First, there is an acute sense of geopolitical vulnerability. It is not uncommon to hear the opinion voiced that the USSR must cope with NATO in the west, China in the south, Japan in the east, and American strategic forces all around. Moreover, there is concern about the tenuous logistical position of the Soviet Far East, connected to European Russia only by the Trans-Siberian Railroad (to be supplemented on its eastern portion by the Baikal–Amur Mainline Railroad [BAM]), air, and circuitous sea routes via the Indian and Arctic oceans. Conversely, it is felt that the United States enjoys the twin advantages of comparatively friendly neighbors along its land frontiers and unimpeded access to the world's oceans.

That spokesmen of the world's largest state profess to feel hemmed in

6. Otto Hoetzsch, *Russland in Asien* (Stuttgart: Deutsche Verlags-Anstalt, 1966), p. 124; Andrei Lobanov-Rostovsky, *Russia and Asia* (New York: Macmillan, 1933), p. 36.

7. On August 21, 1979, *Pravda* carried an article defining Soviet security interests in terms of the range of modern strategic weapons (*Soviet World Outlook*, vol. 5, no. 1 [Jan. 15, 1980], p. 2).

8. Nicholas V. Riasanovsky, "Asia Through Russian Eyes," in Wayne S. Vucinich, ed., *Russia and Asia* (Stanford: Hoover Institution Press, 1972), p. 5.

may sound implausible to outside observers. To be sure, Soviet negotiators do wield the notion of geopolitical vulnerability when bargaining with Washington for a margin of strategic advantage vis-à-vis the United States. Nevertheless, there is a real if unstable nexus of anxieties (vestigial fears of "capitalist encirclement," insecurity about the USSR's great power status) that tempt Soviet leaders to place emphasis on military power to achieve political goals. The incursion into Afghanistan, which from a Western perspective was an act of unprovoked aggression forming part of a geopolitical strategy aimed at the Middle East and Southwest Asia, through Soviet eyes was a response to dangers as well as a probing for opportunities. In Moscow's view, developments in Afghanistan did offer a chance to improve the Soviet position along a portion of its perimeter near the Persian Gulf. But it was also felt that events in Afghanistan in 1979 threatened Soviet credibility globally by jeopardizing the "irreversible" gains of Kabul's 1978 Marxist "revolution."

Second, Soviet views of Asia frequently reflect what a Moscow academic called a "1941 complex": a tendency to see collusion among the USSR's neighbors. The 1941 complex is rooted in events of the 1930s that culminated in Hitler's invasion of the USSR in 1941. Accordingly, Washington is suspected of trying (at its own peril) to use China against the USSR much as Britain and France tried (to their peril) in the 1930s to maneuver Hitler eastward. In the words of Vladivostok analyst Boris N. Slavinsky:

How much our situation today is like that of the 1930's when the western powers armed fascist Germany, trying to push her against the USSR. But, as is well known, Hitler first attacked them! A similar situation could well arise—this time in the Far East—given Peking's geopolitical concepts and expansionist aspirations.[9]

Soviet propagandists exploit the 1941 complex to mobilize popular feelings within the USSR. For example, use of the term *axis* to describe the new relationship among Washington, Beijing, and Tokyo is calculated to evoke images of World War II, which remain very vivid in the general populace. One commentator, in a tactic redolent of the late Senator Joseph McCarthy, portrayed recent contacts between Bonn and Beijing as the work of Nazis among the China specialists within the German Foreign Office.[10]

Third, Soviet attitudes toward Asia betray a craving for status that can be traced to a traditional Russian attachment to rank. Although the

9. S. L. Tikhvinsky, ed., *Istoriya mezhdunarodnykh otnoshenii na Dal'nem Vostoke, 1945–1977* (Khabarovsk: Khabarovskoe knizhnoe izdatel'stvo, 1978), p. 550.

10. Ernst Genri, "Nemetskie revanshisty i Pekin," *Problemy Dal'nego Vostoka* (hereafter cited as *PDV*), no. 4 (1974), pp. 146–58.

original Latin and Manchu documents of the Treaty of Nerchinsk (1689) listed the Chinese (Manchu) emperor before the czar, Peter the Great subsequently reversed the order.[11] A desire to maintain rank among Asian states such as Persia and China is said to have been a stimulus to Russia's late-nineteenth-century reforms.[12] Today, the USSR wants to be treated with the respect it feels it deserves not only as a superpower but as a country with a historically great position in Asia, a position that civil war and revolution eroded but that is now being reclaimed. As an official privately remarked at a recent conference in Khabarovsk: "We are only trying to reestablish our rightful historical interests in Asia and the Pacific." "Rightful historical interests" tend to be equated with the maximum scope of Imperial Russia's interest in any given region—except perhaps Alaska.

The United States plays a special role in the Soviet Union's quest for status in Asia. The United States is expected to deal with the Soviet Union as an equal, to accept the Soviet Union as a major presence with legitimate interests throughout Asia and the Pacific, to include the Soviet Union in regional organizations, and to give priority to relations with Moscow over those with Beijing. Sino–American normalization disturbed Moscow not only because of its geopolitical implications but because by occurring without a corresponding improvement in Soviet–American ties, it suggested that Washington does not give highest priority to relations with the USSR. As Soviet leaders and commentators sense that the USSR is ever closer to realizing its status aspirations in Asia and the Pacific, they increasingly resent any open demonstrations of American superiority. The U.S. mining of Haiphong and bombing of Soviet ships in the harbor still rankle, not so much because of the physical damage sustained but because Moscow suffered a humiliating reminder that the Soviet Union, with all its claims to superpower status, was helpless to deter this naked display of American force. As one Soviet official told the author in 1980: "You'll never be able to do that to us again!" In a broader context a young Soviet diplomat distilled this sense of status restiveness in a remark dropped during a lecture to an American audience on Soviet policy in Asia and the Pacific:

You like being number one, but we are tired of being number two.

Fourth, Soviet views on Asia often exude a half-articulated but one suspects deeply felt expectation of gratitude. To some extent this expectation derives from an unquestioned conviction that the Soviet Union, as heir to the world's first socialist revolution, has borne a major responsi-

11. Gregor Alexinsky, *Russia and Europe* (London: T. Fisher Unwin, 1917), p. 110.
12. Ibid., p. 110.

bility for the growth and defense of a "socialist community." Analogous feelings can be found among prerevolutionary authors who claimed that Russia deserved Europe's gratitude for having held back the destructive forces of Asia before 1600, thereby ensuring Europe's eventual rise to global preeminence.[13] At present the roles of Europe and Asia are blurred and the ideological content has changed, but a consciousness of selflessness and sacrifice persists. Moscow regularly extols itself for contributions to the struggles of Asian peoples against European and American "imperialism" and "colonialism," Japanese "militarism," and Chinese "expansionism." The achievement of Mongolian "independence" in 1921, the defeat of Japan in 1945, the triumph of the Chinese communists in 1949, the survival of North Korea in 1950–53, and the unification of Vietnam in 1975 were all supposedly made possible by Soviet power. Yet one can hear only in Ulan Bator and Hanoi expressions of that gratitude that Moscow seeks to sustain its self-image. Beijing has, in Soviet eyes, added insult to injury by not only showing ingratitude for years of assistance but by "slandering" its benefactor. To make up for the shortage of genuine appreciation of perceived Soviet services to Asia, propagandists have assiduously collected and disseminated pro-Soviet testimonials from prominent Asians, including Mao Zedong.[14]

Finally, history and geography have left Russians with ambivalent feelings about their identity vis-à-vis Europe and Asia. Until 1917 Asia to Russians represented variously a source of terror, an exotic subject of romantic speculations, and an object of imperialist idealism. Throughout a thousand years of vicissitudinous relations, there ran a sense of apartness from Asia, notwithstanding the geographic "Asianness" of much of Russia's territory after 1600. But if Russians did not identify themselves with Asians, they also did not fully assimilate European culture. The result was an uneasy suspension between East and West that led Russians, as Dostoyevsky noted, to be regarded as Europeans in Asia and as Asiatics in Europe.[15]

Following the October Revolution, Russian self-images with respect to Asia underwent a significant change. Lenin set about linking the Bolshevik revolutionary mission with anti-imperialist struggles in Asia and wooing Asian nationalities within the fledgling Soviet state. Russians were subsumed with Slavic and non-Slavic minorities into the "Soviet people," who were supposed to possess special qualifications for assisting in the liberation of all Asians.

---

13. Lobanov-Rostovsky, *Russia and Asia*, p. 24.

14. *What Peking Keeps Silent About* (Moscow: Novosty Press Agency, 1972).

15. Feodor Dostoyevsky, *The Diary of a Writer*, vol. 2 (New York: Scribner's, 1949), p. 1048.

Moscow has tried in various ways to capitalize on the USSR's self-image as a "Eurasian state."[16] Judicious use has been made of Soviet Asians in dealing with Asian countries.[17] Toasting a visiting Japanese foreign minister in 1941, Stalin proclaimed: "You are an Asiatic, so am I."[18] At international conferences throughout Asia, Soviet delegates of unmistakably Russian ethnicity have been overheard stressing that the USSR is an Asian country. Such expressions of solidarity notwithstanding, it is doubtful that the Russian people as a whole (particularly those subject to the current pull of Russian nationalism) feel ethnically or ideologically close to Asia.

Considerable commentary exists about Russian "gut" feelings toward Asians in general and toward the Chinese in particular. This commentary should be treated with caution, based as it is upon limited and not always reliable evidence. Even knowledgeable observers have fallen into the habit of overgeneralizing, asserting variously that Russian racial feeling against Asians is "strong and widespread"[19] or that Russians are virtually immune from racial prejudice.[20]

Some of the ambiguity inherent in Russian attitudes toward Asia is evident in Russian attitudes toward the USSR's own Asian nationalities, especially those in the Central Asian union republics. On one hand there is pride in the material advances of these nationalities under socialism. On the other hand these advances have promoted above-average population growth that portends to alter the ethnic composition of the Red Army and the industrial labor force. Although Russians can take satisfaction in the hostility with which Central Asian Muslims view China (a hostility with deep historical roots), the Islamic revival sweeping the Middle East and Soviet military intervention in Afghanistan raise the specter of an intensification of ethnic consciousness among Muslim intellectuals whose resistance to Russian influence has been greater than any other part of the native population of Central Asia.[21]

Russians, in sum, have complex, ambivalent feelings about Asia and Asians, feelings that are expressed variously under different conditions.

16. M. S. Kapitsa, "Bor'ba SSSR za mir i sotrudnichestvo v Azii," *PDV*, no. 1 (1979), p. 31.

17. Geoffrey Jukes, *The Soviet Union in Asia* (Berkeley: University of California Press, 1973), p. 64.

18. *Asahi shimbun*, Apr. 28, 1941.

19. Sidney Monas, "Amalrik's Vision of the End," in Andrei Amalrik, *Will the Soviet Union Survive Until 1984?* (New York: Harper & Row, 1970), p. 84.

20. George Vernadsky, "The Expansion of Russia," *Transactions of the Connecticut Academy of Arts and Sciences*, vol. 31 (July 1933), p. 396; Klaus Mehnert, *Soviet Man and His World* (New York: Praeger, 1962), pp. 282–83.

21. Alexandre Benningsen and Chantal Lemercier-Quelquejay, *Islam in the Soviet Union* (New York: Praeger, 1967), p. 223.

Essentially, Soviet images of Asia are inextricably bound up with self-images. Asia is simultaneously part of the USSR and an alien entity. Feelings of propinquity and distance, familiarity and exoticism, affinity and repulsion all appear to be widespread, and may even coexist within the same individual.

ASIA IN SOVIET PRIORITIES

Today, Asia occupies à more important position among Moscow's global priorities than it has at any time in the past. This has occurred in part as a result of the development of Siberia, the Soviet Far East, and Soviet Central Asia. In part, Asia's new significance is a consequence of proliferating strategic, political, and economic linkages within and outside the region, linkages that complicate the USSR's task of defending its national security and that challenge the USSR's self-image as the leader of the "socialist community."

Asia traditionally ranked low in the hierarchy of Russian foreign policy priorities. True, the Mongols preempted attention in medieval Kiev and Muscovy but from the sixteenth century the Asian threat receded behind successive waves of Russian eastward and southward expansion. Europe has consistently been accorded the highest military, political, and economic priority in Russian policies, a priority reinforced repeatedly over the last four centuries by challenges from Poland, Sweden, France, and Germany.

To say that Asia occupied an ancillary position in St. Petersburg's priorities should not obscure the integration of Asian with global policies during the last half of the nineteenth century. The stirrings of this integration occurred during the Crimean War, which opened Russian eyes to the vulnerability of Siberia's Pacific littoral to British and French naval forays. Acquisition of the Amur and Maritime regions from China in the treaties of Aigun (1858) and Beijing (1860), followed by conquests in Central Asia in the 1860s and 1870s, dramatically enhanced Russia's presence in Asia and led to a global rivalry with Great Britain in which Asian issues played a conspicuous role.

Since 1917, Soviet leaders have consistently fit Asia into their conceptions of global objectives. The priority assigned to Asia has varied in accordance with policy adjustments designed to promote national interests within a changing international environment. Lenin saw Asia as the "weakest link" of imperialism and sought to utilize the revolutionary struggle of Asian anticolonial and anti-imperialist movements to promote the international goals of Soviet communism. Security considerations, notably Japan's continental expansion and the rise of Hitler, led Stalin to approach Asia within the context of power politics. Stalin's detachment from most of the Chinese communist leaders, his military aid to Jiang Jieshi (Chiang Kai-shek), and his accommodation with Japan in 1941 bespoke a *Realpolitik* in which survival was the highest priority. In the short term Germany's invasion of the USSR and Japan's advance into Southeast Asia in 1941 reduced the perceived importance of Asia to Soviet security. But in the longer run World War II enhanced Asia's significance in Moscow's eyes. The wartime relocation of industries to Siberia, the invasion and occupation of Manchuria and northern Korea, and the acquisition of southern Sakhalin and the Kurile Islands all gave the Soviet Union a significantly greater stake in Northeast Asia by 1945. Subsequent developments (Soviet–American estrangement, the Chinese communist triumph, the Korean War) reinforced Asia's strategic importance for the USSR. By the time of Stalin's death in 1953, his heirs faced a more formidable challenge in Northeast Asia than ever posed by Imperial Japan. The American forces based along an arc from Hokkaido to Taiwan formed part of a Eurasian network that nearly girdled the USSR. Asia consequently became more closely linked to Europe as a security problem; nevertheless, it still did not rank with Europe as a security priority.

Although Stalin appreciated Asia's strategic significance, he showed less interest in Asian nationalist movements. The triumph of the Chinese communists in 1949 failed to trigger a recrudescence of Leninist support for Asian anticolonial movements. On the contrary a rigid "two camps" doctrine announced in 1947 by Andrei Zhdanov inhibited Moscow from exploiting some of the most powerful political currents gathering momentum in South and Southeast Asia in the decade after World War II.

By revising the two-camps doctrine at the Twentieth Party Congress in 1956, Nikita Khrushchev prepared the theoretical groundwork for courting Third World countries that had bourgeois-nationalist regimes. Designed to tilt the global balance of forces in favor of "socialism" by allying the Third World to the "socialist camp," Khrushchev's initiative had the effect of promoting Asia among Soviet global priorities in two ways, one of them unintended. First, Moscow began paying more attention to South and Southeast Asia, with gratifying results in India and (for a while) in Indonesia. Second, this doctrinal departure accelerated China's evolution from a regional ally into a global adversary.

Asia's new importance derives, in the words of one Soviet analyst, from its postwar emergence as an "active participant in a new international-political system" whereas Asia had previously been "an object of imperialist policies."[22] Asia has also become more important in Moscow's

22. D. V. Petrov, ed., *Mezhdunarodnye otnosheniya v Aziatsko-tikhookeanskom regione* (Moscow: Nauka, 1979), p. 4.

eyes as a result of a geographical extension of Soviet power and stakes. Moscow is now deeply interested in the whole region, not merely in those areas adjacent to the USSR's frontiers. Moreover, Soviet analysts see Asia as an area fraught with tension. In the words of E. M. Primakov, director of the Institute of Oriental Studies, Asia has become "the most dangerous zone of the development of global contradictions."[23] Dmitrii V. Petrov, a leading Japan specialist, identified those "contradictions" that arouse particular concern:

> In Asia are interwoven the most important contradictions of our time: between the two main social systems, between imperialist states, between industrialized and developing countries. Asia is a region of incessant territorial disputes and border collisions. National discord and social conflict are especially intense here.[24]

Also compelling in raising Asia's weight in the Kremlin's priorities has been the proliferation of what are seen as linkages within and outside Asia. The most disturbing of these new linkages has been Sino–American and Sino–Japanese normalization, which to many Soviet observers is a step toward a Sino–Japanese–American entente held together by common designs against the USSR.[25] Ties between Japan and Europe, and between China and Europe, add more strands to a worrisome network. At the same time, Moscow perceives linkages that could offer the USSR opportunities to exploit friction among its adversaries. Soviet observers have been quick to catch the potential strains that the Iranian and Afghan crises could put on U.S.–Japanese and U.S.–NATO relations.

The manner in which the USSR ascribes new significance to Asia can be inferred by identifying the Asian component at each level of a hypothetical hierarchy of Soviet global priorities.

Dealing with perceived threats to national security posed by strategic nuclear weapons ranks as the highest Soviet military and diplomatic priority. At present only the United States has the capacity to mount an immediate strategic challenge. Despite its nuclear arsenal China is not commonly regarded as an immediate strategic threat, but some Soviet observers concede that it could eventually become one with technical assistance from the United States, Japan, and Western Europe. Japan, by virtue of its industrial base and high level of technology, also is seen as

23. E. M. Primakov, *International Situation in the Asian Pacific Region: Basic Trends and Developments,* Fourteenth Pacific Science Congress, Khabarovsk, Aug. 1979 (Moscow: Nauka, 1979), p. 2.

24. Petrov, *Mezhdunarodnye otnosheniya,* p. 262.

25. Viktor Tsoppi, "Igra s ognem," *Literaturnaya Gazeta,* Jan. 24, 1979; *Krasnaya zvezda,* Dec. 17, 1978.

possessing the potential to produce and launch nuclear warheads deep into the USSR.

Real and anticipated American deployment of strategic ballistic weapons in the Pacific and Indian oceans promotes Asia's significance at this highest level of national priorities. Trident II is seen as threatening not only the Far East and Central Asia but all of Siberia and portions of European Russia. Conversely, the Soviet deployment of 30 percent of the country's ICBMs along the Trans-Siberian Railroad and one-third of the navy in the Pacific, together with the reported use of the Sea of Okhotsk as an enclave for SS-N-18 missiles capable of reaching most of the continental United States, suggests that greater strategic importance is being attached to Asia and its adjacent oceans.[26]

At a second level of priorities Moscow seeks to project its power and influence abroad by a combination of political, military, and economic means, exercised directly or through satellites and allies. In this context Asia also commands demonstratively more importance today than at any time in the past, thanks largely to the People's Republic of China.

China is the first Asian country to challenge the USSR politically on a global level. Soviet media depict Beijing's Maoist leaders as relentless disrupters of international peace, craving hegemony in Southeast Asia, pushing the United States into nuclear war with the USSR, attempting to poison relations between the USSR and its allies, and systematically undercutting Soviet policies throughout the world in league with imperialists, revanchists, fascists, racists, and Zionists. The intensity of Soviet rhetoric about China to some extent derives from ideological considerations, but within the cloud of hyperbole are suspended particles of genuine anxiety about Beijing's new relationships with the Soviet Union's major rivals. Moscow suspects that China's "reckless" anti-Sovietism could be given teeth by economic, technical, and military assistance from the United States, Japan, and Western Europe. In addition Beijing's strident warnings about Soviet "hegemonistic" aspirations are perceived in Moscow as providing ammunition in Washington, Tokyo, and European capitals that seek to undermine détente, rearm Japan, and strengthen NATO.[27]

From published sources alone it is easy to get the impression that Beijing so preoccupies Soviet leaders that Moscow's highest political priority in Asia must be to contain China. Yet in private, Soviet analysts

26. Japan, Defense Agency, Public Information Division, *Defense Bulletin*, vol. 2, no. 2 (Oct. 1978), p. 7; *Hokkaido shimbun*, Mar. 15, 1977.

27. V. A. Semenov, "Evropeiskaya besopasnost' i pozitsiya KNR," *PDV*, no. 1 (1973), pp. 188–91; V. I. Petukhov, "Problemy Evropy i politika Pekina," *PDV*, no. 2 (1973), pp. 161–66; Yu. I. Mikhailov, "Kitai i zapadnoevropeiskaya integratsiya," *PDV*, no. 4 (1973), pp. 152–59.

assert that China is too weak to pose, alone, a credible threat to the USSR's vital interests. These analysts concede that China is a global irritant but they maintain that Beijing can confront the USSR with a serious challenge only if modernized and armed by the West. That Washington can to a great extent determine Beijing's ability to threaten Soviet interests reinforces on a regional basis what every Russian observer already knows in a global context: that the United States ultimately commands the highest political as well as strategic priority. One specialist went so far as to assert (in private) that if the two superpowers could only resolve their outstanding differences, all would be well—a polite way of signaling that the United States still remains the USSR's main competitor in Asia.

Asia probably plays a bigger rather than a smaller role in Soviet–American competition since the United States withdrew from Indochina. In Moscow's view the United States is trying to compensate for its setbacks in Vietnam and Iran by making a dangerous commitment to counterrevolution in Southwest Asia, a commitment that conflicts directly with a growing Soviet conviction that the USSR has become the protector of "socialist" Afghanistan and "revolutionary" Iran. Moscow also sees a growing American presence in Southeast Asia in the form of more active overtures to ASEAN nations and a closer association with China's ambitions in the region. Washington's strengthened military alliance with Tokyo, its developing strategic partnership with Beijing, and its reaffirmed military presence in South Korea all impress Soviet observers as disturbing evidence of growing tension in Northeast Asia, where the USSR has vital stakes.

Greater Soviet–American tension from Afghanistan to Japan has enhanced Asia's priority relative to other parts of the world. The USSR has higher stakes in Europe but Soviet–American competition there has occurred within a less volatile environment, although recent events in Poland portend otherwise. Africa and Latin America may offer Moscow more opportunities to extend its influence at American expense but Soviet stakes are relatively lower in those regions than in Asia. Perhaps only the Middle East possesses an equivalent combination of tension, opportunities, and stakes.

Asia's higher position in Soviet priorities does not mean that Asia is perceived as a set of problems separate from other parts of the world. Soviet observers explain President Carter's reaction to events in Afghanistan, for example, as but one of a series of deliberate moves (deployment of Pershing missiles in NATO countries, connivance with congressional opponents of SALT II, flurry about the Soviet combat brigade in Cuba) all designed to gather political support from the "military-industrial complex" and its allies.

Japan's growing regional and global profile has also promoted the Asian component in Moscow's priorities. Soviet analysts appreciate the complex international implications of Japan's new economic stature, even as they tend to overdramatize the significance of Japan's increased defense expenditures. Japan's economic penetration of South Korea, Southeast Asia, and the United States, together with its reliance on Middle East oil, has evoked scenarios of Sino–Japanese and Japanese–American rivalry in which some Soviet commentators speculate (in private) on playing a "Japan card" vis-à-vis Washington and Beijing. On the other hand there is a growing recognition that Moscow's own problems with Tokyo have acquired more than a bilateral significance. Official denials notwithstanding, Moscow knows that there *is* a territorial problem in Japan's claims to the southern Kurile Islands; moreover, Moscow knows that the impasse on this issue serves Chinese and American objectives insofar as it inhibits a Soviet–Japanese rapprochement.

Just as economic stature raises Tokyo in Soviet priorities, so do an ability and willingness to pursue a regional power role raise Vietnam's importance in the eyes of Soviet policymakers. Moscow now has a powerful ally in Southeast Asia that fulfills a double function of containing China and providing a base for projecting Soviet influence throughout the region. By expelling the United States from Indochina, replacing a pro-Beijing with a pro-Moscow regime in Cambodia, handling China's retaliatory incursion without invoking the recently signed defense treaty with the USSR, guiding Laos into the "socialist community," and offering Danang and Cam Ranh Bay facilities for Soviet air and naval forces, Hanoi has earned a key place in Soviet regional policy considerations. Moscow, to be sure, pays a price for Hanoi's services in terms of military and economic aid, diminished diplomatic maneuverability toward ASEAN nations, and—for a while—eroded influence in Pyongyang (which condemned Vietnam's invasion of Cambodia but remained silent on China's attack on Vietnam).

Moscow's policies toward Japan and Vietnam suggest, in different ways, that economic factors are growing but still remain subsidiary to political objectives. The USSR has a potentially major economic stake in Asia and the Pacific. There are Soviet officials, especially in Siberia and the Far East, who would like to see their country establish strong economic relationships with Asian and Pacific countries, including the United States. But Moscow planners have not yet seen fit to allow the Soviet Far East to assume more than a modest economic profile in the region. Despite impressive increases in percentage terms during the past twenty years, economic ties with Japan remain limited in terms of what one would expect for two major industrial neighbors with many complementary needs. Trade with other Asian countries collectively constitutes less than that between the USSR and Japan. Sino–Soviet commerce has turned upward after years of stagnation but in 1977 it still had not reached one-quarter of the 1960 volume. Political motivations play a key role in economic relations with Mongolia (a strategically located satellite), North Korea (a self-willed object of Beijing's competitive attentions), Vietnam (an important ally), and the ASEAN nations (where the USSR seeks to increase its own influence and reduce that of the United States, China, and Japan).

Moscow's revolutionary expectations for Asia do not loom so prominently as they did in the early 1920s but they have not been discarded. In general the USSR places a higher priority on maximizing Soviet influence with existing regimes and minimizing that of the United States and China. This does not prevent the Kremlin from assisting Hanoi to export a "revolution" to Cambodia or from "protecting a revolution" in Afghanistan when the risks are deemed affordable. It is even conceivable that under certain circumstances some Soviet strategists might be tempted to take a more direct part in promoting certain elements of the revolutionary situation in Iran, but the risks in provoking a strong Muslim, not to mention American, reaction would seem too formidable for this tactic for the time being. In Southeast Asia, Moscow knows that there is a direct relationship between Hanoi's behavior and ASEAN attitudes toward the USSR. Besides, the revolutionary movements in Thailand, Malaysia, and the Philippines have tended to look to Beijing for aid. Making a virtue out of necessity, Moscow portrays China as a subversive intruder nourishing insurrectionary elements in the region.

It does not appear that the USSR has immediate revolutionary expectations in Northeast Asia. Whatever Soviet publications might say about the late President Park's regime and whatever opportunities some strategists might perceive in recent political unrest in South Korea, Moscow has little desire for an upheaval on the Korean peninsula that could trigger a confrontation with the United States and catalyze Japanese rearmament. However, one specialist did hint privately in the wake of Afghanistan's military investment that any closer coordination of Sino–American strategic policies might oblige the USSR to "re-examine" its attitude towards Kim Il Sung, a euphemism for giving Kim more material and political support to implement his revolutionary mission in the south.

If revolutionary expectations do not figure prominently in Moscow's Asian priorities, a truly revolutionary development unforeseen by Lenin is obliging Soviet leaders to accord new weight to Asia: conflict among communist nations. The Sino–Soviet rift, together with recent hostilities between communist states in Southeast Asia (China and Vietnam, Vietnam and Cambodia) pose knotty political and ideological problems to the party. Ideologues have yet to find a solution to what in Marxist-Leninist theory is impossible. The Politburo's late spokesman on ideological matters, Mikhail Suslov, advanced a semantic solution to this paradox by asserting in 1979 that China is not a socialist state. Yet Leonid Brezhnev discussed China under the category "world socialist system" in the secretary general's report to the Twenty-Sixth Party Congress in February 1981.[28] Analysts privately venture that China is socialist insofar as the state owns and controls the means of production and distribution but that China's foreign policy is "anti-socialist." Debates on this question are veiled from public view but they will probably continue for the foreseeable future.

ASIAN TRENDS IN THE SOVIET PERSPECTIVE

As self-professed Marxists, Soviet spokesmen have little choice but to assert that the course of history is ineluctably moving their way even if it needs a Leninist nudge now and then. Pronouncements about the ascendancy of socialism and the crises of capitalism routinely crop up at party congresses and are ubiquitous features of Soviet publications. This global optimism is applied to Asia, producing regular enumerations of "socialist" gains and "imperialist" reverses in the region.[29]

Soviet observers publicly express satisfaction about recent trends in Asia, citing the following in particular. The United States has been expelled from Indochina, leaving a united Vietnam closely allied with Moscow. Pro-Soviet regimes have been installed in Laos and Cambodia. Political and economic ties with ASEAN nations have been established over the corpse of SEATO. A growing economic relationship with Japan can be seen in both trade and investment statistics. Expansion of the Pacific Fleet and its support bases in the Soviet Far East and Vietnam permits the USSR to enjoy an unprecedented military presence around the Asian littoral. The fall of the Shah in Iran signified a major defeat for American hopes of containing the USSR in Southwest Asia. The ongoing Iranian revolution could eventually move in a direction that would bring "progressive" elements to the fore. The situation in Afghanistan should be "normalized" in the foreseeable future. Indira Gandhi's electoral victory reinforces Soviet–Indian ties and will complicate the American task of arming Pakistan.

On the other hand Soviet expectations in Asia have suffered setbacks, setbacks that the USSR does not always acknowledge publicly but that impinge no less upon perceptions of current trends. No amount of

28. Suslov: *Pravda*, Sept. 19, 1979; Brezhnev: *Literaturnaya Gazeta*, Feb. 25, 1981.
29. Kapitsa, *Bor'ba SSSR.*

rhetoric can conceal the cost to the USSR of China's metamorphosis from a subordinate ally into a vociferously hostile antagonist cultivating political, economic, and military ties with Japan, the United States, and Western Europe. Moscow has had no success in heading off either a Sino–Japanese or a Sino–American rapprochement, both of which in the Kremlin's view are fraught with dangerous implications. Also, Moscow has not been able to weaken the Japanese–American alliance. North Korea's position in the Sino–Soviet dispute is not satisfactory from Moscow's perspective. Moreover, Pyongyang, for reasons that are not yet clear (but no less disturbing), was the scene of declarations by Cambodian exiles with Chinese connections. South Korea has not only survived but is growing economically. Indonesia has rebuffed Soviet tutelage. Professions of friendship notwithstanding, India is no closer to joining the "socialist community." The situation in Iran is unpredictable and potentially dangerous for the USSR. Reaction to the Soviet move into Afghanistan was unexpectedly strong, not only from the United States but from the Third World as well. The intensity of Muslim nationalism in both Iran and Afghanistan is unsettling in its potential infectiousness. Finally, Brezhnev's collective security proposal for Asia, echoed periodically by Soviet spokesmen since its first enunciation in 1969, seems less and less likely to elicit an appeal outside a handful of client states and Vietnam.

The gap between expectation and reality can be illustrated by reference to an article published in 1961 in the party's theoretical journal predicting the growth of the "socialist camp" during the next twenty years.[30] By 1980, the article proclaimed, the "socialist camp" would comprise a majority of the world's population and 60 percent of its industrial production. In fact, the 1 billion members of the "socialist camp" of 1960 has dwindled to 562 million in the "socialist community" of 1980. What was projected to be 54 percent of the world population is barely 14 percent. What was anticipated to be 60 percent of global industrial production is about 30 percent.[31] Much of this discrepancy can be accounted for by developments in Asia. India and Indonesia have not joined, and China has departed from, the "socialist camp."

One of the more delicate assignments undertaken by Soviet commentators is to explain negative trends within an axiomatically optimistic

30. S. Strumilin, "The World 20 Years from Now," *Kommunist,* no. 13 (Sept. 1961), pp. 25–36, in *Current Digest of the Soviet Press* (hereafter cited as *CDSP*), vol. 13, no. 38 (Oct. 18, 1961), pp. 3–7.

31. The official current Soviet statistic is that socialist states account for "more than 40%" of global industrial production. In addition to being a generous estimate, the figure includes China. See *Narodnoe khozyaistvo SSSR v 1978 g.* (Moscow: Statistika, 1979), p. 47.

ideological framework. Under guidelines established by the party, this task is executed in a variety of ways that differ somewhat according to the sophistication of the commentator and of the intended audience.

At a popular level, commentators are wont to portray Asian trends as products of interactions among stereotyped actors: "imperialists" (also "revanchists," "chauvinists"); "socialists" (peace-loving, ever stronger, and led by the Soviet Union); and the Third World (moving ever closer to the socialist countries as the struggle with imperialism deepens). At this level the Sino–American and Sino–Japanese normalizations are treated as a multilevel conspiracy. The Red Army paper *Krasnaya zvezda,* for example, pointed to an emerging alliance of "American imperialists, Japanese revanchists, and Chinese great-power chauvinists."[32] It went on to ascribe grandiose ambitions to all three countries, each of which was said to be temporarily camouflaging its rivalry with the other two in order first to deal with the Soviet Union, which was blocking their "dream of wiping out the peoples' revolutionary gains, redrawing borders, and establishing their own domination in Asia." American imperialists, represented by Zbigniew Brzezinski, are playing the "China card" to create a triangular military alliance while secretly maneuvering Beijing and Moscow into hostilities. Chinese chauvinists are fomenting a Soviet–American nuclear showdown that would "clear the way to world hegemony" for Beijing. Japanese revanchists, restless with postwar subordination to Washington, are nursing expansionist ambitions in Southeast Asia.

At another level of commentary, found mainly in specialized books and journals, one encounters subtler interpretations that share three basic characteristics. First, these analyses do not treat a trend as an isolated phenomenon but relate it to a global "correlation of forces." The correlation of forces embraces a complex interaction between regional and global, political and military, economic and social, and international and domestic issues. Second, close attention is paid to identifying "contradictions" in both bilateral (e.g., Sino–American) and multilateral (Japan–United States–Western Europe) relationships. These contradictions may be temporarily submerged but they are said to resurface inevitably according to "their own logic and law of development" and eventually shift the correlation of forces in favor of the USSR. Third, Soviet analysts distinguish between "subjective" and "objective" trends. The former are supposedly products of political decisions (e.g., Sino–Japanese normalization). The latter (e.g., détente) are said to possess an independent momentum, being part of a historical dialectic.

The single most worrisome subjective trend in Asia today from a

32. *Krasnaya zvezda,* Dec. 17, 1978.

Soviet perspective is the network of new relationships attending diplomatic initiatives in Beijing, Washington, and Tokyo. Neither Sino–Japanese nor Sino–American normalization came as a surprise to Soviet analysts. In a 1965 dissertation V. N. Barishnykov speculated that Washington would move toward a rapprochement with Beijing when Taiwan had lost its military significance.[33] Six years later M. I. Sladkovsky (director of the Institute of the Far East) asserted that Japan's "ruling circles," perceiving a weakening of the U.S. position in Asia, were quietly preparing for an alliance with China.[34] Sladkovsky believed that this alliance would have a racial complexion and as such would not be concluded as long as the U.S.–Japan Mutual Security Treaty remained in effect. What neither Barishnykov nor Sladkovsky envisioned was a simultaneous Sino–Japanese and Sino–American rapprochement without any corresponding attenuation of Japanese–American ties.

Analyses of China's new policies toward Japan and the United States stress the interaction of domestic problems with diplomacy. China's masses are portrayed as tired of Maoist socioeconomic upheavals. Mounting popular dissatisfaction has aggravated power struggles between "ideologues" and "pragmatists" within the ruling elite. These two groups are divided not by foreign policy (all current Chinese leaders are portrayed as chauvinists) but by economic, ideological, and personnel questions. The Gang of Four and Four Modernizations campaigns are but tactics to build up China's military power. By emphasizing material development at the expense of social justice, these campaigns have provoked opposition from officials who came to prominence during the Cultural Revolution. To defuse internal tension, the leadership is whipping up chauvinist sentiment, psychologically preparing the country for war, and launching aggressive ventures in Southeast Asia.[35]

What China seeks in a new relationship with Japan and the United States, according to many analysts, is economic modernization at home and a fulfillment of hegemonistic ambitions overseas. Beijing uses anti-Sovietism as "political dollars" to buy American technical and economic assistance. In fact the arms sought by Beijing in the West are for use not against the USSR but against Vietnam, which Chinese leaders see as blocking their expansive designs in Southeast Asia. Similarly, the Sino–Japanese Peace Treaty (1978) is but a tool for exerting leverage on

33. Cited in Zimmerman, *Soviet Perspectives,* pp. 240–41.

34. M. I. Sladkovsky, *Kitai i Yaponiya* (Moscow: Nauka, 1971), pp. 332–33.

35. M. Yakovlev, "Instability Persists," *Pravda,* Oct. 29, 1978, in *CDSP,* vol. 30, no. 41 (Nov. 22, 1978), p. 8; A. Petrov, "Same Goals, Contradictory Course," *Pravda,* Dec. 28, 1978, in *CDSP,* vol. 30, no. 51 (Jan. 17, 1979), p. 13; "Reshayushchii faktor mirovogo razvitiya," *PDV,* no. 4 (1978), p. 9; "Itogi 'poteryannogo desyatiletiya' i sovremennoe polozhenie KNR," *PDV,* no. 1 (1979), pp. 56–75.

Tokyo. Any Japanese action that incurs Beijing's disfavor can be denounced as a violation of the treaty, making it an instrument to manipulate feelings of cultural affinity and historical guilt that animate segments of Japan's ruling circles and intelligentsia. The U.S.–Japan Mutual Security Treaty is also said to be used by Beijing for its own aims. Beijing in the long run will try to destroy the Japanese–American alliance but for the time being is tolerating it as a device to contain the USSR.

Japan's motives appear to be seen as more complex than those of China because the tactical unity on foreign policy among Beijing's leaders has no counterpart in Tokyo, where different interest groups influence alignments among factions of the ruling Liberal Democratic party and various opposition parties. Moreover, Soviet analysts face phenomena in Japan that do not easily fit into Marxist-Leninist categories. The Japanese communist party, for example, not only has refused to take Moscow's side against Beijing but claims more territory from the Soviet Union than does the conservative Liberal Democratic party.[36]

Published Soviet analyses of Japan's motives for normalizing relations with Beijing stress that elements within the "ruling circles" are seeking to reinforce Beijing's anti-Soviet orientation, increase Tokyo's bargaining leverage vis-à-vis Moscow, secure economic benefits from China, and gain a margin of independence from the United States.[37] For a while these elements were restrained by "thoughtful and realistic" Japanese who are sensitive to the USSR's "growing international authority," anxious about Japan's international image, aware that China cannot be used to extract territorial concessions in the Kurile Islands, and fearful of complicating relations with the United States. Left to themselves, Japan's ruling circles would probably have opted for caution and have preserved diplomatic equidistance between Moscow and Beijing, but this caution was put aside in May of 1978, when Brzezinski told Tokyo to go ahead and sign a peace treaty with China even if that treaty contained an "anti-hegemony" clause aimed at the USSR.

Complexities and anomalies have led to disagreements among Soviet analysts of China and Japan. There is no consensus about the existence of "demaofication." Some specialists are prepared to see a degree of demaofication in the pragmatic, technical-oriented aspects of the Four Modernizations campaigns. Others, however, label the new domestic

36. However, the territorial issue was not mentioned in public communiqués issued after a meeting of Soviet and Japanese communist party representatives in December 1979 (*Soviet World Outlook*, vol. 5, no. 1 [Jan. 15, 1980], p. 6).

37. M. G. Nosov, *Yapono-kitaiskie otnosheniya* (Moscow: Nauka, 1978), pp. 4–7, 169; V. N. Berezin, *Kurs na dobrososedstvo i sotrudnichestvo i ego protivniki* (Moscow: Mezhdunarodnye otnosheniya, 1977), p. 118.

policies as quintessentially Maoist tactics designed to further the Maoist aim of great Han chauvinism. Similarly, there are disagreements on the matter of Japanese "militarism." Some authors play down the subject in their works and privately discount any immediate prospect of militarization, citing the low percentage of armaments expenditures in major corporations and dismissing the far right as an annoyance rather than a powerful threat. Others perceive nationalist tendences in the irredentist movement for the southern Kurile Islands, in textbook revision, and in the rise of Yasukuni and Ise shrine visitations but they stop short of equating these trends with an upsurge of militarism.[38] Still others, including the authoritative party official Ivan Kovalenko ("Ivkov"), depict an ominous scenario of "militarist trends, a buildup of the armed forces, growing production of modern military hardware, wide-scale ideological indoctrination of the masses and the armed forces in the spirit of revanchism, and the propagation of the cult of violence."[39] There are also divergent appraisals of the Japanese–American alliance, which some commentators assert injures Japan's "national dignity and prestige"[40] but which others concede allows Japan to play a larger role in Asia without arousing the fears of Asian countries.

The above differences are alluded to in private conversations but are not articulated in print. Their significance should not be overestimated, for in a larger context Soviet analyses of China and Japan share basic assumptions: internally both countries are beset with economic and social crises, and externally their power aspirations will eventually generate friction with each other and with Washington.

Assessing American policy in Asia presents Soviet analysts with formidable difficulties. A growing awareness of the pluralistic nature of American politics has only complicated the task of determining what Washington seeks in its new relationship with Beijing or how firm Washington's commitment is to South Korea, Thailand, and the Philippines. The enormous volume of raw data is as much a hindrance as an aid to analysis. Pronouncements by administration officials, congressmen, journalists, businessmen, and academics are riddled with inconsistencies that the Soviet observer is unaccustomed to in his own political environment. One specialist wryly confided that it took him some time to realize that the views expressed to him by Asianists at various research institutes and universities were not necessarily those of Washington policymakers.

38. For example, Igor Latyshev, "Natsionalisticheskie tendentsii v politike pravyashchikh krugov Yaponii," *Narody Azii i Afriki*, no. 3 (1971), pp. 40–50.

39. I. Ivkov, "Japanese Militarism Rears its Head," *Far Eastern Affairs*, no. 4 (1978), p. 43.

40. A. P. Markov, *Poslevoennaya politika Yaponii v Azii i Kitai, 1945–1977* (Moscow: Nauka, 1979), p. 234.

Soviet publications treat American policy in Asia as an integral part of the global objectives of the country's "ruling classes": to achieve and preserve political and economic domination, to undermine the "socialist community," to keep the Third World in economic bondage, and to crush anti-imperialist movements wherever they may appear. Without changing these ultimate aims, the United States has shifted its tactics in an effort to compensate for recent setbacks and to exploit opportunities presented by Beijing's current anti-Soviet posture.

According to some observers an important shift occurred in the early 1970s, when the United States recognized its inability to impose its will in Southeast Asia. Searching for an alternative means to contain the USSR and to suppress "national liberation movements," Nixon and Kissinger discarded the "politics of strength" approach to Asia in favor of "balancing centers of power," a tactic that involved taking advantage of the Sino–Soviet rift, inhibiting Soviet–Japanese normalization, and strengthening the military alliance with Japan.[41] The Nixon–Kissinger "Beijing connection," which surfaced in 1971, was cultivated within the framework of détente with the USSR. Under Nixon the United States at least formally remained on the sidelines of Sino–Soviet rivalry. However, the Ford and Carter administrations dropped the "realistic" aspect of the Nixon–Kissinger Asia policy by integrating Beijing's anti-Sovietism into American strategic calculations. Soviet analysts attribute this shift to pressure from "conservative" and "military" circles on Carter to take a tougher stance toward Moscow in the wake of "socialist victories" in Indochina, Angola, Ethiopia, and Afghanistan; American reverses in Iran and Guatamala; and escalating tension between the United States and the Third World.

Washington's new political offensive, according to Soviet analysts, became clear with Brzezinski's visit to Beijing in May 1978, when he remarked that the United States and China shared strategic interests. The new American tactic of "using Chinese expansion for the purposes of fighting socialism and progressive forces in general throughout the world" was again demonstrated in January and February of 1979 by the Carter administration's "factual encouragement of Beijing's aggression against the Democratic Republic of Vietnam."[42]

In Moscow's eyes, closer ties between Washington and Beijing have manifold repercussions on other trends within and outside Asia. One of these is that Japanese trade and investment are growing with China but

41. B. N. Zanegin, "Demokraticheskaya administratsiya i diplomaticheskoe priznanie KNR," *SShA: Ekonomika, Politika, Ideologiya,* no. 3 (Mar. 1979), p. 53; Petrov, *Mezhdunarodnye otnosheniya,* p. 52.

42. B. N. Zanegin, "Vashington i pekinskaya agressiya protiv SRV," *SShA: Ekonomika, Politika, Ideologiya,* no. 5 (May 1979), p. 80.

lagging with the USSR. Although Soviet–Japanese trade has made impressive increases in percentage terms since 1960, the USSR occupied a smaller proportion of Japan's total foreign trade in 1977 than in 1967. Moreover, the pace of Japanese participation in Siberian development has shown definite signs of losing momentum, particularly in the wake of the Afghanistan crisis. Among the many obstacles to Soviet–Japanese cooperation, Moscow ascribes a significant role to the machinations of Beijing and Washington.

Moscow also is disappointed with the low level of Soviet–American trade and of American investment in Siberia. Although one writer recently saw "vast possibilities" involving "fantastic projects" in the Soviet Far East and Pacific,[43] expectations raised by the 1972 Soviet–American Trade Agreement have remained unfulfilled, largely because of the Jackson–Vanik and Stevenson amendments. The granting in January 1980 of most-favored-nation status to China will probably intensify Soviet suspicions about Sino–American collusion.

Trends in Southeast Asia have both pleased and dissatisfied Soviet observers. Moscow is generally pleased with Hanoi's invasion of Cambodia, which Ivan Kovalenko asserted "had a salutary effect on the situation in the region."[44] Kovalenko's "salutary effect" referred not only to the demise of the genocidal regime but to the elimination of Beijing's sole client in Southeast Asia and the gain of a client for Moscow's ally. China's punitive attack on Vietnam probably caused some moments of concern in the Kremlin but eventually brought gratifying results. Vietnam proved itself capable of handling a Chinese challenge without putting the recently concluded defense pact between Moscow and Hanoi to a serious test. Soviet credibility was upheld at a relatively small risk and Moscow acquired a military dividend: the use of facilities at Danang and Cam Ranh Bay.

Yet Moscow is learning that military power does not necessarily translate into political influence in Southeast Asia. ASEAN nations have diplomatic relations and some trade with the USSR but remain cool to closer political ties. The new regime in Phnom Penh has not achieved international legitimacy despite Moscow's efforts at the conference of non-aligned nations in Havana and in the United Nations. However useful as a military ally, Vietnam may prove to be a political liability in a region where distrust of Hanoi runs deep. The expectation of one Soviet commentator that Hanoi will help ASEAN countries move along a "more balanced

43. Boris N. Slavinsky, "Siberia and the Soviet Far East within the Framework of International Trade and Economic Relations," *Asian Survey*, vol. 17, no. 4 (Apr. 1977), pp. 324–25.

44. Ivan Ivkov, "Victory of Immense Significance," *New Times*, no. 5 (Jan. 1979), p. 4.

course" toward "political and economic independence"[45] has no immediate prospect of fulfillment. Even the utility of Hanoi is subject to the unpredictable and ungovernable impulses of Vietnamese nationalism.

If some current trends in Asia have disappointed Soviet observers, the long-term outlook in Moscow is rather optimistic. For one thing, Soviet analysts are skeptical about China's ability to sustain an economic relationship with either Japan or the United States. They feel that the West has overestimated China's economic stature. One specialist remarked privately that China is "objectively" weaker than Italy and will be further behind the USSR in the year 2000 than it is today. Another asserted that China will sooner or later encounter difficulties in repaying Japan with paraffin-rich oil, which the Japanese cannot refine, and the United States with cheap textiles, which will put Americans out of work.[46] These observers are confident that the limits of Sino–American rapprochement will become apparent as Americans recognize China's low trade and investment potential and realize that Beijing, far from being a Far Eastern NATO, is an expansionist power seeking to drive the United States from the western Pacific.

Second, optimism is also evident in long-term prognoses of Soviet–Japanese relations. Japan, it is felt, will become increasingly interested in Siberian resources as OPEC price hikes and Middle East political instability oblige Tokyo to look for alternate sources of petroleum. Moreover, irredentist sentiment about the Kurile Islands is seen as fading with time, thereby removing an obstacle to closer political relations. An anticipated strengthening of "progressive" forces within Japan is also adduced as a factor supporting long-term optimism.

Third, some (but not all) specialists are prepared to entertain the prospect of a limited Sino–Soviet reconciliation in the foreseeable future. This is envisioned as occurring when Beijing, unable to play off Washington against Moscow and denied additional Western credits, turns to the USSR once again for economic assistance. This shift in Beijing will be brought about by the emergence of a more "sober" and "realistic" leadership that recognizes that "reckless anti-Sovietism" works against China's own interests.

Fourth, basic to Soviet confidence about the long-term future is an awareness that the USSR possesses vast untapped natural resources whereas China is economically weak, Japan depends upon imported raw materials, and the United States is becoming increasingly dependent upon imported sources of energy. The USSR may lag behind the United

45. B. Ilyichev, "Southeast Asia: Positive Tendencies," *Pravda*, Oct. 29, 1978, in *CDSP*, vol. 30, no. 43 (Nov. 22, 1978), p. 164.

46. Vladimir B. Yakubovsky, "Soviet Policy in Asia," Lecture at East–West Center, Honolulu, Apr. 20, 1979.

States in technological matters but Soviet observers feel that their country can always "go it alone" in Siberian development. One analyst went so far as to assert that it is the capitalist countries who will need the USSR in order to survive.[47]

Finally, optimism is generated and sustained by what appears to be a genuine belief in "contradictions" that will eventually disrupt the network of linkages that confront the USSR in Asia. The Taiwan problem and rivalry in the Pacific are seen as inevitably pushing China and the United States apart.[48] Economic competition in Southeast Asia will someday reactivate "deep-rooted Sino–Japanese antagonisms."[49] Even the Japanese–American relationship, held together for more than thirty years by military, political, economic, and social ties, will be "irreversibly" weakened by a combination of "basic contradictions unresolved by the Pacific War," rivalry over access to raw materials and markets, Tokyo's regional political ambitions, and growing Soviet–Japanese ties.[50] Similar contradictions are said to be at work among the three centers of capitalism (the United States, the European Common Market countries, and Japan) and between these centers on one hand and the developing nations on the other.[51]

It would be an oversimplification to conclude that Soviet optimism about the long-term future is unclouded by doubts. In private, one analyst confided that there were also unfavorable signs within the present "correlation of forces." At home the USSR is confronted with falling industrial growth rates, endemic labor shortages, transportation bottlenecks, and uncertainties about oil supplies. Abroad, the "progressive forces" are in disarray as a result of unresolved contradictions between the USSR and China, centrifugal tendencies within the "socialist community," and the reformist nature of communist movements in Western Europe. If Beijing were ever successful in securing significant military assistance from the West, he continued, China could mount a serious long-term threat to the USSR. Since these remarks were made (in 1978) the situation in Poland has given grounds for yet more long-term doubts about the correlation of forces, for events there are being watched throughout Asia.

The blend of current disappointments with long-term optimism qualified by residual doubts underlies Moscow's readiness to pursue or pass up opportunities to expand its influence in Asia.

47. Petrov, *Mezhdunarodnye otnosheniya*, p. 6.
48. Ibid., p. 38.
49. Primakov, "International Situation," p. 6.
50. Petrov, *Mezhdunarodnye otnosheniya*, pp. 4, 56, 99; Markov, *Poslevoennaya politika Yaponii*, p. 236.
51. Petrov, *Mezhdunarodnye otnosheniya*, pp. 6, 12, 38.

OPPORTUNITIES AND CONSTRAINTS

Moscow's initiatives in Asia are subject to two contradictory impulses. On one hand a deep commitment to struggle propels Soviet leaders to exploit every opportunity to enlarge the socialist community in general and to promote Soviet power in particular. On the other hand an unwillingness to take serious risks compels policymakers to exercise caution.

The term *struggle* reverberates through the lexicon of Soviet discourse: struggle against capitalism, imperialism, colonialism, revanchism, chauvinism, militarism, fascism, and bourgeois ideology; struggle for socialism, national liberation, and peace. The currently favored slogan, détente (the literal Russian term is "relaxation of tension"), does not signify an abdication of a commitment to struggle. On the contrary, détente is regarded as an "objective" stage in the struggle between socialist and capitalist systems, a decisive stage in which socialism, led by the Soviet Union, is to achieve preeminence without nuclear war. Marxism-Leninism has in this case reinforced a geographical and historical legacy that long ago made struggle a Russian way of life.

At the same time, the current Soviet leadership has shown little propensity to push struggle to the point of taking serious risks. Survivors of a generation baptized by Stalin's purges and World War II, the aging members of the Politburo have developed the habits of patience, persistence, and flexibility. Only when the chances of success seem assured do they act—as in Afghanistan.

Committed to exploiting opportunities yet conditioned to exercise caution, Soviet policymakers have been frustrated by their lack of diplomatic maneuverability in Northeast Asia, where four major powers physically converge, where American strategic weapons are deployed, where Soviet frontiers with China and Japan are unsettled, where a volatile situation exists on the Korean peninsula, and where Moscow hopes to develop some of its richest but most inaccessible resources. During the 1970s Soviet observers witnessed dramatic realignments among China, Japan, and the United States, realignments for which the Kremlin has thus far been unable to devise an antidote. Indeed, recent Soviet behavior has if anything accelerated the very trend that Moscow fears: the formation of a Sino–Japanese–American entente.

Curiously, most Russians, including sophisticated Asian specialists, seem unwilling to entertain the notion that the behavior of the USSR itself might be responsible for the emergence of what Moscow terms "anti-Soviet" coalitions in Europe and Asia. Instead, emphasis is placed on the essential fragility of these coalitions and on how the USSR might utilize their internal contradictions. For example, one analyst has written that the USSR can exploit the divergent national interests of the United

States, Japan, and the European Common Market.[52] Indeed, strong
American reactions to events in Iran and Afghanistan have given Moscow opportunities vis-à-vis Japan and Western Europe. One analyst
adumbrated a strategy that Moscow might adopt if the Reagan administration and Congress took "tough" positions on SALT II, defense expenditures, and arms sales to China:

> If you want another Cold War, we're ready. Only this time, it will be a Cold
> War with just you, not with your allies. This time, you're going to be isolated.

This strategy might prove successful in Asia if the USSR were able to
improve its relations with Japan. In the eyes of Soviet analysts, even a
limited Soviet–Japanese rapprochement would curtail Beijing's ability to
maneuver against Moscow, would weaken the Japanese–American alliance, and would promote greater Japanese participation in Siberian
development.

Improving relations with Japan has not been an easy assignment for
Soviet diplomats. Some Japan specialists in the Academy of Sciences and
the Foreign Ministry have quietly striven to show greater appreciation
for Japanese sensibilities in talks, publications, and broadcasts. Refine-
ments in style alone, however, cannot bridge the distance between Moscow and Tokyo. Soviet bids to improve political relations have repeatedly foundered on the territorial issue, which Tokyo insists must be
solved before a peace treaty can be signed. Insofar as Moscow has little
room or desire to maneuver on this issue, prospects for a political breakthrough with Tokyo are remote.

The political impasse with Tokyo has deprived Moscow of a "Japan
card" to play against Washington. Despite the "Nixon shock," chronic
friction over trade, and varying views on security responsibilities, Japan
and the United States have managed to preserve close political and
economic ties for more than thirty years. The resilience of this relationship puzzles at least one analyst, who asked the author:

> How can it be that Japan, which bitterly fought you in World War II, on whom
> you dropped two atomic bombs, and on whom you imposed a military occupa-
> tion, should like you and not us, even though we were neutral during most of the
> Pacific War, did not bomb any Japanese city, and have no troops on Japanese
> soil?

Opportunities to normalize relations with Beijing have also been limited, in Brezhnev's words, because "the sole criterion which now deter-
mines the Chinese leaders' approach to any major international issue is
their urge to inflict as much damage on the USSR as possible."[53] That

52. Ibid., p. 6.
53. Quoted in *Far Eastern Affairs,* no. 1 (1979), p. 151.

the Soviet leadership has not given up trying, however, is evident from the restraint with which the general secretary spoke about China at the Twenty-Sixth Party Congress early in 1981.

One can assume that Soviet policymakers are quietly seeking out "realistic" elements in Beijing that may come to the fore after the present top leadership passes from the scene. When that time comes, a discreet overture, backed by economic inducements, might elicit a favorable response. Any approach Moscow eventually takes toward China will be conditioned by the prevailing state of Soviet–American relations.

As the USSR's principal global rival, the United States is the ultimate object of any major Soviet initiative in Asia. In the wake of events in Iran and Afghanistan, Moscow can no longer count heavily upon America's post-Vietnam reluctance to become involved in overseas military actions. In the areas where current or potential instabilities offer the USSR opportunities for testing American willpower—Korea, Thailand, the Persian Gulf—Soviet strategists will have to take into consideration the heightened risks of incurring direct American involvement.

Moscow is unlikely to launch any sudden military venture in Asia unless Soviet leaders are confronted with what they perceive as a serious challenge to the USSR's vital interests. Moscow will continue to carry out incremental increases in its military capabilities while probing for soft spots such as Afghanistan, where gains can be had at acceptable risks. There may be more occasions for use of proxies but Moscow will have to take into consideration that Vietnam has its own political and strategic aims, which may not always coincide with those of the USSR, particularly in the event of improved Sino–Soviet relations.

What about the next generation of Soviet leaders? It can be argued that their lack of exposure to the destruction that has made their elders cautious, that their restiveness for more status, emboldened by a perception of American vacillation and a confidence in growing Soviet power, may tempt them to take greater risks. Yet it also can be argued that these same leaders, by shedding some of the insecurity that has gripped their predecessors, may see the logic of giving substance to Brezhnev's 1969 Collective Security proposal and in addition allot higher priority to the problems of food, population, resources, and the environment faced by all Asian nations, including the USSR.

The proportion of challenge, competition, and cooperation in Soviet Asia policy will shift from time to time but the quest for power and prestige is likely to remain a permanent objective. As Asia figures with increasing prominence in the Soviet world view, so should Soviet policies in Asia command more of the world's attention.

3

The Political Influence of the USSR in Asia

ROBERT A. SCALAPINO

Geography and history have combined to make the Union of Soviet Socialist Republics a Eurasian nation. This fact serves to complicate both its domestic and foreign policies and, in some degree, to make of them a continuum. As the Russians projected their nation outward in the course of the nineteenth and twentieth centuries, they encompassed a great variety of peoples, Asian as well as Caucasian. Few of these groups have been thoroughly absorbed, whether the Baltic peoples of the West or the Uzbek and Kazakh peoples of Central Asia. Rather, they have been contained under a Russian-dominated, highly centralized, single-party system with its locus of power in Moscow.

Continued Russian dominance seems reasonably certain, yet the Soviet empire has its elements of fragility. Alien cultures have not been wholly absorbed; ethnic subgroups have not been fully socialized, making for persistent domestic problems. When a neighbor like China challenges not merely the legitimacy of current Soviet leadership but also the legality of Russia's past acquisition of Asian lands and peoples, domestic problems get thrust into the international arena.

Geopolitics dictates that the Soviet Union must pay close attention to both its western and eastern fronts. It is now clear that a third front, on the south, will present increasing and permanent demands. Beyond this, the Russians face the requirement of achieving "equality" with the world's other global power in this nuclear age—the United States. Hence, a fourth front has opened that is geographically unbounded.

In these respects Soviet problems parallel those of the United States. In modern times the United States also has had to direct its attention toward both the Atlantic–European and the Pacific–Asian regions. In addition, issues relating to its northern and southern boundaries, previously somewhat neglected, now demand more attention. The United States too feels the pressure of maintaining matching nuclear strength on the world scene. In the case of both major powers, however, the gravitational pull of the Pacific–Asian region has been ever greater, whether because of threat, opportunity, or some combination of the two.

Thus, in the Soviet perception of areas affecting its national interests,

57

Asia has a priority next to that of Europe and growing rather than diminishing in importance. To understand the contemporary place of the Pacific–Asian region in Russian foreign policy and the political role of the USSR in this half of the world, a brief sketch of the evolution of Asian international politics in their broadest dimensions since World War II is necessary.

THE BACKGROUND

In the immediate postwar period, during the first decade after 1945, the world was dominated by American power despite the fact that these years have often been labeled an era of bipolarism. The Soviet Union, badly wounded by the war, was no more than a regional power. But the region to which its power reached and toward which it exhibited a strong security interest was the central portions of both Europe and Asia, its "borderlands." On the European front Moscow found its situation markedly improved at the end of the war and sought to secure its gains. There, the Kremlin was adamant from the outset: East Europe must be a sphere of Soviet control; West Europe should be, at a minimum, not hostile.[1] In Asia the USSR had to be reconciled initially to cooperation with the Chinese Nationalists under conditions that restored historic Russian privileges. But when the Chinese communists unexpectedly took control, the USSR was prepared to conclude a comprehensive alliance involving substantial aid in order to cement ties with this massive nation on its eastern front. Meanwhile, North Korea was added to Outer Mongolia as a Soviet-sponsored state. During this period, in sum, Soviet policies were based upon an "inner-core" strategy focusing upon the heartland of the Eurasian continent.

In Asia the limited resources of the USSR were largely used to assist two emerging communist states, China and North Korea, and to re-establish the traditional Russian positions in Northeast Asia sanctioned by the Yalta and Potsdam conferences. As a supplement to its inner-core strategy, however, Soviet leaders advanced a revolutionary rhetoric designed to have global appeal, most particularly to what is now called the Third World. This rhetoric drew on Leninism, which called for assaulting the capitalist giants through their soft underbellies—their colonial possessions. It involved full support for "national liberation movements." Here was a minimal risk tactic and one requiring few resources.

1. For a general historical survey of Soviet policies toward Europe and recent developments pertaining to this region, see Stephen S. Kaplan, *Diplomacy of Power* (Washington, D.C.: Brookings Institution, 1981), pp. 1–201, and the sections written by Michel Tatu ("Intervention in Eastern Europe," pp. 205–64).

By the late 1940s the Soviet Union was urging nationalists, hopefully under communist leadership, to take up arms throughout Asia—although the material assistance given them was slight.

Because the United States was the only global power of the period, it fell to Washington to counter Soviet policies, especially Moscow's propensity to advance from the inner-core area outward. First, certain initial premises regarding the postwar world had to be discarded. Three had applied to Asia: Most American authorities had assumed that a rapidly developing China, pursuing the Western political model and assisted by ample U.S. support, could serve as the leader of Asia. Washington had further believed that the wartime alliance with the USSR could be continued, with differences settled amicably. Finally, U.S. leaders thought that the decolonization process would be reasonably swift and peaceful, with a number of new parliamentary states emerging in southern Asia.

None of these crucial premises proved to be correct. China, it was soon discovered, was destined to follow the communist path, in alignment with the Soviet Union. Cooperation with the USSR on such critical issues as Korea and Japan proved impossible, and a cold war climate quickly ensued in Asia as it had in Europe. Decolonization, moreover, proved to be a far longer and more complex process than had earlier been anticipated and one that did not guarantee either stability or political openness.

Once its initial premises were set aside, the United States fashioned policies designed first to shore up those societies on the peripheries of the Soviet–Chinese zone of control—Western Europe and in Asia, South Korea and Japan. It then began the construction of a network of alliances around the Eurasian continent, intended as defensive barriers to communist expansion. It coupled these alliances with aid to a great variety of developing countries in an effort to strengthen their inner defenses. The well-known policy of containment had been born, a policy that was to continue for more than a decade with decidedly mixed results.

The end of this era was signaled by the Sino–Soviet cleavage, that extraordinary event that has so altered the international relations of our times. Progressively, the concept of two ideological camps—and the exclusive, confrontational alliances accompanying them—ceased to reflect reality. Even before the break with Beijing, Russia's post-Stalinist leadership, burdened by domestic difficulties, had begun to explore détente with the United States. This, indeed, was one of the central causes of the break between the two communist giants. As the cleavage worsened, the United States gradually moved into the centrist position within the

Soviet–American–Chinese triangle, communicating with both outside parties and seeking (in the limited degree to which it had leverage) to prevent either war or a restoration of the alliance between them.

The advantages of this development to the United States cannot be underestimated. There were debits, however—some of them substantial. The serious divisions within communist ranks have encouraged adoption of a balance of power strategy by the United States that cuts across ideological lines. Although the dichotomy between the "free" and "communist" worlds was never so pure as its most ardent devotees claimed, earlier policies did provide the ethical or ideological foundation long demanded by the American people in exchange for their support. At present, that foundation is difficult to discern. As one result, the type of public consensus so critical to a coherent American foreign policy cannot easily be constructed or maintained.

The fissures within the communist bloc were also conducive to a declining American perception of threat. This mood also infected America's principal allies, and with it came renewed assertions of nationalism and independence, products of lengthy prosperity and stability, as well as a sense that *international* communism no longer existed.

The fragility of postwar alliances was furthered by the weakened credibility of the United States, especially after Vietnam, coupled with the seeming priority it gave to fashioning closer ties with various communist states. A circular movement of causes and effects has resulted. Domestic and international considerations have reduced the American capacity and propensity to exercise strong leadership in the world. This, in turn, has encouraged foreign countries to doubt American policies and leadership and to hold back from cooperation with the United States. Foreign reluctance to participate in cooperative action, in turn, has reinforced Americans' reservations about entering into cooperative international arrangements.

One of the goals of the Reagan administration is to break the image of weakness, division, and indecision on the part of the United States by tackling internal economic problems, rebuilding American military strength, and giving stronger support to American friends, thereby restoring credibility to U.S. leadership. Only time will tell whether these goals are achieved.

Meanwhile, the Soviet Union has witnessed the destruction of many of its initial postwar dreams and hopes in Asia. Shortly after the close of World War II the USSR had achieved a position in this region far more impressive than that attained at any point by czarist Russia. In addition to regaining territories and privileges long lost, Moscow could look with satisfaction upon the leveling of its historic enemy, Japan, and the achievement of a formidable buffer state/alliance system in Northeast

Asia. Its dominant position in Outer Mongolia was confirmed by treaty. North Korea, established under its aegis, was accounted completely loyal. And most importantly, the far-reaching new alliance with China, East Asia's most massive and potentially most significant state, promised an indefinite expansion of influence. Yet this was not the complete story. In southern Asia the Soviet reach was greatly extended by virtue of the influence that the international communist movement, dominated by the Communist Party of the Soviet Union (CPSU), exercised over the rapidly growing communist parties of the region. In great measure Moscow was able to determine the policies of such parties in the opening postwar years, directing them toward cooperation with noncommunists or struggle. As the newly independent states of Asia began to emerge, Soviet influence was not negligible. The USSR quickly reached out via aid programs and other tactics to associate itself with the nonaligned world.

From the perspective of the early 1980s, the Soviet Union would be justified in regarding the early 1950s as its golden age in Asia. Although mistakes were made (some of them carrying the seeds of future decline) and failures registered, during this period the USSR reached a pinnacle of influence (*not* power) in Asia that remains to be equaled. In addition to the dramatic Sino–Soviet break that has colored every other aspect of the Russian position in this region, the USSR's political relations with most other countries of East Asia have remained static or deteriorated and, with a few exceptions, influence over the Asian communist parties is now negligible. If the Soviet position in South Asia is stronger, here too, the total picture is complex and difficult to forecast, as we shall see. In sum, notwithstanding a few important gains and the rise in its military power within the region, to which we shall refer shortly, the USSR's political and economic position has experienced an overall decline in the Pacific–Asian area during the past three decades. The Soviet Union is aware of these facts and, for the first time since the decline commenced, appears to be contemplating certain new policies to improve its political position. The results remain to be seen.

The factors sketched so briefly above have led to the fluid strategic situation within Asia that exists today. Viewed from a Russian perspective, the inner-core strategy with which Moscow began the postwar era is scarcely viable, at least as long as China moves down its present path and East European nationalism creeps forward. Toward its earlier clients and allies, the Soviet Union often has been forced to respond in a manner primarily defensive, seeking—through the Council for Mutual Economic Assistance (CMEA), the Warsaw Pact, and troop dispositions widely dispersed around its vast borders—to preserve the status quo in the tattered inner zone to the greatest extent possible. As some compensation, however, the Soviet capacity—and will—to project its military power globally is now vastly greater than in the 1950s or 1960s. Indeed, for the first time the Pacific–Asian region must reckon with Soviet military strength, in position or available, roughly equivalent to that of the United States. Thus, in terms of the distribution of military power, this is more nearly a bipolar era than earlier decades; and there is no indication that the massive military superiority of the two superpowers will be seriously challenged from within Asia in this century or well beyond. To label the 1980s as an age of multipolarism is in certain respects highly misleading.

The greatest utility of this power, however, is psychological and political, not military. Its primary service lies in influencing a wide range of economic and political decisions and in deterring opponents, not in its direct employment, at least on a massive scale. The latter event signals failure, not triumph. Never in history has success for major states in their foreign relations depended so fully upon the avoidance of large-scale conflict, while employing all forms of power to influence basic trends.

It is for this reason that the greatest creativity regarding international relations in recent years has related to the camouflages developed to mask major-power involvement in conflict or near-conflict situations. Arms transfers, military training, the use of advisers in the field, the performance of specialized military functions, undeclared war, and the use of surrogates are activities of major and middle powers that have been accelerated and refined in the decades since 1945.

Neither of the two global military powers has lagged in the application of such techniques. The United States took an early lead after 1945, but failures mingled with successes as demonstrated by direct American involvement in Korea and Vietnam. The Soviet Union has come on strong in recent years, and benefited by improving upon earlier American techniques and learning from American failures. Yet it also has had to face the dilemma of escalation or failure. Witness the trauma of Afghanistan. It is clear that for both nations the costs of direct involvement in war now bear heavily upon policymakers. In no sense, however, does this negate the importance of a strategic presence by the two major powers in Asia or the continuing possibility of military intervention. Each superpower must exhibit a willingness under certain circumstances to commit military power directly—preferably on a "quick-strike, single-blow" basis, in such a fashion as to deter further military escalation—or indirectly, in a sustained commitment via Asian allies. These capabilities—and the national will to use them as necessary—will greatly influence the decisions of all Asian states in the years ahead.

Cognizant of these facts, the Soviet Union is dedicated to the augmentation of its military strength in Asia and in the Pacific. In the course of the coming decades it intends to develop Siberia and Central Asia economically and strategically. The USSR also means steadily to increase its Pacific Fleet and air force, as well as its capacity to provide military and economic support to its far-flung allies in the area.[2]

Will its growing military capacities and its demand for recognition as a world power ultimately require that the Soviet Union develop a global strategy? Up to date, Soviet policy has been no more coordinated or carefully constructed than that of the United States. Both major powers have generally accorded greatest priority to Europe and Asia, but both have also taken advantage of "targets of opportunity" elsewhere in an unsystematic and sometimes costly manner. In the coming era, Russia—similar to the United States—will probably put a premium upon stricter priorities, greater burden sharing, and heightened dependence upon economic weapons. Like the United States, although less visibly, the USSR has rising domestic constraints upon the use of its military power. The Soviet people, especially those in European Russia, having had a taste of higher living standards and being exposed in increasing degree to the external world, are beginning to present increased demands to the government for goods and services. This trend can only grow. Moreover, the status quo cannot be maintained with respect to regional and ethnic relations within the USSR. The present distribution of economic and political power that accords predominance to the Russian population based in the European part of the country will not be continued without mounting strains.

Meanwhile, the Soviet alliance system—like the American—is becoming generally less stable and all-encompassing than it was in the cold war era. The ability of the USSR to aggregate power beyond its own forces is similarly less predictable and, in the main, less promising. These factors restrain Soviet actions in Asia, as elsewhere. Thus, despite its commitments to Vietnam, the Soviet Union avoided conflict with China during Beijing's invasion of Vietnam, although the presence (and augmentation) of Russian military power nearby undoubtedly had an indirect effect on China's strategy in that encounter. Soviet policy in this case was comparable to American restraint in responding to the Iranian seizure of the U.S. embassy in November 1979.

In a sense a balance of weakness exists between the two superpowers in spite of the massive armaments they possess. But this balance is no more stable than the balance of power overlaying it. Consequently, limited, indirect military involvements via the medium-sized and smaller

2. One recent estimate of Soviet military power in the Asian–Pacific region and future goals is to be found in *Asian Security—1981* (Tokyo: Research Institute for Peace and Security, 1981), pp. 38–64.

states are virtually assured in the years ahead, with continued risk of escalation to direct major-power conflict when the stakes in these smaller wars become very high.

In the first instance, therefore, it is the domestic and regional components of conflicts within and among the lesser states that represent the critical determinant of major-state relations and general international trends. Poland represents a dramatic illustration of this fact in Europe as does Afghanistan in South Asia. Because of the heavy costs of direct military involvement, the major powers attempt to avoid commitment beyond what seems to be required to preserve their essential interests. Without total involvement each seeks first to turn indigenous developments to its advantage and the advantage of those local forces aligned with it. There is thus a tentativeness to major-power commitments balanced by the tentativeness of alignment among most lesser states. In this general setting, politics—including all that is preliminary to conflict or the threat of conflict—becomes a cardinal element in the situation.

What are the political objectives of the USSR in Asia today, and to what extent have Soviet efforts to achieve those objectives been successful? First and foremost, the Soviet Union seeks to contain China, pending improved relations with some future Beijing government. In this respect the Soviet Union is pursuing policies akin to those carried out by the United States in the 1950s, and for very similar reasons. A second and related objective is to vie with the United States for influence in Asia and, in general terms, to weaken key American alliances by injecting into them elements of complexity and competition. A third Soviet objective in Asia is to project a dual image of the USSR: on the one hand, that of a revolutionary society and developmental model in the tradition of Marx, Engels, and Lenin; on the other hand, that of a responsible but formidable world power, concerned to prevent war and advance state-to-state relations.

SOVIET POLICIES TOWARD CHINA

In assessing the current status of Soviet political relations in Asia with respect to these broad goals, let us begin with the issue of China, so central to all other concerns. The present mood of Soviet leaders—and specialists—regarding the China problem is one of pessimism or at least gloominess with regard to short-term prospects. The Russians assert that Chinese nationalism is still on the rise and that the chances for "rational" policies on the part of Beijing toward Moscow are slim. They hope that at some point in the future a Chinese leadership will come to power prepared to pull Maoism out by the root in the foreign policy arena as well as on the domestic front, enabling the reestablishment of "fraternal relations" with the USSR. Privately, Russian policymakers maintain that they would be satisfied to develop with Beijing the type of relations they currently have with Belgrade. They insist that the Soviet Union continues to have numerous friends in China and that they have a high respect for the Chinese people who have been "betrayed" by their leaders. But they are not forecasting any rapid reversal of recent trends in Sino–Soviet relations, and in this they are probably wise.

Russia and China are two states—or more accurately, two empires—sharing in some measure a common ideology and similar political and economic institutions but differing in ethnicity and culture, timing of revolution, stage of development, and degree of power. Hence, they have very different perceptions of national interests. These are empires, moreover, that are moving toward each other with no buffer-state system to separate them and with nationalist—and racial—feelings strong on each side. Today, moreover, they lack a common enemy, the cement that once held them together, and each is engaged in a fierce struggle to isolate the other, with the Indochina crisis and the Afghanistan invasion being only the latest chapters in what seems likely to be a long-drawn-out and possibly explosive confrontation. The outlook for genuine rapprochement is not promising—at least in the near term.

Negotiations on improving state-to-state relations, first proffered by the PRC in April 1979 in connection with the notification that it was abrogating the 1950 Sino–Soviet treaty, may bear fruit someday but there are no signs that the stalemate will be broken soon. In the talks that got under way in the fall of 1979, Soviet negotiators proposed that Russia and China formally accept certain general principles by signing agreements that would outlaw the use of either nuclear or conventional weapons by one party against the other and that would preclude either state from adopting a policy of hegemony, whether in Asia or elsewhere. This proposal represented a tactical shift for Soviet leaders. Earlier, Moscow had vigorously denounced the term *hegemonism* as a code word used by the Chinese to attack the USSR. Now, the USSR was proposing to the Chinese that the two communist countries bilaterally forsake hegemonism while at the same time introducing a resolution in the United Nations to outlaw hegemonism globally. Clearly, the Soviet Union was seeking to challenge China's monopoly of the term and to undermine the political advantages Beijing was gaining.

The Chinese have responded to Soviet proposals by insisting that prior to any agreement on general principles, the Russians must act on specific grievances. The Chinese spokesmen have demanded, among other things, that Russia withdraw its troops from Mongolia, cease military assistance to Vietnam, and remove troops from Afghanistan. Because the USSR is not prepared to meet any of these conditions, the impasse continues. Russian spokesmen say they suspect that the Chinese do not want an improvement of relations at this time.

Certainly the Soviet Union would like to reduce the tension on its eastern borders, thereby alleviating one of the many pressures with which it is confronted. Undoubtedly, this desire has been heightened by the specter of a more formidable military/political cluster of states gathering to oppose it in Asia with China at the vortex. Russian strategy, therefore, has been to start with "agreement on general principles," allowing "intractable" specific issues to be taken up subsequently—whether they be resolved or remain unsettled. Its precedents include the American–Soviet agreement of 1972 and illustrate the Russian penchant for such approaches. Yet it has not been a strategy acceptable to current Chinese leaders. The specific issues upon which the latter have chosen to focus, moreover, are among those upon which the Russians are least likely to yield, at least at this point.

Given the current situation, therefore, the containment of China both militarily and politically remains the central task as viewed from Moscow and continues to color all other aspects of Soviet policies in Asia. For these purposes Russia first must manifest its own power to the north and west of the PRC. The Soviet forces kept on or near these borders have numbered about 46–51 divisions in recent times, with front-line troops between 450,000 and 600,000 and with additional rear reserves, all supplied with the Soviet Union's most modern conventional and nuclear weapons.

In these vast border regions, only one possible buffer state exists: the Mongolian People's Republic (MPR), a state long under extensive Soviet control. The Russians achieved dominance in Outer Mongolia in the early 1920s as a by-product of their civil war. In recent times the Mongols have never had a realistic option of complete independence. They have had only the choice between Russian or Chinese primacy, or at one time (in the 1930s) possibly Japanese "protection." Today the Mongols of the MPR number approximately 1.5 million, whereas the Mongol population of Inner Mongolia and other provinces of China is about twice that figure. The Chinese, whatever their political persuasion, have accepted the Mongolian People's Republic reluctantly. Privately, they believe Mongolia is a legitimate part of greater China. This leaves the Mongols in the MPR with the alternative of becoming an ethnic minority in China, a status few of them are prepared to accept. Hence, a strongly Russianized Mongol political elite in Ulan Bator probably will remain in authority, backed by Soviet power and loyal to Soviet policies. Here, nationalism works to the advantage of the USSR.

Elsewhere in the area the Soviet Union may have been tempted from time to time to take advantage of the PRC's repressive policies toward its minority peoples and to abet the emergence of other buffer states. In the early 1960s, for example, border troubles in Xinjiang caused substantial numbers of Kazakhs to migrate from China to Russia. Tibet also offered possibilities for maneuvering because of the long-standing Tibetan resentment of Chinese dominance that burst out in the uprising of 1959, when the Dalai Lama took flight. Nor could Manchuria—historic site of Russian influence and locus of initial Soviet assistance to the Chinese communists—be overlooked.[3]

On careful reflection, however, the Russians must have concluded that support for nationalist causes within the Chinese empire held limited prospects for success and carried multiple risks. The ethnic minorities of China constitute substantially less than 10 percent of the total population, and those most likely to represent a point of political resistance are generally separated geographically and culturally. The Chinese capacity to control such dissidence, moreover, is vastly greater than earlier, despite the mistaken policies of the recent past. Thus, support for separatism might well involve the Soviet Union in an unending guerrilla-type struggle even if the initial phases of the operation went well. And the Russians have their own ethnic problems to consider. Would not a separate Xinjiang Republic, for example, prove attractive to peoples on the Soviet side of the border? For these reasons, although the USSR has not been reluctant to play upon ethnic problems within the PRC in its propaganda, careful limits have been placed on Soviet actions.

Apart from the border regions of China, an additional area of immediate strategic importance for Sino–Soviet relations exists in the north, namely, the Korean peninsula, and more specifically, North Korea.[4] The Democratic People's Republic of Korea (DPRK) has a very short border with the USSR but that border is extremely close to Russia's key military facility at Vladivostok. If Pyongyang were to be aligned closely with Moscow, China could be made highly vulnerable since it shares an extensive border with North Korea along the Yalu River, near where some important Chinese industrial centers are located. In any policy dedicated to the containment of China or in the event of a Sino–Soviet conflict, the orientation of North Korea is crucial.

Both Russia and China have long been aware of this fact. Until recently, however, Beijing has overwhelmingly scored the gains in the

3. For a careful study of Chinese policies on nationalities, see June Dreyer, *China's Forty Millions* (Cambridge: Harvard University Press, 1976).

4. The Korean issue is extensively discussed from various perspectives in William J. Barnds, ed., *The Two Koreas in East Asian Affairs* (New York University Press, 1976). For a more recent appraisal, see the author's article, "Current Dynamics of the Korean Peninsula," *Problems of Communism,* Nov.–Dec. 1981, pp. 16–31.

competition for influence over Pyongyang. Currently, the situation is less clear.

Actually, it is ironic that the Soviet Union has lagged behind in North Korea inasmuch as this small state was initially created by Soviet power, and Kim Il Sung, then a young man largely unknown to the Korean people, was put in office by his Russian mentors. However, the Korean War, and more particularly postwar internal political struggles in Pyongyang, strained relations between Kim and the Russians and in the longer run abetted the rise of Chinese influence.

Thus, while there have been various twists and turns, Soviet–North Korean relations have been troubled for more than two decades despite Pyongyang's continued reliance on Moscow for military and economic support. The Russians have neither liked nor trusted Kim Il Sung, a sentiment the Korean strongman strongly reciprocates. Moscow regards the cult of personality in North Korea as extreme and believes that various domestic policies pursued by the Kim government have been mistaken. But most of all, the Russians have bitterly resented the regularity with which North Korea appeared to support the PRC in recent years. Kim aligned himself with Beijing in its attacks on Khrushchev's policies in the early 1960s, and by the close of the Khrushchev era relations between the DPRK and the USSR were extremely bad. Some temporary improvements then took place in the mid-1960s, and at the height of the Cultural Revolution in China, North Korean–Chinese relations worsened. But with Zhou Enlai restored to power in the Chinese foreign ministry, from 1970 Pyongyang tilted sharply toward Beijing and relations with the Soviet Union ranged from cool to hostile. In 1975, for example, when Kim Il Sung visited the PRC and various countries in East Europe including Bulgaria, he did not go to Moscow (whether because he chose not to go or was not invited). More recently, the DPRK has recognized the Chinese-backed Pol Pot regime in Cambodia and also serves as the official host of Prince Sihanouk.

The Soviet Union has not appreciated such North Korean actions but it has tolerated them. Indeed, until recently at least, the USSR seemed resigned to accepting the PRC's greater influence on the DPRK, noting its cultural and geographical proximity and hinting that Kim shared many of Mao's idiosyncracies. Restraint was the rule in providing military and economic assistance to Pyongyang; the Russians furnished essential items and supported certain industrial projects primarily with a view to retaining leverage for the future.

By 1978 the DPRK was obtaining as much of its oil from the PRC as from the USSR, with Chinese aid in other fields mounting. Therefore, although North Korea then faced default on its international debt payments, Moscow made no move to bail out its former protégé; it let Pyongyang default. In the mid-1970s, in fact, the Russians winked at South Korea, permitting its nationals to enter the USSR for cultural meetings and sports events and suggesting privately that the only long-term solution for the Korean peninsula was some variant of the German formula. During this period Soviet support for Kim's reunification proposals was very muted in comparison with the elaborate praise given the plans by Beijing.

With the U.S.–PRC normalization, however, and the deterioration in U.S.–USSR relations, the status of Chinese–Soviet competition for influence over North Korea has undergone some changes. On the one hand, there are indications that Pyongyang has been decidedly unhappy with certain of China's recent policies in a manner not unlike Albania. At the same time, the Soviet Union—deeply concerned about what it regards as the efforts to build a united front in Northeast Asia against it—has powerful incentives now to soften its earlier policies toward Pyongyang notwithstanding all its reservations regarding Kim and his regime. In the summer of 1979 a high-level Korean Workers' Party (KWP) delegation led by Politburo member Kim Yong Nam visited Moscow, with reports that expanded cooperation between the KWP and the CPSU was mutually accepted. Russian trade with North Korea has risen in the past several years as have scientific-cultural exchanges. Recent Soviet pronouncements, moreover, have treated Kim's reunification proposals with greater solicitude. China, concerned about the attrition taking place in its position, has launched a counteroffensive proclaiming its allegiance to North Korea in very strong terms and exchanging high-level missions with the DPRK leaders. The North Koreans appear to be profiting from the intensified wooing of both communist neighbors at present with the ultimate outcome unclear.

The competition with respect to Japan does not involve any such uncertainties at this point.[5] Here, China's successes in recent years have been in striking contrast to the disaster marking Soviet policies. Moscow's record on Japan is one of unblemished harshness, starting with its initial post-1945 policies on the handling of the emperor, prisoner repatriation, and reparations. In more recent years the issues have been the four disputed islands, fishing rights, and Japan's relations with China. While the issues have changed, the basic Soviet approach remains the same and the Russians have been caught in a trap of their own making. They have believed that it is necessary to be tough with the

5. For perspectives on past Soviet–Japanese relations, see the work edited by this author, *The Foreign Policy of Modern Japan* (Berkeley: University of California Press, 1977).

Japanese, that this is the only tactic that produces results (a view by no means exclusively Russian, it might be noted). Yet at the same time they have strongly resented what they regard as a Japanese anti-Soviet bias.

The events of recent years with respect to Sino–Japanese relations have been especially disturbing to Moscow. After sternly warning Tokyo not to sign the treaty of friendship with Beijing if it contained an anti-hegemony clause, Russian leaders chose largely to disregard the concession obtained by the Japanese in the provision stipulating that the treaty should not be regarded as directed against either party's relations with third nations. Japan was accused of capitulating to American and Chinese pressure. Meanwhile, Japanese trade with China mounted rapidly while various obstacles stood in the way of comparable Soviet–Japanese economic expansion. Public opinion polls continued to reflect the deep distaste among the Japanese people for Soviet politics and policies, whereas enthusiasm for closer relations with China remained high despite a decline in euphoria after the Chinese invasion of Vietnam and Beijing's scaling down of its overly ambitious economic program. China has managed to link itself with Japan on the northern islands question while setting aside the issue of the Senkaku Islands. It was thus able to gain ground with a younger, more nationalistic generation of Japanese.

One can now detect signs that the Soviet Union may, as a result of repeated failures in the past, change its policies toward Japan. Russian leaders have always believed that ultimately Japan could be attracted by the prospects of participating in the development of Siberia without the need on the part of Moscow to make major political or strategic concessions. Recent trends in Soviet–West German economic relations have strengthened that conviction. Thus, the USSR has given signs of being prepared to bring Siberian economic development more prominently into play during the 1980s, with the major agreement upon Sakhalin oil and gas development and export to Japan achieved in 1981 an example. Whatever future potentials are contained in such a policy, however, today the Soviet Union continues to labor against severe obstacles in its efforts to prevent closer Sino–Japanese collaboration. Indeed, recent trends have appeared generally to confirm its supreme fear that a Sino–Japanese–American entente directed against the USSR is in the making.

Yet some Russians are aware of the fact that the Japanese government does not wish to turn to a hazardous foreign policy that would be likely to produce deep fissures in the Japanese political arena. They realize that despite numerous Soviet provocations, most Japanese leaders continue to hope that they can find a rough balance in relations with China and Russia at some point, notwithstanding the enormous difficulties of achieving and maintaining such a position. Is the Soviet Union willing to provide the economic carrot to accompany the military stick in playing to such Japanese sentiments? Or will Japan represent for the USSR a self-fulfilling prophecy—a nation made increasingly hostile and turned toward a military path initially not intended or desired, as a result of Soviet rigidity?

The situation to the south is more favorable to the USSR but here too the balance sheet is mixed. In Southeast Asia the Russians have achieved an alliance with Vietnam and, through Vietnam, with Laos and Cambodia, thereby making Indochina the linchpin in their drive to contain China on this front. The situation was well designed for Soviet involvement. First, there was the heritage of massive Russian assistance during the North's campaign against South Vietnam and the United States. With victory in that war Hanoi was certain to demand hegemony over its two small neighbors. The history of the region and of the Indochinese communist movement, together with the growth of Vietnamese military power by the close of the war (both its position within Cambodia and Laos and its troop strength and armaments), made this inevitable. Only the timing and the means were in doubt. These were determined in large part by the extraordinary stupidity and brutality of the Pol Pot government.

Just as predictably, Vietnamese hegemony over Indochina was certain to be resisted by the Chinese. No large state with interests in a neighboring region wants to see the emergence of a small empire on its borders. Historically, the Chinese have regarded Southeast Asia as a legitimate sphere of influence. Even if Vietnam were not aligned with their most dangerous opponent, therefore, they would have opposed Hanoi's expansionist policies. The stage was thus set for a Soviet-backed Vietnamese initiative and for a Chinese response, with some hope on both sides that an ambivalent, perplexed world would sit on the sidelines.

Up to now the USSR can view its assistance to Indochina as worth the price, measured in terms of its rivalry with China. A hostile front has been opened up on the PRC's southern borders, one stretching for hundreds of miles and not involving the deployment of Soviet soldiers. The Chinese have been forced to spread out their military forces while Soviet units remain at peak strength on China's northern and western borders. At the same time, the Soviet Union has constructed what may be a long-term economic, political, and strategic alliance with a nation having the military capacity to play a dominant role in the region. By inducing Vietnam to join CMEA, the Russians simultaneously have sought to commit Hanoi to economic relations having structural implications for Vietnam and providing an additional international component to an economic organization that was almost exclusively European up to this point. Moreover the new strategic ties have provided the Russians with base facilities at such important places as Cam Ranh Bay and Danang.

In contrast, China has witnessed a deterioration of its position through-out Indochina. During the North Vietnam wars with France and with South Vietnam and the United States, China provided major assistance to Hanoi at considerable sacrifice while seeking to demonstrate to the Viet-namese communist leaders that alignment with China was crucial to their future. Meanwhile, the PRC cultivated various Cambodian factions, in-cluding the Khmer Rouge, and at the close of the Vietnam War it took a leading role in underwriting the Pol Pot regime. Beijing's hope was that, at a minimum, Vietnam could be induced to maintain a neutrality be-tween the PRC and the USSR and to concentrate upon its massive task of economic development while Chinese influence would be predominant in Cambodia and would continue in Laos, especially in the northwest, where a Chinese presence had long been accepted. In sum, Beijing sought an Indochina composed of three reasonably separate units, all having the most limited ties with the Soviet Union.

At present, however, the PRC faces the prospect of long-term hostility with Vietnam and, because of Vietnam, with Cambodia and Laos, states now fully subordinate to Hanoi. The Soviet Union, furthermore, now has an extensive presence throughout the region and, as I have indi-cated, one not likely to diminish in the foreseeable future. Thus, a sec-ond front against China has been opened, and one can understand why Chinese leaders refer to Vietnam as the Soviet Union's Cuba in Asia. Yet what can be done? The effort to "punish" Vietnam—that phrase with such a traditional ring, applied by the Chinese over the millennia toward bad barbarians on their borders—was unsuccessful. Vietnamese with-drawal from Cambodia could not be forced. On the whole, Chinese military forces performed in a relatively mediocre fashion, revealing the fact that their weapons were antiquated, their coordination was poor, and their tactics and leadership were outmoded. Moreover, despite boasts that the threat of Soviet intervention did not materialize, the Chinese admitted privately that they were inhibited from striking with greater force because of the Soviet threat.

If the attack was not a great military success, it also was not a political triumph for the PRC. In comparative terms the USSR appeared the more moderate major power, and even among some of Beijing's most ardent supporters in Japan and the United States, the Chinese invasion raised serious questions. Chinese efforts to repair relations with India were set back, and within the Third World, which China seeks to culti-vate, reactions were strongly mixed.

The current balance sheet thus seems to favor the Soviet Union as against China in this critical theater, and by a considerable measure. The USSR, especially when it calls upon the assistance of certain East Euro-pean countries, has the military and economic resources to underwrite

Vietnamese domestic and regional programs, at least in sufficient degree to sustain them. China has neither the resources nor, under present conditions, the desire to undertake this task, even if it wished to do so.

Nevertheless, the risks with respect to Indochina are very substantial for all parties involved, including the Soviet Union. The Chinese may prove to be both patient and daring: patient in their commitment to a protracted, many-faceted struggle to bring Indochina into their sphere of influence; daring in some of the techniques that they employ. What cost will the USSR ultimately pay, economically and militarily, to uphold Hanoi and its satellites?

Publicly and privately, Chinese leaders have insisted that the struggle for Indochina has only begun, although they do not commit themselves to a second "punishment" like that of February 1979. If the battle does indeed become a protracted one, the USSR–Vietnam alliance can expect very limited support from other states within Southeast Asia. To be sure, these states have strong qualms in many cases about their long-term relations with the PRC. They recognize the fact that Beijing has a political, even a territorial interest in the region. China, for example, has already ousted the Vietnamese from the Paracel Islands. It lays claim to all islands in this group and to the Spratley Islands as well. The Southeast Asians know their history. They know that whenever China has been strong and united, it has extended its suzerainty southward. And most of the ASEAN states have their overseas Chinese problem similar to that of Vietnam. Thus, ASEAN–Chinese unity over the Indochina issue will be difficult to sustain.

Nevertheless, the suspicions throughout Southeast Asia regarding Vietnam and the Soviet–Vietnamese alliance generally equal, and in some cases exceed, the concern over China. The Vietnamese problem is immediate; the Chinese problem lies down the road. The prospect of Soviet bases, or an augmented Soviet military presence in the area, also seems considerably more real in the short term than that of a militarily powerful PRC. It is for these reasons that a state such as Thailand—now on the front line—moved closer to China as Vietnamese operations in neighboring Cambodia became even more threatening. Thus, Sino–Soviet competition in Southeast Asia continues to be complex, with the final costs and gains to each side yet to be determined.

In South Asia the Soviet Union counts heavily upon the stability of its relations with India, combined with its new position in Afghanistan, to offset the special relations between China and Pakistan that have endured various upheavals within the latter country, and China's continuous efforts to cultivate the Himalayan states that mark the buffer between Asia's two massive societies. On the whole, Soviet strategy has been successful, partly because India has few alternatives in its quest for external assistance. The United States, as we shall note, has not been interested in competing for Indian support in recent years, and China is neither interested in nor capable of playing a major role with respect to the Indian subcontinent.

In the past China has sought merely to soften India's far-flung borders. This has involved efforts to cultivate governments that might be expected to resist or resent overweening Indian power. Its special relations with Pakistan, which have survived various crises within that country, have been directed to that end, as have its overtures to Nepal, Bangladesh, Sri Lanka, and even Bhutan. In part also, the effort to soften Indian borders has involved small-scale military training and supplies furnished to such separatist tribes of the northeast Indian frontier as the Mizo and Naga. In addition, Beijing occasionally has smiled upon Indian communist factions other than the staunchly pro-Soviet Communist Party of India (CPI), thereby exploring another route to possible influence.

None of these efforts has been highly productive, although the aid to tribals has constituted a constant and costly annoyance to New Delhi. Such activities, in any case, are currently at a low ebb, with clear indications that Beijing now wants to improve relations with New Delhi—if this can be done without making sizable concessions. Discussions on the boundary controversies have at last begun. A new Chinese involvement in the region relates to Afghanistan. The Soviets charge that China is providing assistance to the Afghan rebels who are challenging the Marxist government in Kabul, and this is highly probable.

The long-term Soviet position in South Asia, however, is less likely to be affected adversely by China than to be determined by developments indigenous to the region and Soviet responses, as we shall soon indicate. China is nearly as remote from India culturally and geographically as is Russia. Its capacity to compete militarily or economically with Moscow is very limited. For the most part, political currents within the region are not running in its direction—although it can expect to benefit on occasion from anti-Indian sentiments, as in the case of Pakistan; all the states of this region, including India, would like to evolve toward a position of greater symmetry with respect to the major external states. For China, however, South Asia is of secondary importance compared to East Asia.

Taking the Asian region as a whole, how should one assess the results of the Soviet Union's goal of containing China pending the establishment of a more satisfactory relationship with this huge society? Some successes have been achieved but, on balance, the results have fallen extremely short of what must have been Moscow's hopes. Far from being isolated, the PRC is closer today to an alignment with Japan and the United States, the two most powerful societies of the Pacific–Asian region, than at any other time since its establishment, although the Taiwan issue has suddenly been elevated to complicate matters. Moscow's problems are most graphically illustrated by the situation in Northeast Asia, where political and military tides generally continue to run against it in spite of efforts to reverse them. In Southeast Asia the USSR has scored its most significant gains by bolstering an emerging Vietnamese empire that threatens to create long-term problems for Beijing. But the final costs and risks to Moscow of this commitment remain to be determined, and here too countercurrents have been set in motion. In South Asia Moscow's hopes center upon India and seem well-grounded at this point, but even New Delhi scans the skies periodically for signs that Washington and Beijing may be interested in raising their posture so as to provide India with more options and leverage.

Russian spokesmen insist that they do not fear China and, indeed, there is no reason that such a fear should exist, if the reference is to China alone. The PRC is destined to be poor and weak for the foreseeable future. There is, of course, a certain tendency among Russians to conjure up the specter of the yellow peril, recalling a history of invasions from the East across the thinly, diversely populated Siberian and Central Asian lands. As we have observed, the China problem can become enmeshed in Soviet ethnic issues of a domestic character. Yet what must be worrisome to Soviet leaders is the prospect of the lengthy and costly program necessitated to contain even a weak China. And beyond this, the greater concern is a China abetted and bolstered in various ways by Japan and the West, most particularly the United States.

VYING WITH THE UNITED STATES

The second major objective of the USSR in Asia is that of competing with the United States for influence and hence of seeking to weaken or complicate the key American alliances. It must be emphasized at the outset that gains or losses on this front for Russia are registered for the most part independently of Soviet initiatives. The policies of the United States itself, domestic as well as international, are the primary determinants of American influence in Asia.[6] The rise of Soviet military power in the region has, to be sure, contributed to doubts concerning the credibility of American security pledges. But the greater cause of these doubts lay in the American abandonment of Vietnam, the initial decision relating to troop withdrawal from South Korea, the derecognition of the Republic of China on Taiwan, and other indications that strategic withdrawal from the East Asian region was in process, including the Pen-

6. The status of the United States in Asia as of the beginning of the 1980s was summarized in the article by this author entitled "Asia at the End of the 1970s" (*Foreign Affairs*, special issue, 1980, *America and the World—1979*, pp. 693–737).

tagon's acceptance of a one-and-one-half war strategy, with its priority on Europe.

Another caveat is in order. The Soviet desire to weaken American influence varies in intensity in accordance with global conditions, most especially the general status of Soviet–American relations. For example, there was once a greater Soviet acceptance of the American–Japanese relationship than exists at present. Furthermore, the Russian desire for a decline in American involvement is not applied uniformly. As we shall note, both Taiwan and Vietnam represent areas where Moscow desires an American presence.

Finally, one must put in perspective the rhetorical patterns characterizing Soviet propaganda. Cold war terminology persists in the Soviet media and even in published scholarly works but private conversations often reveal subtlety, understanding, and a relative absence of polemics. In times of tension, such as exist now, these disparities are especially prominent.

Nonetheless, the USSR remains continuously alert to competition with the United States in this vital part of the world. Soviet tactics in advancing this competition involve three interrelated policies: an augmentation of military power in the region, to which reference already has been made; a propaganda campaign focusing upon the problems encountered by the United States in its Asian relations, with failures and points of strain emphasized; and finally, policies aimed at providing an alternative to the United States via programs of economic assistance, cultural exchange, and political-military commitments.

How successful have these Soviet policies been to date? On the military front Soviet advances, coupled with signs of a growing crisis of confidence in Asia over American power and will, caused Washington to reverse earlier policies of strategic withdrawal. By 1978 the United States had halted its retreat and had given pledges that it intended to remain a Pacific–Asian power with both the capacity and the determination to meet its treaty obligations. Increasingly, the U.S. emphasis has been shifting from a reliance upon fixed bases and extensive manpower to mobility and advanced strategic weapons systems, but currently it is American policy to match Soviet military power in all critical regions of Asia, from the Japanese archipelago to the Indian Ocean.

Moreover, the United States has taken specific steps in an attempt to reassure Asian allies or other countries considered threatened by Soviet power that it will not remain indifferent to their fate. Thus, further troop withdrawal from South Korea has been delayed indefinitely. The protracted negotiations with the Philippines over a renewal of base agreements have been concluded successfully. Thailand, living in the lengthening shadow of the Indochina conflict, has been given assurances of American assistance in the event of attack, and arms shipments to Bangkok have been hastily stepped up. Perhaps most importantly, joint defense planning and military exercises have been undertaken both with South Korea and with Japan. Moreover, the first contacts between Japanese and South Korean defense leaders have been encouraged as part of the effort to strengthen Northeast Asia. Finally, Washington has moved steadily toward a security relationship with Beijing. In addition to placing no obstacles in front of European arms sales to the PRC, the United States first authorized the sale of certain items with clear military relevance such as advanced computers and a satellite system. The message of Vice-President Mondale during his PRC trip in early 1979 that the task ahead in Sino–American relations was to build "concrete political ties in the context of mutual security," and that any nation seeking to weaken or isolate China "assumes a stance counter to American interests," was not missed by the Russians. The subsequent visit of Secretary of Defense Brown represented an additional signal of concern to Moscow. Finally, Secretary of State Haig, in a major policy decision set forth in June 1981 in the course of his visit to Beijing, indicated that the United States was prepared to sell weapons to China.

The Reagan administration has thus not only continued but advanced the policies toward China initiated in the latter stages of the Carter era. Policies toward the PRC, to be sure, remain to be clarified, and it is likely that the China issue will continue to evoke controversy in the United States. Moreover, as indicated earlier, the Taiwan issue has suddenly been raised into a major matter threatening U.S.–PRC relations, with the initiative having been taken by Beijing. Yet, considering Asia as a whole, American military strength and support for allies are being sustained, indeed substantially bolstered.

Despite this fairly dramatic reversal of U.S. strategic policies in the recent past, doubt concerning American capacities and intentions remains widespread in Asia. New or augmented issues now confront the United States in its relations with both China and Japan, moreover. The years ahead promise to be filled with complex problems in Asia for Washington. Among Asian leaders, however, the evidence suggests that some degree of confidence in the United States relating to Pacific–Asian security issues has been regained as a result of Washington's recent foreign policy decisions. In addition to specific bilateral issues, the chief Asian concern is currently with the domestic scene in the United States, namely, whether economic and political conditions will permit strong leadership and an American consensus sufficient to sustain international commitments.

In any case the persistence of doubts within Asia regarding U.S. foreign policies and domestic health has not produced a turn toward the

Soviet Union for security support with the exception of the very special cases of India and Vietnam. On the contrary, it has generally heightened the concern about the Soviet threat and hence encouraged moves in the direction of both greater self-reliance and increased regional cooperation. Japan, South Korea—and, one might add, Taiwan—all have increased defense expenditures, in some cases by a sizable amount. The PRC, while giving a low priority to military expenditures in the face of its serious economic problems, also seeks assistance from the advanced West. In all cases the premium is upon modernization programs. The fact that relations between China and Taiwan as well as South Korea remain minimal and potentially hostile adds complications to the scene—and to American policies. For the latter two states, the Soviet Union is not currently the primary concern. Nevertheless, the commitment of Japan and the PRC to improved military capabilities relates almost solely to a perceived Soviet threat.

The response of the USSR to these and related developments has been one of great alarm. Indeed, more than at any other time since World War II the Soviet Union perceives that an effort is now under way, spearheaded by the PRC and the United States, to confront it with a second front, a powerful new Northeast Asian military alliance as a companion to NATO in the West. As seen from Moscow, this new alliance is designed to consist of the United States, Japan, and South Korea, coupled with China, and to be directed specifically against the Soviet Union. For some time Soviet authorities have spoken about "the rise of Japanese militarism," crediting the United States with the aggressive fostering of this trend. More recently they have underlined the fact that Japanese military interests are being directed toward Korea. But of all the developments, the one that causes the Soviet Union the greatest anxiety is the fact that the United States has moved in the direction of advancing military commitments to the PRC.

In the main, the Soviet response to these developments has been militant. Throughout Northeast Asia Russian military operations have been expanding. Japan is being treated to the specter of close-in Soviet power. Fortifications on the disputed islands have been augmented. Extensive Soviet military maneuvers have been conducted in the near vicinity of Japan, with occasional overflights of Soviet aircraft. The Chinese also have been confronted with massive Soviet power on their borders, with no indication that Moscow will be receptive to troop withdrawal unless and until meaningful agreements between the PRC and the USSR are in sight. Meanwhile, a double track has been built on the Trans-Siberian Railroad and improvements in Siberian air and naval bases are going forward, together with steady additions to the Soviet Pacific Fleet.

The situation thus increases in potential danger, given the heightened militarization taking place on all sides. It is always possible that the USSR may succeed in convincing one or more of the states of the region that its military strength, coupled with the uncertainties surrounding American power and policy, make accommodation to Soviet interests the only sane and logical policy. Up to date, however, the trend has been the reverse. The movement is toward alignment against a perceived Soviet threat, albeit with a pronounced Japanese reluctance to accept a confrontational policy. Increased Soviet military power has neither isolated the United States nor reduced its influence. On the contrary, reliance upon the United States has had a higher premium even as self-strengthening takes on new importance.

In Southeast Asia a similar result has flowed from the increased Soviet strategic presence connected with the new Indochina conflict. As noted earlier, recent developments have heightened the worries among ASEAN states regarding the short-term actions of the Soviet-backed Vietnamese without removing the concern about the long-term role of China in the region. Most ASEAN leaders doubt that Hanoi will allow Cam Ranh Bay and Danang to become Soviet-controlled bases, given the xenophobic nationalism of the old Vietnamese communists in power and their fear of the long-term repercussions upon Sino–Vietnamese relations. However, there is a general recognition that the USSR has acquired a new set of strategic commitments in their area, one more likely to grow than to shrink. Consequently, the strategic presence of the United States is assigned as high a priority as at any time since these states achieved independence. The extension of the Philippine base agreement was generally applauded by the ASEAN community, and the Carter administration's pledge to Thailand was widely welcomed.

As in Northeast Asia strong doubts about the willingness of the United States to risk direct military involvement exist, and it is generally believed that the Guam Declaration represents the outer perimeter of American commitment. Few expect American ground troops to be involved in any Southeast Asian conflict. But no one believes that Russian ground forces will be involved either, and the relative caution characterizing the Soviet Union in regard to military engagement with China has not passed unnoticed. The desire, therefore, is for an American strategic presence that, at a minimum, balances the Soviet presence, enabling the indigenous states to negotiate with assurances of U.S. support.

Soviet leaders may hope that their heightened military presence in the region, together with that of Vietnam, will serve to deter ASEAN alignment with any hostile power, especially China. To some extent this strategy may prove effective. For example, both Thai and Malaysian leaders have visited Moscow in an effort to effect some balance in their position. Yet with respect to the Soviets' competition with the United States, their increased strategic presence in the region and the Soviet–Vietnamese alliance thus far have served to alarm the ASEAN states, thereby increasing American influence.

In South Asia the picture is different up to this point. Here, American efforts to match Soviet military activities in the Horn of Africa and South Yemen, and to offset the collapse of American power in Iran by increasing its presence in the Indian Ocean, generally have met with opposition from the indigenous South Asian nations, especially India. Various other issues have abetted the widening of the cleavage between Washington and New Delhi. Throughout this region, moreover, it was assumed until recently that the United States would continue its low military posture in South Asia despite some augmentation in the surrounding waters. The Reagan administration's major military and economic aid proposals for Pakistan, however, signal a more active American presence on the subcontinent itself. But as long as Soviet activities in Afghanistan and elsewhere do not appear to Indian leaders to project Soviet power too close to their borders and as long as Soviet military assistance serves Indian interests, the heartland of South Asia will remain a region where increased Russian influence can be ascribed in some degree to the advent of the USSR as a global power. And the major U.S. assistance to Pakistan now being projected may make more difficult extensive improvements in Indian–U.S. relations, despite Mrs. Gandhi's new interest in a more equidistant foreign policy.

On balance, however, the rise of the Soviet Union as a military power in Asia has served to enhance the importance of the United States as a countervailing force in the eyes of most Pacific–Asian states, notwithstanding their anxieties about American performance. This is particularly true in East Asia, where the Russians stand in an adversary posture toward many of the states of the region. Here, indeed, countermeasures are under way involving growing cooperation between the United States and the indigenous nations. In sum, there is no evidence at this point that the Soviet Union can generally translate its growing military power into rising political influence in the region, thrusting the United States aside in the process. Much hinges, however, on the relative skill with which both the USSR and the United States mesh economic, political, and strategic policies in the years that lie ahead.

Hence, in analyzing the Soviet effort to reduce American influence, we must turn to the other components of Russian policy, namely, its attacks upon specific American programs coupled with its projection of Soviet policies of a positive nature. Here, the issues can best be introduced on a case-by-case basis. Let us begin with Japan. As might be expected, the Soviet media have focused primarily upon two aspects of the American–Japanese relationship. They have been quick to call attention to the economic tensions between the two nations and to ascribe these to systemic weaknesses that cannot be fundamentally altered. At the same time, they have featured "American efforts to steer Japan down the path of militarism," as noted earlier, seeing this as part of a broader attempt to create a Northeast Asian alliance with the collusion of the PRC.

Each of these critiques, of course, has a basis in fact. There are good reasons to suspect that future American–Japanese economic relations will involve competition as well as cooperation and will produce periods of considerable tension. Structural changes, moreover, are required from both societies—changes that cannot be made quickly or easily. On the military front many Americans do believe that Japan must play a larger role on behalf of its own security and that of its region. Exponents of a united front strategy directed against the USSR, moreover, are to be found both within the current American administration and in influential circles out of government. And if such a strategy prevails, it will provoke serious strains within Japan and in American–Japanese relations, as is now clear.

The Russians are in a weak position to exploit these issues, however, given their record. By blandly asserting that "no territorial dispute exists," the Soviet government has managed to rekindle Japanese nationalism, directing it strongly against the Soviet Union. Russian military policies, meanwhile, have induced an increased sense of threat among Japanese of diverse political perspectives. Protests by Soviet spokesmen that they are merely responding to the rising crescendo of American–Japanese military operations in the region have a very limited effect.

It would be unwise, however, to assume that the Soviet Union is reconciled to the permanent hostility of Japan, or incapable of deviating at all from its poorly conceived policies of the past. As indicated earlier, Soviet leaders show signs of becoming more imaginative in their approach to Japan, offering carrots along with the military stick. Siberian resources will soon begin to flow to Japan on an expanded scale, and Japanese involvement in Siberian development will grow. By these means Moscow can hope to move Japan to a more independent position between the Soviet Union and the United States. It can also hope that its massive, close-in military presence will deter Japan from moving toward confrontation and will provide additional strains on U.S.–Japanese relations.

With respect to the Korean peninsula, Soviet attacks upon the South Korean government continue to be extremely shrill. Moscow has branded the new government of Chun Tu Hwan as a militarist, fascist junta. It has castigated U.S. policies in Korea with equal fervor. Meanwhile, support for Kim Il Sung's reunification program has appeared to grow stronger, after a long period of great Soviet restraint with respect to Kim and his policies. Given the economic needs of North Korea and the prospects of a widening gap between North and South on the military as well as the economic front, it would not be difficult for the USSR to put together an almost irresistible economic-military assistance program for Pyongyang. In this manner it might seek to further its containment of China, as suggested earlier, while providing at least a partial answer to any political/military coalition encompassing South Korea along with the larger societies of the region. Such a policy, to be sure, would increase both costs and risks for the USSR on yet another front, and it is very unlikely that the underlying suspicions between the Russians and the North Koreans, particularly Kim Il Sung, would be dissipated, but mutual advantage—if so perceived—might override the latter consideration. Yet it is also clear that North Korea at this point would like to establish at least informal relations with the United States, not only in the hope of weakening U.S.–Republic of Korea ties but also to increase its own options. And the Soviets also have an alternate strategy that could be pursued, that of seeking contacts with South Korea, thereby expanding Russian presence on the Korean peninsula.

To compete with the United States in the broader arena of China is vastly more difficult for the USSR, at least at present, and there can be no doubt that Moscow is deeply worried about trends in the Sino–American relationship, especially its strategic implications. The Soviet media regularly assail both "the Maoist foreign policies being perpetuated by China's leaders" and epitomized in Soviet eyes by Deng Xiaoping, and "the anti-Soviet, united front policies of certain American opponents of détente" recently symbolized in the Soviet mind by Zbigniew Brzezinski. One Soviet message to Americans is that to build up China will not be to set it against the Soviet Union, because Chinese power cannot hope to match that of the USSR whatever Western assistance is given, but to encourage Chinese expansionist policies in Asia. Yet another message is that policies aimed at a Sino–American military alliance will wreck any prospects for détente and move the world closer to war.

Meanwhile, Moscow—seeking to take advantage of recent U.S.–PRC tensions—has renewed its overtures to China, and has sent key China specialists to Beijing to test the waters. Small USSR–PRC trade increases and some cultural exchanges are en route. It is to the Chinese advantage to have at least a small Russian card in their hands when they seek concessions from the United States. Beyond this, if the PRC could get Soviet pressure upon it reduced, sustantial benefits would flow. Yet it appears impossible at present for the USSR to meet such major PRC demands as those pertaining to Vietnam and Afghanistan. Thus, the Soviet bid to improve relations with China, thereby challenging the new U.S. effort, faces major obstacles. For their part, the Chinese have asserted that even if relations with the United States were to be downgraded, ties with the USSR would not be strengthened under present conditions.

Until recently, Soviet spokesmen were silent on the Taiwan issue, but in March 1982 Brezhnev pointedly asserted that Russia did not challenge Chinese sovereignty there. In point of fact, the USSR has no wish to see Taiwan revert to China. PRC control of the Taiwan Straits and portions of the west Pacific via Taiwan would have adverse strategic implications for the Soviet Union as for neighboring states, particularly if it were accompanied by further Chinese acquisitions of South China Sea islands. One may also assume that Moscow would be grateful if the Taiwan issue could remain alive as a point of contention between Washington and Beijing. But there are no signs that the USSR itself intends to make significant overtures to Taiwan. In addition to the likelihood of a negative response from Taipei under present conditions, Soviet authorities have little desire to involve themselves in an issue that could only complicate possible future improvements in Sino–Soviet relations.

Soviet competition with the United States in Southeast Asia naturally has scored its greatest gains in Indochina. The USSR was one vital factor in Vietnam's military victory over the United States, and now it has replaced the United States as the dominant external power in the area. Thousands of Soviet and East European technicians and advisers are currently in residence. Russian economic and military assistance has been variously estimated to total between $2.5 and $3 million dollars (U.S.) per day. In partial recompense, Hanoi, Phnom Penh, and Vientiane all loyally support the Soviet Union internationally and accept the Soviet model in many aspects of their domestic programs.

It should be noted, however, that the Soviet Union has not sought to exclude the United States from Vietnam in recent years. On the contrary, in private conversations Russian officials have urged American recognition of the Democratic Republic of Vietnam and participation in Vietnamese economic rehabilitation. There are probably several reasons for this. Given the magnitude of its own support to Hanoi and the strength of its position in Indochina, Moscow need not fear American competition. An American presence would help legitimize the Indochinese governments. It could also help complicate U.S. relations with Beijing. In addition American aid would relieve the Soviet Union of some of the economic burden of rebuilding Vietnam.

The Soviet Union faces a dilemma in Southeast Asia. Soviet leaders have always considered the region to be of secondary importance strategically, except insofar as it served to weaken or contain the United States and China. Now, in order to pursue these objectives, Moscow is making commitments and bearing costs that exceed those in more important regions, with no end in sight. Soviet leaders must wonder whether the long-term political gains warrant such expenditures. They must ask such questions as: Will historic Cambodian and Laotian antipathy to Vietnamese overlordship again manifest itself, or have these two peoples been thoroughly crushed? Will this or the next generation of Vietnamese leaders seek to jettison their Soviet benefactors once the critical need for their aid has passed, or will the relationship be more like the one that the Soviet Union has achieved with India? The answers remain difficult to predict and the Indochinese situation remains fluid. Here, the Russians ride the back of a tiger and they must know it.

Furthermore, the wider Southeast Asian scene is hardly of great comfort to the Russians as they seek to reduce American influence. Once, following the Vietnam War, the USSR was prepared to compete with Washington for greater influence within the ASEAN community. Reversing their earlier position that this organization was an American-devised, SEATO-type alliance, Moscow and Hanoi asserted that they were prepared to accept and work with ASEAN economically and politically. Now the USSR has returned to its old hostility and it is faring badly in efforts to offset American influence. Political gains here at the expense of the United States are problematic.

Once again South Asia provides the greatest solace to the Soviet Union in its quest to counter the American role. In considerable measure, however, this results from the different priorities assigned this region by the two nations. For the United States, as has been observed, South Asia remains an area of lesser importance, particularly in comparison with East Asia. Events in the Middle East, and especially in Iran, have heightened the importance of the Indian Ocean. Recently, moreover, Soviet involvement in Afghanistan has caused the United States to seek a significant expansion of its relations with Pakistan. Even now, however, there is little inclination in Washington to compete with the USSR as chief counsel and benefactor to the Indian government. In the past the United States had been prepared to accept India's primacy on the subcontinent, and it earlier abandoned the effort to preserve a balance between New Delhi and Islamabad. It was also ready to encourage multilateral efforts to abet the economic modernization of this major society. But it did not regard Soviet–Indian relations as posing a political or military threat. In part this has been because it believes that the Indians possess and use an assertiveness in such relations, limiting the Soviet impact, and indeed there is little evidence to indicate strong Soviet influence on Indian domestic political trends. Washington also considers India's potential influence to be almost wholly regional, and within the regional context, Indian interests now coincide with those of the United States in certain respects, namely, in a desire to see a further dismemberment of Pakistan avoided or to see other developments that would strengthen Soviet power within the region as a whole.

In this setting South Asia remains a fascinating testing ground for a number of alternative possibilities that could affect the future of American–Soviet relations in much broader terms. In India the Soviets appear to be applying lessons learned from the debacles of China and Egypt. They seem relatively content with a level of influence considerably lower than that of strong control. They pay substantial homage to Indian politics by rendering support to the government in power. Clearly, there are degrees of alignment in the contemporary world. In spite of its insistence India is not a nonaligned nation at present. Yet Indian alignment with the Soviet Union is not the same as that of Bulgaria or the People's Republic of Mongolia, and it is not likely to become so.

Once, in days of greater compatibility, the United States and the Soviet Union were moving toward an implicit acceptance of the fact that each had the right to maintain "special relations" with certain countries and regions, taking into consideration various historical, geopolitical, developmental, and cultural circumstances. In that era, for example, the Soviet leaders tacitly accepted the special ties between the United States and Japan in a manner similar to the recent American acceptance of the ties between the USSR and India. It was even acknowledged informally that the two great powers should seek to avoid being used by small states, that each should refuse to be pushed into a situation where the two were bidding against the other at ever higher levels to secure dubious, and quite possibly temporary, favors. In comparison with the current tendency for intense global competition—a competition that threatens to deplete resources rapidly and divert them from critical domestic uses—a return to that earlier era should have deep mutual attraction despite the obstacles that would currently beset such an effort.

Meanwhile, in any survey of the ongoing competition between the Soviet Union and the United States within Asia as a whole, one must conclude that the Soviet position in East Asia remains precarious and far from satisfactory, notwithstanding the gains achieved in Indochina. In this region the Soviet Union continues to pay a heavy price for past errors. On balance it has run against indigenous political and nationalist tides, Vietnam being the exception. Thus, although the United States remains very much on trial, given its own errors and shortcomings, its influence recently has been rising. In contrast, the Soviet Union has operated in South Asia with greater sophistication and a closer attunement to indigenous trends, particularly in India. It also has operated with relatively minimal competition from the United States in recent years. Hence, its gains appear to be more firmly grounded, although it must worry about the internal political and economic trends in nations that are as volatile and unpredictable as any in the world, and about the long-range impact of its intervention in Afghanistan.

For the United States, however, one significant issue looms ahead. In striving to overcome the image of a declining and an indecisive power—unwilling and unable to compete effectively with the USSR—Washington runs the risk now of appearing overly belligerent and preoccupied with military approaches to problems that require coordinated military, political, and economic policies. Subtlety and sophistication are required in a degree not yet established by the Reagan administration, and this could serve to disrupt American alliances and alignments in Asia as well as in Europe.

THE SOVIET IMAGE IN ASIA

The final broad goal of the USSR in Asia, as set forth earlier, is to present a dual image: that of a revolutionary leader and model and that of a responsible yet powerful nation, committed to peace and security in the world. In connection with the former task the Soviet problems are as follows. First, despite the continued use of Marxist-Leninist rhetoric at home and abroad, the USSR itself is a deeply conservative society—bureaucratic, hierarchical, and structurally geared to painfully slow progress. Consequently, the Soviet model appears neither revolutionary nor attractive to most of the developing nations of Asia. If Western-style parliamentarianism has failed to take root in much of the region, Soviet-style communism is also widely acknowledged to be a failure—even by the Chinese, who spent years seeking to adapt it to their society. The quest for viable political institutions continues. Few answers have yet been found but the Soviet Union does not now offer a path to the future.

Of equal importance is the fact that the Asian nationalist revolutions have been completed. There are no more "liberation movements" in this region to support. Attention is now being directed to consolidation and development. The first generation nationalist-radical leaders of Asia are gone. That group, deeply politicized, frequently substituted foreign adventurism or visionary schemes of a regional or global nature for desperately needed domestic programs. Living by words more than deeds, they were moved by ideological appeals.

Today, power is in the hands of second- or third-generation figures, generally pragmatic and intent upon economic and social achievements at home. Vietnam represents an exception, being led by the last remnants of an earlier era. The old men of Hanoi have spent their lives in revolution and warfare, so it is perhaps natural that they now seek to ensure Vietnam's security by dominating Cambodia and Laos. But this is not representative of the rest of contemporary Asia.

Among Asia's remaining revolutionaries—for example, the guerrilla communists or separatist movements like those of the Islamic rebels of the Philippines or the Karen of Burma—Soviet influence is negligible. It is instructive to note that the Communist Party of the USSR has its closest ties in Asia with the parliamentary communist parties today, namely, those of India (CPI) and Sri Lanka (SLCP). Long ago, it lost its influence with the guerrilla parties to the Communist Party of China. For them, Maoist tactics have had far greater relevance, and in addition many have had strong ethnic components connecting them with China, making Soviet influence virtually impossible. Needless to say, neither the Soviet government nor the CPSU is likely to have great influence among the religious and separatist rebels of Asia. As a revolutionary force, therefore, the USSR is at a low ebb throughout the region.

However, the Soviet image as a major power has been steadily rising. At present the USSR is recognized by virtually every nation of East and South Asia. Moreover, increasingly it is recognized as a global power, as is its desire. In this new role, what are Moscow's principal policies? Two characteristics stand out. First, the Soviet Union seeks status as a responsible state dedicated to the cause of peace and stability. In this regard the earlier Soviet proposal for an Asian collective security system has been quietly dropped. This proposal, always vague, and regarded by many as an anti-Chinese ploy, never received Asian support. Instead, Soviet leaders have launched a campaign to secure universal condemnation of hegemonism as "an inadmissible policy in international relations." Yet the Soviet invasion of Afghanistan along with a number of other measures, such as bringing military forces onto the northern islands in dispute with Japan, have currently caused a major setback to Soviet efforts to achieve a peaceful image in Asia.

The USSR also has sought to align itself with the Asian-formulated principles of peaceful coexistence. Repeatedly, in speaking to Asian states including China, Soviet leaders advance the proposals that both parties reaffirm their dedication to mutual respect for each other's sovereignty, equality, noninterference in each other's affairs, and strict observance of generally accepted standards of international law. Moscow has repeatedly asserted that the Soviet Union has no intention of attacking any Asian state. It couples these assurances with such traditional Soviet proposals as a world treaty outlawing the use of force.

Proposals are also advanced toward individual countries or regions. Japan is urged to sign a treaty comparable to the one that it signed with the PRC. A zone of peace is proposed for South Asia. Increased economic and cultural relations are proffered to ASEAN. To the PRC the USSR suggests an agreement on general principles using earlier agreements with the United States and France as its models.

These proposals have met with varying degrees of support and opposition, hope and cynicism in Asia, depending upon the source. In the light of recent events, doubt has predominated over belief in most quarters. Yet one question continues to be debated within Asia: Is the Soviet Union on balance prepared to accept the existing situation and prevailing trends or will it challenge these by force? No doubt the correct answer to this question is complex, requiring various caveats. Some trends, even if they are a product of Soviet policies, deeply concern Moscow—for example, the growing security network among the United States, Japan, and the PRC. Yet few changes plausible under present circumstances—especially if undertaken with violence—would benefit the USSR. Of course, Moscow would be delighted if a pro-Soviet faction came to power in China, or if the Japan Socialist party succeeded the Liberal Democratic party in Tokyo. It also would welcome pro-Soviet governments elsewhere. None of these outcomes, however, is likely. On the contrary, those forms of Asian radicalism most likely to succeed, whether they come in a communist or religious-fundamentalist form, would probably reduce Soviet influence. Victory for the Filipino, Malaysian, or Burmese communists, for example, would be more likely to give additional influence to the PRC than to the USSR.

Naturally, this does not mean that the Soviet Union is uninterested in inducing certain changes. As we have seen, it is profoundly dissatisfied with PRC foreign policies, with the attitudes of the Japanese government, and with many other aspects of the present scene. But it is difficult to envisage how the use of Soviet force would alter the situation to the Russian advantage. Concerning their own boundaries, the Soviets are exceedingly defensive—and with reason. They hold territory in dispute, with both China and Japan presenting revisionist claims. No changes are desired here. And the Soviet Union cannot contemplate large-scale military involvement with any of the major states except with aversion. Defeat or occupy China, now a nation of 1 billion people? Seize additional territories from China and be subject to prolonged guerrilla war? Establish a "friendly" government and suffer the same fate? Or challenge Japan, thereby facing the United States in a frontal confrontation?

Neither these nor other scenarios for a direct involvement of the Soviet Union in a major war can be defended logically. The principal risk, now as in the past, is an escalatory development, quite possibly involving one of the middle powers aligned with the USSR, with the boundary between indirect and direct involvement impossible to maintain.

The USSR now seeks to avoid such an event by advancing its second general policy, namely, the establishment of a strong military presence, so that whether the test be one of negotiations or hostility short of war, Soviet power—together with its credibility regarding the use of that power—will serve to advance Soviet interests and deter opponents. In playing its role as major power, the Soviet Union is thus pursuing policies not dissimilar to those followed by the United States in past decades. Its primary attention is devoted to seizing upon targets of opportunity, fashioning from these such alliances and alignments as are possible, and, in the course of these developments, committing a considerable measure of Soviet resources. The principal objective also parallels that long held by the United States, namely, the containment of a foe perceived to be dangerous. Thus far, however, Russia has been both less generous in its economic assistance and less bold in its military commitments than America. Much aid is in the form of loans, and although the Russians have long placed advisers throughout the military, economic, and political structure of aligned states, they generally have refrained from sending ground forces or highly visible, participating air and naval units on a major scale. These latter forms of involvement had been confined to East Europe and Mongolia until the Afghanistan intervention.

Nevertheless, the movement of Soviet military power, accompanied by economic and political support, from Soviet Asia to the Pacific–Asian peripheries, land and sea, is one of the significant developments of recent decades, an event that is likely to have a long-term impact upon Asian domestic politics and international relations. As evidence of the Russian intention to be a truly global power, it is both impressive and of concern to many Asians.

What final balance sheet on the political role of the USSR in the Pacific–Asian region is appropriate? On the positive side of the ledger from a Soviet standpoint, the USSR has benefited recently from certain actions and inactions of the other major states. Following the Vietnam debacle, American policy in Asia has seemed to many Asians generally lacking in cohesion, unpredictable, and without credibility. American strategic withdrawal from Asia now has been halted and certain new initiatives have been begun, but U.S. actions will be watched skeptically in the period immediately ahead, with successes on the domestic front equally crucial to those in the international arena if U.S. prestige is to be reestablished, and with a need for policy sophistication and closer coordination with aligned states than in the past.

Meanwhile, the PRC, even in a period of economic and political fragility, by "punishing" Vietnam has heightened the age-old suspicions held by many of its neighbors, including some who harbor no love for Hanoi. Beijing's willingness to use military force beyond its borders to advance its influence—and possibly its territorial claims—can only be disquieting to the ASEAN states and to most nations of South Asia. The PRC's seeming insistence that American sales of defensive military equipment to Taiwan be halted adds a further uncertainty to the scene. Finally, Japan evokes a mixture of admiration and antagonism as it wrestles with the issue of how far to diverge from its past pursuit of a minimal-risk foreign policy, one separating economics from politics to the greatest possible extent. Yet few Asians see Japan as a regional leader in the strategic sense in the near future.

In this atmosphere the Soviet Union has been able to hold or advance its strategic political position in such diverse societies as Afghanistan, India, and Vietnam. In each instance, employing different techniques, it has seized upon or helped to create the opportunities afforded by indigenous or regional conditions. There is no reason to believe, moreover, that the Russians can learn nothing from their mistakes of the past. The era of the "ugly Russian" may be ending. Much emphasis is given to providing Soviet technicians going abroad with some linguistic and cultural appreciation and, at the same time, causing them to assume a low profile in the societies to which they are sent. Reports vary, but in certain areas such as India, Russians in residence get reasonably high marks for decorum at present.

On the other hand, the negative side of the ledger seems considerably heavier. From a Soviet perspective, China must be accounted a disaster and one not likely to be altered greatly in the near term. Relations with Japan are appallingly bad and, once again, changes in both attitudes and policies are likely to come slowly even if new Russian initiatives are mounted. On the Korean peninsula also, the Soviet position vis-à-vis North Korea is one of mutual wariness despite current Soviet efforts to improve relations. Moreover, the USSR cannot now adjust its policies toward South Korea to accord with the realities.

Meanwhile, the costs and risks of Russian alignment with Vietnamese nationalism remain to be calculated but there is no reason to believe that they will be slight, given Chinese pressures to the north and ASEAN doubts to the south. In South Asia the political gains seem more secure—but the uncertainties surrounding India, the oncoming tide of Islamic revivalism, the heavy costs of the Afghan venture, and the possibility that the United States and/or China might exercise new political initiatives in this region render the current Russian strengths tentative.

In addition the Soviet Union faces more fundamental obstacles in any drive to establish greater political influence in this vitally important part of the world. Its culture remains distinctly foreign to most of Asia. Even within its own borders, the unfinished assimilation of Asian peoples remains an issue. Its diplomacy in Asia, moreover, has been notably lacking in flexibility, subtlety, and sophistication with rare exceptions. As we have implied, this may change. The USSR has a sizable group of younger specialists on Asia who are intelligent, well-equipped in terms of linguistic and area training, and vastly more flexible than their older superiors. But the Soviet system inhibits their exercise of great influence at present and, quite possibly, for the future as well.

Finally, the Soviet model—with its record of having sacrificed agriculture for early, spectacular gains in heavy industry and of employing an extensive centralization that enfeebled initiatives elsewhere—has very limited appeal in Asia, even to those states that are committed to a "socialist" future. And now there are other models, suggesting that a number of intermediate systems between those of communism and Western-style liberalism are available for those seriously committed to economic modernization.

Besides the problems of relating the contemporary USSR to Asia, developments within the Soviet Union itself inhibit an extension of Russian influence externally. The increasing porousness of the Soviet Union, its widening contacts with Europe and with many other parts of the world, including the United States, are preparing the stage for another Russian revolution at the end of the twentieth century. The new revolution is not likely to be bloody, and it will not necessarily overturn the political institutions of the past. The theorists who foresee convergence between communism and liberalism probably will be disappointed. But this rolling revolution that rides on the needs and desires of younger generations, with its center in Moscow and its vortex within the relatively affluent, well-educated classes, already has begun to show itself. To those historic forces essentially inward looking, even xenophobic, will now be added a new insistence upon looking inward so that a greater share of Russia's resources can be directed toward an improved quality of Soviet life. And this ultimately will require a frontal assault upon bureaucratism and those other forces stifling incentives in so many sectors of the Soviet system.

The balance of weakness that currently governs international politics is compounded out of two elemental conditions: the internal problems now preoccupying every major state and the extraordinary complexity of the postcolonial world. The fact that these weaknesses are in some degree camouflaged by massive stores of arms should not mislead us. All major nations—particularly the United States and the USSR—now recognize that direct involvement in military conflict bears risks and costs likely to be greater than any conceivable gains.

Thus, as was underscored earlier, the primary purpose of military power on the part of the major states today is to influence political developments short of conflict and, if this fails, to influence the ensuing conflict short of direct involvement.

Soviet leadership has demonstrated an awareness of these facts even if it has not always been constrained by them. The activities of the USSR in Asia have been generally characterized by caution and restraint to date—Afghanistan, on the Soviet border, being the exception, and an expensive one. On balance, however, despite its rising military capabilities in Asia, the Soviet Union has little reason to be happy with its current political position in the region. It is estranged from all the major states of eastern Asia and it must worry about the possibility of a hostile coalition of these states operating against it, if not formally, then in de facto terms. Most of its Asian alliances and alignments, moreover, while requiring significant Russian commitments, are uncertain in strength and duration because they rest upon a limited commonality of interests. Generally, Asian societies have completed their revolutions and are seeking developmental policies suitable to their own traditions and current needs.

In sum, the ingredients for extensive, continuous Russian political influence are not present in the Pacific–Asian region. Yet this same period marks the advent of the Soviet Union as a global power. It is the tension between these two facts that in different ways is worrisome both to the USSR and to most Asian states.

4

The Sino–Soviet Conflict:
The Soviet Dimension

SEWERYN BIALER

Sino–Soviet relations were one of the focal points of world politics in the 1970s and will certainly continue to be so during the 1980s. While the Soviet–American contest will for the foreseeable future remain the central focus of international relations, the Sino–Soviet conflict influences all aspects of those relations. At the same time, though it is significantly influenced by the changing international environment, the Sino–Soviet conflict has an impetus and internal logic of its own.

This chapter is devoted to the analysis of the Sino–Soviet conflict as it evolved in the 1970s and to its prospects for the 1980s. To the extent that analysis of the Soviet and Chinese sides of the conflict can be disaggregated, I will focus in these pages on Soviet perspectives. A voluminous literature that traces the Sino–Soviet conflict through all its turns and twists in the 1970s is available, and I see no reason, therefore, to engage in a similar exercise.[1] Instead, I would like to examine briefly a limited number of questions that bear on the present and future of the conflict, primarily from the Soviet point of view.

First, from the Soviet perspective, what are the nature and goals of Chinese domestic and foreign policy, particularly in the post-Mao period?

Second, how can one explain the persistence of the conflict from the Soviet side, and why are the Soviets unwilling or unable to meet the basic Chinese demands for its alleviation and for normalization of relations?

Third, what are the prospects—from the Soviet side—for the evolution of the conflict in the 1980s?

---

1. The most extensive treatment of the Sino–Soviet conflict in the 1970s can be found in the brilliant essay by Kenneth G. Lieberthal, *Sino–Soviet Conflict in the 1970's: Its Evolution and Implications for the Strategic Triangle* (Santa Monica: Rand Corporation), R-2342-NA, July 1978. Other general overviews are given by Harry Gelman, "Outlook for Sino–Soviet Relations," *Problems of Communism*, vol. 28, no. 5-6 (Sept.–Dec. 1979) (special issue), pp. 50–66, and Steven I. Levine, "The Unending Sino–Soviet Conflict," *Current History*, vol. 79, no. 459 (Oct. 1980), pp. 70–75, 104.

SINO–SOVIET RELATIONS IN THE 1970S

Sino–Soviet relations of the 1970s commenced in the aftermath of the bloody clashes on the border near Chenpao Island. Those clashes, in all probability precipitated and provoked by the Chinese side, elevated tensions from a political and an ideological struggle into the realm of a military conflict. From that moment on, Chinese behavior became a key Soviet security concern; Soviet middle-range hopes for change in Chinese behavior disappeared as the Soviet Union started to view the conflict from a long-range strategic perspective.

By the mid-1970s the basic ideological formula of Sino–Soviet relations had changed dramatically: neither side perceived the other as truly socialistic any longer. The Soviet Union reluctantly accepted the Chinese definition of the relationship and ceased to regard long-term prospects in terms of relations between socialist states and between communist parties. This redefinition signaled a radical lowering of hopes regarding the eventual resolution of the conflict and, more specifically, the nature of the solution. Prior hopes for a restoration of the alliance and "fraternal ties" with the Chinese party were replaced by efforts to achieve the normalization of state relations and to decrease the intensity of antagonistic behavior on both sides.[2] Thus, the Twenty-fifth Congress of the CPSU declared that henceforth Sino–Soviet relations would be based on the principles of "peaceful coexistence."[3] For the Chinese, on the other hand, this redefinition precluded any further Soviet claims, on the basis of the Brezhnev Doctrine, to intervene legitimately in internal Chinese affairs.

The 1970s ended even less auspiciously than they began. The Chinese military attack on the Soviets' principal Asian ally, Vietnam, in February 1979, although far from successful from the Chinese point of view, humiliated the Russians, who for all practical purposes stood by idly and

2. At the 24th Party Congress of the CPSU, Brezhnev expressed his hopes about relations with China in the following words: "We are prepared in every way to further not only the normalization of relations but also the restoration of good-neighbor relations and friendship between the Soviet Union and the Chinese People's Republic, and we express the conviction that this will ultimately be achieved" (prolonged applause) (*Pravda*, Mar. 31, 1971). Brezhnev's formula for relations with China at the 25th CPSU Party Congress was as follows: "I would like to reiterate that in relations with China, as with other countries, we adhere firmly to the principles of equality, respect for sovereignty and territorial integrity, noninterference in each other's internal affairs and the non-use of force. In short, we are prepared to normalize relations with China on the principles of peaceful coexistence" (*Pravda*, Feb. 25, 1976).

3. The Soviets reserve the term *peaceful coexistence* to describe their relations with countries that have different sociopolitical systems and that are perceived to be antagonistic or potentially antagonistic. Where the potential for long-range friendly relations appears to exist, the term is not applied.

looked on as their ally was being invaded. China's abrogation of the thirty-year Friendship Treaty symbolized the end of the troubled decade. Soviet hopes that the death of Mao would create an opening for a movement toward reconciliation with China were dashed ignominiously. During Mao's lifetime some Soviet leaders and analysts had still entertained the hope that, to a crucial extent, the conflict was intimately linked to Mao's biases and cunning and to his domination of the Chinese political scene. However, by the end of the decade the truth was inescapable: the conflict is basically a clash of national purposes and interests. This is a fact of life with which the Soviets will have to live for the foreseeable future.

Between the sets of events that opened and closed the 1970s the Soviet Union pursued a multifaceted policy toward China. The primary objective of this policy was to minimize, through intimidation, the probability of increased tension on the Sino–Soviet border in order to avoid redirecting Soviet resources toward the containment of China. At best this policy counted on a shift in Chinese attitude and policy toward the Soviet Union; at worst, it aimed at the military, political, diplomatic, economic, and ideological isolation and neutralization of China. Both the maximal and minimal goals of Soviet policy toward China in the 1970s were to a large extent unobtainable.

In his brilliant report for the Rand Corporation, Kenneth Lieberthal characterized Moscow's policy toward China in the 1970s as a "carrot and stick" policy.[4] But primarily because of Chinese unresponsiveness to the Soviet carrot, Soviet policy toward China was and continues to be heavily weighted toward the stick.

As William G. Hyland remarked:

Where Khrushchev had relished polemicizing with the Chinese and set some store by his ability to persuade other Communists of the righteousness of his own cause, the Brezhnev regime downgraded the purely polemical aspects of the contest with Beijing. Whereas Khrushchev brought primarily political and psychological pressures on China, without any real threat of military action, the Brezhnev regime began building up its military forces, with the implicit threat of intervention. Where Khrushchev wanted to win over the majority of the Communist movement and reestablish Soviet preeminence, the Brezhnev regime came to see the contest more in conventional power terms. In short, in the years that followed Khrushchev's removal, the Soviet leadership began to pursue policies designed to contain and counter Chinese influence. The conflict was transformed from an ideological contest to a power struggle between two potential enemy states.[5]

4. Lieberthal, *Sino–Soviet Conflict,* p. vi.
5. William G. Hyland, "The Sino–Soviet Conflict: A Search for New Security Strategies," *Strategic Review,* vol. 7, no. 4 (Fall 1979), p. 52.

The carrot side of the Soviet policy toward China consisted of many initiatives that, while falling far short of Chinese demands, nevertheless were consistently pursued by the Soviet side. These initiatives included the following:

1. Intermittent border negotiations with the Chinese during which the Soviets made many concessions. For example, immediately after one round of negotiations on this subject would break off, the Soviets would make genuine efforts to start a new round of negotiations as quickly as possible, relaxing slightly the details of their position on individual items of the border dispute.[6]

2. A proposal to conclude with the Chinese a nonaggression treaty that would preclude the use of military means in the solution of issues under dispute.[7]

3. Attempts to expand trade with China and promises for the resumption of deliveries of industrial equipment to China on beneficial terms.

4. The cessation of polemics in the Soviet press against Chinese internal and foreign policy directly after Mao's death as a signal that the Soviets were ready to talk business with the new Chinese leadership.[8]

5. Proposals to resume and broaden cultural, technological, and scientific exchanges with China and to broaden the exchange of journalists.

6. Invitations to convene a summit meeting between the two leaderships that may provide an impetus to the resolution of the conflict that meetings at the lower level do not provide.[9]

As Ken Lieberthal remarked: "The *substance* of the offers was consistent with the continuing Soviet effort to communicate the USSR's willingness to engage in a far-reaching rapprochement with the leadership in Peking should leaders who were willing to tread this path come to the fore in the Forbidden City."[10]

The stick side of Soviet policy toward China in the 1970s included the following:

6. The latter round of negotiations between China and the Soviet Union on the border dispute started on October 17, 1979, and ended inconclusively in the spring of 1980. A Chinese source close to the negotiations informed me that Deng Xiaoping instructed the delegation to stonewall the Soviet proposals.

7. The Soviets proposed such a nonaggression treaty to China on June 14, 1973.

8. This halt in Soviet attacks lasted for approximately six months and resumed only after Chinese invectives and polemics increased in intensity rather than ceased. These events are analyzed in Robert Horn, "China and Russia in 1977: Maoism without Mao," *Asian Survey*, vol. 17, no. 10 (Oct. 1977).

9. The last Soviet proposal for a summit meeting between the Chinese and Soviet leaders was issued in the fall of 1973 and received no response from the Chinese side. It is very unlikely that a new invitation will be issued from Moscow until Brezhnev's death or retirement and the consequent change of leadership in the Kremlin.

10. Lieberthal, *Sino–Soviet Conflict*, p. 18.

1. The conclusion of the Soviet–Mongolian Defense Treaty, which led to the stationing of Soviet troops in Mongolia, the strengthening of Mongolian defenses, and the consequent increasing danger to China's security on its northern border.[11]

2. A very significant and dramatic military buildup along the Soviet side of the border that involved the deployment of more than forty Soviet divisions constituting a self-contained force including major air and armored elements.[12]

3. Whereas in numerical terms most of the Soviet military buildup occurred during the early 1970s, in recent years a dramatic upgrading of troops deployed on the Chinese border has taken place, their control and communications capacities were improved dramatically, and their modernization brought them up to the qualitative level of Soviet troops deployed against the NATO alliance in Europe.[13]

4. The deployment and upgrading of the Soviet military presence along the Sino–Soviet border went hand in hand with major fortification efforts and with upgrading of both the command system and the second line troops stationed in the Far Eastern, Siberian, and Central Asian military districts.

5. The significant buildup of the Soviet Pacific Fleet, which for the first time included nuclear submarines.[14]

6. An increase in the Soviet naval presence in the Indian Ocean, on China's southern flank.

7. Retargetting of significant Soviet strategic rocket forces against China and the introduction of new intermediate-range ballistic missiles (the SS-20) aimed at Chinese targets.[15]

8. The inclusion of Vietnam in the Soviet sphere of influence, the conclusion of an alliance with Vietnam, and major economic and military efforts to strengthen it as a thorn in China's side.[16]

11. This defense agreement was stipulated in article 5 of the Treaty of Friendship, Cooperation and Mutual Aid between the Soviet Union and Mongolia (see *Pravda*, Jan. 16, 1966).

12. Concerning the deployment, strength, and disposition of Soviet forces on the Chinese border, see Central Intelligence Agency, National Foreign Assessment Center, *Estimated Soviet Defense Spending*, SR-78-10121, June 1978.

13. For a discussion of the recent upgrading and modernization of the Soviet troops facing China, see the first annual report of the Research Institute for Peace and Security, *Asian Security 1979* (Tokyo: Nikkei Business Publishing Co., 1979), pp. 45–47.

14. The buildup of the Soviet Pacific Fleet and its primarily anti-Chinese character is treated in ibid., pp. 47–52.

15. On the question of Soviet strategic deployment against China and its buildup in the last few years, see Uri Ra'anan, "The USSR and the 'Encirclement' Fear: Soviet Logic or Western Legend?" *Strategic Review*, vol. 8, no. 1 (Winter 1980), pp. 48–49.

16. The Soviets concluded a 25-year friendship and cooperation treaty with Vietnam on November 3, 1978. In addition to the usual stipulations concerning economic, scientific-

9. Although the Soviet presence in Vietnam is still insignificant, efforts are continuing on the Soviet side to secure naval and probably also air bases on Vietnamese soil. If successful, such a step would improve markedly the Soviet military deployment against China.

10. Hand in hand with the military efforts went repeated Soviet attempts to isolate China diplomatically and to expel it from the international communist movement.[17]

11. A continuing Soviet effort is being made to create an Asian Collective Security System, which in fact will be directed against China.[18]

12. The Soviets increased their efforts to counteract Chinese activities in Third World countries, sometimes even going so far as to condition their help for a particular Third World country on its taking the Soviet side in the conflict with China.

13. Vociferous polemics against, and clashes with, the Chinese in international forums, especially the UN, and attempts to mobilize the support of Third World UN members against the Chinese.

14. Pressure on Japan and Western European countries to limit their economic help to China and to abstain from military deliveries to China, making it clear that such deliveries would be considered a highly unfriendly act by the Soviet Union and would meet with the appropriate response.

15. During the early 1970s détente with the United States was partly motivated by an attempt to minimize or preclude the danger of a Sino–American alliance. In the late 1970s, when détente crashed, major political pressure was brought to bear on the United States partly through its allies to preclude the development of relations between the United States and China into a full-fledged military alliance.

---

technological, educational, and cultural cooperation, the treaty stated: "In the event that one of the parties is the object of an attack, the . . . parties will immediately begin mutual consultations with a view to eliminating that threat" (article 6, cited in *Pravda*, Nov. 4, 1978).

17. The last such effort by the Soviet Union was made at the international conference of communist parties that convened in East Berlin in late June 1976. Like all previous attempts it ended unsuccessfully. Indeed, some of the communist parties, notably the Italian and the Romanian, conditioned their attendance on the Soviet promise not to attempt to excommunicate China from the movement.

18. The Soviets began their effort to create an Asian Collective Security System in 1969. Elaborating on the essence of the Soviet proposal, Leonid Brezhnev stressed in his speech at the 15th Congress of Soviet Trade Unions in March 1972 that a collective security system in Asia "must . . . be based on such principles as renunciation of the use of force in relations between states, respect for sovereignty and inviolability of frontiers, noninterference in each other's internal affairs and wide development of economic and other forms of cooperation on the basis of complete equality and mutual benefit" (*Pravda*, Mar. 21, 1972).

16. Finally, one should mention the meagerly documented, but nevertheless probable, Soviet attempts to subvert the upper echelons of the Chinese party from within by the Soviet intelligence apparatus.[19]

The carrot and stick policy was directed at influencing the behavior of the Chinese leadership, the carrot through positive incentive and the stick through negative reinforcement. Yet, to repeat, while both these were used, the clear stress of Soviet policies during the 1970s was on dealing with China from a position of strength. Two assumptions underlay the Soviet dual policy toward China: (1) the conviction that Chinese leadership circles were, and remain, badly split on the question of what policy to pursue with regard to the Soviet Union, and (2) that both the peaceful initiatives and the threatening actions by the Soviet Union would provide ammunition for those among the Chinese leaders who want normalization of relations between the two countries.[20]

If my definition of the basic goals of Soviet policy toward China in the 1970s through positive and negative incentives is valid, then one should, in my opinion, conclude that at the beginning of the 1980s this policy has proved to be essentially a failure. The Soviets have failed completely to push the Chinese to a successful resolution of the conflict. To date, the negotiations have been characterized by either a token Chinese presence or an intransigent Chinese position. Simultaneously, a major cornerstone of the Soviet policy to isolate China through détente with the West has disintegrated—at least as far as the United States is concerned.

Relations between the United States and China have developed rapidly during the 1970s, having achieved a momentum of their own partly independently of the triangular Soviet–American–Chinese relationship. The first steps were taken by the United States in extending militarily significant aid to China. Although the possibility of a formal or de facto Chinese–American military alliance is still far removed and not at all certain, the nightmarish specter of such an alliance has been introduced into Soviet thinking and calculations. Despite major Soviet efforts to the

19. For a comprehensive review of the Soviet subversion effort in China, see Lieberthal, *Sino–Soviet Conflict,* pp. 25–30.

20. Khrushchev's memoirs provide innumerable examples indicating that the Soviet leadership was convinced that at least one dimension of the continuing power struggle in China was the attitude toward the Soviet Union itself. See *Khrushchev Remembers,* trans. and ed. Strobe Talbott (Boston: Little, Brown, 1970), and *Khrushchev Remembers: The Last Testament,* trans. and ed. Strobe Talbott (Boston: Little, Brown, 1974). In a number of conversations with Soviet specialists in international affairs I had ample opportunity to confirm that they were convinced that the Peng Dehuai and Lin Biao affairs were connected with the differences within the Chinese leadership concerning their policy toward the USSR. For a Western account of the possible factional alignments in the Chinese leadership, see Thomas W. Gottlieb, *Chinese Foreign Policy Factionalism and the Origins of the Strategic Triangle* (Santa Monica: Rand Corporation), R-1902-MA, July 1977.

contrary, a Japanese–Chinese treaty was concluded with the inclusion of an "anti-hegemonistic" clause clearly directed against the Soviet Union.[21] In contrast to China's diplomatic and political isolation during the late 1960s, the late 1970s saw a significant revival of Chinese foreign policy initiatives with developed as well as underdeveloped countries.[22] Efforts to expel the Chinese from the international communist movement ended in failure. Whereas the appeal of Chinese communism to the ultraleft revolutionary groups has declined visibly, its appeal to established communist parties who want to find a counterweight to Soviet domination of the international movement has increased immensely. China developed rapidly its economic ties with developed capitalist countries and can count on significant help in its program of internal modernization.[23] The Chinese plan of internal development, the Four Modernizations, even if only partly successful, will increase significantly China's military and economic potential to oppose the Soviet Union. After a long period of debilitating upheavals China is finally moving toward stabilization of its internal situation.

It is not easy to answer fully the question of why Soviet policy toward China in the 1970s was basically a failure. Let me offer some brief observations that seem crucial for understanding this failure.

Of course, the most general reason lies in the lack of Chinese response to either the carrot or the stick. The carrot offered too little to satisfy the Chinese and to provide ammunition for those within the leadership who allegedly support normalization of relations with the Soviet Union. The stick had the opposite effect than the one intended, i.e., the intimidation of China. One doubts that such Soviet intimidation can affect China in the desired direction. The Chinese sense of greatness, their concept of popular warfare, and above all a contempt for the Russians bred by a deep awareness of past injustices and humiliations, doom to failure a policy of threat and intimidation. It is also possible, although by no means certain, that the Soviet leadership has vastly overestimated both

21. The Sino–Japanese peace treaty was concluded on August 12, 1978. Its anti-hegemony clause states the following: "The Contracting Parties declare that neither of them should seek hegemony in the Asian–Pacific region or in any other region and that each is opposed to efforts by any other country or group of countries to establish such hegemony" (article II of the Treaty of Peace and Friendship Between the People's Republic of China and Japan, in *Peking Review*, vol. 21, no. 33 [Aug. 18, 1978], p. 8).

22. The most visible signs of Chinese diplomatic activity were the visits of Chinese leaders to foreign countries in the last few years, including the United States, Japan, Romania, Yugoslavia, France, Great Britain, and West Germany.

23. Chinese trade with the capitalist West has increased considerably in the 1970s. See Central Intelligence Agency, National Foreign Assessment Center, *China: Real Trends in Trade with Non-Communist Countries Since 1970*, ER77-10477, Oct. 1977. From the West and Japan the Chinese received access to $29 billion worth of credits, yet in actuality have drawn very little. The sum will undoubtedly increase substantially in the coming years.

Mao's personal role in the continuation of the Sino–Soviet conflict and the degree to which the Chinese leaders are split on the issue of China's policy toward the Soviet Union.

But in the final analysis the basic failure of Soviet policy toward China in the 1970s lies in the nature of overall Soviet foreign policy, the behavior of the current generation of Soviet leaders in the international arena, and the inability of Soviet decisionmakers to order in any clear way the priorities of their international policy. In other words the reasons for the failure of the Soviet Union's China policy are similar to the reasons for the failure of détente with the United States.

On the one hand the Soviet Union suffers from a feeling of insecurity, which it counteracts by upgrading its military potential beyond the levels that would satisfy its reasonable defense needs without provoking its adversaries to embark on a cycle of counter-buildups. The Soviet concept of total security is unattainable and provides the wrong prescription for normalization of relations with its adversaries, both Chinese and American.

Contradictory results obtain not only from the Soviet quest for total security but also from the deep and insoluble contradiction between the Soviet desires to avoid confrontations with its major adversaries and to normalize relations with the great powers while simultaneously engaging in a program of external expansionism in which military power plays a dominant role. It is a Soviet illusion that stable relations with America or China are compatible with the displayed inability to resist the temptation to seize and exploit available targets of opportunity in the Third World. Such behavior confirms the worst fears of their adversaries and nullifies the effects of their friendly gestures and peaceful initiatives.

POST-MAO CHINA: THE SOVIET PERSPECTIVE

Inconsistencies, hesitations, and ambiguities are evident in the Soviet view of the post-Mao internal situation in China, especially regarding developments since the CCP's December 1978 Central Committee Plenum.[24] This is in contrast to the more consistent Soviet evaluation of the changes that have taken place in the international activity of the Chinese leadership.[25] Indeed, authoritative Soviet sources emphasize that the

---

24. The most authoritative Soviet statement about Chinese internal developments in the post-Mao period can be found in "Kitai: nekotorye tendentsii vnutrennego polozheniya," *Kommunist*, no. 3 (Feb. 1980), pp. 95–106. Because of the large volume of Soviet literature devoted to the analysis of China, I will henceforth quote only the most authoritative and interesting items.

25. One of the most telling Soviet analyses of the foreign policy of China in the post-Mao period can be found in B. Pyshkov and B. Starostin, "Ot 'Ul'trarevolyutsionnosti' k soyuzu s imperializmom i reaktsiei," *Kommunist*, no. 16 (Nov. 1978), pp. 98–109.

new course in Chinese internal policies is directly linked with Chinese foreign policy changes and its goals are primarily foreign oriented. In Soviet terminology, the goal of the Chinese course toward modernization involves the creation, with the help of the United States, Japan, West Germany, and other imperialistic states, of a stronger, stabler military, economic, and scientific-technological basis for accomplishing the Great-Han (*velikokhanskie*) expansionist plans.

According to the Soviets a qualitative change of a counterrevolutionary nature occurred in the international activities of the Chinese leadership. The title of an editorial in the main theoretical journal of the Soviet Communist party neatly summarizes the Soviet position: "Beijing: Yesterday—reserve of imperialism, today—its ally."[26] The "Chinese problem" is portrayed by the Soviets as not only encompassing Sino–Soviet relations but also directly threatening the peace and security of other nations.

With regard to the states that compose the world communist/socialist system, the Chinese problem finds its expression in the sharpening of an open and a direct confrontation with an increasing number of socialist countries and an attempt to intervene in their internal affairs. This intervention sometimes even takes the form of military action.[27]

With regard to world capitalism the problem is expressed in an open convergence of Beijing's foreign policy orientation with the anticommunist strategy of imperialism, in the coordination of actions with the most reactionary historical forces, in open opposition to the world socialist system, against both the national-liberationist movement and the developing countries that have a socialist orientation. It finds its expression in various cooperative ventures with the imperialists and in the buildup of China's military/economic potential.

With respect to the developing countries the problem finds its expression in the increasing economic, political, and military support given by China to reactionary regimes in the development of good relations with such regimes, and in the help given by China to forces of internal reaction.[28]

The goals and methods of Beijing's present policy are perceived by the Soviets as differing very little from the policies of imperialist states. If

26. See "Pekin: vchera—rezerv imperializma, segodnya—ego soyuznik," *Kommunist*, no. 4 (Mar. 1979), pp. 71–84.

27. On Chinese attitudes toward the world socialist system and its allies, see A. Kruchinin and V. Feoktistov, "Kak preemniki Mao voyuyut protiv sotsializma i ego soyuznikov," *Kommunist*, no. 5 (Mar. 1978), pp. 89–100.

28. See, for example, T. M. Kotova, A. S. Krasil'nikov, and A. V. Pedin, "Gegemonism Pekina—ugroza svobode i nezavisimosti stran Azii i Afriki," *Narody Azii i Afriki*, no. 4 (Apr. 1979), pp. 3–16.

some time ago one could still speak about the desire of the Chinese leaders to exploit the contradictions between the two world systems for their own profit, today the situation is quite different. China has moved from the ideological struggle against the socialist countries to a political, an economic, and even a military struggle. Viewed in class terms, China's coordination of its activities with those of the imperialists signifies that China has been transformed into a link of the world capitalist system.

The Soviet leadership's view of the internal changes that have taken place following Mao's death and the defeat of the Gang of Four can be expressed as follows. The Chinese leadership, without changing its basic strategic goals, is engaged in broad tactical maneuvers in search of more effective ways to realize its hegemonic plans. Policy changes have been instituted by the Chinese leaders in order to preserve and strengthen their power over the country and the party, to search for more effective ways to transform China into a militaristic superpower, and to attempt to reduce the growing social tension that aggravates the political instability of the "militaristic-bureaucratic" regime.

The main directions of the maneuvers and changes adopted by the Chinese leadership are in conformity with the goals outlined above and can be explained by them. However, when evaluating these developments we must remember that they are taking place under conditions in which China finds itself economically unstable, torn politically by factional struggles, and ideologically confused and chaotic. Economically, the leadership is attempting to redirect the activity of the party, government, and military apparatus toward the modernization of not only agriculture, industry, the military, science, and technology but also the improvement of the political system and the revision of existing economic programs. Whereas during the initial post-Mao period this revision consisted of an attempt to proclaim a new Great Leap Forward, at present the center of gravity has switched to the "regulation" of the national economy. Politically, an attempt is being made to increase the effectiveness and efficiency of government. Ideologically, a change in the attitude toward class struggle has taken place, according to which it is no longer proclaimed as the main contradiction in Chinese society. Chinese leaders assert that although the class struggle has not withered away, it should not at the same time be "artificially sharpened." Furthermore, a selective rephrasing and reinterpretation of some of the slogans and "truths" of Maoism are being conducted according to current needs.

The period after Mao's death and the defeat of the Gang of Four is distinguished by a symmetry between Russian and Chinese views of each other. The ideological substance and formulas that constituted a major part of the struggle between these two countries has declined and even disintegrated. The leadership in both countries is looking frantically for an ideological underpinning for the current conflict. Obviously, the conflict today is one of national interests, a clash between the two great powers. But both powers derive their integral legitimacy from the communist ideology and both need an ideological justification and rationalization for their conflict.

The Soviet spokesmen make a major distinction between the official and the popular anti-Maoism in China. They see, on the one hand, maneuvers by the present leadership to readjust Mao's teaching to current needs in order to minimize the impact of his teachings on Chinese society, and to revise them in the interest of their own power struggles. At the same time, they discern a wave of popular disillusionment with China's Maoist past and a growing sentiment among all strata of the population that undermines not only Mao's heritage but also the political position of his successors. The Soviets tend to be realistic in the evaluation of the chances of success of this popular wave. They stress the strength of the Chinese state's coercive apparatus and of the force of nationalism in keeping this movement under control. Nevertheless, they evaluate this movement as at least delaying the efforts to modernize and stabilize the country.[29]

The general Soviet view on post-Mao China is that the situation has gone from bad to worse. On the one hand it is grudgingly recognized that Chinese internal policy moved away from the extremes of Maoist "permanent revolution," from the great leaps and cultural revolutions, and that the internal behavior of the Chinese leadership became much more rational and coldly calculating. But from the Soviet point of view this is exactly a change for the worse because the opponent has become much more formidable. Early hopes following Mao's death that the new-found rationality of the changing Chinese leadership would lead to the tempering of Chinese hostility toward Russia have not been fulfilled. They now see a China that is becoming stronger internally, a China that is moving from absolute faith in the force of revolutionary slogans to faith in what it can accomplish through the process of modernization. This China has abandoned its isolation and anti-Western xenophobia and increased its activities in the international arena immensely. It is a China that enters into virtual alliances with developed Western countries—particularly the United States—and that, as much as being used as a card by the United States against the Soviet Union, is itself using the American card in its struggle with Russia.

To any independent observer the significant break with Maoism by the current Chinese leadership is beyond question. The consequent

29. See V. Lazarev, "Antimaoistskoe dvizhenie v KNR," *Kommunist,* no. 8 (May 1980), pp. 101–12.

change in Chinese internal policies is probably clear to the Soviet leaders also but they cannot admit it publicly. Instead, their official announcements proclaim the virtual continuity with Maoism in post-Mao China.[30] However, a shift in emphasis is reflected in a partial reversal of their previous argument. While Mao was alive they emphasized that the internal policies of the Chinese leadership were at the source of China's deviation and led, in turn, to its "hegemonistic" foreign policy. Today, the focus of their criticism has switched to Chinese foreign policy, now portrayed as anti-Soviet and in search of world domination. A subordinate role is assigned to China's internal policies, which are designed merely to serve and support foreign policy goals.

According to Soviet views, the changes in the method of economic management that were forced on the Chinese leadership by the bankruptcy of their previous efforts does not alter the antisocialist essence of China's economic activity. The absolutely central goal of the modernization program concerns an accelerated increase of the military-economic power of China. Soviet figures suggest that in 1979 China occupied third place in the world with regard to total military expenditures. While investment in China's national economy declined in absolute figures in that year, direct military expenditures increased 20 percent. Thus, the Soviets reason that the Chinese modernization program is in fact a program of forced militarization.[31] It has to be said, however, that these assertions are purely propagandistic. In fact there is no major increase, if any, in Chinese military spending.

Despite its new economic policy the Chinese leadership, in Soviet eyes, has no new "scientifically valid" overall program of economic development. Moreover, in the last two years some of the changes that were instituted by the Chinese leadership—in both the domestic and international spheres—are proof of a growing danger to the "socialist accomplishments" of China. As Moscow sees it, China is at a new, dangerous stage, where "socialist" forms of development are being diluted by the encouragement of private enterprise, by the introduction of elements of market socialism, and especially by the risky decision to enter into joint ventures with capitalist firms. Beijing's decision to create mixed companies is part of its general political line of allying with imperialism. Previously one could speak about the deformation of the socialist bases of Chinese society as a result of the exploitation of China's economic resources for antisocialist goals. Today, says Moscow, one can speak

30. "Maoism Without Mao," *Far Eastern Affairs*, no. 3 (1978), pp. 14–22.

31. An American government publication denies this Soviet assertion, which is clearly used for propaganda reasons. See Central Intelligence Agency, National Foreign Assessment Center, *Chinese Defense Spending, 1965–79*, SR80-10091, July 1980.

about the danger of the growth of spontaneous tendencies toward a private economy in China, about the overall weakening of both the state and the collectivist economic sectors, and about attempts to introduce into China forms of economic activity foreign to socialism and belonging to a market economy.[32]

In its present form the modernization program impels the Chinese leadership to seek support primarily among such groups as skilled workers, rich peasants, the intelligentsia, and remnants of the national bourgeoisie. The urban and rural "poor," in neither their economic nor political characteristics, can serve the goals of modernization with the necessary effectiveness. Moreover, modernization will not result in the improvement of the masses' material situation insofar as it is aimed primarily at the buildup of Chinese military power.

It is not entirely clear how the Soviets judge the prospects of the Four Modernizations. Impressed by the Chinese commitment to this program, the Soviets are deeply afraid that the Chinese will eventually succeed and that within half a century they will become a powerful adversary. Indeed, there exists a genuine belief among the Soviet leaders and the population as a whole that the Chinese are committed to a long-term, aggressive, anti-Soviet policy.

According to the Soviet view, the official Chinese line, which is anti-Maoist in words but in deeds follows slavishly in Mao's footsteps, masks the authentic, broad, and spontaneous anti-Maoist movement developing in China. This movement is being fought fiercely, using extreme methods of coercion and intimidation.[33] The Soviet leaders are placing their hopes on the destabilizing potential of this movement, a potential that may even force the Chinese leadership to change its basic policies. Yet those hopes are not very high, because, as the Soviets often repeat, one should not exaggerate the forces of the anti-Maoist movement in China. The fact of its existence does not signify that it can undermine the basis of the military-bureaucratic dictatorship in the near future. But it would also be wrong, the Soviets assert, to underestimate the importance of this movement, especially under China's present very unstable conditions.

Soviet analysts pay considerable attention to the factional struggle within the top Chinese leadership. According to the Soviets the divisions within the leadership have not decreased at all as a result of the purge of the Gang of Four; factionalism still splits China's Communist party from

32. V. Akimov and V. Potapov, "Results of the 'Lost Decade' and China's Economic Situation," *Far Eastern Affairs*, no. 2 (1979), pp. 53–70; idem, "'Four Modernizations': Outlines and the Reality," *Far Eastern Affairs*, no. 3 (1979), pp. 52–63.

33. K. Yegorov, "Punitive-Repressive Apparatus in the System of Maoist Dictatorship," ibid., no. 2 (1976), pp. 70–77.

top to bottom. It is quite interesting that both in their published material and in private conversations, Soviet observers of the Chinese power struggle see its greatest value for the Soviet Union in the weakening of China. They do not contend that any of the factions that are now fighting one another represent diverse opinions on the basic direction of Chinese policies, particularly foreign policy and especially relations with the Soviet Union. The Soviet judgment is that the struggle is primarily a fight for personal power and only secondarily involves tactical differences concerning the party's internal policies.

Soviet observers do not ignore the ideological revisions of Maoism that have taken place in China. Yet in their opinion the recent ideological "modification" of Maoism does not change its basic nature. Moreover, they stress that the revisions reinforce those elements of Maoist ideology that are most hateful to the Soviets: militant great-power nationalism, unbridled hegemonism in foreign policy, anti-Sovietism, and reliance on war and coercion as the key means of solving China's international and domestic problems.

THE SOVIET RESPONSE

The acute Sino–Soviet conflict has become a permanent fact of life with which the Soviets have learned to live. It colors their view of international relations and influences their domestic and foreign policies.

Although the conflict's significance did not overshadow the basic dimension of Soviet foreign policy—U.S.–Soviet relations—it became intertwined with those relations and added a new dimension to overall Soviet policies. It is my contention that while in the 1960s the influence of the conflict on Soviet policies had largely a temporary, ad hoc effect, in the 1970s the conflict and the question of the Soviet response to it in the political, economic, and ideological arenas have acquired a long-range nature—a permanency—that will not be basically influenced even if a breakthrough comes in the 1980s and normalization of relations between the Soviet Union and China is accomplished. For the foreseeable future, regardless of whether the efforts for normalization succeed, the Soviet policymakers and strategic planners are acting, and will be acting, under the assumption of a potential two-pronged danger to the Soviet Union and its ambitions—from the West and from the East.

Let me list some of the more important influences of the Sino–Soviet conflict, in its present form, on the Soviet situation and politics.

A number of scholars and journalists concerned with Sino–Soviet relations engage in speculation about the divisions in the Soviet leadership and elite concerning Soviet policy toward China. When, for example, the head of the Supreme Soviet, Podgornyi, was dismissed from his post in

1977, some analysts suggested that he favored a more conciliatory attitude toward China in the wake of Mao's death. (One has to add immediately that there was even widespread speculation, with greater basis in fact, that the reason for his dismissal involved differences regarding Soviet African policy.) A recurrent theme in the speculations about divisions within the Soviet leadership concerns the question of a Soviet preemptive strike against Chinese nuclear facilities. As rumor has it, there were during the late 1960s and mid-1970s major discussions among the Soviet leadership in which one group in alliance with the military high command advocated such a preemptive strike. It is clear, however, that all rumors regarding divisions among the Soviet leadership and elite about policies toward China are no more than rumors for which absolutely no evidence can be found. Moreover, Soviet experts on international relations with whom I have had the opportunity to discuss these rumors, and some of whom are usually reliable, deny unequivocally that major differences exist among Soviet leaders on their China policy. One has to assume not only that there is no Chinese connection in the CPSU but that differences—if they exist—are of a purely tactical nature.

Of course, among serious Soviet students of China, both in personal conversations and in their writings, one finds a less polemical tone toward China than in the speeches and writings of authoritative Soviet sources. One can discern among Soviet sinologists a wistfulness and regret that things have gone so far from bad to worse in the relationship between the Soviet Union and China, as well as a thinly concealed desire for an improvement in their relations. But one has to be clear that it is not these sinologists who shape (or even influence significantly) Soviet foreign policy; it is the political leadership, the ideologues, and the military. There is no evidence to suggest that the Sino–Soviet conflict has become an issue in Soviet domestic politics. We saw in the 1970s new signs that there were basic differences of opinion among the Soviet leadership and political elite about the causes of the conflict and about the policies that the Soviet Union should adopt to deal with it. One has an overwhelming impression that the Soviet leadership and the political elite are unified in their basic outlook on this subject and in their basic policy prescriptions. One even has the impression that the Sino–Soviet conflict acted as one of the primary elements in stabilizing and solidifying the elite consensus about the basic conduct of Soviet foreign policy in general. Students of Soviet foreign policymaking are well aware of differences of opinion among the leadership and the political elite with regard to some major aspects of Soviet foreign policy, particularly with regard to the United States. Under these conditions the apparent unanimity of attitude among the leadership and the elite toward China and Soviet China policy acts as a basic unifying force.

The Soviet Union has developed a large group of experts on Chinese affairs who serve both in an advisory capacity to the decisionmakers and as propagandists of the Soviet point of view. The opinions expressed by Soviet China experts in their writings and personal contacts with Western colleagues reflect the official position and, at the same time, could serve as a guide to discern the nuances and differences that may exist in particular aspects of China policy among the political elite. In connection with this, one should remark that the writings and conversations of those experts do provide a picture of slight differences in the harshness of the treatment of China's policies and situation, slightly varied explanations of the causes and sources of Chinese behavior, and especially lesser or greater hopes for peaceful solutions of the conflict and of the prospects for change in Chinese positions. Yet these differences are primarily differences of stress, not of basic substance. Moreover, one has a clear impression that these differences are much less pronounced than the variations in treatment that one encounters in expert Soviet writings and conversations concerning the other enemy of the Soviet Union—the United States. The evidence is not conclusive but one is led to assume that the advice that the Soviet decisionmakers get from the professional China hands is basically in tune with their own views and is rather homogeneous.

The Soviet authorities have been quite successful through their propaganda machine at creating in the Soviet population—particularly among the Slavs—a mood of general agreement with Soviet China policy. One has the impression that broad popular strata, particularly the Russians, have been successfully mobilized to support their government's position on China. One has a feeling of a widespread genuine dislike and fear of China; of strong elements of even hatred toward China that has racial overtones; of a common view of the Chinese leadership as ingrates who betrayed the Soviet Union and are trying to push the Soviet Union toward war, and with whom one should deal from a position of strength. If this impression is correct, it differs very considerably from Soviet popular attitudes toward the West. The conclusion must be that Soviet public opinion does not provide a restraint on the policies adopted by the Soviet leadership vis-à-vis China.

One of the most significant influences of the Sino–Soviet conflict and its intensity on Soviet behavior is Soviet military policy. The perception of the Chinese danger, reflected for example in the deployment of new nuclear weapons, particularly the SS-20, is not simply a component of Soviet military policy but influences importantly the overall Soviet military buildup. There is a discussion raging in the West whether the Soviet Union has as its military goal the attainment of strategic parity with the United States and the improvement of its global capacities to match those of the United States or whether the Soviet goal is the achievement of superiority over the Western alliance. It is a question that is extremely difficult if at all possible to answer, in light of the Soviet concept of security. As it is often remarked, the Soviet concept of security is highly exaggerated and includes tremendous military redundancy. What the Soviets, traditionally and at present, are aiming for is nothing less than a nonattainable total security. By doing so, their military buildup reaches a point where the Soviets can feel secure only if other nations feel insecure. This crucial dilemma and contradiction of the Soviet quest for security does not take into account other nations' reactions to what the Soviets may consider defensive steps but which the outside world sees as a growing danger and to which it reacts accordingly. This vicious spiral of Soviet perceptions and behavior, reflected in their military policy, is quite clear in its behavior toward the United States and its Western allies.[34] The Sino–Soviet conflict acts as a powerful reinforcer of this type of Soviet behavior and therefore makes the regulation of the arms race much more difficult and the stabilization of the Soviet military buildup much more unlikely (this is incidentally one of the reasons that I am not at all certain whether some degree of normalization of Sino–Soviet relations would not also be in the interest of the United States and its allies).

The Sino–Soviet conflict and the imperatives that it imposes on Soviet priorities regarding budgetary expenditure obviously increase the burden of the military buildup on the Soviet economy. It should be remarked, however, that in all probability it otherwise influences the Soviet economic policy only to a very limited degree. The development of the BAM railway system, the efforts to build an infrastructure in eastern Siberia, and the efforts to increase settlement in the areas adjacent to the Sino–Soviet border are only in a coincidental way connected with the Sino–Soviet conflict. The Far Eastern territories of the Soviet Union and Siberia are anyway the natural and logical targets of Soviet economic expansion. In the period of increased scarcities of raw materials, particularly oil, any rational Soviet economic expansion plan has to redirect its investment resources from the European part of the Soviet Union to those areas.

The Soviet Union has become a global power with global political interests. Yet, obviously, there exists in the Soviet foreign policy strategy an order of priorities that reflects Soviet fears and ambitions. One may suggest that without a chronic and an intense Sino–Soviet conflict the attention paid by Soviet foreign policy to Central and Southeast Asia

34. For a discussion of the Soviet concept of security, see Seweryn Bialer, *Stalin's Successors: Leadership, Stability and Change in the Soviet Union* (New York: Cambridge University Press, 1980), chap. 12.

would have been less pronounced. Undoubtedly the main direction and the main preoccupation of Soviet foreign policy, whether as part of its competition with the United States or on its own merits, is directed toward Western Europe. In its activities in the Third World countries, however, one can notice an increase in Soviet attention toward the Asiatic countries adjacent to China. It is part of a concerted Soviet effort to isolate China in Asia.

The Sino–Soviet conflict and its intensity seriously influence Soviet dealings with the international communist movement and with left-wing and revolutionary groups. It introduces a major complicating and aggravating element into those dealings and minimizes the Soviets' effectiveness in their attempt to influence those movements. Until Mao's death and the recent changes in China, the principal danger to the Soviet Union in this respect consisted of a partial ability of the Chinese to capture the ultraleft wing of the leftist movement, to create ultraleft movements that competed with Soviet-sponsored activities, and to put the Soviets on the defensive in trying to reassert their revolutionary credentials. After Mao's death and the reorientation of Chinese domestic and foreign policy in a rightist direction, this danger from the Chinese has subsided. On the other hand the Chinese have increased their efforts to develop closer ties with the Eurocommunist parties and to identify with those groups in the international communist movement that are opposed to the oppressiveness of the Soviet regime, Soviet expansionism, and military buildup. In other words, while the ultraleft splinter activity of the Chinese has diminished in its effectiveness, its danger as a reinforcing factor in the disputes between the Soviet Union and the established communist parties has increased. It is a factor that seriously complicates Soviet freedom to maneuver in the international communist movement.

Logically, the Sino–Soviet conflict and its intensification should have pushed the Soviet Union to a greater effort to preserve and strengthen détente with the United States. Without détente with the United States, and with closer relations between the United States and China, the Soviet Union finds itself in the worst position in the strategic triangle. As a matter of fact, in the early 1970s it was the American opening to China that provided an additional and important inducement for the Soviet Union to enter into a détente with the United States. Yet, throughout the 1970s the deterioration of relations between China and the Soviet Union did not affect their lack of restraint in pursuing their aims in the international arena by means contrary to the American understanding of détente. It seems to me that this signifies first of all that, from the Soviet point of view, the American China card is almost played out and can have little influence in tempering Soviet behavior. Second, it signifies at least partial reevaluation of the centrality of U.S.–Soviet relations in the international arena in Soviet eyes, and their assignment of higher priority to their expansion in the Third World and intimidation of Western Europe than to détente with the United States. In this sense the extent to which the intensification of the Sino–Soviet conflict pushes the Soviet Union visibly toward an improvement of relations with the United States can serve as a barometer of the Soviet view of the correlation of forces between the United States and the Soviet Union.

SINO–SOVIET RELATIONS: THE 1980S

What are the prospects for Sino–Soviet relations in the 1980s? Quite clearly, they depend not only on Soviet intentions and behavior but also on a number of other factors that may influence Soviet behavior.

A key factor here is American behavior, primarily because it will influence the Chinese attitude to any Soviet overtures. The question simply stated is: To what extent and how successfully will the United States be able to resist Soviet expansionism and to achieve a more balanced relation of military strength with the Soviet Union in the 1980s? The Chinese interest in opening toward the United States is not, I feel, primarily based on a desire for American help in Chinese modernization or, even more narrowly, an American sale or grant of major quantities of weapons to China. Rather, the Chinese want an American resolve and ability to resist Soviet worldwide expansionism. If during the 1980s China becomes convinced that the balance of power continues to tilt dangerously in favor of the Soviet Union, the vital interest of its own security may make it amenable to attempt to at least partly reconcile its differences with the Soviet Union.

On the other hand a strong and resolute American foreign policy vis-à-vis Soviet expansionism would be, in my view, the single most important factor in preventing a Chinese positive response to possible Soviet reconciliation attempts. (Obviously a central factor in influencing Sino–Soviet relations in the 1980s will be developments within China itself: the extent to which the modernizations program is successful; the success in renewing and maintaining a unified leadership, and so forth.)

What I would like to concentrate on in my discussion of the prospects for Sino–Soviet relations in the 1980s, however, are not the important factors mentioned above but rather the pressures on the Soviet domestic and international situation that may influence Soviet behavior toward the Chinese adversary.

It seems to me that there are three sets of circumstances and pressures that may shape Soviet policies toward China during the 1980s. The first has to do with the state of the competition between the United States and the Soviet Union during this period; the second concerns the coming succession in the Soviet Union; and the third concerns the growing pressures on the economic resources that the Soviet Union will encounter in the 1980s.

The first factor that should have decided influence on Sino–Soviet relations in the 1980s is the state and prospects of U.S.–Soviet relations. Détente between the United States and the Soviet Union, which started to unravel during the last year of the Carter administration, came to a decisive end with the advent of the Reagan administration. While there is no doubt that Soviet actions in the field of arms buildup and especially in the attempts to expand in the Third World were key contributing factors to bringing about the end of détente, the initiative to depart from détente and to resume a confrontational stance toward the Soviet Union was, just as clearly, an American decision.

The Reagan administration's policies and its lack of commitment to arms control, as well as its general attitude toward Soviet international ambitions, create new conditions for Soviet international activity quite different from those of the 1970s.

The value of détente, as perceived by the Soviet Union, was not only—or perhaps not so much—in the implied economic relations with the West but primarily and foremost in the final Western recognition of the Soviet empire and the concomitant contribution to the stability of that empire. Second, it was expected in Moscow that détente would permit the expansion of Soviet power and influence in various parts of the globe through means that would include military action without a high probability of creating a dangerous confrontation with the United States.

The first expectation concerning Eastern Europe has collapsed regardless of détente's fate. The situation in Poland, if it continues, endangers not only the stability of the whole of Eastern Europe but also the strategic position of the Soviet Union. Even in the absence of any actions to strengthen NATO, the conditions of the Soviet Western front will be perceptibly worse in the 1980s than they were in the 1970s.

The Soviet leaders' expectations concerning the chances of expanding their influence and power in the international arena without major confrontations with the United States are also not very realistic if the rhetoric of the Reagan administration reflects a policy direction that can be backed up by the will and means to act forcefully in the international arena. At the time of this writing, Fall 1981, it is yet too early to say, but in all probability the Reagan administration's decisions constitute in this respect a major shift in American post-Vietnam policies. If this is the

case, the incentives for the Soviet Union to try to lessen tension in Sino–Soviet relations and to attempt to achieve at least a partial reconciliation with the Chinese are very high indeed—much higher than in the
1970s.

A most important stimulus and pressure for changes in Soviet policy
toward China will not originate in new political issues but in the policymaking process itself—in the impending turnover of the leaders and
elites in the 1980s.[35] The consequences of succession for the Soviet
political system are profound. The probabilities of deep personal and
policy conflicts within the top leadership structure are increased. The
possibilities for resolving these conflicts in more extreme ways are max-
imized. The tendency toward large-scale personnel changes within the
leadership itself and among the top elites and bureaucratic hierarchies is
heightened.

The period of succession offers a high potential for destroying the
bureaucratic inertia of the departed leaders and for changing the initial
drift of their policies. It is a period with a high potential for ferment, for
greater responsiveness to pressures, real and anticipated, for broaden-
ing of political participation, and for opening of the political process. In
sum, the succession, aside from its own intrinsic importance, acts as a
catalyst for pressures and tendencies that already exist within society but
that previously had limited opportunity for expression and realization.

The approaching succession is in many respects different from those
in the past. It combines a number of characteristics that make it fraught
with very important political implications in the 1980s, for better or for
worse from the Western point of view. The foremost of these characteristics is the fact that it almost inevitably will combine the replacement
of the top leader with that of the core leadership group and a large part
of the central elite and with the beginning of a generational turnover
among the Soviet elites. Moreover, the age-cohort characteristics of the
Soviet leadership and elites is such that the replacement will not only be
massive but also will be compressed in a relatively short time span.

If the advanced age of this leadership group has no precedent in
Soviet history, there is also no precedent for the clustering of such a high
proportion of the members of this group in the highest age bracket.
What is even more significant from the point of view of our inquiry is the
lack of a precedent for the described type of age configuration on the
eve of succession. The approaching succession will not consist simply of
the replacement of the top leader but also of a massive replacement and
reshuffling within the highest echelons of the Soviet hierarchy during
the coming years.

35. See Seweryn Bialer, "Succession and Turnover of Soviet Elites," *Journal of International Affairs,* 32, no. 2 (Fall/Winter 1978): 181–200.

The age structure of the top leadership, far from being limited to that group, is very nearly mirrored in the case of the central elite, both with regard to its advanced age and the clustering of this age group. Its massive replacement in the 1980s is also unavoidable.

Massive replacements at the levels of the top leadership and central elite, which would certainly accompany the second if not the first stage of the upcoming succession, will most probably produce political conflicts over policies and procedures regardless of who the new leaders will be. On the one hand such a prospect is especially likely because the succession will follow a period of extraordinary and long-lasting stability, during which policy differences were submerged in the name of unity, stability, and compromise, and bold initiatives, especially on the domestic scene, were lacking. On the other hand, the succession will come at a time when the Soviet Union will begin to face difficult economic choices, when the possibility of satisfying diverse interests and pressures through compromise solutions will become more difficult than in the Brezhnev period.

I believe that the massive turnover of elites, especially when compressed into a short period of time, can in itself be significant in determining the formation of the styles and behavior of the new leadership and elites. By breaking the official routine inculcated in a bureaucratic and centralized structure, by undermining the inertia of a set style of work, by disrupting the existing and fixed informal ties, and by weakening the interests vested in long-established substantive policies, this turnover will provide a setting that will facilitate the elaboration of changed modes of political behavior. Yet the key questions still remain. Will the newcomers be favorably disposed to make use of the opportunity to be different? How much pressure will they exert, and in which direction, in order to change the policies and processes of the Soviet government? In short, just how different will they be from their predecessors?

The most important question, then, is whether and to what extent the succession and the subsequent replacement of large segments of the elites will coincide with the emergence of distinctive differences between the incoming group and the outgoing group, irrespective of the diverse personalities within each group. I would like to suggest that in the approaching succession such a coincidence will occur. In addition to the imminent replacement of the top leader and a large part of the highest leadership, a generational change within the Soviet elite will also occur; a large proportion of the new elite will have entered politics after Stalin's death.[36] The approaching succession, whatever the form and results of

---

36. The post-Stalin generation is still represented to only a very small degree in the central leadership and elite in 1980, comprising only 12.5% of these leaders whereas the Great Purge, World War II, and late-Stalin generations make up 67.5, 10, and 10% of the

its initial stage, will eventually involve a replacement of the top leadership and the central establishment on a scale much greater than the last two successions and will be combined with an increased generational turnover of the Soviet political elite. This conjunction of succession, in both the broad and the narrow sense, has no precedent in Soviet history. It will be a political development of long-term duration and significance.

The stability and longevity of the existing pattern of leadership have been conditional on two internal structural factors: gradualism in major policy changes and gradualism, to say the least, in personnel replacement. We do not know whether the first condition will still obtain during the succession or whether, after the cycle of cautious adjustment and traditionalism of the last decade, the mood of the leadership and the elite will swing toward revitalization and major reforms, just as the frozen conditions of Stalin's Russia were replaced by the flux of the Khrushchev period. Certainly, during the succession, the nature of this tendency will depend ultimately on whether the Soviet leaders and elite will become more aware of the pressures and frustrations stemming from failures or dangers at home or abroad. We do know, however, that the second condition—gradualism in personnel replacement—will most probably not persist.

The effects of the pressures created by the forthcoming succession, in combination with the political issues that will become part of the political agenda, may become significant. They may, and in all probability will,

---

members, respectively. However, on the republican and provincial levels the post-Stalin generation already has significant representation among the leadership. Listed below are the data indicating the percentage of post-Stalin generation representatives occupying the top positions in various institutions in 1978: Presidium, Council of Ministers (RSFSR): 30.7%; first *obkom* secretaries (RSFSR: Russian provinces): 32%; second secretaries of republics (Russians): 45.4%; republican and first obkom secretaries (Ukrainians and Belorussians): 47.6%; Russian first obkom secretaries in non-Russian areas of RSFSR and non-Slav republics: 38.5%; all above-mentioned institutions: 36.9%. Seventy-five percent of the leading party and soviet officials of Moscow and Leningrad are in this category. Among the elites of the seven non-Slav republics of Uzbekistan, Tadzhikistan, Kirgizia, Latvia, Lithuania, Estonia, and Moldavia, the average age and representation of the post-Stalin generation run as follows. The Republican Secretaries have an average age of 55.3, and 27% of the positions are filled by representatives of the post-Stalin generation. The median age within the Presidium of the Council of Ministers is 55.7, with 33.3% of the bureaucrats having entered the party after Stalin's death. The Central Committee's department heads average 50.1 years of age, with 46.1% of this group being comprised of post-Stalin generation representatives. Members of the Council of Ministers have a median age of 54.2, and 35.2% of the leaders represent the generation in question. The percentage of *raykom* and *gorkom* first secretaries having entered the CPSU after 1953 is 66%, with the average age of this group of bureaucrats being 47.8. *Rayispolkom* and *gorispolkom* chairmen (including also some chairmen of provinces) average 47.2 years of age, with 73.2% of the group representing the post-Stalin generation.

lead to the destabilization of the central policymaking system, which, in a highly centralized polity such as the Soviet Union, may have very serious consequences. The destabilization will involve a breakdown of the consensus among the leadership and the elites, the intensification of factional struggles at the top and middle levels of the bureaucracy, possible realignments of existing alliances, the exploitation of policy issues for the accumulation of power by individual leaders and groups, and sharp twists and turns in central policies.

The third set of pressures will originate in the Soviet economy. There exists a basic consensus among students of Soviet economics that in the 1980s the Soviet Union will face grave economic problems.[37]

A secular decline in economic growth rates involving all sectors will confront the Soviets in the coming decade. Extensive development has reached such limits that retention of the high growth rates of the past is no longer possible. Even without the intervention of other negative factors and assuming no decline in the quality of the traditional Soviet leadership of the economy, the growth of Soviet GNP in the 1980s will be approximately 2.5 percent per year.

The Soviet political-economic system of management, pricing, and incentives is ill-prepared to maximize the possibilities for intensive growth. The conditions for a relatively rapid change would require fundamental changes in the economic-political system and are unlikely to be accomplished in the foreseeable future. Among the steps already undertaken by the Soviet government to counteract the declining tendencies of growth, none will have any major impact on the Soviet economy.

The Soviet Union in the 1980s is also facing unfavorable demographic trends. There will be a rapid decline in the growth of new labor resources. The situation will be further complicated by changes in the composition of the new labor force, which will be overwhelmingly non-Russian.

---

37. These tendencies and trends are well presented in Congress of the United States, Joint Economic Committee, *Soviet Economy in a Time of Change*, 96th Congr., 1st Sess. (Washington, D.C.: U.S. Government Printing Office, 1979), vols. I and II. A number of papers by the CIA also provide a basis for an analysis of the Soviet outlook for the 1980s. They are: Testimony of the DCI Admiral Stansfield Turner before the U.S., Congress, Joint Economic Committee, Subcommittee on Priorities and Economy in Government (96th Congr., June 26, 1979); National Foreign Assessment Center, *Simulations of Soviet Growth Options to 1985*, ER 79-10131, Mar. 1979; idem, *SOVISM: A Model of Soviet Economy*, ER 79-10001, Feb. 1979; idem, *Soviet Economic Problems and Prospects*, ER 77-10436U, July 1977; idem, *Prospects for Soviet Oil Production*, ER 77-10270, Apr. 1977; and idem, *USSR: Long Term Outlook for Grain Imports*, ER 79-10057, Jan. 1979. A representative nongovernmental study of the prospects for the Soviet economy in the 1980s can be found in Holland Hunter, ed., *The Future of the Soviet Economy, 1978–1985* (Boulder, Colo.: Westview Press, 1978).

The Soviet Union will face an energy balance unfavorable to its economic growth. This is especially true in the production of oil. It is a matter of major contention among economists as to how much this production will fall. Nevertheless, there is a growing consensus that a decrease will take place. Even if one rejects the worst-case scenarios, which predict an 8-million-barrel-a-day oil production, the decline will be sufficient, it seems, to impose major constraints on the Soviet economy and to limit Soviet ability to fully utilize their existing economic capacities.

The enormous agricultural investments of the Brezhnev era have produced limited and, at best, uncertain results. Soviet agriculture in the 1980s will remain a highly volatile economic sector. Moreover, because of reduced secular growth in other sectors, the unavoidable agricultural fluctuations will have a growing influence on the size of the Soviet GNP.

In sum, there can be little doubt that the Soviet Union faces a difficult economic situation in the 1980s. How difficult it will be is a matter of conjecture. According to the worst-case scenarios, it will be a period of low growth intermingled with economic stagnation. But even according to the more optimistic scenarios, the Soviet Union will face an economic crunch far more severe than anything it encountered in the 1960s and 1970s.

During the 1980s the Soviet Union will in all probability be unable to pursue a policy in which military expenditures, investments, and consumer spending will all grow steadily and sometimes even rapidly. The consensus among Soviet leaders and elites, made possible by high growth rates in the past, will give way to fierce competition, which in a situation of leadership succession can become very intense. In the context of the present discussion the most important aspect of the growing Soviet economic difficulties will be the increasing pressures placed on military expenditures. One should not have any illusions. If the Soviets feel that their security is threatened, they will make any sacrifices necessary to keep up their military strength. Yet the cost of such effort will be immeasurably higher than in the past. Soviet economic problems will require enormous and costly investment in renovating technological plants and developing tremendously expensive energy resources. At the same time, throughout the 1960s and 1970s social constraints developed with regard to how much the leadership could depress the growth rate of the standard of living. With the abolition of mass terror during the post-Stalinist period, the stability of the system and the compact between the leadership and the broad strata of the population became increasingly based on a steadily growing consumption and on the expectation of the population that such growth would continue. Neither the Soviet leaders nor Western analysts know how the working classes, and especially industrial workers, will react to a stagnating standard of living. In light of the events in Poland the specter of labor unrest must hound the Soviet leadership.

All three pressures described here—the Soviet succession, the Soviet economic situation, and the state and prospects of Soviet–American relations—should, logically speaking, exert a major influence on the Soviet leadership in the direction of accommodation and partial reconciliation with the People's Republic of China. There is little doubt that in the coming years, especially given the conditions of a political succession, it is almost unavoidable that the new Soviet leaders will once again make serious efforts to determine whether a reconciliation is possible.

It is my opinion, however, that for a number of reasons the present level of hostilities, suspiciousness, and conflict between the USSR and the PRC will in all probability remain unaltered in the 1980s.

First of all, in view of the deep, negative feelings toward the Chinese held by both the Soviet leadership and the population as a whole, it is unlikely that the Soviet Union will go far enough in its offers of peace and reconciliation with the People's Republic of China to satisfy the minimal requirements for basic changes in policy toward the Chinese.

Second, the Chinese themselves know very well that overtures toward the Soviet Union or positive responses to Soviet overtures would critically endanger the American connection—especially in a situation where a highly conservative and ideologically anticommunist government such as the Reagan administration continues to govern in the United States. The Chinese value highly their newly acquired American connection and see in it—rightly or wrongly—the necessary condition not only for improving their security but also for successfully conducting the Four Modernizations.

5

The Northern Territories: 130 Years of Japanese Talks with Czarist Russia and the Soviet Union

FUJI KAMIYA

The territorial dispute between Japan and the Soviet Union over the four islands, that is, the Habomais, Shikotan, Kunashiri, and Etorofu, that lie off the northeastern tip of Hokkaido has been one of the principal stumbling blocks in the relations between the two countries since the end of World War II. To gain some perspective on what is likely to be the future of Japanese–Soviet relations, it is necessary to review the evolution of this dispute in some depth, to assess the prospects for some eventual compromise, and to discuss the constraints on Japanese–Soviet relations in the absence of any compromise. This is what I propose to do in this chapter.

In the spring of 1951 General Omar Bradley, then chairman of the U.S. Joint Chiefs of Staff, criticized General Douglas MacArthur's proposal to expand the Korean War into China as "the wrong war against the wrong enemy in the wrong place at the wrong time." In a similar way things seem generally to have been wrong with Japan's approach to the Northern Territories.

The first "wrong" thing is Japan's protagonist in the negotiations: the Soviet Union. The Soviet Union is a tough bargainer on any question but on territorial issues it has shown a toughness unlike that of any other major power. Alone among the Allied powers, the Soviet Union gained territories through World War II. It went along with the Allies in disclaiming territorial ambitions and suggested that it might relinquish its occupied territories after the war. But whereas the other Allies did eventually give up their territories, if belatedly—it was not, for example, until 1972 that the United States finally turned back the Bonin (Ogasawara) Islands and Okinawa to Japan—Moscow distinguished itself by disregarding the Allied declarations and holding firmly onto the

This chapter was translated into English by Kazuo Takahashi and the Council on National Security Problems (Tokyo). It was edited by Janet D. Zagoria.

121

vast bulk of territories it took. Indeed, the Soviet Union has shown conspicuous intransigence on all territorial questions. Although it appeared somewhat conciliatory on certain territorial questions at different times, in general the Kremlin has seemed to consider nearly every piece of land acquired as vital to Soviet strategic security.

Japan, by contrast, has shown (by international standards) a very timid attitude about security matters. For the past fifteen years it has staunchly refused to permit its defense budget to rise above 1 percent of its gross national product. It has been extremely reluctant to build up the weaponry of its 240,000-man Self-Defense Forces. It has tended to put a low strategic value on disputed territories, particularly the Northern Territories. The growing interest Japan has shown in regaining the Northern Territories has been for entirely different reasons, which are historical and political. The two countries have thus approached the territorial question from opposite perspectives.

Timing has also been wrong in the Northern Territories dispute. There have been periods—as immediately after World War II, after Stalin's death in 1953, after the Cuban missile crisis in the early 1960s and Khrushchev's ouster soon after, and even until 1968—when the Soviet Union was politically vulnerable or militarily weak enough so that it might possibly have been pressured into negotiating on the issue. There have been periods—notably, in the mid-1950s, for a time in the 1960s, and during the heyday of détente in the early 1970s—when the Soviet Union showed a certain willingness to negotiate over at least some of the Northern Territories. There have been times when the Soviet Union wanted something from Japan, and an exchange of some sort might have been struck. Each time, however, either Japan has been caught ill-prepared to seize the opportunity to strike a bargain, or, for some other reason, the moment when negotiations might have been fruitful has passed without resolution of the dispute. The two countries have been consistently out of kilter, one might say, on the Northern Territories issue. And, as time goes on, the possibility of resolving the issue in Japan's favor is lessened, if indeed it ever existed.

There is another wrong thing one could mention about the issue. It is that Japan and the Soviet Union have not alone controlled the outcome of the dispute, which has been affected by other powers as well. The United States, China, and Europe have all, at different times and from different perspectives, played a role in the Northern Territories dispute, complicating the issue and helping to prevent it from being resolved.

The Northern Territories issue remains, therefore, extremely contentious. There is no doubt that Japan has a traditional claim to the four islands, and most Japanese regard them as Japan's inalienable lands. It is also clear that the Soviet Union has physical control of the islands, and

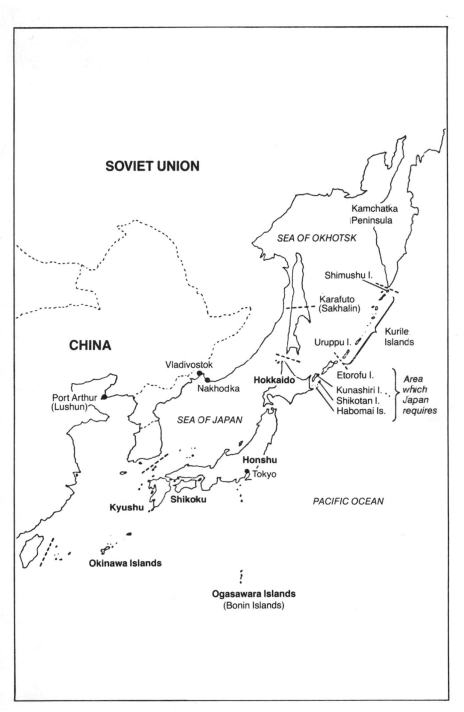

Fig. 5.1. "A border yet unresolved": Japan's Northern Territories.

Japan does not possess the means to secure its claim. With these basic difficulties in mind, I would like to provide a brief history of Japan's negotiations with czarist Russia and later with the Soviet Union on the Northern Territories before making some observations about the likely outcome of this dispute.

BEFORE THE PACIFIC WAR

Japan and Russia concluded two treaties in the pre-World War II period that bear directly on the Northern Territories issue. The first, concluded in the Tokugawa period, was the Treaty of Commerce, Navigation and Delimitation signed in 1855. The second, signed in the early Meiji period, was the Treaty for the Exchange of Sakhalin for the Kurile Islands of 1875.

Article 2 of the first treaty reads:

Henceforth the boundary between Japan and Russia will pass between the islands Etorofu and Uruppu. The whole island of Etorofu belongs to Japan and the whole island of Uruppu and the other Kurile Islands to the north constitute possessions of Russia. As regards the island Karafuto (Sakhalin), it remains unpartitioned between Japan and Russia, as has been the case up to this time.[1]

Thus, by the treaty Russia acknowledged the islands from Etorofu southward as being exclusively Japanese.

The Treaty of 1875 lists, in its article 2, eighteen islands of the Kuriles from Uruppu north to Shumshu, making it clear that they would be transferred to Japan. In exchange, Russia was to get all of Sakhalin. The four islands—the Habomais, Shikotan, Kunashiri, and Etorofu—were not mentioned (p. 10). The Japan–Russia Treaty of Commerce, Navigation and Delimitation therefore remained in force on the Habomais, Shikotan, Kunashiri, and Etorofu. These four islands were evidently to remain Japanese.

Two other treaties concluded in the pre-World War II period should be mentioned. Although they do not deal directly with the Northern Territories as defined here, they do deal with nearby Sakhalin and they serve to mark the twists and turns in the fortunes of Japan and Russia.

The first of these is the Portsmouth Treaty, which marked the end of the Russo–Japanese War of 1904–05. Negotiated through the good offices of U.S. President Theodore Roosevelt, this treaty changed the status of Sakhalin: by its article 9 the treaty divided the island between Russia and Japan at the 50° north latitude (p. 17). Russia thus lost the southern half of Sakhalin as a result of its ignominious defeat in the war.

1. *Hoppo Ryodo Mondai Shiryo Shu* (*Documents on the Northern Territories Problem* [henceforth *Documents*]) (Tokyo: Hoppo Ryodo Mondai Taisaku Kyokai, 1972), p. 1. Unless otherwise indicated, page citations in the text refer to *Documents*.

Russian rights to northern Sakhalin as well were threatened by a development that took place during Russia's Civil War. In the summer of 1918, taking advantage of the turmoil in Russia, Japan intervened in the struggle to occupy northern Sakhalin, along with parts of the Soviet Far East. The Russians thereby lost physical control even of that part of the island accorded to it under the Portsmouth Treaty.

The second Russo–Japanese treaty, concluded in 1925, merely reversed this new development. In 1925 Japan formally recognized the communist government of what had become the Soviet Union. The same year, the two nations signed a treaty setting out fundamental rules to govern their relations. Article 2 of the treaty says:

The Union of Soviet Socialist Republics agrees to continue honoring in its entirety the Portsmouth Treaty of September 5, 1905. (p. 27)

In other words, the status quo ante—whereby Japan controlled all of Sakhalin south of the 50° latitude and the Russians controlled Sakhalin north of that latitude—was to prevail.

By these various agreements, then, Japan and Russia acknowledged Japanese claims to the four islands of the Habomais, Shikotan, Kunashiri, and Etorofu and to southern Sakhalin, while they agreed that the northern part of Sakhalin should be Russian. A division of territory had been arrived at. All this was to change dramatically with Japan's defeat in World War II.

WORLD WAR II AND THE PEACE SETTLEMENT

Preparations for the postwar settlement in the Far East may be said to have begun with the Cairo Declaration, signed by Jiang Jieshi (Chiang Kai-shek), Churchill, and Roosevelt in November 1943. It announced the Allies' intention to "restrain and punish the aggression of Japan," which was to be "stripped of all the islands in the Pacific which she has seized or occupied since the beginning of World War I in 1914" and "expelled from all other territories which she has taken by violence and greed" (p. 35). This would have covered the northern half of Sakhalin, but not the Kuriles that Japan acquired by peaceful means in the abovementioned Treaty of 1875.

The Soviet Union was not represented in Cairo but Stalin had hastened—as soon as the Soviet Union joined the Allies in Europe—to press Soviet territorial claims there. Thus, when Stalin agreed at the Teheran Conference in December 1943 to enter the Pacific War, the Allies assumed he had a price. This price emerged in late 1944. The Russians wanted southern Sakhalin and all the Kurile Islands. And at Yalta, in February 1945, the United States accepted this price. President

Roosevelt agreed that the southern half of Sakhalin and the Kurile Islands would be handed over to the Soviet Union at the end of the war (p. 35). (The U.S. State Department had in fact prepared a memorandum for Roosevelt's use at Yalta, saying that the Russians had no legitimate claim to the four islands, although they did have a claim to the eighteen ones north of the four islands. Unfortunately, FDR did not read this memorandum: he assumed that the Russians had a legitimate claim to all the Kuriles and apparently misunderstood that the four islands were part of it. The United States also agreed, at Soviet insistence, to keep this part of the Yalta agreement secret.[2]

The Yalta agreement was confirmed at Potsdam, in August of the same year. Meeting with Stalin, the leader of Britain's new Labour government, Clement Atlee, and Harry S Truman, who had acceded to the U.S. presidency at FDR's death, agreed that "Japan shall consist only of Honshu, Hokkaido, Kyushu and Shikoku, along with such minor islands as we shall determine."[3] Japan was to be reduced virtually to the Japanese homeland. Its "unconditional surrender" was to be made clear.

Japan's actual surrender took place at a ceremony aboard the U.S. battleship *Missouri* on September 2, 1945, at which time the United States accepted Japan's surrender in behalf of the Allies. The same day Joseph Stalin issued the following statement:

On this day, Japan has admitted defeat and signed an unconditional surrender. This means that Southern Sakhalin and the Kurile Islands pass into the hands of the Soviet Union. Henceforth, the Kurile Islands shall not serve as a means to cut off the Soviet Union from the ocean or as a base for a Japanese attack on our Far East, but as a means to link the Soviet Union with the ocean and as a defensive base against Japanese aggression.[4]

Stalin thus made clear his conviction that the Allied agreements covered the four islands of the Habomais, Shikotan, Kunashiri, and Etorofu and southern Sakhalin, and his determination to retain control of the new Soviet acquisitions.

Stalin's conviction was doubtless strengthened by two subsequent developments. In 1951 the San Francisco Peace Treaty was signed. By this treaty Japan abandoned claims to certain territories. Its article 2(c) said:

---

2. For details, see John J. Stephan, *The Kurile Islands: Russo–Japanese Frontier in the Pacific* (Oxford: Clarendon Press, 1974), chap. 5.

3. *Documents*, p. 37.

4. See Shigeto Yuhashi, *Senji Nisso Kosho Shoshi (A Short History of Japanese–Soviet Negotiations during War)* (Tokyo: Kasumigaseki Shuppan, 1974), p. 228. See also Tsuguo Togawa, "Hoppo Ryodo no Rekishi (History of the Northern Territories)," in Hiroshi Kimura, ed., *Hoppo Ryodo o Kangaeru (Thinking on the Northern Territories)* (Hokkaido: Hokkaido Shimbun Sha, 1981), p. 68.

Japan renounces all right, title and claim to the Kurile Islands, and to that portion of Sakhalin and the islands adjacent to it over which Japan acquired sovereignty as a consequence of the Treaty of Portsmouth of September 5, 1905.[5]

The Soviet Union was not a party to the San Francisco treaty and in fact was highly critical of it. The treaty does not specify to whom Japan should relinquish its claim over the territories. Furthermore, even at the time, the Japanese raised doubts about some of the treaty provisions. Japan's chief delegate at the San Francisco conference, Shigeru Yoshida, said:

Whereas the Japanese people accepted cheerfully the terms of this treaty, it is undeniable that we feel some anguish and concern with regard to a few of its provisions. This treaty is just and magnanimous to a degree rarely seen in history, and we dutifully acknowledge the position we find ourselves in. Nevertheless, in view of the responsibilities vested in me by the Japanese people, I must take the liberty of inviting your attention to a few points.

First, the territorial issue. . . . It is more difficult for us to acquiesce in the allegation by the chief Soviet delegate that Japan seized the Kurile (Chishima) Islands and southern Sakhalin by force. Upon the opening of Japan to foreign intercourse, Imperial Russia took no exception whatsoever to Japanese ownership of Etorofu and Kunashiri. Only the Kurile (Chishima) Islands north of Uruppu and southern Sakhalin were at that time areas of mixed habitation by Japanese and Russians.

On May 7, 1875 the Russian and Japanese governments agreed through peaceful diplomatic negotiations that Japan would get the northern Kurile Islands in compensation for southern Sakhalin, which would be Russian. Whereas compensation was the term used, the Kuriles were received in return for concession with regard to southern Sakhalin. Southern Sakhalin itself became Japanese as a result of the Portsmouth Treaty concluded on 5 September 1905 through the mediation of President Theodore Roosevelt.

Then, upon Japan's surrender on September 2, 1945, the Kuriles and southern Sakhalin were unilaterally taken over by the Soviet Union. Moreover, the islands of Shikotan and Habomais, which form an integral part of the Japanese homeland, were similarly occupied by Soviet forces because they happened to have Japanese military forces stationed on them. (pp. 113–14)

As a representative of a defeated nation, however, Yoshida spoke at the very end of the conference. Without further comment by the other delegates, therefore, the treaty was signed the following day.

5. *Documents*, p. 118.

The famous *Yoshida Memoirs* and other written materials detail the period from preparation of documents for the treaty by Yoshida's staff to his final speech.[6] They indicate that the Japanese side prepared explanatory materials amounting to seven volumes on the territorial issue alone in order to substantiate the Japanese claims to everything south of Iturup Island and to southern Sakhalin. These Japanese efforts bore no fruit.

Japan's pleas at the time to the U.S. chief negotiator were also in vain. The United States had decided upon a so-called one-sided peace, which excluded the Soviet Union from the postwar settlement in the Pacific. But the Americans also had to preserve the appearance of a general peace. The United States therefore felt constrained to accommodate the harsh anti-Japanese sentiments of other Allies, such as Britain and Australia. Understandably, U.S. negotiators did not award high priority to Japanese claims to the Northern Territories. The Japanese, for their part, keenly aware that their surrender was unconditional and that their most likely means of recovering sovereignty over disputed territories lay through the United States, did not press their claims. Japan contented itself with entering Yoshida's speech in the record.

Not long after the San Francisco conference a second development occurred, which was to weaken the Japanese case. A Japanese government official, speaking during a Diet interpellation, stated with some confusion that the term *Kurile Islands* in the treaty referred to both the southern and northern islands.[7] Other Japanese officials may well have differed with this interpretation or at least had doubts about it. But— stunned by Japan's defeat and chaos for the first time in its history—they did not dare to speak out in opposition to it. Furthermore, Japan would not have had the clout to make good on any claim it might have made at this point. This ambiguous attitude was permitted to stand for years while the Yoshida government bent its efforts toward regaining Japanese independence and developing stronger relations with the United States.

It was, in fact, not until after peace negotiations with the Soviet Union in 1955–56 that an official Japanese interpretation emerged that the "Kurile Islands" renounced in the peace treaty included only the eighteen islands north of Uruppu, while the Habomais, Shikotan, Kunashiri, and Etorofu remain inherently Japanese.

6. Shigeru Yoshida, *Kaiso 10-nen* (*Memoirs: Ten Years in Retrospect*) (Tokyo: Shincho Sha, 1957), pp. 23–41.

7. Research Office of the Foreign Affairs Committee of House of Representatives, *Territorial Problems of Japan* (Tokyo: House of Representatives, 1971), p. 77.

THE 1955–56 PEACE NEGOTIATIONS

Throughout Stalin's lifetime the Soviet Union remained intransigent on the disputed islands. But with the thaw in East–West relations that developed after his death, the new Soviet leaders showed an interest in normalizing relations with the countries defeated in World War II. They also showed some flexibility on territorial issues to the extent that they sought to gain reconfirmation of the boundaries established at Yalta in the name of peace.

Toward this end Moscow took diplomatic initiatives aimed at countries on the dividing line between East and West. Thus, in April 1955 the Russians suddenly declared their willingness to sign a peace treaty with Austria, and one was signed in May. In September of the same year, they had discussions with West German Chancellor Adenauer and they recognized his country. The Japanese–Soviet negotiations of 1955–56 on restoration of diplomatic relations and settlement of the territorial issue were part of the same process. The Russians initiated these talks. Their initiative, unfortunately, caught Japan, now led by Prime Minister Ichiro Hatoyama, totally unprepared.

Hatoyama himself wanted to follow up Yoshida's pro-American policy with a normalization of Japanese relations with the Soviet Union. But a realignment of political parties then seemed imminent in Japan. Many Japanese leaders expected a radical shift in Japanese policies. This expectation induced them to concentrate their energies on strengthening their positions against domestic rivals rather than attempting to increase Japan's bargaining power with Moscow.

In addition the Ministry of Foreign Affairs was in a poor position to deal with Soviet overtures. Ministry officials were confused by the transition from the "liaison diplomacy" practiced under the American occupation to the more autonomous diplomacy appropriate to an independent country. The ministry also appears to have been divided on Soviet policy. Some officials, such as Prime Minister Hatoyama, evidently were willing to engage in talks with the Russians at this time; they looked toward a restoration of relations and settlement of outstanding issues in the near future. A "mainstream faction" in the ministry, however, remained very fearful that an early settlement with Moscow might produce an unfavorable outcome for Tokyo.

As a result of these differences Japan was drawn into negotiations but it then vacillated throughout the 1955–56 talks, only to end up in the end with a semi-"Adenauer formula" that shelved the major issues for future negotiation while establishing diplomatic relations through a joint declaration. But let us look at these talks more closely.

The talks began in London in June 1955 with Shunichi Matsumoto negotiating for the Japanese side and Yakov Malik for the Soviet. At the outset, the Japanese side presented a seven-article memorandum as a basis for the negotiations; the Japanese also pressed for a separate solution, on a priority basis, of the problem of returning Japanese internees in the Soviet Union. The Soviet Union, for its part, offered a twelve-article peace treaty draft and advocated combining the question of a peace treaty with that of the internees.

On the territorial issue, the Japanese memorandum said:

The Habomais, Shikotan, the Kurile Islands and southern Sakhalin are historically Japanese territory, but upon the restoration of peace we propose a frank exchange of views regarding future disposition of those areas.

The intention of this wording, according to Matsumoto, was not to achieve complete reversion of all territories to Japan but rather to negotiate with flexibility.

By contrast the Soviet draft said, predictably:

Japan recognizes that southern Sakhalin, the Kuriles, and all adjacent islands and straits are completely under the sovereignty of the U.S.S.R., and renounces all sovereignty and the right to claim the above territories. The boundary between the U.S.S.R. and Japan is . . . the midline of the Nemuro [Habomais] Straits and the Goyomai Straits. (p. 184)

This Soviet position put the Habomais and Shikotan on the Soviet side, along with all the rest of the Kuriles and southern Sakhalin. Moreover, the Soviet position was forcefully presented, along with Soviet opposition to the U.S.–Japan security pact signed in 1951, and the Russians remained firm on both points for a number of weeks.

Suddenly in August 1955, however, the Soviet Union shifted ground. Its delegation said then that the Soviet Union would cede to Japan the Habomais and Shikotan—that is, the islands closest to Japan, which Yoshida had described as part of the Japanese homeland. The Russians also made a statement to the effect that they would not continue to insist on a draft article demanding the dissolution of the Japan–U.S. military alliance formed in 1951.

"I could hardly believe my ears at first," Matsumoto recalls. "I thought that once both sides had come this far, a little more compromise would bring the negotiations to an early end."[8] Matsumoto obviously had not expected that the Soviet Union at that time would agree to cede any islands and thought negotiations would proceed apace.

However, at the end of August Tokyo instructed Matsumoto not to

8. This quotation and the extracts cited above are from Shunichi Matsumoto, *Moskwa ni Kakeru Niji (Rainbow toward Moscow)* (Tokyo: Asahi Shimbun Sha, 1966), pp. 43, 184, and 30, respectively.

agree to a compromise that provided for the return of the Habomais and Shikotan alone. The instructions specified that the Habomais and Shikotan were part of Hokkaido while Kunashiri and Etorofu were inalienable lands of Japan; as to the Kurile Islands and Sakhalin, the states concerned should determine their disposition at an international conference. Matsumoto had to proceed on the basis of these instructions. The Soviet Union responded by hardening its position. The room for compromise narrowed, and the talks recessed in September, not to reconvene until January 1956.

The situation did not improve when talks resumed in Moscow at that time. For, in November 1955 Japan's two conservative parties merged to form the Liberal Democratic party. The new ruling party then advanced so strong a demand that the talks could only fall through.

The 1956 negotiations were like a two-act play. Act 1, extending from January to August, was performed on the Japanese side by a delegation with two heads: Foreign Minister Mamoru Shigemitsu and Matsumoto, now ambassador to the Soviet Union. This delegation was invested with full powers to negotiate and sign a peace treaty. Shigemitsu, formerly a hardliner on Soviet policy, at first adhered to Japan's previous tough bargaining position. Subsequently, however, he moved toward a more conciliatory stance that would have allowed return of only the Habomais and Shikotan to Japan while temporarily deferring settlement of the other territories. Then, in the face of Soviet stubbornness, Shigemitsu went further; he decided to accept the Soviet proposal for a peace treaty in which Japan would recover the Habomais and Shikotan but relinquish its claim to the other territories. Shigemitsu planned to take personal responsibility for signing the peace treaty.

But at the last minute Matsumoto intervened and solicited new instructions from Tokyo, where government officials, the ruling Liberal Democratic party, the press, and the public were all against precipitous acceptance of the Soviet terms. The Hatoyama government did not have the courage to defy this climate of opinion. Accordingly, Tokyo rejected Shigemitsu's move. Sorry end of Act 1.

Act 2 was only minimally more productive. It took place in October 1956, when Prime Minister Hatoyama visited Moscow. Hatoyama wanted to visit the Soviet capital himself so as to negotiate a peace treaty. The Liberal Democratic party was ready to endorse the visit if five conditions were met: (1) the end of a state of war were announced, (2) a fishery treaty went into effect, (3) embassies were established, (4) the Japanese internees were immediately returned, and (5) the Soviet Union agreed to support Japan for membership in the United Nations. But opposition developed within the party from hardliners who disapproved of a Hatoyama visit, and the party was finally unable to agree to endorse the visit. In the end the cabinet had to appoint a delegation that lacked formal party backing.

By September Hatoyama's leadership of the Liberal Democratic party was so weak that four influential big business organizations called on him to resign, and he did announce his resignation. This evidently helped persuade party hardliners to permit him to go to Moscow as his political swan song. This agreed upon, the party leaders turned their main attention from fretting over the impenetrable wall of Soviet intransigence to deciding who would be the next prime minister. Hatoyama was already a lame duck.

Another factor that turned the hardliners around was the so-called Gromyko–Matsumoto letter. This letter, sent by Soviet First Vice-Minister of Foreign Affairs Andrei Gromyko to Ambassador Matsumoto, held out the prospect of a peace treaty and resolution of the territorial issue as soon as diplomatic relations were normalized. It said specifically that after such relations were established, "negotiations on conclusion of a peace treaty would be continued, including territorial problems."[9]

The letter gave Hatoyama ammunition for his argument that Japan should not yet give up hope of settling the Northern Territories issue and that he himself should go to Moscow to negotiate. Accordingly, Matsumoto twice went to Moscow to pave the way for the prime minister's visit. It finally took place in October, at which time Japan and the Soviet Union signed a joint declaration. The declaration provided for diplomatic relations between the two countries; in fact, in the absence of a peace treaty it still is the sole basis for diplomatic relations. In addition, in a watered-down version of the Gromyko statement the declaration said that "negotiations on conclusion of a peace treaty will be continued" (pp. 174–75). Japan continued to maintain that a peace treaty should be concluded only in conjunction with resolution of the Northern Territories issue. The Soviet Union still refused to give any commitment on the territorial issue, except for the Gromyko promise that negotiations on a peace treaty would include talks on the territorial question.

MARKING TIME IN THE 1960S

In August 1961 Soviet Communist Party General Secretary Khrushchev sent a letter to Prime Minister Ikeda that showed new Soviet interest in normalizing relations with Japan. The letter said:

The Soviet Union desires to completely normalize relations with Japan, resolving through discussion all outstanding issues. Regrettably, however, the full opportunity for cooperation and improvement of relations is not adequately being

9. *Documents*, pp. 168–69.

utilized. Your Excellency Mr. Prime Minister, I would be less than sincere in this connection if I failed to point out that . . . [the reasons are] Japan's military alliance with the United States of America and continued maintenance of foreign military bases on Japanese soil. (pp. 230–31)

Prime Minister Ikeda replied to this "domestic interventionist language" by pointing out that the Japan–U.S. security alliance was already in force at the time of the Japanese–Soviet joint declaration of 1956, and that the joint declaration itself affirmed the right of individual and collective self-defense enunciated in article 51 of the UN Charter. It was not the Japan–U.S. Security Pact that was impeding normalization of relations, Ikeda said, but the Sino–Soviet alliance, which was directed against Japan, and the mutual aid treaty just concluded between the Soviet Union and North Korea. Ikeda went on to link the questions of a peace treaty and the Northern Territories once more:

Your Excellency has alluded to the complete normalization of diplomatic relations between Japan and the Soviet Union, but that requires a peace treaty. The position of the Japanese people is that the way to conclusion of a peace treaty will be cleared when the Soviet government returns to Japan its own native territory. (p. 231)

There followed another exchange of letters on the territorial issue. Khrushchev's letters (dated September 29 and December 8) said that "the territorial issue was solved a long time ago by a series of international agreements." The Soviet leader referred to the Cairo Declaration, the Yalta and Potsdam agreements, and the San Francisco Peace Treaty (pp. 232, 234–36). Ikeda responded by referring (in a letter dated November 15) to the same conventions, saying they prove that "it is all too clear that territorial issues outstanding between Japan and the Soviet Union have not already been solved" (pp. 233–34).

Letters were again exchanged between Khrushchev and Ikeda in 1964, but no fresh arguments were put forward on either side and both the Russian and the Japanese governments seemed to have lost interest in the issue for a time (pp. 241–44). People outside the governments, however, did begin participating in the debate. For example, a Japanese Socialist party delegation to the Soviet Union discussed the matter with representatives of the Soviet Communist party. Then in October 1964 a group of Japanese Diet members visiting the Soviet Union met with Khrushchev, who explained the Soviet position on the Northern Territories issue. Because the Sino–Soviet conflict intensified at this time, China began to take a vocal part in the controversy on Japan's side. Mao Zedong himself brought it up during a meeting with a visiting Japanese Socialist party delegation in July 1964. Meanwhile, the Japanese government remained relatively quiet about the territorial issue.

It was not until the latter half of the 1960s, with the government of Eisako Sato, that official Japanese interest in the Northern Territories question was revived, and then it was an offshoot of the Okinawa issue. As the government pressed for the United States to return Okinawa to Japanese control, it also began to think again of the Northern Territories. The prime minister and foreign ministers began to refer to the Northern Territories in their speeches at the UN General Assembly. The Diet dispatched a commission charged with investigating the issue to Hokkaido.

Sato's central concern was always over Okinawa, which was a matter of lively concern to the Japanese largely because Japanese live there, whereas no Japanese live in the Northern Territories. There is keen attention to the Northern Territories issue by people, especially fishermen, in the neighboring area of Hokkaido. But the effort to regain the Northern Territories was at this stage more a government-sponsored issue than a popular one. Still, concern over Okinawa did serve in the late 1960s to spark new interest in the Russian-held islands to the north.

This interest was reflected in July 1967 in a visit by Foreign Minister Takeo Miki to Moscow that caused something of a flurry in Japan. For halfway through a meeting with Miki, Soviet Premier Alexei Kosygin observed:

As the Japanese side is well aware, the Soviet Union also hopes for conclusion of a peace treaty. This is only my personal view, but I feel that neither side is yet quite sure how to approach the matter of a treaty. Therefore, how about exploring through diplomatic channels the possibility of concluding an interim measure?[10]

Kosygin was speaking exclusively about a peace treaty, as seems clear from the fact that the joint statement issued at the end of the Miki–Kosygin talks made no reference to the territorial issue. But the Japanese inferred that the term *interim measure* might suggest a more flexible Soviet policy on the islands and that therefore some movement on that question might be possible. This served to keep Japanese hopes alive as the two countries entered the 1970s.

THE ISSUE BECOMES MORE COMPLICATED

As Japan and the Soviet Union entered the 1970s two developments seemed to augur well for Japan on the Northern Territories issue. For one thing the Soviet Union was pursuing détente with the West. Second, Japan was making an effort to maintain "equal distance" in its relations with Moscow and Beijing. It had an interest in normalizing its relations with the Soviet Union in order to balance a developing dialogue with

10. *Yomiuri Shimbun* (henceforth *YS*), July 23, 1967.

China. So, on its side Japan might have been ready to resolve the territorial problem.

Unfortunately, these two conditions were offset by a series of other developments that complicated Russo–Japanese relations and prevented the two sides from finally coming to terms on the issues outstanding between them. First, the period of détente coincided with a Soviet effort to build up militarily, to reach nuclear parity with the United States. This reach for military power was accompanied by a grab for territory. In the nineteenth century, when colonialism was rampant, territory was high among the stakes in the game of power politics. In the postcolonial 1970s it no longer commanded the interest of other major powers, but the Soviet Union still seems to see territory as an important status symbol. In this respect it is not yet a "developed" country. So, it has adopted a naked policy of expanding influence into Eurasia and Africa, seeking and gaining "colonies," in Vietnam in 1975, in Angola in 1976, in Ethiopia and South Yemen in 1977, and in Afghanistan in 1978. The Soviet invasion of Afghanistan at the end of 1979 merely capped a process that was already under way.

But the invasion prompted the United States to wake from its post-Vietnam lethargy and adopt a harder line toward the Soviet Union. By the spring of 1980 the United States was going even further, showing a desire to "punish" the Soviet Union for its misconduct in Afghanistan. Americans were talking of the "end of détente" and a second "cold war," if not worrying about the possibility of World War III. And they were attempting (with some success) to pull Japan along in a campaign to combat Soviet expansionism. This deterioration in the general international political environment was one factor undermining the resolution of Soviet–Japanese issues. In such a climate neither side could be flexible about the territorial question.

Second, the developing Sino–Japanese rapprochement and, with it, the threat of a Chinese–Japanese–U.S. alliance aroused Soviet fears, further undermining the chances of Soviet–Japanese negotiation. In September 1972 Prime Minister Kakuei Tanaka visited China to normalize Sino–Japanese relations. This did not go down well with Moscow, by then acutely if prematurely concerned about the potential Chinese military threat on its eastern borders and Chinese political attacks on Moscow. Relations between Japan and the Soviet Union began to show increasing strain.

In October 1973 Tanaka went to Moscow in search of some epoch-making event to enhance his already strong domestic popularity. His visit was the first by a top Japanese leader since the Hatoyama visit of 1956, and it generated a great deal of enthusiasm in the Ministry of Foreign Affairs.

During the Japanese–Soviet talks, General Secretary Brezhnev apparently called for joint cooperation on development of natural resources in Siberia. Tanaka tenaciously pressed for the return of the Northern Territories. A subsequent joint communiqué was not exactly brimming with new developments. The first clause read as follows:

The two sides recognized that to conclude a peace treaty by resolving the yet unresolved problems remaining since World War II would contribute to the establishment of truly good-neighborly relations between the two countries and conducted negotiations on matters concerning the content of such a peace treaty. The two sides agreed to continue negotiations for the conclusion of a peace treaty between the two countries at an appropriate time during 1974.[11]

There are certain witnesses to the fact that the Soviet leader himself at that time orally acknowledged to the Japanese premier that the "yet unresolved problems remaining since World War II" included the four islands. But one can ask a couple of questions here.

Did the Soviets really agree that "yet unresolved problems" actually included the territorial one? The answer is yes. Several Japanese involved in the negotiations were clear and optimistic on this point, as were reporters covering the negotiations. The Japanese also made it clear from the beginning that without a reference to the territorial issue, Japan would not agree to a joint statement. It is true, furthermore, that the term *yet unresolved "problem"* in the draft communiqué was subsequently revised to read *yet unresolved "problems"* in the final version. These considerations make it unlikely that the Soviet side did not understand where Japan stood on this question. They suggest that there might well have been an oral understanding that the Northern Territories issue would be included in peace treaty talks.

But there is a second question. Did the Soviet agreement to discuss the issue represent a change of their policy toward the four islands demanded by Japan? Premier Tanaka painted a hopeful picture on this point during a press conference held after his return to Tokyo. Other mass media coverage was similarly hopeful. Both gave the impression that there was movement on the Soviet side.

On this point I am more doubtful. Here, I think, one must give weight to what Foreign Minister Masayoshi Ohira said at a press conference soon after the talks. Recognizing Tanaka's accomplishment in going to the Soviet Union, Ohira went on to express regret over the failure of his visit to achieve a clear breakthrough on the territorial question (*YS*, Oct. 11, 1973). Moscow could also not possibly have felt friendly toward Tanaka, who, as noted above, had dared to normalize relations with its

---

11. *A Border Yet Unresolved: Japan's Northern Territories* (Tokyo: Northern Territories Issue Association, 1981), p. 110.

archenemy Beijing. It therefore seems unlikely to me that the Russians would have made any real concession to the Tanaka government.

Moscow did take an initiative with the Miki government that followed. In a personal message from General Secretary Brezhnev, handed by Soviet Ambassador Oleg A. Troyanovsky to Prime Minister Miki, the Russians proposed a friendship pact between Japan and the Soviet Union (*YS*, Feb. 14, 1975). The Miki government, however, promptly rejected this proposal, arguing that the conclusion of a peace treaty between the two states would, before anything else, strengthen the basis for friendly relations. Foreign Minister Kiichi Miyazawa's visit to Moscow in January 1975 served only to affirm the 1973 joint communiqué without bringing about any further progress toward a peace treaty.

By this time the issue of an "anti-hegemony" clause in the Sino–Japanese peace treaty had already appeared. The issue arose on November 13, 1974, at a preliminary meeting in Tokyo between Vice-Minister of Foreign Affairs Fumihiko Togo and his Chinese counterpart, Nianlong Han. It was kept from the Japanese public until January 1975. Soon after, however, the mass media in Japan gave wide coverage to the Chinese demand for such a clause (*YS*, Jan. 26, 1975). On February 3, 1975, Ambassador Troyanovsky called on the vice-president of the Liberal Democratic party, Etsusaburo Shiina, to try to restrain the government from agreeing to the clause, which the Soviets saw as an anti-Soviet move engineered by China. They began a vigorous effort to check Japan's negotiations with Beijing. By mid-1975 Moscow was putting substantial pressure on Tokyo not to concede to the anti-hegemony clause.

On June 12 of that year Foreign Minister Gromyko handed an "announcement of the government of the Soviet Union" to the Japanese ambassador to Moscow, Akira Shigemitsu. It strongly opposed the inclusion of the clause in the prospective Sino–Japanese peace treaty and bitterly condemned Chinese efforts to put the clause in. "It is increasingly more apparent of late," the Soviet message said,

that the Chinese leadership is trying to exercise its influence on Japan in order to complicate its relations with third countries, including the Soviet Union. This is shown by its naked method of forcing Japan in every possible way to include a clause in the Sino-Japanese Peace and Friendship Treaty whose negotiations are currently going on. As a leader of China himself admits, this clause regards the Soviet Union with the deepest hostility. (*YS*, June 18, 1975)

The Soviet "announcement" expressed hope that the Japanese government would not take measures "detrimental to Japanese–Soviet relations." It went on to conclude that "it is the common interest of both the Soviet Union and Japan to make an appropriate counterattack against narrow-minded moves of a third country to obstruct an improvement of

Japanese–Soviet relations." The Soviets thus made clear that Japanese accession to Chinese demands on this point would poison Japanese–Soviet relations.

On June 19, 1975, the Japanese response to the Soviet "announcement" was a visit from Ambassador Shigemitsu to Foreign Minister Gromyko. He said that it was the consistent policy of Tokyo to establish good-neighborly and friendly relations with the Soviet Union. He also emphasized Japan's position that the Sino–Japanese treaty was not aimed at a third country. Finally, he reiterated that it was Japan's fundamental policy that Moscow and Tokyo should solve their outstanding issues since World War II (meaning the territorial dispute) as soon as possible, and they should proceed to conclude a peace treaty.

Despite these disclaimers, Japan had been drawn, through the negotiations with China, into the Sino–Soviet controversy. Soviet–Japanese negotiations for a peace treaty came, during this period, to a complete standstill although two meetings were held between leaders of the two countries.

The first meeting took place when Foreign Minister Miyazawa and his Soviet counterpart Gromyko visited New York to attend the UN General Assembly in September 1975. The second meeting was during Gromyko's visit to Tokyo in January of the following year. On both occasions Gromyko expressed Soviet opposition to a Sino–Japanese treaty that included an anti-hegemony clause and repeated the Soviet proposal to conclude a treaty of good-neighborliness and cooperation while shelving the territorial issue.

In response Japan argued for an early resolution of the territorial issue. The Soviet Union then further hardened its attitude. In an article by Gromyko the Russians branded Japan's demand for the return of the Northern Territories as "groundless and unreasonable" (YS, Oct. 4, 1975). The following February General Secretary Brezhnev used the same phrase in his keynote speech at the Twenty-fifth Congress of the Soviet Communist Party. This period saw also an increase of movements by the Soviet navy and air force north of Hokkaido in an apparent Soviet effort to intimidate Japan. The Sino–Japanese rapprochement undoubtedly aroused Soviet fears of a Sino–Japanese and perhaps eventually a Sino–American alliance against the Soviet Union while the rapprochement may also have stiffened Japanese demands on the Northern Territories. As a result, relations between Japan and the Soviet Union cooled even more at this time.

In this situation Japan decided it needed to expand its flexibility by stepping back somewhat from China. On July 7, 1976, Foreign Minister Miyazawa criticized China in a House of Councillors foreign affairs committee session. Referring to a report that Chinese visitors to Hokkaido had criticized Moscow for refusing to return the Northern Territories, Miyazawa said:

The Northern Territorial issue is a purely bilateral problem between Japan and the Soviet Union. From any perspective, interference by another country will not prove beneficial. And it will not help provide an amicable settlement of the dispute. (*YS*, July 10, 1976)

The Soviet Union promptly responded. A political commentator of TASS analyzed Miyazawa's remarks over Radio Moscow. He remarked to the effect that

Foreign Minister Miyazawa made this comment of late in order to show domestic and international public opinion afresh that Japan is in need of no self-appointed advisers and intends to carry out independent diplomacy. (*YS*, July 21, 1976)

China then proceeded to make its own comments on the Miyazawa remarks. In a commentary by a New China News Agency reporter the Chinese criticized the Gromyko article, Brezhnev's February 1976 speech, and Soviet naval and air force exercises in the vicinity of Japan. They went on to attack Miyazawa, saying:

After the Soviet Union threatened Japan by a show of force in its large naval and air exercise, in order to curry favor with the Soviet Socialist Imperialists-Revisionists, Foreign Minister Miyazawa misleadingly called this hegemonic move of demonstration of force to Japan a "routine operation" and he further made the statement slandering people of China. (*YS*, July 19, 1976)

Again, the Soviets responded. In a *Pravda* article the Kremlin said:

[The] New China [News] Agency severely criticized the government of Japan and Foreign Minister Miyazawa, and in a form almost similar to an ultimatum demanded that Japan should adopt a policy line convenient to the Maoists. This is not the first time for the Chinese leadership to meddle in the internal affairs of other countries and instruct them on what kind of policy they should take. (*YS*, July 26, 1976)

Japan had been caught in the crossfire of Sino–Soviet polemics, with Miyazawa being praised by the Russians and condemned by the Chinese. Japanese ties with China were undermining relations with the Soviet Union. In such a climate any movement on the Northern Territories question was highly unlikely. Sino–Japanese talks stalled.

It was at this point that the Lockheed bribery scandal came to light, submerging all other issues in Tokyo. Factional struggle developed within the ruling Liberal Democratic party, culminating in the resignation of the Miki cabinet en bloc. Japan's U.S. ties thus intervened to distract the government's attention and prevent it from pursuing discussion of Soviet–Japanese questions.

At the same time, Mao Zedong's death on September 6, 1976, put China's internal situation into flux. These parallel developments in the two Asian capitals brought negotiations for the Sino–Japanese peace treaty to a temporary halt. Both countries became preoccupied with domestic politics.

A third factor complicating the Japanese effort to resolve the territorial issue was West European acceptance of the territorial status quo on the Soviet Union's western borders. The Russians had long sought to have their gains at Yalta and in the postwar period sanctified by Western Europe so as to stabilize their strategic and political position in Eastern Europe. To this end they wooed former West German Chancellor Willy Brandt, who responded with his "Ostpolitik." A Soviet–West German goodwill treaty was signed in 1970. More significantly, West Germany also agreed with Poland to accept its control of the territory east of the Oder–Neisse. It was the first lock, one might say, on the East European door. The other locks came later, in 1975, when the Conference on Security and Cooperation in Europe agreed at Helsinki to legitimize the general Soviet position in Eastern Europe.

The territory east of the Oder–Neisse abandoned by Bonn is much larger in both area and population than the Northern Territories. But the two areas are comparable in that they were promised to Stalin at the Yalta Conference as spoils gained from those defeated during World War II. Japan maintains that the two are separate questions. Nonetheless, by renouncing its claim to the larger territory in the West, West Germany helped to undermine Japan's claim to the smaller territory in the East.

WEAKENING JAPANESE CLAIMS IN THE 1970S

As a result of these three factors—the deterioration of East–West relations, the developing Sino–Japanese relationship, and European settlement of outstanding territorial issues with the Soviet Union—talks on the Northern Territories question were not fruitful in the 1970s. On the contrary, during this period Japanese–Soviet relations sank to their lowest point since the normalization of 1956.

This was partly because an event suddenly occurred to worsen relations. On September 6, 1976, a Soviet MIG-25 pilot defected with his plane to Hokadate Airport on Hokkaido. He requested—and was quickly granted—political asylum in the United States while the plane was dismantled and examined by Japanese and American technicians.

The Soviet Union lodged repeated protests with Japan over its handling of the incident and pressed for the immediate return of the pilot and the highly secret MIG-25, under threat of retaliation. Instead, on

September 9 the Japanese government permitted the pilot to go to the United States in accordance with his wishes and delayed returning the plane for two months, sending it back then in parts after the technicians had found the plane to be of a surprisingly low order of technology.

On September 28, 1976, Soviet Foreign Minister Gromyko met with Japanese Foreign Minister Zentaro Kosaka. In evident pique over the plane incident, Gromyko stressed that his country was not considering at all the conclusion of a Soviet–Japanese peace treaty with a prerequisite of return of the Northern Territories. He also flatly rejected Japan's three-year-old invitation to Brezhnev to visit Tokyo, saying that such a visit could be contemplated only when relations between the two countries were friendly.

Two months later the Soviet Union unilaterally declared a 200-nautical-mile exclusive fishing zone. Subsequent negotiations between Tokyo and Moscow for an interim fishery agreement saw rough water. On February 24, 1977, the Council of Ministers of the Soviet Union made a formal decision to draw the 200-mile line; it included the disputed four Kuriles on the Soviet side, thereby giving the fishery negotiations a conspicuously political character.

There is no need here to detail the fishery negotiations, which lasted until the end of May 1977. But one point in them is relevant to the territorial issue. Article 1 of the proposed treaty defined the 200-mile zone in which the agreement was to apply, a zone that Japan acknowledged. But article 8 explicitly qualified article 1 by stating that the demarcation would not affect the positions or views of the contracting parties on other issues (*YS*, May 18, 1977). Japan read this as meaning the territorial issue. It maintained that the Soviet 200-mile zone applied only to fishing and did not undermine Japan's claim to the Northern Territories.

Nonetheless, at the final stage of bargaining in May Japan did permit a change that diluted its case. The draft of article 8 read to the following effect:

Any provision in this agreement shall not be interpreted in such a way as to injure the positions or the views of either government in regard to the issues being discussed in the Third U.N. Conference on the Law of the Sea and other issues in their bilateral relations. (*YS*, May 17, 1977)

On Soviet insistence, Japan agreed to eliminate the word *other* from the draft, leaving the article to read "issues being discussed . . . and issues in their bilateral relations." Japan had stepped back from the joint communiqué of 1973, which had said "outstanding issues" instead of the original "outstanding issue," while the Soviet Union had not moved an inch from its original position in the fishery negotiations. As a result of the fishery negotiations, Japan was accepting what one might call a "creeping political jurisdiction" over everything in the economic zone. Meanwhile, Soviet control of the Northern Territories was tightening.

SOVIET–JAPANESE TRADE RELATIONS

Improved trade and economic relations between the two countries have not helped in the last decade, because both the Soviet Union and Japan have sought to keep their economic ties businesslike and to separate economics from politics. Development of the Soviet–Japanese trade relationship since 1974 is shown in table 5.1.

The current legal framework for this trade is defined by two instruments. One is the Japan–Soviet Trade Treaty of 1957, which, inter alia, stipulates that the two countries grant each other most-favored-nation treatment. The other is the fourth Japanese–Soviet trade and payment agreement signed in Moscow on May 22, 1980, which covers the period 1981–85. Under these agreements Japan exports heavy industrial and chemical products such as steel, machinery, plants, and chemical items. The Soviet Union, on its side, exports raw materials and energy sources, such as oil, coal, lumber, platinum, palladium, and cotton. The trade has thus been complementary.

To put the Japanese–Soviet trade into perspective, one may usefully compare it to Japan's trade with China. Table 5.2 shows recent figures for Sino–Japanese trade.

China's trade with Japan caught up with that of the Soviet Union around 1964–65. Since then, Japan's exports to China have surpassed those to the Soviet Union in value. Since 1975 Japan's imports from China have also exceeded those from the Soviet Union in value. For example, in 1978 Japan's exports to China amounted to $546 million more than its exports to the Soviet Union; its imports from China were worth $588 million more than its imports from the Soviet Union al-

Table 5.1. Development of Trade between Japan and the
Soviet Union ($1,000)

	Japan's exports	Japan's imports
1974	1,095,642	1,418,143
1975	1,626,200	1,169,618
1976	2,251,894	1,167,441
1977	1,933,877	1,421,875
1978	2,502,195	1,441,723

Source: Ministry of International Trade and Industry of Japan, *Tsusho Hakusho (White Paper on International Trade),* 1977, 1978, 1979.

Table 5.2. Development of Trade between Japan and China
          ($1,000)

	Japan's exports	Japan's imports
1974	1,984,475	1,304,768
1975	2,258,577	1,531,076
1976	1,662,568	1,370,915
1977	1,938,643	1,547,344
1978	3,048,748	2,030,292

Source: See table 5.1.

though neither communist country looms large in Japan's total trade picture.

By contrast Japan is a fairly important trading partner for the Soviet Union. Of all members of the Organization of Economic Cooperation and Development (OECD), Japan ranked second only to West Germany in 1977 as an exporter to the Soviet Union. In imports Japan was third after West Germany and Italy.

Japan is even more important as a trading partner for China. Japan's share of the OECD countries' trade with China is by far the largest in both exports and imports. In 1977 Japan absorbed as much as 49 percent of China's total exports to OECD. Japan's share of China's imports was almost as high at 47 percent. Thus, Japan is more important to both the Soviet Union and China for trade than either country is to Japan.

Moreover, the Soviet Union is especially interested in Japan's help in developing Siberia although Japan's own interest in Siberia has waned. In this respect it may be noted that the Tyumen oil project in Western Siberia once drew substantial Japanese interest because Japanese participation in Siberian development promises access to a long-term, stable supply of essential raw materials and offers hope of significant and much needed markets for Japanese machinery and plants. But since the summer of 1975 Japan has shelved the Tyumen project and has paid scant attention to Siberian development generally. As the spirit of détente has dissolved, Tokyo has shown interest in additional joint Soviet–Japanese projects only if American capital is involved.

The Soviet Union, on the other hand, has remained quite interested (for several reasons) in obtaining Japanese help in developing Siberia. The Russians want to secure advanced Japanese technology so as to accelerate Siberian development for the raw materials they need for domestic purposes. They want to sell raw materials to the Japanese in order to develop a stable source of foreign currency. The Russians are interested also in freeing Soviet capital for other uses. For these reasons

Moscow has not permitted its displeasure over the Sino–Japanese peace treaty negotiations to interfere with economic relations.

THE SIGNING OF THE PEACE TREATY

Some observers were convinced that the settlement of the fishery question in May 1977 had for the time being reversed the deterioration of Soviet–Japanese relations in the wake of the MIG-25 incident and the Soviet declaration of a 200-mile zone that included the Northern Territories. But the resumption of negotiations for the Sino–Japanese Peace and Friendship Treaty in the fall of 1977 and the subsequent acceleration of Chinese–Japanese talks caused the Soviet Union to repeat its harsh warnings with ever increasing urgency. Moscow was intent on restraining Japan from signing what it regarded as a treaty of "anti-Soviet alliance" because of the anti-hegemony clause.

At a regular foreign ministers' meeting between the Soviet Union and Japan held in Moscow in January 1978, Foreign Minister Sunao Sonoda once again proposed to proceed to conclusion of a Japanese–Soviet peace treaty after the Northern Territories were returned. Gromyko repeated the Soviet position that there was no territorial issue to be discussed. Gromyko went on to press Japan to conclude a good neighbor treaty with Moscow while continuing negotiations for a formal peace treaty. The Soviet side presented its draft of such a treaty for Japan's consideration.

Sonoda took the draft, retorting: "We will keep it but cannot study it." At the same time, he presented a draft of a peace treaty to the Soviets to emphasize Japan's stand that the peace treaty should be at the top of the foreign ministers' agenda.

The Soviet side, in turn, refused to study Japan's draft. An apparent impasse had been reached. At a meeting between Premier Kosygin and Foreign Minister Sonoda, Moscow once again stated that no territorial issue existed between the two countries. The Russians then proceeded to press their idea of a good neighbor treaty to precede any other.

The following month the Russians presented their idea at a higher level. On February 23, 1978, Brezhnev sent a letter to Prime Minister Takeo Fukuda arguing for conclusion of a good neighbor treaty. The next day Moscow unilaterally published its draft of such a treaty in the government newspaper *Izvestiya* (Feb. 24, 1978). The draft, it should be made clear, makes no reference at all to the Northern Territories although it calls for the continuation of peace treaty negotiations, to which the territorial issue had previously been linked. The draft also clearly interferes with Japan's security policy inasmuch as its article 3 says that the Soviet Union and Japan "undertake not to allow the use of their territories for any actions which could prejudice the security of the other party." Article 5 then goes on to say:

The Union of Soviet Socialist Republics and Japan shall maintain and expand regular contacts and consultations on important international problems affecting the interests of the two states, through meetings and exchanges of opinions between their leading statesmen and through diplomatic channels. If a situation should arise that, in the opinion of both parties, is dangerous to the maintenance of peace, or if peace is violated, the parties shall immediately contact one another with the aim of exchanging opinions on the question of what can be done to improve the situation. (*YS*, Feb. 24, 1978)

The language shows that, in the final analysis, the Soviet Union aims to draw Japan away from the United States and place it under Soviet influence, because this draft article specifies that threats to the peace of both countries should be a matter for joint consultations, whereas under the Japan–U.S. Mutual Security Treaty of 1960 Japan is bound to consult with the United States.

The second sentence of the article, which refers to mutual "contact," is particularly worrisome to the Japanese. It could be interpreted to mean that some sort of joint action would follow. After the Soviet invasion of Afghanistan in December 1979 the Japanese have been very apprehensive about what form "joint action" might take and how it might be implemented. The Soviet draft treaty has therefore served only to intensify Japanese concern vis-à-vis the Soviet Union, a concern that was fed by other Soviet moves during this period.

On June 19, 1978, the Soviet government once more warned Japan against conclusion of the peace treaty with China (*YS*, June 19, 1978). At about the same time, in late May, Moscow carried out a military exercise around the Northern Territories on a scale never before seen in the area. Judging from its timing, the Soviet action was clearly meant as a blunt message to Japan not to sign the peace treaty with China.

The Soviet exercise had, however, the opposite effect, touching off considerable anti-Soviet sentiment in Japan. It is reported that after his trip to China in the spring of 1978, U.S. National Security Adviser Zbigniew Brzezinski strongly encouraged Japan to sign the peace treaty even with the anti-hegemony clause, and in any case Washington's eagerness to see the treaty signed is evident from the fact that the U.S. State Department welcomed the treaty before it had been formally signed (*YS*, Aug. 11, 1978). Combined with such U.S. persuasion to Japan to sign the treaty the maneuvers ensured that Japan would go ahead, and on August 12, 1978, Sino–Japanese talks were consummated with the signing of the Treaty of Peace and Friendship.

The Soviet reaction was predictable. On August 23 Boris M. Zinoviev,

chargé d'affaires at the Soviet embassy in Tokyo, visited Vice-Minister
for Foreign Affairs Keisuke Arita and orally conveyed a notification on
the Sino–Japanese treaty:

The Soviet Union cannot remain uninterested as long as the contents of this
treaty go beyond the framework of bilateral relations between China and Japan.
The Soviet Union will take necessary action to protect its interests. (*YS*, Aug. 24,
1978)

Arita replied by reiterating the Japanese contention that the treaty "does
not affect Japan's relations with third countries at all."

The Soviets are not satisfied with this Japanese explanation. They have
found particularly unacceptable Japan's argument on article 4, which
stipulates that the treaty is not aimed at any third country. The Japanese
say that this article cancels out the "danger" of the anti-hegemony clause.
The Russians counter that the treaty may draw Japan into China's adventurous policy of anti-Soviet expansionism. They say they will assess
whether Japan's Soviet policy has changed in terms of "specific and real
actions." The Russians are obviously concerned that the signing of the
Sino–Japanese treaty and the normalization of U.S.–Chinese relations
that followed soon after will give rise to an anti-Soviet alliance in the Far
East that would be a nightmare for the Kremlin.

Nonetheless, the Russians did not permit the signing of the Sino–
Japanese treaty to interfere with their economic relations with Japan. It
is true that in September 1978 a chilly atmosphere pervaded the foreign
ministers' meeting held by Gromyko and Sunao Sonoda. But even then
Gromyko made it clear that the Soviet Union desired to continue to have
trade and other economic relations with Japan on the basis of mutual
benefit. In view of the harsh criticism Moscow made of the peace treaty,
this position was remarkable. It shows the heavy weight the Kremlin
gives to Siberian economic development.

Soviet military actions have also proceeded on a track independent of
the economic one. On January 29, 1979, Japan's Defense Agency announced that the Soviet Union had deployed about 2,300 ground troops
on the two northernmost disputed islands, Kunashiri and Etorofu, and
that full-scale bases were being constructed there (*YS*, Jan. 30, 1979).[12]
Although the Soviet buildup had its own place in Soviet global military
strategy and was certainly designed to strengthen the Russians' strategic
situation in the Far East, it also represented a response to the conclusion
of the Chinese–Japanese peace treaty.

Japan protested to Moscow about its activities in the Northern Territories. Moscow flatly turned aside the protests (*YS*, Feb. 2, 1979). It has

12. As of 1980–81 Japanese defense specialists generally estimate that the Soviet Union
holds approximately one division on the four disputed islands.

since expanded its military facilities to Shikotan Island as well. Meanwhile, air, ground, and naval exercises have been conducted around Sakhalin, and the Soviet Pacific Fleet has been bolstered by a new helicopter carrier, *Minsk*, and an attack landing ship, *Ivan Rogov*. These Soviet actions have elicited new Japanese protests. The Soviet buildup has thus brought an additional irritant to Japanese–Soviet relations.

Yet in February 1979 Moscow sent a delegation headed by I. F. Semichastov, deputy minister of foreign trade, to Japan to propose some joint projects for copper mining, development of forests, and steel-building (*YS*, Feb. 26, 1979). The visit was consistent with Moscow's desire to have Japanese participation in Siberian economic development continue. But it indicated, too, that the Soviets wanted to keep the door open to improvement of their relations with Japan. They were trying to cool the "China fever" of the Japanese public and pull Japan back from its tilt toward China to forestall the feared "triple entente." In this situation, what are the prospects for resolution of the Northern Territories issue?

CONCLUSION

Clearly, Japan has a legal claim to the four islands. The peace settlement after World War II sometimes seems to undermine Japan's case for the Northern Territories. By the Allied agreement at Yalta the territories were conceded to the Soviet Union, and by the San Francisco Peace Treaty Japan agreed to relinquish its claim to the "Kurile Islands." But, as noted above, Japan was not a party to the Allied agreement, the Soviet Union was not a party to the San Francisco treaty (which also did not specify to whom the territories should be relinquished), and Japan at the time raised doubts about how the term *Kurile Islands* was to be interpreted.

However, the Northern Territories question is not primarily a legal question but a political one. And here the Japanese case is less strong. The Hatoyama government entered negotiations with the Soviet Union before Japan was ready; it vacillated during the 1955–56 negotiations, possibly missing an opportunity to get the Habomais and Shikotan alone. The government finally consented to a vague formula that shelved the territorial issue while permitting diplomatic relations to be established through a joint declaration. It subsequently accepted a watered-down statement that said negotiations on a peace treaty would be continued without mentioning the territorial issue.[13]

Then, during the 1970s, Japan staunchly maintained that the four disputed islands are historically as well as legally part of Japan. Japan

13. *Documents*, pp. 174–75.

also consistently contended that the territorial issue cannot be separated from talk of a Japanese–Soviet peace treaty.

Unfortunately, during this period Japan's claims to the Northern Territories were complicated by the retreat from détente that began in the mid-1970s, the Sino–Soviet conflict, and the European settlement of outstanding territorial issues at Helsinki. These developments had the effect of involving others in the Japanese–Soviet dispute, weakening Japan's ability to make good on its claim to the territories, and—above all—hardening the Soviet position on the territories.

Nonetheless, twenty years of Liberal Democratic pressure for the return of the Northern Territories has made the issue an increasingly popular one in Japan. At present it would be very difficult for any Japanese government to abandon claim to the islands without paying a substantial price politically.

During these twenty years Japan has not been fully conscious of its economic position as a leading industrial power. As it becomes fully aware of its position as the most developed industrial country in the region, however, it could attempt to seek some sort of quid pro quo. For example, Tokyo has already moved back from cooperation in Siberian development as Japanese–Soviet talks on a peace treaty and other issues have flagged. The Soviet Union has proposed a long-term economic cooperation agreement to Japan. Tokyo, however, maintains that negotiation for a peace treaty that resolves the territorial issue should take precedence over such an agreement.

There is also the question of what policies Japan might pursue if it becomes militarily stronger. As indicated above, the conservative governments Japan has had since 1967 have staunchly refused to permit Japan's defense budget to rise above 1 percent of GNP, the lowest percentage for any major industrial power. These governments have also refused to consider equipping the Self-Defense Forces with certain kinds of modern weapons. They have been extremely reluctant even to talk about a Japanese role in the Asian–Pacific regional defense beyond its own self-defense, and this despite American efforts to get Tokyo to do all these things.

But the dissipation of the détente spirit after the Soviet invasion of Afghanistan, and, more particularly, Soviet military activities just north of Japan in recent years, have fueled a debate over defense that has now broken into the open. It is likely that Japan's military strength will be beefed up in future and that Japan, as a major power in the North Pacific, will be called upon to play a larger role in the defense of that area. Just how it will approach the Northern Territories at that time is not clear.

As for the Soviet Union, it is questionable that the Kremlin would ever have given up the disputed islands after they were acquired at the end of World War II. Certainly, Stalin would never have willingly relinquished his newly won booty, and the sudden apparent offer of the Habomais and Shikotan (made during the thaw of the 1950s) was never renewed after Soviet–Japanese discussions aborted in mid-1956. Instead, the Russians pursued a joint declaration to establish diplomatic relations rather than pressing for a peace treaty to which Japan had attached the territorial question.

During the 1960s the Russians began to try to separate the issue of the Northern Territories from any discussion of a peace treaty, insisting that the territorial issue was resolved long ago by the various agreements that settled World War II. They also broached at this time the possibility of some "interim measure" that might be taken short of a peace treaty (*YS*, July 23, 1967). All the while, however, the Russians sought to keep Japanese hopes alive that some resolution of the territorial issue might come about, much as a striptease artist seeks to keep her audience hoping that she will in fact divest herself of the last concealing item. Thus, as late as 1973 the Russians permitted the joint communiqué signed by Brezhnev and Tanaka to read "yet unresolved problems remaining since World War II," evidently knowing that Tokyo understood this to include the territorial issue (*YS*, Oct. 11, 1973). But whereas for Japan the Northern Territories were and remain an end of diplomacy, for the Soviet Union the islands had become by the 1970s merely a means to something else.

All along, the Kremlin has wanted primarily to normalize relations with Japan. It originally expressed willingness to talk about the territorial issue only in order to bring about its main goal: a peace treaty with Japan. At the beginning of the 1970s it began to try to separate these two questions entirely. Japan would not agree.

Accordingly, the Russians began to try to bypass the peace treaty issue by proposing an "interim measure," that is, a good neighbor pact. This was the theme struck in the mid-1970s by Brezhnev in his personal message to Prime Minister Miki (*YS*, Feb. 14, 1975). It has been presented periodically since. Japan has not been responsive to this proposal either, insisting that a peace treaty is the best way to establish friendly relations between the two countries. Meanwhile, Japan went ahead and—with U.S. support—assented to a peace treaty with China that included the reviled anti-hegemony clause, something the Soviet Union interprets as a directly anti-Soviet move portending a dual, if not triple, alliance against itself in the East.

The Soviet Union proceeded, on the one hand, to try to drive a wedge into the U.S.–Japanese alliance by offering a good neighbor pact that provides for mutual "contact" between the Soviet Union and Japan in case of a threat to the peace of either country. On the other hand, the Kremlin moved aggressively, declaring a 200-mile economic zone that extends nearly to Hokkaido, expanding its military facilities in the Northern Territories, and building up its general military posture in the Pacific. At the same time, in November 1978 the Soviet Union signed a treaty of friendship and cooperation with Vietnam, and it supported the Vietnamese invasion of Cambodia in December and has since backed the Heng Samrin government there. Farther west the Soviet Union went on to invade Afghanistan.

Moscow is now attempting to turn the political and military balance in its favor in the Far East. Always supercautious about its security and fearful of the worst, it now seeks to consolidate its footholds in the Eastern and the Western Pacific and to bolster its overall strategic strength to counter growing U.S. cooperation with Japan and China. In this process it is helping to spur that cooperation, which in both cases has now taken on a military aspect as the United States conducts joint military exercises with Japan and agrees to make specific defense equipment sales to China. The Russians are thus helping to fulfill their own prophecy. But the point here is that in such a climate the Soviet Union will be less conciliatory than ever on territorial questions.

Previously, the Soviet Union has been willing to negotiate with Japan on the Northern Territories only if Japan would pay a price. This price has now gone up to abrogation of Japan's alliance with the United States. Such a price is clearly exorbitant in Japanese eyes, and even if a more "progressive" government should come to power in Tokyo in the 1980s, there is no chance that it would abrogate the U.S. alliance. The Russians should know this. Although they may harbor fleeting hopes that they can shake Japan loose from its American allies, it is unlikely that they think this will come about and that they will not have to negotiate on the Northern Territories at all.

On March 5, 1980, Soviet Ambassador to Japan Dimitri S. Polyansky had his first press meeting in four years (*YS,* Mar. 6, 1980). At that time he defended the Soviet military involvement in Afghanistan, saying it is intended to protect the country against external threats. He also stated that Japan should not join the United States in economic sanctions against the Soviet Union. Polyansky then remarked: "In these four years, Japanese–Soviet political and diplomatic relations have experienced not a few periods of cooling and retreat." Polyansky brushed aside the charge that the Soviet military buildup in the Far East was directed against Japan. He said that worsening relations, epitomized by the prevailing apprehension in Japan over the Soviet threat, were due instead to the "unfriendly attitude of the government of Japan." He reiterated the well-known

Soviet stance that the Northern Territories issue does not exist and that a good neighbor treaty should take precedence over a peace treaty.

Polyansky thus made it crystal clear that the Soviet Union has now abandoned even a pretense of acting on the territorial issue and is determined to lay the blame for worsening Japanese–Soviet relations at Tokyo's door. As long as the Soviets adhere to this new tougher-than-tough policy, it still seems that no one can expect resolution of the territorial issue for the time being at least. Finally, I just want to ask which country eventually gets more or loses more from this frozen state of affairs—the Soviet Union or Japan.

6

Soviet Policy in Southeast Asia

DONALD S. ZAGORIA AND SHELDON W. SIMON

For most of the postwar period Southeast Asia was a backwater for the Soviet Union, a region in which it had little influence and one that did not assume a high priority in Soviet strategic thinking. Since the mid-70s, however, the Soviets have acquired a greater strategic stake in the region and new opportunities to expand their influence and power. There are several reasons for this.

First, it has become increasingly obvious to the Soviets since Mao's death in 1976 that even a limited détente with China is unlikely in the near future. On the contrary, China is turning to the West, and an incipient strategic partnership directed against the Soviet Union may be in the making. For this reason the Soviets seek now to contain China with even greater urgency than before, and they have found a natural ally in Vietnam because of Vietnam's own burgeoning conflict with China. Second, Southeast Asia's waterways are assuming growing importance for the rapidly growing Soviet Pacific Fleet. The South China Sea, the Malacca Straits (claimed as national waters by Malaysia and Indonesia), and the waterways adjacent to Vietnam are all vital passageways between the home port of the Soviet Pacific Fleet in Vladivostok and the Indian Ocean. With regular access to Vietnamese naval and air facilities the Soviets can more effectively project their military power throughout Southeast and Southwest Asia. Third, the new Soviet alliance with Vietnam provides Moscow with a key client state in the region, one that is already the strongest military power in Southeast Asia and one whose power and influence are certain to grow in the 1980s. Finally, the decline of American power and prestige in Southeast Asia after the U.S. defeat in Vietnam has created a vacuum of power that the Soviets can aspire to fill, all the more so because China is regarded with suspicion in many parts of the region.

In sum, viewed in terms of Moscow's two foremost global objectives—containing China and competing with the United States for worldwide influence and power—Southeast Asia is acquiring new strategic importance.

Moreover, the new Soviet alliance with Vietnam seems likely to flour-

153

ish, at least in the short run, thus providing the Soviets with both increased stakes and increased opportunities in the region. The Vietnamese share several common interests with Moscow. Vietnam's conflict
with China, like that of Moscow, seems deeply rooted. For some years to
come, therefore, the Vietnamese will require a Soviet security blanket to
protect their newly acquired Indochinese communist empire against
Beijing. Vietnam is also increasingly dependent on Soviet economic and
military assistance and there is little likelihood that that dependence will
diminish in the years immediately ahead. Finally, like the Soviets, Vietnam would like to reduce American influence in Southeast Asia, and
especially to force the United States out of its key air and naval bases in
the Philippines. Thus, the Soviets and the Vietnamese are coming closer
together because of common concerns about China and the United
States, concerns that are not likely to diminish in the near future.

SOVIET REGIONAL OBJECTIVES AND TACTICS

Soviet interests in Southeast Asia can be summarized as follows:
• to contain Chinese power and influence in the region;
• to weaken American power and to separate the United States from its
allies and friends as part of a continuing effort to shift the global balance
of power more in the Soviet favor;
• to prevent ASEAN from developing into a pro-Western bloc with
security ties to the West and/or China;
• to help consolidate a group of pro-Soviet communist states in Vietnam, Laos, and Cambodia and to draw those states into the Soviet orbit;
• to gain increased and regular access to air and naval facilities in Vietnam and elsewhere in the region in order to facilitate the projection of
Soviet power.

The Soviets pursue these goals in a variety of ways. They are providing considerable economic and military assistance to Vietnam. They are
steadily building a powerful Pacific Fleet, which now has access to Vietnamese ports, and they are seeking access to other ports in Southeast
Asia (so far without success). They are trying to exploit the widespread
fear of China and the overseas Chinese throughout the region. And they
are seeking to reinforce doubts among the noncommunist states in the
region about American credibility as a security partner.

Over the longer run, the Soviets undoubtedly want to break up the
Western alliance system in the Pacific. The United States has security
treaties with Japan, Australia, and New Zealand; the Manila Pact provides it with security links to the Philippines and Thailand; the United
States has military bases in Japan and the Philippines; all five ASEAN
countries, as well as many others in the Pacific, purchase their arms from

the West and have a pro-Western orientation; finally, the Five-Power Defense Pact links New Zealand, Australia, Britain, Singapore, ard Malaysia. The Soviets want to break up this pro-Western grouping in the Pacific and to enter the region themselves as a major security guarantor. This is the meaning of the *Asian collective security* concept that the Soviets have been advancing since the late 1960s.

Soviet Strategy and Tactics

Moscow seeks to achieve its goals in Southeast Asia in a variety of ways, but among the most important is massive military, economic, and political support of Vietnam. This serves a variety of Soviet objectives in the region.

1. By helping Vietnam consolidate an Indochinese empire on China's southern border, Moscow helps complete the encirclement of China.

2. By gaining increased access to military facilities in Vietnam, Moscow demonstrates that it is now a major agent in the region. These facilities provide the Russians with new opportunities to intervene in Southeast Asia in times of crisis. During the Chinese incursion into Vietnam in February 1979, for example, the Soviets deployed ten ships from the Soviet Pacific Fleet to the South and East China seas, evidently as a warning to China against going too far in Vietnam.

3. Support for Vietnam identifies the Soviets with a state that is by far the strongest military power in the region. When the Soviet Union's own military power in the region is added to that of the Vietnamese, it represents a formidable combination that the Soviets hope to use for political leverage on all the states in the region.

The Soviets seek to achieve their objectives in Southeast Asia in a variety of other ways as well.

• Quite apart from their relationship with Vietnam, the Soviets have steadily built up their military power in East Asia since the 1960s. It is safe to assume that this military buildup will continue steadily from now on and that the Soviets will seek to use it for political gain. For example, as Soviet naval power in the region grows, the Russians will continue to exert pressure on the ASEAN governments to allow port calls for Soviet combatants. They will argue that if ASEAN were truly nonaligned, as it claims to be, it would allow Moscow the same rights that it allows Washington.

• In a variety of ways the Soviets will seek to exploit widespread fear of China and the overseas Chinese in the region. Such a stratagem can be used to some advantage in countries such as Malaysia and Indonesia, where Chinese minorities are viewed by the majority of the population with suspicion and resentment.

• The Soviets can offer themselves to the ASEAN governments as a great power willing to provide the smaller powers of the region with an "insurance policy" against a China that might one day become too powerful and an America whose leadership has in the past been viewed in the region as unreliable and erratic.

• The Soviets can selectively encourage radical or opposition groups in some countries in the region that are politically fragile. By selectively encouraging opposition groups in such countries, the Soviets can hope to reap handsome rewards if and when these groups come to power. In sum, the Soviets have a variety of levers they can use in an effort to insert themselves increasingly into the region as one of the great-power "security managers" whose views and interests must be taken into account.

Obstacles to Soviet Advance in the Region

There are, however, serious obstacles to the further spread of Soviet influence in Southeast Asia. Therefore, much will depend on how well the Soviets overcome these obstacles and on how adroitly those who wish to inhibit the further spread of Soviet influence manage their affairs.

The Soviets will have difficult problems in consolidating their relations with the proud and fiercely independent Vietnamese communists. The Vietnamese leaders fought a thirty-year war against the French and the Americans. They are deeply nationalistic. It is unlikely that they will surrender their independence to the Russians. If the Kremlin insists on subordinating and dominating Vietnam, as it has in the past insisted on dominating many other of its client states, it is bound to run into trouble. Moreover, the Soviets are not in a strong position, because of their own economic difficulties, to provide Vietnam with the grain and other kinds of assistance that the Vietnamese require to pull their weak economy out of the doldrums. This could complicate future Soviet–Vietnamese relations.

Elsewhere in the region, among the noncommunist states, the Russians have little if anything of a positive kind to offer. Their trade is minimal; their ideology is irrelevant; their cultural impact is nil. By comparison the West has enormous advantages. The ASEAN countries are conservative, market-oriented, anticommunist states. Most of them have booming economies, and throughout the region, generally, there is a growing sense of interdependence and common destiny with Japan and the United States. Since the Soviet-supported Vietnamese invasion of Cambodia and the Soviet invasion of Afghanistan, the ASEAN and ANZUS countries have drawn even closer to the Western powers. There is now a common effort on the part of the United States, China, Japan,

ANZUS, and ASEAN to force the Vietnamese to withdraw from Cambodia and to protect Thailand from any military spillover of the war in Cambodia. Finally, and not least important, there is an increasingly large degree of regional cooperation and cohesion that will inhibit the Soviet and Vietnamese efforts to play off the countries against one another and against the United States. In sum, the obstacles in the way of further Soviet advance in the region are many.

Degree of Risk that the Soviets Are Willing to Assume

In the past the Soviets have pursued their objectives in Southeast Asia with an exceptional degree of prudence. This pattern is likely to continue for a variety of reasons.

First, the Soviets do not want a war with China or the United States, or a confrontation with either power that might lead to a major war. This is why the Soviets acted with such great circumspection when the Chinese invaded Vietnam in 1979. And this is also why the Soviets have evidently cautioned the Vietnamese against carrying the war in Cambodia into Thailand.

Second, the Soviets do not want to push too aggressively in Southeast Asia for fear of driving ASEAN into the hands of China and the United States.

The Soviet invasion of Afghanistan and recent developments in Poland may incline the Soviets even more in the direction of prudence in Indochina. At a time when the Soviets are engaged in heavy fighting in Afghanistan and when they are faced with great dangers in Poland, they will not want to stir the pot in Indochina.

Still, the Soviets are increasingly locked into a situation over which they may lose a degree of control. If, for example, China were to mount another invasion of Vietnam, as it did in 1979, the Soviets might feel compelled to take military action of some kind in defense of Vietnam. Also, the degree of risk that the Soviets are prepared to take in the region may rise if the Soviets come to believe that their adversaries are coming together in an anti-Soviet coalition.

Limits Imposed on the Soviets in the Future

There are two major limitations imposed on the Soviets by their new alliance with Vietnam.

First, the Vietnam connection makes any Soviet effort to improve relations with China much more difficult and helps drive China closer to the United States and Japan.

Second, the Vietnam connection makes any Soviet effort to improve relations with ASEAN more difficult and helps drive ASEAN closer to

China, the United States, and Japan. The ties between Thailand and China have grown substantially as a result of the Vietnamese invasion of Cambodia. And even Indonesia—since 1965 the most anti-Chinese government in the region—has reopened trade ties with China and is reportedly considering the reestablishment of diplomatic relations.

But these limits, substantial as they are, are probably viewed in Moscow as acceptable. First, in the Kremlin's view China is not now seriously interested in improving relations with the Soviet Union. Second, ASEAN remains divided on the best long-run approach to Vietnam. Singapore and Thailand are most concerned about the threat from Vietnam to the region and are therefore more inclined to cooperate with China. But Malaysia and Indonesia look upon Vietnam as a potential barrier against Chinese expansion and do not want to foreclose the possibility of improving relations with Vietnam. As long as the future direction of ASEAN remains fluid, the Kremlin will find sufficient room for maneuver despite its commitment to Vietnam.

SOVIET–VIETNAMESE RELATIONS

Because so much of the Soviet stake in Southeast Asia is now tied to Moscow's alliance with Vietnam, let us consider this alliance in more detail.

The Origins of the Soviet–Vietnamese Friendship Treaty

The Soviet treaty with Vietnam was signed in November 1978. The operative clause in the treaty is article 6, which calls for consultation in case either party is attacked or threatened with attack. It calls for "appropriate and effective measures" to safeguard the security of the two countries. Press reports indicate that a second secret military protocol was added after the start of the Vietnam–China border war in February 1979, but such a protocol, if it has been signed, has never been made public.

The political and strategic contexts in which the treaty was signed make it evident that both the Vietnamese and the Soviets had anti-Chinese motives in mind when they signed. By November 1978 the Chinese had halted all economic and military assistance to Vietnam and were massing troops on the Vietnamese border. The Vietnamese, in turn, had begun to expel ethnic Chinese from Vietnam and were reinforcing their side of the frontier with China. Perhaps even more significantly, the Vietnamese had plans under way for an invasion of Cambodia, then led by Pol Pot and supported by China. Thus, the Vietnamese needed the security treaty with Russia in order to neutralize China. As events turned out, Hanoi made a successful gamble. Vietnam invaded Cambodia shortly after signing the treaty with the Soviet Union, overthrew the pro-Chinese Pol Pot government, and replaced that government with Cambodians of its own choosing. Although Beijing subsequently launched a month-long incursion into Vietnam, the Chinese withdrew without shaking Vietnamese control over Cambodia. Thus the Vietnamese bet that the Russians would neutralize China while Hanoi completed its plans to unify all of Indochina was vindicated.

The Soviets, for their part, also had China in mind when they signed the treaty with Vietnam in late 1978. By that time the Chinese had signed a peace treaty with Japan that contained the famous anti-hegemony clause and they were moving to normalize relations with the United States, a process that was completed by January 1979. Thus, by late 1978 Moscow was concerned about the emergence of a new anti-Soviet coalition in the Pacific. The Russians must have viewed their own treaty with Vietnam as a response to such a development and as a means of shoring up their own position in the Pacific.

Developments in Soviet–Vietnamese Relations since November 1978

Since the signing of the Soviet–Vietnamese treaty in November 1978 economic, military, and diplomatic relations between the two countries have become increasingly close.

On the economic and military fronts, Hanoi has become increasingly dependent on Moscow:

• About 65 percent of Vietnam's total trade is now with the Soviet Union.
• The Vietnamese, having joined the Soviet-bloc Council for Mutual Economic Assistance in June 1978, are increasingly integrating their economy with those of the Soviet Union and its East European allies.
• At least 20 percent of the rice eaten in Vietnam (and possibly as much as 30%) must now be supplied by the USSR. Without these rice shipments Vietnamese food intake would fall below the 1,500 calories a day per person considered by the United Nations to be subsistence level.
• Hanoi depends on the USSR for vital imports such as petroleum, steel, iron, chemical fertilizer, and spare parts for its transportation system.
• The USSR is funding more than half Vietnam's current five-year plan at a cost of about $3.2 billion and including about forty major industrial projects. In addition about 30,000 Vietnamese students and technicians are studying in the Soviet Union.
• The Soviets are also now supplying almost all Vietnam's arms. Soviet naval assistance has increased most rapidly. Moscow has given Vietnam at least five naval combat vessels. The Soviets have helped modernize the Vietnamese air force and they have contributed to Vietnamese air de-

fense with antiaircraft missiles and radar stations. The Soviets have also
provided logistical support for the Vietnamese military campaign in
Cambodia.

Finally, the Soviets are providing a good deal of diplomatic support to
Vietnam. The Russians have been the leading backer at the United
Nations and elsewhere of the Vietnamese effort to legitimize its client
government in Cambodia led by Heng Samrin. Moscow has opposed
ASEAN resolutions in the UN calling for the withdrawal of all foreign
troops from Indochina. And it has worked assiduously on Third World
nations to get them to recognize the Heng Samrin government. India
recently did so.

In sum, the Soviet Union and Vietnam have in the past few years
developed relations that are far closer than the two countries have had
with each other at any previous time in their history.

Implications of the Soviet–Vietnamese Alliance for China

The Soviet–Vietnamese alliance has potentially grave implications for
China. With a hostile Vietnam on its southern border and a hostile
Soviet Union on its northern border, both of them tied together by a
military alliance, China is now virtually surrounded by adversaries.

To counter this alliance, the Chinese have forged closer ties with the
United States, Japan, and the noncommunist ASEAN countries, particularly Thailand. Beijing has warned Hanoi that any Vietnamese invasion
of Thailand would be countered with Chinese force. At the same time,
the Chinese supply arms and aid to the Pol Pot guerrilla forces still
fighting inside Cambodia against the Heng Samrin government. And,
along with ASEAN and the majority of Western countries, the Chinese
seek to deny international legitimacy to the Heng Samrin government.

Although the Chinese realize that the struggle against their Soviet and
Vietnamese adversaries will be long and complex, they contend that the
best way to break up the Soviet–Vietnamese alliance is to bog the Russians and Vietnamese down in a long war of attrition in Indochina. Over
the longer run, they argue, the proud and independent Vietnamese will
become as disenchanted with their Soviet alliance as the Chinese themselves became in the 1960s.

This Chinese calculus may or may not prove to be correct. Much of
what happens in Indochina during the next five to ten years will be
outside China's control. And there are many intangibles. Will the Pol Pot
guerrilla forces remain a viable force inside Cambodia? Will Thailand
and the other ASEAN countries remain opposed to accepting a Vietnamese-dominated government in Cambodia or will they come to terms
with that government? Will the Soviet–Vietnamese alliance strain under

the stresses of a protracted conflict in Indochina or will the Soviets and Vietnamese be driven closer together as a result of a common antipathy to China? The answers to these questions were not clear as the 1980s began.

Implications of the Soviet–Vietnamese Alliance for ASEAN

For the noncommunist countries of Southeast Asia the new Soviet–Vietnamese alliance poses a dilemma. Who is the greater adversary for ASEAN: China, or Vietnam supported by the Soviet Union? Both Indonesia and Malaysia look with considerable suspicion at China. Both countries have Chinese minorities that are not fully assimilated. In both countries communist insurgents, with some indigenous Chinese support and some support from Beijing, have in the past sought to overthrow the local government. The military now leading Indonesia has particularly vivid memories of the abortive communist coup in 1965, which led to the murder of many Indonesian generals and to hundreds of thousands of casualties. Rightly or wrongly, they are convinced that Beijing was implicated in this abortive insurrection. Malaysia, a country with a delicate balance of Chinese, Malays, and Indians, fears that the Beijing government could use the sizable Chinese minority inside Malaysia as a fifth column. Thus, both Indonesia and Malaysia regard China as a long-range threat to their security.

The Indonesians, moreover, are convinced that they understand the Vietnamese better than Westerners because they, like the Vietnamese, had to fight against Western colonialism in order to gain their independence. And they believe that the Vietnamese are more nationalist than they are communist. Thus, they want to build Vietnam up as a barrier to the spread of Chinese influence in Southeast Asia. For such reasons they are eager to reach some compromise with Vietnam over the Cambodian issue, and they are not so fearful of a Cambodia dominated by Vietnam.

These perspectives are not shared by Thailand, Singapore, or the Philippines. Thailand has a historic rivalry with Vietnam that goes back more than a thousand years. The Thais regard Cambodia as a traditional buffer against Vietnamese expansion in Indochina. Since 1979 the Thais have lost their buffer and they are determined to restore it by forcing the Vietnamese to withdraw from Cambodia. To gain support in this effort, the Thais have drawn closer to China, much to the discomfort of Indonesia and Malaysia. Singapore and the Philippines share the Thai view. They do not dispute the idea that, over the longer run, China may prove to be an adversary but they both believe that, in the existing situation, Vietnam represents the greater threat and that Thailand must be protected even if this means drawing closer to China.

Because of their differing perceptions about who is the main long-term adversary of ASEAN, the ASEAN countries have different ideas about how best to ensure their future security. Indonesia and Malaysia are inclined to continue the dialogue with Vietnam and to seek out some compromise solution in Cambodia that will leave Vietnam as the predominant power there, although preferably with a client government more acceptable to Thailand. Their idea is that a Vietnamese-dominated Indochina will be a reliable buffer against China and, once Chinese pressure is reduced, Vietnam will be less dependent on the Soviet Union. Thailand, on the other hand, supported by Singapore and the Philippines, refuses any compromise that does not include a complete Vietnamese withdrawal from Cambodia.

Implications of the Soviet–Vietnamese Treaty for the United States

The United States has both global and regional concerns over the new Soviet–Vietnamese alliance. On the global level the United States is worried about the new ability of the Soviet Pacific Fleet, by using naval facilities in Vietnam, to project its power throughout the Western Pacific and into the Indian Ocean. On the regional level the United States is concerned about the prospects for further Soviet–Vietnamese expansionism in Southeast Asia. If the Vietnamese are able to consolidate their grip on Cambodia, might they not then proceed to bring additional pressure to bear on Thailand? Already the Soviets and the Vietnamese have given their blessings to the formation of a new pro-Vietnamese Thai Communist party.

Over the longer run, too, the United States is concerned about the ability of the Soviets to use their navy as a vehicle for mounting political pressure against all the ASEAN countries. In the entire period since the end of World War II up to the beginning of the 1980s, Thailand and offshore Southeast Asia have been firmly tied to the Western world. All five ASEAN countries have free market economies that conduct most of their trade with the West; all have staunchly anticommunist governments, often led by the military; and all are fearful of the spread of any type of communism. Now that the Soviets are stepping up their naval activity in Southeast Asian waters, however, and now that they have a military foothold in Vietnam, their ability to put political pressure on ASEAN will grow. In 1979, for example, the Soviets sought the permission of the ASEAN countries to allow port calls of Soviet naval combatants. So far ASEAN has refused these Soviet requests, but it is unlikely that the Soviets will give up the effort to have their Pacific Fleet enjoy the same privileges that the American Seventh Fleet now enjoys. Thus, over the longer run, the Soviets—aided by the Vietnamese—are certain to want to change the existing pro-Western balance of power in offshore Southeast Asia, and the United States will be faced with the challenge of preventing such a change from taking place.

Implications of the Soviet–Vietnamese Treaty for Vietnam

For Vietnam the treaty with Moscow has produced a number of advantages. Armed with that treaty, the Vietnamese were able to depose the pro-Chinese government of Pol Pot in Cambodia and to realize their dream of unifying all of the former French colony of Indochina under their control. The Vietnamese have also received vast quantities of military and economic assistance from the Soviets. And the Soviets have supported the Vietnamese on the most pressing diplomatic issues. Over the longer run, barring a radical turn in Soviet policy, the Vietnamese can expect continuing Soviet support in Vietnam's struggle against China. These are all significant gains.

Still, dependence on the Soviet Union is not an unmixed blessing for Hanoi. It virtually rules out any substantial Vietnamese accommodation with China even though such an accommodation is in Vietnam's long-term interests. It also makes much more difficult any Vietnamese accommodation with the United States even though it is in Vietnam's interest to have American recognition and American assistance in rebuilding its war-torn economy. And it makes more difficult any Vietnamese accommodation with ASEAN even though such an accommodation is necessary if Vietnam wants to play a more prominent role in the future of the entire region. Finally, the price of Soviet aid is high. Vietnam has been forced into an unnaturally close and excessive dependence on the Soviets. Hanoi had to join CMEA, the Soviet bloc economic organization, and now it relies almost exclusively on Soviet economic and arms support. Such an extraordinary degree of dependency on a European power cannot be easy for the fiercely independent Vietnamese leaders, who have struggled for more than three decades against foreign domination.

Implications of the Soviet–Vietnamese Treaty for the Soviet Union

Although the Soviet alliance with Vietnam has some negative aspects for the Kremlin—it makes more difficult any accommodation with China, increases the risk of a confrontation with China in Indochina and diminishes the Soviet ability to project a peaceful image to the ASEAN countries—its positive aspects almost certainly outweigh the negative.

The Soviets are now solidly aligned with the strongest military power in Southeast Asia. They have access to military facilities that allow them to project their military power throughout the region and into the Indian Ocean. They have virtually completed the encirclement of China.

Also they are on their way to weakening U.S. influence in the region. In sum, the Soviets have become a key player in a region of the world that was once a Western lake, a region that is, moreover, bound to grow in strategic importance.

Strains in Soviet–Vietnamese Relations

Although the ties that bind Moscow and Hanoi are likely to remain strong as long as the two have common adversaries, there were already indications in early 1981 that the two-year-old marriage was under considerable strain.[1] Differences between Vietnam and the Soviet Union centered in five areas: the quantity and quality of Soviet economic aid, Vietnamese economic planning, control over Laos and Cambodia, Vietnam's regional objectives versus Moscow's global objectives, and Vietnamese resentment over Soviet efforts to dominate Vietnam.

There are many signs of deep Vietnamese dissatisfaction with the Soviet inability or unwillingness to provide greater levels of economic assistance. The Soviets reportedly told the Vietnamese in 1981 that they wanted to provide 40 percent less aid during Vietnam's third five-year plan period (1981–85) than they provided during the second plan period.

The Vietnamese are evidently dissatisfied, too, with the terms of Soviet economic assistance. A high-ranking Vietnamese official complained to a reporter in early 1981 that the Soviet Union had raised its price for oil and that this would increase Vietnam's trade imbalance with the Soviet Union and force it to export more of its scarce agricultural products.[2]

A second area of tension between the two allies is Soviet dissatisfaction over the Vietnamese management of Vietnam's economy. In June 1980 the Soviets sent a delegation to Vietnam to assess the Vietnamese use of Soviet aid. After the inspection the Soviet delegation concluded that Vietnam did not have the proper management capability to absorb advanced Soviet equipment. It was this decision that evidently encouraged the Soviets to cut their aid to Vietnam's third five-year plan.

Yet another source of tension between the two partners concerns their respective roles in Laos and Cambodia. The Vietnamese are disturbed by Soviet efforts to increase their presence in Cambodia and Laos, and Hanoi is trying to limit Soviet influence in those two countries. However, the Vietnamese are on the horns of a dilemma. On the one hand they

1. See Nayan Chanda, "Bickering Begins as Old Friends Fall Out," *Far Eastern Economic Review,* vol. 111, no. 10 (Feb. 27, 1981), pp. 32–34; Howard Simon, "The Tree Wants Quiet, But the Wind Doesn't Stop," *Manchester Guardian Weekly,* Jan. 25, 1981; Carlyle A. Thayer, "Vietnam: Beleaguered Outpost of Socialism," *Current History,* vol. 79, no. 461 (Dec. 1980), pp. 165–69, 196–97; Frances Starner, "Blunder and Disaster: Measuring the Cost," *Asiaweek,* Aug. 1, 1980.
2. Chanda, "Bickering Begins," pp. 32–34.

have little capacity to help the Laotian and Cambodian communists restore their economies. Therefore they want the Soviets to help. On the
other hand the Vietnamese want the Russians to distribute their aid
through the Vietnamese. But the Soviets are seeking to establish an
independent presence in Cambodia and Laos. The Laotian air force is
now mainly trained by the Russians and there are Soviet military advisers with the Laotian air force. The Soviets also maintain a ground
satellite reception station in Laos. And the Russians have been seeking to
train Cambodian army officers in Moscow. These developments must be
viewed warily by the Vietnamese because the Laotian and Cambodian
communist leaderships may well look upon a Soviet presence in their
countries as a welcome counterweight to that of the Vietnamese.

Still, the possibility for either Cambodia or Laos escaping from Vietnamese control and playing Hanoi off against Moscow remains only a
long-range possibility. Vietnamese control over both countries is strong.
In Cambodia the recent purge of a pro-Soviet faction in the Cambodian
Communist party led by Pen Sovan has led to an even tighter Vietnamese grip on Cambodia. The Vietnamese have advisers at every level
of Cambodian government. Even all local government in Cambodia is
controlled by a Vietnamese working group. In addition there are
200,000 Vietnamese troops still in Cambodia.

In Laos the communist strongman, Kaysone, had a mother of Vietnamese origin, lived in Vietnam for a long time, and was a secretary of
Ho Chi Minh and a battalion commander of Vietnamese troops during
the Vietnam War. As in Cambodia, the Vietnamese have advisers in all
the ministries. About 40,000 Vietnamese troops occupy Laos. Under
these circumstances, it is difficult to see how Laos or Cambodia can get
out from under Vietnamese control. Nevertheless, over the longer run,
tension between Moscow and Hanoi over Laos and Cambodia is likely to
grow. The Vietnamese are clearly determined to limit Soviet influence in
Laos and Cambodia whereas the Soviets, for their part, will probably
want to increase their presence in those two countries both as a hedge
against possible future difficulties with the Vietnamese and as a way of
extending their own influence.

Yet another important difference between Moscow and Hanoi has to
do with their conflicting objectives in the Southeast Asian region. The
Soviets see this region largely through the prism of their relations with
China and the United States. One of their biggest concerns is that an
excessively militant Vietnam may push ASEAN into the arms of the
United States and China. Moreover, if an opportunity arose for an improvement in Moscow's relations with Beijing, the Russians might well
be tempted to reduce their support for Vietnam against China. Thus,
the Soviets will remain loyal to Vietnam only as long as that loyalty does

not interfere with Moscow's larger great-power interests. This is defi-
nitely a source of concern to the Vietnamese. For their part the Vietnamese see Southeast Asia largely in terms of their narrow preoccupation with consolidating their control over the former French colony of
Indochina. They are not concerned about the costs this may involve in
terms of their own, or Moscow's, relations with ASEAN, the United
States, and China.

Finally, and not least important, there is the question of Vietnamese
resentment over Soviet attempts to dominate Vietnam. So far, the historical record suggests that Moscow has an urge to dominate its allies and
that this urge ultimately leads to serious tensions with those allies. Such
was the case in Soviet relations with China, North Korea, Egypt, Somalia,
and the Sudan. Given this Soviet urge to dominate, on the one hand,
and, on the other, a passionate Vietnamese nationalism resulting from
several decades of struggle against foreign invaders, one finds it difficult
to believe that the path of Soviet–Vietnamese alliance will be smooth.

Moreover, a basic lack of trust seems to permeate the relationship
between Vietnam and the Soviet Union. Soviet consular officials and the
several thousand Soviet advisers in Vietnam, like other foreigners, are
restricted in their movements. Soviet naval ships reportedly have to go
through lengthy procedures before they can enter Vietnamese waters.
All this is evidence of a basic Vietnamese lack of trust of the Russians.

Despite this impressive list of tensions between Moscow and Hanoi,
however, the ties that bind the two together will probably prove stronger
than the frictions that divide—in the short run at least. As long as Vietnam is faced with a hostile China and is so dependent upon Soviet
economic and military aid, it has few alternatives to its alliance with
Moscow. Over the longer run, however, it would not be surprising to see
a rift develop between the two countries once Hanoi is able to reduce its
dependence on the Russians.

THE CAMBODIAN ISSUE

If one of the critical elements determining Soviet policy in Southeast
Asia is the new Soviet–Vietnamese alliance, a second concerns the future
of Cambodia. The Vietnamese invasion and occupation of Cambodia
have become the major stumbling block to regional stability. All the
ASEAN countries, China, and the United States refuse to recognize the
Heng Samrin government of Cambodia and insist on a complete withdrawal of the twelve Vietnamese divisions inside Cambodia. The Vietnamese, supported by the Soviets, insist, on the contrary, that the Cambodian situation is "irreversible," that the new Vietnamese client government in Cambodia should be recognized by the world community,

and that Vietnamese troops will withdraw only when the country is free from challenge by the Chinese-supported Pol Pot insurgency.

The Vietnamese invasion of Cambodia has led to chronic instability in the region for a variety of reasons. First, in 1979 it produced hundreds of thousands of Cambodian refugees who fled war-torn and food-short Cambodia to refugee camps inside Thailand and on the Thai–Cambodian border. If the refugee problem were to grow, it could contribute to the undermining of Thai political stability. Second, the Thai–Cambodian border has become a battleground for the contending forces—the Pol Pot guerrillas and the Vietnamese army. The Pol Pot forces have encamped along the border and go back and forth from Cambodia into Thailand in order to obtain sanctuary and supplies. If the Vietnamese army along the border were to mount a large-scale hot pursuit effort into Thailand in an effort to finish off the guerrillas, this could trigger a Thai–Vietnamese war. In June 1980 the Vietnamese crossed the Thai border in a raid on one of the refugee camps.

A third source of instability is rooted in the fact that the ASEAN countries, China, the United States, and most other Western powers have refused to recognize the new government in Cambodia, which the Soviets and the Vietnamese insist is the lawful government of the country. Finally, the Vietnamese have so far been unable completely to consolidate control inside Cambodia. Pol Pot and other anti-Vietnamese guerrilla forces continue to fight on, and there are not enough trained and educated Cambodians left to govern the country, thousands of them having been murdered or starved by the barbaric Pol Pot government. Thus, if the Vietnamese are intent on dominating Cambodia, as they appear to be, they will probably require a large military presence there indefinitely. But such a Vietnamese military presence inside Cambodia represents a serious potential threat to Thailand.

Thus, for a great many reasons the Vietnamese invasion of Cambodia has produced a number of new problems in the region and there are no compromise solutions now on the horizon that are likely to be acceptable to all the parties concerned.

A variety of possible outcomes of the present conflict over Cambodia can be envisaged. A protracted war between Vietnamese troops and Pol Pot guerrillas supported by China could go on for years with no final resolution, or some compromise solution acceptable to some or all of the parties might yet emerge. In 1981 the Vietnamese floated a solution in which Vietnam would in effect guarantee Thai security in exchange for Thai recognition of a broadened Heng Samrin government. The Thais have so far rejected such a solution.

Soviet policy on the Cambodian issue has been fully supportive of the Vietnamese diplomatic position, but Moscow has been wary of any increase in fighting along the Thai–Cambodian border that might trigger a Thai–Vietnamese war. There is even some indication that the Soviets have been urging restraint on the Vietnamese on this issue. The Soviets have good reasons to want to avoid an escalation of the conflict in Cambodia. A Vietnamese–Thai war might bring China and the United States in on Thailand's side. If this were to happen, the Soviets would be forced to honor their treaty with Vietnam. But the Russians have no desire to be sucked into a war in Indochina as a result of Vietnamese adventurism. Also, a war between Thailand and Vietnam would only push ASEAN even further into the arms of China and the Western powers. This is not in the Soviet interest.

SOVIET RELATIONS WITH THE ASEAN COUNTRIES

For several reasons the Soviet Union has not been very successful in extending its influence into noncommunist Southeast Asia during the thirty-five years since the end of World War II. All five ASEAN countries have free-market economies that are highly dependent on Western trade and investment; they are led by military-technocratic alliances that are extremely wary of communism of whatever variety; all these countries have been struggling against communist insurgents for much of the postwar period; all of them purchase their arms from the West and some of them are tied into the Western alliance system; and finally, the Soviets have little to offer them in aid, trade, or investment.

One big question for the 1980s is, however, whether the Soviets, with Vietnamese assistance, can begin to make inroads into this increasingly important region. There are several reasons that such inroads might be possible. First, Soviet military power in the Western Pacific is growing very rapidly. Second, during the late 1970s confidence in the United States was declining throughout the region. The United States was widely perceived as an unreliable and erratic partner with no long-range commitment to the region. Third, fear of China is widespread in the region. Finally, some of the ASEAN governments are potentially unstable. An Iranian-type backlash against Western-style modernization is conceivable in Indonesia and the Marcos government in the Philippines is opposed by communist and Islamic opponents. Thus, it is possible—albeit unlikely—that anti-Western governments may come to power during the 1980s in some ASEAN countries. Now we will review Soviet economic and political relationships with the ASEAN countries and assess the prospects for an increase of Soviet influence among the five.

Soviet Economic Influence in ASEAN

As suggested above, Soviet economic influence in the ASEAN states is a weak reed on which to build influence. American trade with the five

Table 6.1. Value of Selected Southeast Asian Countries' Trade with the USSF and Eastern Europe as a Percentage of Their Total World Trade (Comared with U.S. trade)

Country		1973	1974	1975	1976	1978
Burma	U.S.	3.9	2.9	7.3	—	—
	USSR and E. Europe	0.5	0.2	0.4	—	—
Indonesia	U.S.	19.0	15.9	14.0	17.4	—
	USSR and E. Europe	0.5	1.9	2.9	0.8	1.1
Laos	U.S.	5.4	4.7	—	—	—
	USSR and E. Europe	0.1	0.0	—	—	—
Malaysia	U.S.	8.6	9.9	10.7	12.6	—
	USSR and E. Europe	0.6	0.5	0.4	0.6	0.4
Philippines	U.S.	28.3	24.1	22.4	22.2	—
	USSR and E. Europe	0.1	0.3	0.2	0.4	0.2
Singapore	U.S.	15.1	14.0	15.7	13.2	—
	USSR and E. Europe	0.4	0.4	0.3	0.5	0.5
Thailand	U.S.	14.0	13.5	14.4	13.4	—
	USSR and E. Europe	0.7	1.0	0.9	0.8	1.0

Source: United Nations, *Yearbook of International Trade Statistics, 1977* (New Yak, 1978). Compiled from tables on pp. 252, 500, 582, 622, 756, 833, 896, and United Nations, *Yearbook of International Trade Statistics, 1978* (New York, 1979), pp. 595, 733, 889, 974, 1045.

ASEAN countries remains many times that of the miniscule Soviet economic activity in the area (see table 6.1). For several reasons Soviet trade is generally treated as either irrelevant or unattractive by ASEAN government officials. The quality of Soviet manufactured goods is generally low and service arrangements are virtually nonexistent. Because the Soviets do not permit rubles to be converted into hard currency, trade is conducted by barter—a tedious process frequently leading to ill will. Added to these obstacles are Moscow's continued refusal to provide preferential access to socialist bloc markets for Third World products and its insistence that because the Soviet Union bears no special responsibility for Third World poverty, it need not concern itself with concessional terms of trade. Moscow's angry denial that it is part of the "industrial north" that has exploited the "agrarian south" has not endeared it to ASEAN; it only reinforces ASEAN's reluctance to expand commercial relations.

There is only one endeavor within ASEAN where the Soviets have engaged in successful trade and investment: shipping. About half of Soviet "imports" from Singapore consist of ship repairs. And the Russians have joint shipping companies on a 50–50 arrangement with Thailand and Singapore. Both have greatly increased tonnage moved over the last decade. The lines do not belong to the Far East Freight Conference and hence substantially undercut Conference freight rates. The lines' operations also provide an institutional framework for the expansion of Soviet shipping in Southeast Asia. In Thailand, for example, Soviet ship dockings increased from 56 in 1972 to 240 in 1978, while for Singapore the number rose from about 200 in 1969 to 885 Soviet ships in 1977. The most recent addition to Moscow's Southeast Asian bilateral shipping companies is the Philippines.

Soviet Political Influence

The Russians must overcome massive suspicion of their interest in the region if their relations with ASEAN are to be improved. Direct Soviet aggression in Afghanistan, the growing Russian Pacific naval contingent, and Soviet-backed aggression in Cambodia have served not only to put the ASEAN states on their guard but also to drive them closer to the United States and—reluctantly—even toward China. All ASEAN states have increased their arms procurement budgets. And a number of ASEAN officials support the idea of a future combined United States–Japan–China arrangement to keep Asian maritime routes open in the face of a growing Russian naval challenge.

As long as the Russians appear to give carte blanche to Vietnam's efforts to consolidate its Indochinese position and threaten Thailand, Moscow will be unable to prevent ASEAN's tilt toward China and its call for a renewed American commitment to the region's protection. The Soviets' weak propaganda counter to these developments has been to remind the ASEAN states of their desire for a neutral zone and the incompatibility between this goal and a continued U.S. military presence. How the neutral zone is enhanced by the activities of a growing Soviet fleet operating from Vietnamese bases, however, is a question Moscow does not raise.

Thailand has served as a regional center for Soviet diplomatic and intelligence activities for some years with an embassy staff much larger than the complement normally required to conduct the USSR's business. Thai suspicion of Soviet activities was high even before Vietnam's invasion of Cambodia. Now, as the "front-line state," Thailand has especially poor relations with the USSR. In September 1979, for example, Thailand prohibited unauthorized Soviet overflights of its airspace to Cambodia and Vietnam, requiring that each cargo flight request advance permission and list its manifest before being approved. While grumbling privately, the Russians have apparently complied with the Thai regulations. Moreover, Moscow has not openly condemned the Thai leadership's anti-Vietnam and pro-China policies, as it has those of Singapore. It has chosen instead to blame Washington and Beijing for "using" Thailand as a "staging area" against the "legitimate government" of Cambodia.[3]

The USSR, then, probably desires to keep lines of communication with Thailand open. Bangkok was undoubtedly relieved that the Russians did not intervene directly during the 1979 Chinese incursion into northern Vietnam; Russia's caution suggested there were limits to its backing of Vietnam's regional ambitions.

As has Thailand, *Malaysia* also sought to negotiate with Moscow over Indochinese developments. The Malaysian prime minister visited the USSR in September 1979, as had his Thai counterpart earlier. However, neither received any encouragement that the Russians might be interested in a compromise solution for Cambodia.

Singapore has been the most outspoken ASEAN member in its condemnation of the Soviet–Vietnamese challenge. Minister of Foreign Affairs Dhanabalan has warned that his country might abandon nonalignment if the Soviet–Vietnamese alliance threatened noncommunist states in the region. Singapore also was the first ASEAN member to chide the Russians publicly after Vietnam's brief June 1980 incursion into Thailand. The Soviet ambassador was upbraided for his country's violation of the guarantee given the preceding April that Vietnamese forces would not cross into Thailand. Interestingly, Singapore has also been willing to invoke a form of economic sanction against the Soviet Union by cutting back on the repair of Soviet merchant vessels—the major economic relationship between the two.

The only other ASEAN member with which the USSR has had significant ties is *Indonesia*. Until the mid-1960s, of course, Moscow was Indonesia's primary military supplier, providing more modern equipment than that given to any other military establishment in the region. The abortive Indonesian Communist party coup in 1965, however, despite the absence of any Russian involvement, resulted in the severance of military links between the two states and Indonesia's reorientation toward the West. Since 1966 Jakarta's military government has been suspicious of Soviet motives, and relations between the two governments, although correct, remain at a very modest level. Because Indonesia is even more apprehensive of China than of Russia, however, the possibility of Soviet–Indonesian talks that could lead to a wider ASEAN–Soviet dialogue over Indochina should not be ruled out. As the self-styled leader of the association, Suharto's government would be a logical starting place for any major Soviet diplomatic effort to obtain ASEAN backing for a compromise Cambodian arrangement.

In sum, Soviet influence among the ASEAN states was quite limited in

3. *Izvestiya*, July 6, 1980.

the early 1980s and is likely to remain so as long as the five remain
united in their opposition to Vietnamese expansion.

AMERICAN POLICY IN SOUTHEAST ASIA

American policy in Southeast Asia during the 1980s will be faced with a
number of difficult challenges and choices. What follows are some
guidelines that flow from what has been said earlier in this chapter and
in other portions of this volume.

1. The highest U.S. priority in Southeast Asia should be given to
maintaining the viability, unity, and continued development of ASEAN.
ASEAN is a counter to a Russian-backed expansionist Vietnam; it is an
important trading partner for the United States, Japan, and other members of the developing Pacific community; it is a moderate and generally
friendly grouping within the more radical Third World; its strategic
waterways control the access from the Pacific to the Indian Ocean; it will
be, according to at least one authoritative estimate, the most rapidly
growing region of the world in the 1980s; it provides to the Third World
an example of rapid growth via a free market economic system; it is the
first successful regional grouping in the postwar history of Southeast
Asia. In short, the United States has an enormous stake in ASEAN's
continued prosperity and unity. A great deal more needs to be done to
acquaint the American people with the strategic importance of this region in the post-Vietnam War era.

2. In seeking a resolution of the Cambodian issue, the United States
should allow ASEAN to lead. If ASEAN comes to the conclusion that the
time is ripe for a negotiated settlement of the Cambodian question, the
United States should support it. If ASEAN comes to the conclusion that
the time is not yet ripe, and that Vietnam must make further concessions, the United States should support that position. Whether ASEAN
takes a soft or hard line toward Vietnam on the Cambodian issue is less
important than that whatever line it takes does not lead to a split within
ASEAN.

3. ASEAN leaders are encouraging a stepped-up American military
presence in Southeast Asia and increases in American military assistance. These are desirable. The United States has an interest in signaling
to its friends and allies in the region, as well as to its adversaries, that
America's Vietnam trauma is over and that the United States is prepared
once again to assert its power in Southeast Asia as in other important
regions of the world.

4. At the same time, the challenge to Western interests in the region
should not be defined exclusively in military terms. To do so will be to
neglect the critical internal dimension of security in the region. Much of

that security in the future will depend in each country on the legitimacy of the incumbent government, on the stability of political institutions, on more equitable growth, on greater sensitivity to the needs of minority ethnic and regional groups within each country, and so forth. These are the issues that will determine the viability of most of the ASEAN regimes, and they are only marginally related to Vietnam's actions in Indochina, to the growing Soviet naval presence, or to the provision of American conventional weapons to ASEAN militaries.

5. The United States should encourage Japan to increase its economic role in the region. After Prime Minister Zenko Suzuki assumed office in 1981 he made his first trip abroad to the ASEAN countries. The ASEAN countries want greater levels of assistance than Japan is yet prepared to offer. At the same time, they are suspicious of Japan's interest in the region. Southeast Asia was colonized by the Japanese during World War II and there remain deep scars as a result. But at a time when American economic aid resources are increasingly limited and when the United States is asking its Japanese partner to share some of its Pacific security burden, what better way for the Japanese to share the burden than to invest more heavily in assistance to ASEAN?

6. As long as Vietnam refuses to enter into an agreement on Cambodia that is satisfactory to Thailand and the other ASEAN countries, the United States should continue to oppose Vietnam. Over the longer run, however, American policy should be sensitive to the serious strains that are now developing in the Vietnamese–Soviet alliance and to the possibility of reaching an accommodation with the Vietnamese. Such an accommodation could come about if Hanoi were to reach a peaceful settlement with Thailand over Cambodia, to adopt an independent policy in the East–West struggle, and, eventually, to reach a modus vivendi with ASEAN.

7

The Soviet Union and the Two Koreas

RALPH N. CLOUGH

The fundamental Soviet interest in Korea is strategic, stemming from the location of the peninsula on the border of the Soviet Union. Here, as elsewhere along their borders, the Soviets have wanted a friendly government, as responsive as possible to their wishes. In unfriendly hands the Korean peninsula could pose a serious threat to the principal Soviet naval base in the Pacific at Vladivostok.[1] Its warm-water ports, if made available to the Soviets by a friendly government, would be a valuable strategic asset.

In economic terms a united Korea could be an important trading partner for the Soviet Union, contributing significantly to the development of Siberia and the Maritime Provinces. North Korea, alone, however, has not made a very significant economic contribution since 1945. It makes no products that the Soviets could not readily obtain elsewhere, the volume of trade has not been large, and from 1968 through 1976 exports to North Korea exceeded imports from that country by a large margin.[2] The trade has been much more valuable to North Korea than to the Soviet Union, for it was essential both in the rebuilding of the

1. For an official formulation of Soviet interests in Korea, see the statement of Colonel General T. F. Shtikov, head of the Soviet delegation, at the opening session of the U.S.–Soviet Joint Commission charged with establishing a provisional government in Korea, March 20, 1946: "The Soviet Union has a keen interest in Korea being a true democratic and independent country, friendly to the Soviet Union, so that in the future it will not become a base for an attack on the Soviet Union" (U.S. Department of State, *Foreign Relations of the United States, 1946*, vol. 8 [Washington, D.C.: U.S. Government Printing Office, 1971], p. 653). Shtikov candidly informed the U.S. representative on the commission, Lieutenant General John R. Hodge, that the Soviet Union could not risk individuals hostile to the Soviet Union coming to power in Korea; it wanted a government that would be "loyal" to the Soviet Union (Carl Berger, *The Korea Knot* [Philadelphia: University of Pennsylvania Press, 1957], p. 69).

2. Total trade between the Soviet Union and North Korea grew gradually from about $100 million in 1956 to $365 million in 1970. Trade was balanced through 1967 but during the three years 1968–70 exports to North Korea from the Soviet Union exceeded imports by more than $200 million. See Joong-Koon Lee, "North Korean Foreign Trade in Recent Years and the Prospects for North–South Korean Trade," *Journal of Korean Affairs*, vol. 4, no. 3 (Oct. 1974), p. 20. See also analysis below of trade in the 1970s (pp. 132–85).

economy after the Korean War and in the subsequent industrialization of the country.

As an ideological and a diplomatic ally, North Korea has proved a disappointment. Although it adds to the number of socialist countries in the world and lines up with Moscow on some issues, it is not a malleable and responsive satellite like Soviet-controlled Mongolia. Kim Il Sung has shown a stubborn independence in his dealings with the Soviets and in recent years has tilted toward China. In Third World conclaves the North Koreans champion the independence of small countries, encouraging resistance to big-power dictation.

Soviet interests in Korea are, of course, affected and complicated by Soviet relations with China, Japan, and the United States. In 1950, when the Soviet Union and the People's Republic of China were close allies, they shared common interests, first, in approving Kim Il Sung's attempt to unify the peninsula under a communist regime, and later in preventing the destruction of Kim's government and the unification of Korea under a noncommunist regime. But as the conflict between them over other issues developed in the late 1950s, their interests in Korea diverged. Rivalry for influence over Pyongyang came to dominate their policies toward Korea. Moscow sought, sometimes by threats, sometimes by rewards, to prevent Kim Il Sung from taking the Chinese side in the Sino–Soviet struggle within the world communist movement. In this the Soviets were only partially successful. The scope for Kim Il Sung to maneuver between the two contestants and his own determination to maintain a substantial degree of independence prevented either Moscow or Beijing from turning North Korea into a completely reliable ally. Although the Soviets would doubtless prefer a more responsive regime in Pyongyang, the continued existence in North Korea of a communist buffer state demonstrating considerable independence from Beijing probably meets minimum Soviet needs.

The Russians once saw the Japanese as their principal rivals for domination over the Korean peninsula. Today, however, with Korea divided into two independent states and Japan no longer bent on military expansion, the peninsula is not a highly contentious issue between the Soviets and the Japanese. Although Moscow recognizes North Korea and Japan recognizes South Korea, they appear to share an interest in peace in the peninsula.

Korea is a secondary interest in terms of Soviet relations with the United States, not comparable in importance with the global strategic balance or the confrontations in Europe or the Middle East. Although the Soviet Union probably would prefer the withdrawal of U.S. forces from Korea, assuming that there was little risk of a conflict that would draw them back in, it probably does not regard those forces as a significant threat to its own territory. The United States has not established a permanent military base in Korea on the scale of those on Okinawa or in the Philippines, and the level of its forces there has been declining since the end of the Korean War. The Soviets have expressed routine, low-keyed support for the North Korean demand for withdrawal of U.S. forces but have not made it a significant issue in U.S.–Soviet relations. The Soviet Union appears to share with the United States, as well as with Japan and China, an interest in forestalling any resumption of large-scale conflict in Korea.

Although the Soviet Union officially supports Kim Il Sung's call for "peaceful reunification" of Korea, there is little evidence that the Soviets consider Kim's goal achievable in the foreseeable future. Speaking privately, Soviet scholars see no prospect of early reunification. They criticize Kim's position on reunification as unrealistic and express the view that an agreement on peaceful coexistence between the two Koreas roughly comparable to that between the two Germanies would serve Soviet interests better than the military confrontation and high state of tension that now exists.

Whether Soviet leaders would regard reunification of Korea as a desirable long-term goal for the Soviet Union is difficult to judge. In 1950 Stalin presumably was confident that a united Korea under Kim Il Sung would be a reliable satellite. But after the experience of the past thirty years, present-day Soviet leaders must doubt that the Soviet Union could compete effectively with China and Japan in exerting influence on Korea. A united Korea of more than 50 million people, highly industrialized and with a powerful military force, could adopt an independent course with substantial freedom to choose whether to cooperate most closely with China, Japan, the Soviet Union, or the United States.

Recent trends in East Asia may raise further doubts in Soviet minds as to the desirability of a united Korea. Moscow has expressed concern over the drawing together of China, Japan, and the United States represented by the Sino–Japanese peace treaty and the normalization of relations between Washington and Beijing.[3] Whether the Soviet Union

3. An authoritative TASS commentary criticized the Japanese for "capitulating before Beijing's insistence on the inclusion of an anti-hegemony" clause in the treaty. It declared that "the treaty is in conflict with the interests of peace and détente, it is fraught with tremendous dangers primarily to the peoples of Southeast Asia, who have already long been the target of aggressive aspirations of Peking leaders" (*Washington Post*, Aug. 13, 1978). Subsequently, the Soviets officially notified the Japanese government of their dissatisfaction with the treaty (Foreign Broadcast Information Service [hereafter cited as FBIS] *Daily Report, East Asia and Pacific*, Aug. 23, 1978, p. C1 [Washington, D.C.]). Shortly after Washington announced the agreement on normalization of relations between the United States and the People's Republic of China, Leonid Brezhnev, in a letter to President Carter, expressed concern over the anti-Soviet implications of the anti-hegemony clause in the

could maintain predominant influence over a united Korea under conditions of growing cooperation among China, Japan, and the United States is very doubtful. Such a triple entente would exert a powerful attraction on a united Korea. A divided Korea would have less freedom of choice. North Korea, confronted by a larger and stronger South Korea, could not afford to distance itself too far from the Soviet Union and thus would continue to function as a buffer.

SOVIET RELATIONS WITH NORTH KOREA BEFORE 1970

The Soviets installed Kim Il Sung in North Korea in 1945 and helped him overcome rivals among local communists and the group returned from China. They saved his regime from destruction during the Korean War by providing large amounts of military equipment and supplies to his forces and those of the Chinese. They also played an essential part in rebuilding North Korea after the war and were the main contributor to the country's industrial expansion and growing military strength. Yet the course of Soviet–North Korean relations has not been smooth. Each party believes itself to have been ill-used by the other.[4]

The aspect of Soviet behavior that Kim Il Sung must resent most keenly was the attempt in the late 1950s to dominate North Korea by interfering in its domestic politics. Soviet-oriented Korean rivals of Kim sought to weaken his position by espousing Soviet criticisms of the cult of personality following Khrushchev's secret speech to the Twentieth Congress of the CPSU in 1956. The Soviets also criticized North Korean economic policies. In 1963 and 1964, when attacks on each other by Moscow and Pyongyang came into the open, the North Koreans accused the Soviets of arrogance and big-power chauvinism in trying to force their views on North Korea. Moreover, they denounced the Soviets for buying North Korean goods cheaply and sending in return Soviet goods priced far above international market prices. Soviet foreign policy also came under attack, especially what the North Koreans regarded as Khrushchev's craven knuckling under to the United States in the Cuban missile crisis. Khrushchev's crude attempt to bring the Koreans in line by

---

joint U.S.–PRC communiqué (*New York Times*, Dec. 22, 1978). A typically critical Soviet view of recent trends in United States–China–Japan relations is presented by I. Ivkov in "USA: Playing the 'Chinese Card' in Asia," in the Soviet journal *Far Eastern Affairs*, no. 2 (1979), pp. 71–87. Ivkov is the pen name of Ivan Kovalenko, a senior specialist on Japan in the International Department of the CPSU Central Committee.

4. For more detailed discussions of Soviet–North Korean relations before 1970 than is possible here, see B. C. Koh, "North Korea and the Sino–Soviet Schism," *Western Political Quarterly*, vol. 22, no. 4 (Dec. 1969), pp. 940–62, and Joungwon Alexander Kim, "Soviet Policy in North Korea," *World Politics*, vol. 22, no. 2 (Jan. 1970), pp. 237–54.

cutting economic aid intensified Kim Il Sung's bitterness and strengthened his determination to make North Korea as self-reliant as possible.

For their part the Soviets regarded North Korea as an ungrateful and a cantankerous neighbor. They particularly resented its support for aspects of the Chinese position in the acrimonious Sino–Soviet dispute of the early 1960s.

By 1964 both parties began to realize that prolongation of the highly publicized dispute was not in their best interests. The ouster of Khrushchev provided an opportunity for reconciliation. The new Soviet premier, Alexei Kosygin, visited Pyongyang in February 1965 and substantial quantities of Soviet economic, technical, and military aid flowed into North Korea in the latter half of the 1960s. The rapprochement between Moscow and Pyongyang was facilitated by a falling-out between Beijing and Pyongyang during the Cultural Revolution in China

By 1970 each party had a better appreciation of the value of the relationship and a more realistic understanding of its limits. The North Koreans recognized that access to Soviet industrial and military technology was essential to their country's security and development Even though their refusal to be subservient limited their access, the existence of Sino–Soviet rivalry ensured some access as long as they avoided swinging too far toward the Chinese position. The Soviets recognized that neither threats nor gifts would give them control over Kim Il Sung, but also that their superiority over the Chinese as actual or potential suppliers of industrial and military technology would prevent Kim from committing himself exclusively to the Chinese camp.

SOVIET RELATIONS WITH NORTH KOREA IN THE 1970S

In April 1970 Zhou Enlai visited Pyongyang to restore the friendly relations between North Korea and China that had been disrupted by the Cultural Revolution. The warming up of Beijing–Pyongyang relations that followed was accompanied by a gradual cooling in Moscow–Pyongyang relations. The cooling of relations between Moscow and Pyongyang can be perceived in the treatment that they have accorded each other in official statements, in high-level visits, and in other aspects of their relationship. The contrast between Pyongyang–Moscow and Pyongyang–Beijing relations was marked and the tilt toward Beijing increased up to 1979.

Political Relations

A basic difference between the Soviets and North Koreans lies in their appraisals of the situation on the Korean peninsula. Although the Soviet Union has officially declared its support for the North Korean position on reunification, it has not, like the PRC, endorsed the view that the Democratic People's Republic of Korea is the sole legitimate sovereign Korean state. On the contrary, it has referred publicly to "both Korean states." A Soviet commentary in 1972 warmly welcomed the opening of talks between North and South, declaring that "both sides have many problems to solve if they want to remove the old obstacles in order to bring the two sides together. This can only be done if the two parties take realistic attitudes and show goodwill." The commentator referred approvingly to the precedent of East and West Germany.[5]

Soviet interest in the German precedent has come up in the private comments of Soviet scholars, as referred to above. It was also reflected in the visit to Pyongyang by Erich Honecker, chairman of the State Council of the German Democratic Republic, in December 1977. Honecker, while expressing support for the withdrawal of foreign troops from Korea and the peaceful reunification of the peninsula, placed great stress on the importance of spreading détente throughout the world and of maintaining a close alliance with the Soviet Union. Kim Il Sung felt called upon in his speech to dwell at length on the differences between Germany and Korea that, in his view, made the arrangement between the two Germanys correct but a similar arrangement in Korea wrong. He pointed out that Germany was divided as the result of the defeat of its aggression against other countries and that a Germany reunified along militarist lines might emerge again as an aggressive force. Thus, the existence of a separate workers' and farmers' state in the eastern part of Germany was a good thing for the German people and the people of the world. Korea, on the other hand, had never invaded other countries. It was divided "as a consequence of the occupation of half its territory by imperialists." A reunified Korea, Kim said, would threaten no one; on the contrary, reunification would consolidate peace and security in East Asia.[6]

The generally low-key treatment of Korea in official Soviet speeches and the press is evidence of the low priority given the Korean problem. Most statements on the subject appear on ceremonial occasions and are much more mildly worded than typical North Korean diatribes. Brezhnev's lengthy report on the world situation to the Twenty-fifth CPSU Congress in February 1976 made no reference to the Korean question.[7] The subject was also omitted from Andrei Gromyko's October 1978

5. Commentary by Ligonov in FBIS, *Daily Report, Soviet Union*, Nov. 22, 1972, pp. C2, C3.
6. FBIS, *Daily Report, East Asia and Pacific*, Dec. 12, 1977, pp. D6, D7.
7. Donald S. Zagoria, "Korea's Future: Moscow's Perspective," *Asian Survey*, vol. 17, no. 11 (Nov. 1977), p. 1108.

speech to the United Nations.[8] The greetings from Brezhnev and Kosygin on the August 15, 1978, anniversary of Korean liberation departed from past practice by dropping any reference to the Democratic People's Republic of Korea in the body of the message, referring only to the friendship between the Soviet Union and "Korea" and to the accomplishments of the "Korean" people.[9]

The North Koreans have demonstrated their displeasure with the Soviet Union principally by aligning themselves with the Chinese on important issues. For example, during Hua Guofeng's visit to Pyongyang in May 1978, the North Korean media reported a PRC protest to the Soviet Union over a border incident but ignored the Soviet reply. The North Koreans also adopted a critical attitude toward Moscow's close ally, Cuba, and declined to participate in the World Festival of Youth in Havana in July 1978.[10] During 1978 Pyongyang frequently attacked "dominationism." In a speech on September 9, Kim Il Sung defined the term broadly to include efforts by any nation, large or small, to control another,[11] but it has been used in contexts where it was clearly aimed at the Soviet Union, as during Romanian premier Ceauşescu's visit to Pyongyang in May 1978 and North Korean Foreign Minister Ho Tam's speech to the nonaligned conference in Belgrade in July 1978.

The most stinging rebuke to the Soviets was the publication and broadcast in early August 1978 of excerpts from an article by the PRC defense minister, Xu Xiangquian, denouncing the Soviet Union in harsh language. The excerpts propounded the Chinese view that the Soviet Union is no longer a socialist nation and called on all Second World and Third World countries to expose and attack "the aggressive and war policies pursued by Soviet social-imperialism."[12]

The greater political distance between Moscow and Pyongyang than that between Beijing and Pyongyang during the 1970s could be seen in the level and frequency of official visits back and forth and in the relative

8. Beijing, New China News Agency broadcast, Oct. 3, 1978, FBIS, *Daily Report, People's Republic of China*, Oct. 4, 1978, p. A10. The Chinese broadcast seized on the omission of Korea "for the first time in decades" from Gromyko's UN speech, portraying it as further evidence of "surreptitious relations between Moscow and Seoul."

9. FBIS, *Trends in Communist Media*, Aug. 23, 1978, pp. 8–9.

10. Ibid., Aug. 2, 1978, p. 16.

11. FBIS, *Daily Report, Asia and Pacific*, Sept. 12, 1978, p. D15.

12. Ibid., Aug. 1, 1978, p. D1. When the Vietnamese vice-minister of foreign affairs protested references in the Xu article to mistreatment of Hoa people in Vietnam, the North Korean ambassador in Hanoi blamed the incident on irresponsibility of the newspapers concerned and said that these issues were being withdrawn from circulation (see ibid., Sept. 13, 1978, p. K6). However, there is no report of similar disclaimers having been offered to the Soviets.

cordiality of statements made on such occasions. No Soviet Politburo member visited Pyongyang after Mazurov's visit in 1971 until D. A. Kunayev went in January 1978. Kunayev presented Kim Il Sung with an Order of Lenin awarded by the Supreme Soviet *in 1972*. No communiqué was issued after the visit and the two sides were said to have discussed "urgent international problems" in a "sincere and fraternal atmosphere," language not suggestive of full and enthusiastic agreement. Kunayev's banquet speech, as reported in Korean by Pyongyang's domestic service, did not even contain a ritualistic endorsement of North Korea's policy toward South Korea, although Vice-President Pak Song Chol, speaking at the same banquet, asserted that during the visit the Kunayev delegation had extended support for the Korean people's struggle to compel U.S. forces to withdraw and to achieve the independent and peaceful reunification of Korea.[13] The Chinese sent senior Vice-Premier Deng Xiaoping to represent them at the thirtieth anniversary of the DPRK in September 1978. He was enthusiastically welcomed and received by Kim Il Sung. Deng was listed as number 3 among the distinguished guests, after two heads of state, while the Soviet representative, N. M. Matchanov, vice-president of the Supreme Soviet, was number 80 on the list and was not seen by Kim.

Visits by high-level Koreans to Moscow were somewhat more frequent than the reverse flow but still relatively few. A proposed visit by Kim Il Sung to Moscow after his visit to Beijing in 1975 was turned down by the Soviets and he has not gone since. The top-ranking Chinese leader, Hua Guofeng, was warmly received on his visit to Pyongyang in May 1978. The Chinese were referred to in a *Nodong Sinmun* editorial on the visit as the DPRK's "closest comrades in arms."[14]

Economic Relations

Trade between the Soviet Union and North Korea showed a substantial increase from 1968 through 1971, then a decline until 1978, when it rose above the 1971 figure (see table 7.1). The decline was greater than the dollar figures show because of price increases in 1976 and 1977 amounting to about 35 percent. Thus, the actual volume of trade in 1977 was not much above the 1968 level. A notable phenomenon during this period was the bulge in the value of Soviet exports to North Korea in 1971–73, which produced a trade deficit for the Soviet Union of half a billion dollars. The cumulative Soviet deficit for the period 1968–77 was more than $900 million.

Soviet–North Korean trade not only declined by 1977 to a little above

13. Ibid., Jan. 23, 1978, pp. D2–D6.
14. FBIS, *Trends in Communist Media*, May 17, 1978, p. 5.

Table 7.1. North Korean Trade with the Soviet Union, 1968–77 ($U.S. million)

	Two-way trade	Exports	Imports	Balance
1968	293	121	172	−51
1969	329	127	202	−75
1970	373	143	230	−87
1971	503	136	367	−231
1972	461	156	305	−149
1973	482	180	302	−122
1974	453	197	256	−59
1975	470	210	260	−50
1976	405	160	245	−85
1977	448	224	224	—
1978	555	296	259	+37
1979	750	390	360	+30

Sources: American University, *Area Handbook for North Korea* (Washington, D.C. 1976) p. 301; CIA, *Korea: The Economic Race between the North and the South,* Jan. 1978, p. 12. Figures for 1974 and 1977–79 are also from CIA, converted into U.S. dollars from ruble amounts given in Soviet foreign trade yearbooks.

the 1968 level, it was also a much smaller proportion of North Korea's total trade. In 1970 it had constituted 50 percent of North Korea's trade but only about 25 percent in 1977. Chinese trade with North Korea increased as Soviet–North Korean trade declined, until by 1978 they probably were approximately equal. In a further effort to diversify North Korea's trade, Kim Il Sung began in 1972 a large-scale program to import industrial machinery, including some complete plants, from West European and Japanese suppliers. Inexperience and a decline in the prices of North Korean export products as the result of the world recession caused the North Koreans to pile up debts to noncommunist suppliers amounting to about $1.4 billion by the end of 1976, which they were unable to repay on schedule.[15]

Several conclusions can be drawn from the pattern of Soviet–North Korean trade in the 1970s. Moscow permitted a large indebtedness to develop, presumably covered in part by long-term, low-interest loans. But the debts could not be allowed to increase indefinitely; hence, the decline in trade was balanced in 1977. Trade in 1978 and 1979 produced a small surplus in favor of the Soviet Union. The Soviet Union continues to be an important trading partner for North Korea even though less important than ten years ago. Moscow must continue to

15. *Korea: The Economic Race between the North and the South* (Washington, D.C.: Central Intelligence Agency, Jan. 1978), ER 78-1008, p. 8.

trade at a substantial level in order to maintain some degree of influence relative to the Chinese and also in order to collect its debt over a period of time.

There is no evidence of Soviet willingness to help Pyongyang reduce its large hard-currency debt to noncommunist countries.[16] The North Koreans renegotiated the terms of their $390 million indebtedness with their largest creditor, Japan, in 1976 but soon fell behind in their payments and stopped them altogether in 1978. In August 1979 Japanese creditors, after prolonged negotiations, agreed to a lengthened repayment schedule for principal and interest extending through 1989. Pyongyang kept up its payments through June 1981 and trade with Japan, conducted on a cash basis, increased steadily.[17]

Pyongyang's fundamental problem has been its inability to increase its exports rapidly. In 1976 total exports were only 76 percent above the 1970 level, whereas, by way of contrast, South Korea's exports increased by 800 percent during the same period. Exports of military equipment to Third World countries have become a significant item in North Korea's foreign trade and may ease its balance of payment problems somewhat, although the extent to which the recipients of military equipment pay for it in hard currency is uncertain.

Little is known about details of Soviet–North Korean negotiations on trade matters, but the pattern of the trade in the 1970s and the reputation of the Soviets as hard bargainers with socialist states dependent on them suggest that differences over trade issues probably are a major cause of strain between the two countries.[18] North Korea's inability to meet payments on its large debt to noncommunist countries closes the door to new credits from those sources and compels the North Koreans to rely heavily on the Soviets and Chinese as trading partners. But the Soviets have insisted on balancing trade with North Korea and will doubtless press in the 1980s for at least a partial repayment of the debt to them. The Chinese, very short of foreign exchange for their own ambitious modernization program and unable to compete effectively with the Soviets in the export of modern technology, are in no position to replace them as a lender and supplier to North Korea.

---

16. A senior Soviet specialist on Northeast Asia told the author in July 1979 that when the North Koreans asked the Soviets for hard currency to help them pay off their debts to Western countries, they were turned down with the advice: "You're always talking about self-reliance, why don't you practice it?"

17. *Far Eastern Economic Review,* vol. 105, no. 36 (Sept. 7, 1979), p. 56; *Washington Post,* Mar. 21, 1981; *Asian Wall Street Journal Weekly,* June 29, 1981.

18. The Soviet specialist referred to in n. 16 criticized the North Koreans for not fulfilling their commitments to supply certain commodities in exchange for Soviet shipments to North Korea. He said that some of the promised goods had been shipped to China instead.

The economic difficulties besetting North Korea and its inability to obtain Soviet or other help in overcoming them are reflected in the frequent exhortations to North Koreans through the media to achieve economic goals through increased exploitation of their own human and material resources. North Korea's serious economic problems seem to offer an opportunity for the Soviets to increase their influence on the country by offering more help. However, past Soviet experience with Kim Il Sung's stubbornly independent behavior, perhaps combined with a low opinion of North Korea's economic policies, may cause Soviet leaders to feel that little is to be gained by extending more credits. They may believe that a relatively low level of balanced trade will suffice to maintain a necessary foothold in the country.

Evidence of economic cooperation between North Korea and the Soviet Union despite the strains between them has been the construction going on at the port of Najin in the extreme northeastern part of Korea since 1977, as first reported in a Soviet economic journal. The Soviets appear to be using the port to relieve congestion at Soviet Pacific ports by landing cargo there and shipping it by rail into the Soviet Union. The two countries signed a protocol in December 1978 providing for increased use of the port.[19]

Military Relations

In the past the Soviet Union has been North Korea's primary supplier of military equipment. From 1964 to 1973 about three-fourths of imported weapons came from the Soviet Union and one-fourth from the PRC. But after 1973 Soviet military aid declined to a low level while Chinese aid increased. The Chinese began to supply T-59 medium tanks (the Chinese version of the Soviet T-54) and Chinese-produced fighter aircraft. Although these weapons are obsolescent, they were the best the Chinese had. The Soviets have provided no new planes or missiles since 1973. MIG-23 aircraft and SA-6 and SA-7 surface-to-air missiles, which the Soviets sent to their Middle Eastern allies, and T-72 tanks, which they are reportedly selling to India,[20] have not appeared in North Korea.

North Korea's own military production capability increased substantially in the 1970s. The North Koreans can now produce small arms, recoilless rifles, mortars, rocket launchers, artillery, antiaircraft weapons, armored personnel carriers, ammunition, tanks, and submarines. The quantitative increase in North Korean weapons during the 1970s has come in great measure from home production. Sometime in the

19. FBIS, *Daily Report, Soviet Union,* Jan. 8, 1979, pp. M1, M2.
20. *Far Eastern Economic Review,* vol. 101, no. 39 (Sept. 29, 1978), p. 5. According to newspaper accounts, advanced MIG-25 jets, as well as T-72 tanks, have been supplied to Syria, Libya, and Algeria (*New York Times,* Nov. 4, 1979).

mid-1970s the Soviets provided the technology that enabled Pyongyang to produce the T-62 tank, which began to appear in North Korea in 1978. The T-62 is less advanced than the T-72 but it is superior to South Korea's M-48 tanks.[21] Thus, the Soviet Union made a significant contribution to modernizing North Korea's forces during the 1970s but continued to withhold advanced aircraft and missiles, which North Korea is incapable of producing. Reports that North Korean pilots have been flying MIG-23's in Libya have not been confirmed.[22]

In view of Kim Il Sung's emphasis on building a powerful military force, the refusal of the Soviets to supply advanced weapons such as they have provided to other allies must have provoked deep resentment. It must also have strengthened Kim Il Sung's determination to increase North Korea's own military production capability as much as possible in order to reduce somewhat dependence on the Soviet Union. It was probably one of the principal causes for the coolness in relations between Pyongyang and Moscow and for Pyongyang's tilt toward Beijing in the 1970s. Soviet reasons for withholding such weapons are not known. It seems probable, however, that the Soviets distrust Kim and fear that he might be tempted to attack South Korea if he had a much stronger military force. It is also possible that the Soviets, offering new weapons as a quid pro quo, pressed Kim, as they once did the Chinese, to permit the establishment of Soviet bases on Korean soil and that Kim rejected the proposal. Finally, the Soviets may simply feel that Kim has no need for the weapons for defensive purposes and that supplying them would give them no increased leverage on him.

SOVIET AND NORTH KOREAN PERCEPTIONS OF EACH OTHER

That Soviets and North Koreans do not get along very well with each other is apparent from the foregoing analyses of their political, economic, and military relations. Their attitudes are implicit in their behavior and public statements and sometimes explicit in private comments by Soviet scholars and officials.

There seems to be little personal rapport between Soviets and North Koreans. Soviets privately speak slightingly of Kim Il Sung's policies, especially his grandiose cult of personality. The Soviets have not re-

21. Larry Niksch, *Korea: U.S. Troop Withdrawal and the Question of Northeast Asian Stability* (Washington, D.C.: Library of Congress, Congressional Research Service, Jan. 2, 1980), p. 9.

22. Korean Information Office, Embassy of Korea, Washington, D.C., *Korean Newsletter*, vol. 2, no. 4 (Feb. 19, 1979), p. 2. According to intelligence sources in Washington, the North Korean pilots in Libya were not flying MIG-23's, but an advanced model of the MIG-21.

ferred publicly to Kim's promotion of his son, Kim Chung Il, as his successor; they are unlikely in principle to look favorably on this attempt to bring about a dynastic succession in a socialist country. They see Kim not only as uncooperative and arbitrary but also as irresponsible and capable of reckless behavior that could involve the Soviet Union in a dangerous situation. The patent Soviet disinclination to give prompt and full backing to North Korea in the Pueblo incident, the shooting down of the U.S. EC-121, and the ax murders of two American officers in the demilitarized zone reflects Soviet distaste for Kim's adventurism.

The Soviets have been irked by North Korea's refusal to join COMECON and link its economic policies more closely with those of the Soviet Union. They particularly resent Kim's tilt toward China and his refusal to respond to Soviet pressures for more balanced treatment. Soviet gestures toward South Korea, discussed below, may be intended as a demonstration of Soviet displeasure.

In short the Soviets find the North Koreans intractable, ungrateful, and difficult to manage. They have often gone contrary to Soviet wishes and sometimes openly attacked Soviet policies, but the Soviets find themselves in a dilemma. Because of the strategic importance of North Korea they cannot read the country out of the socialist camp, as they did Albania. Harsh treatment would push the North Koreans further into the Chinese embrace. On the other hand, what the Soviets perceive as generous treatment in the past has not won them over either.

Kim Il Sung sees the Soviet Union as a big, threatening neighbor that would like to dominate North Korea as it does Mongolia. He has declared directly his opposition to great power chauvinism and domination.[23] He is determined to maintain North Korea's independence to the greatest possible extent and his tilt toward China has served to demonstrate this independence to the Soviets. At the same time, he recognizes that North Korea must depend on the Soviets to some extent, economically and militarily, and in a more basic sense, as the primary counter to U.S. support for South Korea. This unavoidable dependence breeds frustration and resentment. Moreover, the Soviets keep North Korea on a short rein, providing neither the military nor the economic support that it would like to have.

In personal relations the North Koreans appear to reciprocate the frosty attitude of the Soviets toward them. The lack of rapport probably results in part from the arrogance displayed by Russians visiting North

23. See particularly Kim Il Sung's notable report of October 5, 1966, to the Korean Workers' Party Conference, in which he champions the independence of each communist party and condemns at length interference by the big communist powers in the affairs of communist parties in smaller countries (FBIS, *Daily Report, Far East [Supplement]*, Oct. 12, 1966).

Korea. A Polish observer, who visited North Korea in the late 1960s, commented that the Soviets behaved "like British colonialists."

There is also an element of distrust and suspicion in North Korean attitudes toward the Soviet Union. Whenever a small nation is dependent on a big power for its security, there is always a lurking fear that the big power might sell it out if the big power's interests so dictated. Consequently, the North Koreans have been suspicious of Moscow's policy of détente with Washington. Suspicions have been heightened by Moscow's failure to support completely and enthusiastically the North Korean position on reunification and by the gestures toward South Korea despite vehement North Korean protests.

North Korean attitudes toward the Soviets cannot be disentangled from their attitudes toward the Chinese. Given the intensity of Sino–Soviet rivalry, favoring one inevitably means disfavoring the other. Although China is also a large and potentially threatening neighbor, the Koreans have more in common culturally and politically with the Chinese than with the Russians. Greater personal rapport between North Koreans and Chinese is evident from public statements and from the treatment accorded visitors back and forth. The fact that the Chinese lost many lives in defending North Korea during the Korean War, while the Soviets gave only material support, makes a qualitative difference in the relationship. The Chinese–Korean "friendship sealed in blood" is frequently referred to on ceremonial occasions.

NEW SHIFTS IN THE BALANCE: 1979–80

Pyongyang's public denunciation of the Soviet-supported Vietnamese invasion of Cambodia in December 1978 accentuated its already pronounced tilt toward China. Subsequently, however, signs appeared that Kim Il Sung was seeking to redress the balance by overtures to the Soviet Union while, at the same time, the Pyongyang–Beijing relationship began to show evidence of strain.

Pyongyang's attack on the Vietnamese invasion of Cambodia was caustic. Scattered signs of North Korean sympathy for the Cambodians had already appeared after the visit of Pol Pot to Pyongyang in 1977, but when Vietnam invaded Cambodia, North Korea cast aside its caution and explicitly denounced Hanoi's "outrageous" action in a *Nodong Sinmun* editorial as "a crude violation of the publicly recognized international law."[24] The editorial did not, however, hint that the Soviet Union had anything to do with it. The subsequent Chinese invasion of Vietnam was not criticized by North Korea despite the statement in the editorial condemning Vietnam that differences among "fraternal parties and fra-

24. FBIS, *Daily Report, Asia and Pacific,* Jan. 12, 1979, pp. D1–D3.

ternal countries... must not be solved by a coercive method with the mobilization of armed forces, but must be solved through negotiations *under all circumstances.*"[25] The Soviet press called attention to the DPRK's failure to denounce the PRC's aggression. While not condemning the PRC for invading Vietnam, North Korea did not applaud the action. It simply failed to mention it in the media. Furthermore, the North Koreans did not criticize the Soviet Union for backing Vietnamese aggression. Thus, although leaning toward the Chinese position, the North Koreans exercised a degree of restraint, unlike, for example, Mongolia, which shows little restraint either in its support of Soviet actions or in its criticisms of Chinese moves.

The Soviet invasion of Afghanistan late in December 1979, which was bitterly denounced by the PRC, placed new strains on North Korea's relations with its big power supporters. As in the case of the Chinese attack on Vietnam, the North Koreans neither supported nor condemned the action; they simply did not report it in their news media. They did, however, show initial disapproval of the Soviet-installed Afghan government by withholding from the new leader, Babrak Karmal, a congratulatory message such as had been sent to his two predecessors, Taraki and Amin, on their assumption of power. Moreover, at a February meeting of Soviet-bloc countries in Sofia, North Korea joined Romania in refusing to back a resolution supported by ten other countries expressing solidarity with the new Afghan government.[26] The occupation of a Third World, nonaligned state by Soviet forces clashed with the principles of independence and nonintervention long advocated by Kim Il Sung within the nonaligned movement. In an authoritative communiqué issued in June 1980 the senior leaders of North Korea, while aiming their principal volleys at "the imperialists" and not mentioning the Soviet Union by name, condemned interference in the nonaligned movement by "the great powers" and called on the nonaligned states to "strongly demand the unconditional withdrawal of foreign troops from the territories of other countries for the relaxation of international tension and the maintenance of peace."[27]

However, despite their distaste for Soviet behavior in Afghanistan the North Koreans bowed to the reality of their dependence on Soviet support. They recognized the Karmal government and acknowledged in their press that they maintained diplomatic relations with it. A senior North Korean official, Hyon Chung Kuk, in an effort to draw a distinc-

25. Ibid., p. D2. Italics added.
26. *Washington Post*, Feb. 9, 1980.
27. Pyongyang, *Communiqué on the Joint Meeting of the Political Committee of the Central Committee of the Workers' Party of Korea and the Central People's Committee of the Democratic People's Republic of Korea*, June 1980, pp. 2, 8.

tion between the Vietnamese invasion of Cambodia and the Soviet invasion of Afghanistan, told a visiting Japanese Socialist party delegation that the Soviet Union had intervened at the request of the Afghan government, pursuant to a Soviet–Afghan treaty.[28]

Signs of strain in the relations between Pyongyang and Beijing appeared as early as 1978 over the signing of the Sino–Japanese peace treaty on August 12 of that year. Differences of view concerning Japan had been developing for a long time. In 1970, during Zhou Enlai's visit to Pyongyang, the Chinese and North Koreans had denounced in similarly harsh terms "the revival of Japanese militarism" and the alleged schemes of "U.S. and Japanese reactionaries" to attack North Korea. Following the normalization of relations between Beijing and Tokyo in 1972, however, Chinese and North Korean attitudes toward Japan diverged. The Chinese have expressed approval of the U.S.–Japanese security treaty and of strengthened Japanese military forces as needed to counter the Soviet menace. The North Koreans, on the other hand, have continued to denounce the "Japanese militarists" and to voice dark suspicions of their designs on Korea.

One would assume, therefore, that the signing of the Sino–Japanese treaty would not elicit cheers from the North Koreans. The media in North Korea did not report the signing. Moreover, during the visit of a high level "military friendship" delegation from China in late August, the North Korean vice-minister of defense used the occasion to condemn attempts by "Japanese reactionaries" to "run amok in Korea." To so criticize the Japanese in the presence of a visiting Chinese delegation was unusual.[29] On the other hand, Kim Il Sung himself was reported in the Japanese press to have told a Japanese visitor in October that the Sino–Japanese treaty should be welcomed and would be good for peace in Asia.[30] What the North Koreans may be saying officially to the Chinese and Russians about the treaty we have no way of knowing. In any case North Korea's public attitude has been cautious.

During 1979 and 1980 various other signs of some cooling in the relations between Pyongyang and Beijing appeared. For example, on September 9, 1979, the anniversary of the founding of the DPRK, the *People's Daily* editorial omitted the usual call for the withdrawal of U.S. forces from Korea, and the *Nodong Sinmun* editorial on the PRC national day, October 1, did not claim as it had in 1977 and 1978 that the PRC backed the U.S. force withdrawal. On October 25, the anniversary of the

28. Young C. Kim, "North Korea in 1980," *Asian Survey*, vol. 21, no. 1 (Jan. 1981), p. 122.

29. FBIS, *Trends in Communist Media*, Sept. 7, 1978, p. 7.

30. Kim Il Sung to Ryosuke Yasui, editor of Japanese monthly *SEKAI, Asahi,* Oct. 28, 1978.

Chinese entry into the Korean War, the *Nodong Sinmun* again failed to mention Chinese backing for the withdrawal of U.S. forces, although its editorial on the Soviet national day, November 7, noted Soviet support for the withdrawal. A *Nodong Sinmun* editorial on October 1, 1979, revived a Kim Il Sung quotation last used in 1971, which ranked the Chinese Revolution second to the Great October Revolution in Russia.[31]

The clearest and most authoritative evidence of disenchantment with China appeared in Kim Il Sung's report to the Sixth Congress of the Korean Workers' Party in October 1980. Kim warned the socialist countries against making any "unprincipled compromise with imperialism." He said that the socialist countries "must not bargain with the imperialists on matters of principle... must not give up their anti-imperialist stance in order to improve their diplomatic relations with the imperialist countries nor must they sacrifice the interests of other countries in their own interest."[32] There is little doubt that these strictures were aimed primarily at the PRC, which has compromised with the United States over the Taiwan issue and is earnestly engaged in expanding its relations with the United States, North Korea's chief enemy.

Both Beijing and Moscow reported without comment the emergence of Kim Chung Il, Kim Il Sung's son, at the Sixth Party Congress in positions very close to the top of the party hierarchy. But shortly thereafter a Hong Kong journal closely associated with Deng Xiaoping supporters in Beijing published a harsh denunciation of Kim's attempt to set up a dynastic succession. The adoption of such a feudalistic system by "a professed socialist country truly makes a great mockery of that name," the article said.[33]

While the Pyongyang–Beijing relationship was showing signs of strain, Kim Il Sung was taking steps to improve relations with Moscow. On the 1978 anniversary of the Bolshevik Revolution the messages to Brezhnev and to the Soviet defense minister used warmer language than had been used in previous years. In June 1979 a North Korean Politburo delegation visited the Soviet Union. On August 15, 1979, the anniversary of the liberation of Korea from Japan, the North Koreans resumed the practice, discontinued since 1976, of sending a message from the defense minister to his counterpart in Moscow. Kim Il Sung's message to Brezhnev on the same occasion said he would make "every effort" to improve relations, language that had been used in recent years only with the Chinese and Cambodians.[34] The Soviets sent a Politburo member,

31. FBIS, *Trends in Communist Media*, Oct. 3, 1979, p. 8.
32. FBIS, *Daily Report, East Asia and Pacific*, Oct. 15, 1980, p. D14.
33. *Zheng Ming*, Nov. 1, 1980: FBIS, *Daily Report, PRC*, Nov. 21, 1980, p. U-1.
34. FBIS, *Trends in Communist Media*, Aug. 22, 1979, p. 18.

V. Grishin, to represent the CPSU at the KWP party congress in October 1980. Although he ranked somewhat lower than Li Xiannian, a vice-chairman of the Chinese Communist party, he was received by Kim Il Sung and was treated with almost as much deference as Li was. The North Koreans reciprocated by sending Politburo member and premier Yi Chong Ok to represent them at the Soviet party congress in February 1981, a higher level representation than in 1976.

Except for sending a high level representative to the KWP party congress, the Soviets have shown little disposition to respond to Kim Il Sung's overtures. They may be holding out for a more pronounced move away from China and toward the Soviet Union than Kim has been willing to make.

The moderation of Pyongyang's tilt toward China in 1979 and 1980 probably was caused by disillusionment with China on the one hand and a greater sense of both vulnerability to and dependence on the Soviet Union on the other. The waning of ideological commitment in China, the expansion of relations with the United States and Japan, and the downgrading of Mao all must have made Kim Il Sung uneasy. He may also have been disturbed by reports of trade between the PRC and South Korea.[35] At the same time, Soviet military occupation of a Third World neighbor and the installation there of a Soviet puppet leader must have caused grave misgivings in Pyongyang, recalling past Soviet interference in North Korea's domestic politics as well as Soviet military intervention in Hungary and Czechoslovakia. It served to underline the importance for North Korea of maintaining a balanced position between Moscow and Beijing, not swinging too far toward either. Although the Soviet Union is in a position to do more for North Korea than China is, it must also appear to Kim Il Sung as posing a greater threat to its independence than China does. After all, it was the Soviet Union, not China, that intervened in Korea in the 1950s in an attempt to undermine Kim's position. It was the Soviet Union that used military force to impose on Hungary and Czechoslovakia governments of its own choosing. It was the Soviet Union that helped Vietnam invade Cambodia in order to replace an independent communist government with a pro-Vietnamese, pro-Soviet puppet regime. And it was the Soviet Union that invaded Afghanistan. These precedents argue for a moderate tilt toward China as a warning to the Soviets that North Korea prizes its independence and cannot be cajoled or forced into the Soviet camp. China's military

35. The PRC has denied reports in the *Asian Wall Street Journal* of substantial trade between the PRC and South Korea. The Soviet press, which gleefully played up the reports, was castigated by the Chinese press for seeking to drive a wedge between Beijing and Pyongyang. See *Korea Herald* (Seoul), Mar. 14, 1981.

"punishment" of Vietnam, although demonstrating that China too can be a dangerous neighbor, seems unlikely to modify the probable North Korean view that the more powerful Soviet Union has the stronger tendency toward "dominationism."

Consequently, Kim Il Sung has little choice but to continue the balancing act he has followed for decades if he is to maintain his nation's independence. He may be forced by growing South Korean economic and military power to make concessions to the Soviets that he declined to make in the past in order to obtain increased economic and technical assistance, but he will do so only with great reluctance and will continue to rely on a relationship with China to prevent the Soviet Union from gaining dominance over North Korea. Somewhat warmer relations with Beijing than with Moscow, although less rewarding than the reverse stance, may be less dangerous. The most critical test for Pyongyang's relationships with its big power allies is likely to come during the transition to Kim's successor. If the top North Korean leaders should disagree and Moscow and Beijing intervened to support rival claimants, not only would political stability in North Korea be lost but the nation's independence and peace in Northeast Asia would also be gravely threatened.

SOVIET RELATIONS WITH SOUTH KOREA IN THE 1970S

As early as 1969–70 the South Koreans began to give serious thought to the possibility of trade and political relations with communist countries. In 1971 the government announced that it was prepared to have diplomatic relations with the Soviet Union and the PRC if they ceased "hostile activities," recognized the sovereignty of the Republic of Korea, and suspended aid to North Korea. In that same year South Korean diplomats were authorized to have contacts with their Soviet counterparts, and regulations were modified to permit trade with "non-hostile" communist states. In June 1973 President Park Chung Hee withdrew South Korea's objection to the membership of both Koreas in the United Nations. He also declared that "the Republic of Korea will open its door to all the nations of the world on the basis of the principles of reciprocity and equality" and urged countries with ideologies and social systems different from those of South Korea "to open their doors likewise to us."[36]

The Soviet Union has not responded officially to the South Korean proposal but it has in modest ways "opened its doors" to the South Koreans. In 1973 a South Korean businessman was allowed to visit Leningrad with a tour group and a dramatist was admitted in order to

36. Research Center for Peace and Unification, *Korean Unification: Source Materials with an Introduction* (Seoul: 1976), p. 339.

attend a theater meeting in that city. Later that year a South Korean team was permitted to participate in the World University Games in Moscow despite vehement protests by the North Koreans.

In subsequent years South Korean officials were admitted to the Soviet Union to attend international conferences and South Korean teams took part in international athletic events in the USSR. The most significant of these signs of flexibility by Moscow toward Seoul was the admission of the South Korean minister of health and his delegation to attend a WHO conference in Alma Ata in the summer of 1978. Not only did the Soviets admit the cabinet minister, they also issued visas to two newsmen who accompanied him and allowed one of the journalists to make a phone call from Moscow to Seoul, the first such communication. Moreover, the local newspaper, *Kazakhstanskaya Pravda,* referred to the "Republic of Korea" by name in reporting the meeting.[37] South Korean visitors to the USSR during 1979 included two sports officials who attended the congress of the International Ice Hockey Federation, two newsmen who attended the congress of the International Press Service, and sixteen scholars who attended the International Political Science Association conference. Moreover, in April 1979 an international telephone link with the Soviet Union via the United Kingdom was opened. Soviet courtesies to the South Koreans were noted by the Chinese, who condemned this "increased flirtation" as support for the U.S./South Korean scheme to create "two Koreas."[38] The Chinese have refused to admit South Korean athletes to international meets on their territory, as a result of which at least one international sports competition, the World Ice Hockey Championship (Group C), originally to be held in Beijing in March 1979, was shifted to another country.[39]

Although the Soviet Union has admitted South Koreans to international gatherings on its territory, it has so far declined to allow its citizens to participate in similar activities in South Korea. Soviet and East German marksmen refused to take part in the World Shooting Championships in Seoul in October 1978, as a result of which the Soviets and East Germans lost their seats on the International Shooting Union's Administrative Council.[40] The Soviets also declined to participate in the World Women's Basketball Tournament in Seoul in April 1979.

One reason for Soviet willingness to permit a few contacts with the South Koreans probably is a desire to avoid interfering with the choice of the Soviet Union as a desirable location for international conferences

37. FBIS, *Daily Report, East Asia and Pacific,* Sept. 7, 1978, p. E6.
38. FBIS, *Daily Report, PRC,* Sept. 15, 1978, p. A3.
39. *Korea Herald,* Feb. 18, 1979.
40. FBIS, *Daily Report, East Asia and Pacific,* Oct. 3, 1978, p. E5.

and athletic meets. No doubt the Soviets justify their action to the North Koreans by pointing out that the rules of sponsoring organizations require the host country to admit participants from all countries belonging to the organization. It would detract from the Soviet Union's international prestige if it were to forgo hosting important international meetings out of deference to North Korea's political sensitivities. The Soviets have, however, gone beyond what was strictly required of them for this purpose, perhaps motivated by a wish to impress on the North Koreans that they are not being realistic in refusing to deal with South Korea. Soviet gestures toward South Korea could also be a means of chiding the North Koreans for tilting too far toward China.

In fact, the Soviets have been quite restrained in their responses to the overtures made by the South Koreans. Officially, they have supported the North Korean position on reunification and have shown no interest in the concept of cross-recognition pushed by the United States and Japan. On October 12, 1978, *Pravda* condemned attempts at "dismembering" Korea, specifically referring to cross-recognition in this connection. *Pravda* went on to say that the Soviet Union recognizes "only one Korea—the DPRK," which, it said, "symbolizes the bright future of the entire Korean people."[41]

In the future, Soviet contacts with South Korea probably will gradually increase as South Korea comes to play an increasingly active and important international role. But rivalry with the PRC places severe constraints on how far the Soviets can go. Although the PRC itself may eventually find desirable abandonment of its strict policy of no contacts with South Koreans, under the present circumstances of intensified Sino–Soviet hostility over Indochina no early Chinese move in this direction seems likely.

SOVIET PERCEPTIONS OF THE KOREAN QUESTION

For the Soviet Union, Korean policy is subordinate to its policies toward the United States, China, and Japan. Soviet relations with the two Koreas are important primarily because of the effect they have on Soviet relations with the larger powers. Theoretically, either of the Koreas could adopt policies that helped the Soviet Union achieve its goals in regard to the big powers; in practice, however, the probability is greater that actions they take in their own interests will make Soviet goals more difficult to achieve. Consequently, from the Soviet viewpoint Korea is more a nuisance to be controlled than an opportunity to be exploited. The complexity of the Korean problem severely limits policy options and

41. FBIS, *Trends in Communist Media*, Oct. 18, 1978, pp. 6–7.

tends to defer to the distant future hopes for basic changes in Korea that would serve Soviet foreign policy objectives. Possible Soviet options include the following:

Close Collaboration with North Korea.   Soviet interests would be best served by a regime in Pyongyang that collaborated as closely with Moscow as Mongolia, Cuba, and Vietnam do. It would align itself firmly with the Soviet Union on Sino–Soviet differences and would cooperate in advancing Soviet influence throughout the world. Such a regime would be closely tied to the Soviet Union and Eastern Europe economically, would depend to a significant degree on Soviet aid, and would provide the Soviets with military bases at warm-water ports. During the 1970s, however, the trend in Soviet–North Korean relations has been away from, rather than toward, the achievement of this level of cordiality and cooperation. The prospects for turning Kim Il Sung into a useful collaborator of this type are dim.

Preventing North Korea from Collaborating with Adversaries.   If the most desired goal of converting Pyongyang into a close collaborator cannot be achieved under present circumstances, what about the lesser goal of preventing North Korea from collaborating with Soviet adversaries? Failure to prevent undesired collaboration between Pyongyang and Beijing no doubt has been disappointing to the Soviets but so far that collaboration has not exceeded tolerable limits. Total dependence on Beijing is no more desired by Kim Il Sung than total dependence on Moscow, which provides a built-in regulator of his swings toward one communist capital or the other.

The confrontation between the two Koreas, Kim Il Sung's ambition to unite Korea on his terms, and the nature of South Korea's relations with the United States and Japan provide assurance against North Korea's collaborating with the United States or Japan against the interests of the Soviet Union. Thus, Moscow can have reasonable confidence that North Korea will not develop dangerously close ties with any Soviet adversaries. North Korea does not have the freedom of maneuver to become a Yugoslavia.

Promoting Coexistence of the Two Koreas.   Hints that the Soviets would feel more comfortable with the institutionalized acceptance of coexistence by both Koreas have been apparent, as discussed above. The Soviets are aware of the shortcomings in North Korean policies and of the fact that over the next decade the balance of economic strength and perhaps also of military productive capability will shift decisively in favor of South Korea. Whether by design or not, they have exerted some pressure on Kim Il Sung to accept peaceful coexistence with South Korea, but they seem to believe that the costs of publicly backing such a position would outweigh the benefits. They may consider Kim Il Sung immovable on this question and also may fear the gains that Beijing would make at their expense in Pyongyang if they were to espouse "two Koreas." Moreover, they appear relatively relaxed about Korea, not particularly worried that the arms race there will lead to the resumption of large-scale warfare. Therefore, they probably see no pressing need to respond to U.S. proposals for cross-recognition or to take other steps toward a stabler form of coexistence between Seoul and Pyongyang.

Promoting Unification of Korea.   A unified Korea might be a long-term goal of Soviet policy but only according to conditions under which Moscow could be reasonably confident of having predominant influence over it, for reasons explained earlier. The routine nature of the lip service given to North Korean reunification policies, taken together with private Soviet comments, indicates little expectation that unification of Korea is a practicable goal for the next decade. It seems less likely to be adopted as a Soviet tactical goal for this period than the promotion of peaceful coexistence between the two Koreas.

Watch and Wait.   The complexity of the Korean problem, Moscow's disillusionment with Kim Il Sung, and the absence of any strong pressures to resolve the Korean problem for the sake of Soviet relations with the big powers, argue for a policy of watching and waiting. The Kremlin's aging leaders, who have many more urgent problems on their agenda, seem unlikely to come forward with any bold initiatives aimed at transforming the Korean situation. They have lived with it for more than twenty-five years since the Korean War. There have been alarms and excursions but no serious threat to the stability of the peninsula. Consequently, it is easy for them to rationalize the necessity of continuing to live with the situation, unsatisfactory as it is in some respects, and to avoid unnecessary risks.

Given their tendency to place confidence in the long flow of history to favor their cause, Soviet leaders seem likely to follow a policy of awaiting crucial changes in the Korean situation and then seeking to turn the changes to their advantage. One such change will be the accession of a new leadership in North Korea.

POLICY IMPLICATIONS

Such is the complexity of the Korean problem, involving six governments and their interactions with one another, that the ultimate effects of possible changes in U.S. policy toward Korea are very difficult to predict. This chapter has dealt with two of the relationships: Soviet–

North Korean relations and the minimal relations between the Soviet Union and South Korea. Certain inferences for U.S. policy can be drawn from the analysis of these relationships, but policy recommendations would require consideration of U.S. relations with all five governments, extending far beyond the reach of this study.

On the assumption that U.S. objectives vis-à-vis Korea are to lower tension and create a more peaceable state of coexistence between the two Koreas, what U.S. policies might cause the Soviet Union to take steps toward the same goal? A basic difficulty is that although the Soviets appear to share with the United States a desire to avoid the resumption of conflict, they seem confident that war will not break out in Korea. They do not seem to regard the military confrontation there as a pressing international problem requiring early solution. They exhibit more concern over Korea as an element in their rivalry with the PRC than as a problem in U.S.–Soviet relations. Thus, the Soviets are unlikely to be particularly receptive to U.S. efforts to enlist their cooperation in reducing tension in Korea. Moreover, the current state of Soviet–North Korean relations suggests that even if the Soviets were responsive to U.S. proposals, their ability to persuade or encourage Kim Il Sung to accept coexistence with South Korea is not great.

Suppose the United States were to try to exploit and intensify the strains between the Soviet Union and North Korea by establishing official contacts and communication with the North Koreans. In view of the present political climate in the United States and the state of U.S. relations with South Korea, the U.S. government could at most take only a few hesitant steps down that road. Such a tentative approach would be unlikely to have a significant impact on Moscow–Pyongyang relations, which are determined primarily by their bilateral dynamics and secondarily by the Chinese factor. Moreover, even if political circumstances did not constrain the United States from moving decisively to establish a variety of relations with North Korea, it probably would be contrary to U.S. interests to do so for other reasons. Kim Il Sung is less cautious than the Soviet Union and has a much stronger motivation to act against U.S. interests in dealing with South Korea. To the extent that a U.S. connection increased his capacity for independent action, diminished Soviet influence on him, and increased his leverage on the Soviet Union, it might easily produce results contrary to U.S. intentions and interests.

United States relations with South Korea will have a significant effect on Soviet–North Korean relations. The arms race between the two Koreas has been fueled to a great extent by the contributions of the superpowers in weapons and in technological aid to the arms industries. Both superpowers have shown restraint in the types of weapons provided. As weapons production capacity increases on each side of the demilitarized zone, the influence of the superpowers will decline but they will retain an important residual influence through their ability to provide or withhold advanced weapons. The United States and the Soviet Union can exert some restraint on the arms race in Korea by declining to provide new generations of weapons. Even if such restraint does not significantly reduce tension and the danger of war, it would limit somewhat the defense burden borne by the people of the two Koreas.

The decision of the Reagan administration to sell F-16 aircraft to South Korea, approved earlier "in principle" by the Carter administration, may cause the Soviets to supply more advanced aircraft to Pyongyang, thus escalating the arms race another notch.

Although the Soviet Union officially endorses North Korea's rejection of South Korea's proposals, which are supported by the United States and Japan, for the admission of both Koreas to the United Nations and the cross-recognition of both by all four big powers, the Soviets seem uncomfortable with this position. They recognize that separate Koreas are likely to exist for a long time and that the position maintained by South Korea and its allies is more realistic than the North Korean position. Because the South Korean position accords with reality, the United States and Japan can hold firmly to it and mobilize world opinion to support it. As South Korea becomes increasingly active and important in world affairs, it will become increasingly difficult for the Soviet Union and the PRC to refrain from dealing with it. When the support of North Korea's allies for its hardline position weakens, even the North Koreans themselves may come to recognize the inevitability of accepting long-term coexistence with South Korea.

Despite Soviet unreceptiveness to U.S. initiatives on Korea, periodic discussions of the Korean question with Moscow (and Beijing) are desirable. Reminding the Soviets and Chinese of the firmness of the U.S. commitment to South Korea is crucial. In addition, if they are truly interested in preventing any miscalculation by Kim Il Sung, such discussions provide an opportunity for them to communicate U.S. statements to the North Koreans. United States discussion of Korea with Moscow and Beijing also tends to make Seoul and Pyongyang uneasy concerning big power intentions and exerts some pressure on them to reach agreement themselves on the future of Korea.

8

The Soviet Union's Economic Relations in Asia

ED. A. HEWETT AND HERBERT S. LEVINE

There is enormous variation in the magnitude and importance of Soviet economic relations with the countries of East and Southeast Asia.[1] For North Korea and Vietnam, the Soviet Union has played a crucial role as a trade partner, a source of credits, and a source of military and economic aid. The Soviet–Japanese economic relationship has developed from virtually nothing in the last two decades to an important one, but not nearly so important as it could be if significant political differences were to be resolved. Simultaneously, Soviet–Chinese relations have lost much of the importance they had in the 1960s. For the rest of the countries of Southeast Asia the Soviet Union is a minor economic factor *now*, although its superpower status and its constant interest in the region suggest the possibility of a much more significant economic role in the future.

This chapter assesses the economic role of the USSR in East and Southeast Asia. First, we review available data on the nature of Soviet economic contacts with this region in the last several decades. The data are rather poor, but there is sufficient information to gain a general picture of the state of these relations. Later we discuss, respectively, Soviet economic relations with Japan, China, North Korea, and Vietnam—these being the major Soviet trade partners in this region. We analyze the evolution of bilateral economic relations and their implications for the rest of the region, with an emphasis on the recent past and the near-term future.

AN OVERVIEW OF THE SOVIET ECONOMIC PRESENCE IN ASIA

The three major aspects of the Soviet economic presence in Asia are merchandise trade, shipping, and credit. We will discuss each of these—

We are indebted to David Neumark, Yoshinobu Shiota, Phillip Rothman, Elissa Kapell, and Mina Mohammadioun for their research assistance.

1. The countries of Asia covered in this paper include Japan, China, North Korea, Vietnam, Thailand, Singapore, Malaysia, Indonesia, the Philippines, Australia, and New Zealand.

although the major emphasis is on merchandise trade—in order to place them in the context of Soviet and Asian economic relations with the world as a whole.

Merchandise Trade

Table 8.1 contains data on Soviet trade with Asia for selected years (1955–78) based on Soviet foreign-trade statistical yearbooks. The values are in millions of foreign-trade rubles. The table's Total Asia row gives total Soviet exports to, or imports from, Asia, and the Total World row gives total Soviet exports to or imports from the world. The last row in the table is derived from the previous two and shows the proportion of all Soviet exports or imports accounted for by Asia.

The relative importance of Soviet trade with this region has fallen throughout the 1955–78 period, most dramatically in the aftermath of the break with China. In recent years 5 percent or less of total Soviet exports have gone to Asia, and no more than 9 percent of its imports have originated there. In 1978 Soviet trade turnover with Japan, its largest trading partner in Asia, constituted only 3.3 percent of total Soviet trade. No other country in Asia accounted for even 1 percent of Soviet trade turnover in that year.

Table 8.2 shows that in most cases the Soviet Union accounts for an insignificant portion of the total trade of individual Asian countries. With only two exceptions, no country in Asia receives more than 4 percent of its export proceeds from the USSR, and Soviet shares of Asian imports are even smaller. The Soviet Union is, however, a very important trade partner for North Korea and Vietnam. In 1976 they both delivered 37 percent of their exports to the Soviet Union, and Vietnam received 42 percent of its imports from the USSR while North Korea's imports from the USSR constituted 31 percent of its total imports.

Returning to table 8.1, note how the relative importance of the Soviet Union's various Asian trade partners has changed over time. In the mid-1950s practically all the Soviet Union's trade in Asia was conducted with socialist countries: China, North Korea, North Vietnam, and also with Malaysia and Indonesia. These countries accounted for 99.6 percent of Soviet exports to Asia and 96 percent of its imports from the area. These proportions slipped to 92 percent of exports and 82 percent of imports in 1960, with the beginning of the rise in Soviet trade with Japan and Soviet imports from Malaysia (primarily rubber). In the 1960s and 1970s the proportions changed dramatically so that by 1978 the Soviet Union was shipping only 45 percent of its exports in Asia to socialist countries (China, North Korea, and Vietnam) and buying barely 20 percent of its total Asian imports from the socialist countries.

This reflects a shift in Soviet motives for trade from almost exclusively political ones to increasing emphasis on economic objectives, which in turn was accompanied by a changing Soviet perception of the potential economic benefit of international trade and of the Soviet Union's proper role in the world economy. In the 1950s Soviet leaders based their approach to trade on the theory that there were two separate world economies—the socialist world economy and the capitalist world economy—and that socialist countries could benefit most from international trade if they built up a socialist trading bloc. This approach began to change in the 1960s, and by the early 1970s a number of Soviet economists were stressing the argument that the coexistence of the two different social systems does not mean that there is not a single world economy. Quite the contrary, they argued, the world economy is an objective reality, within which the two world systems interact, compete, and cooperate.[2] Moreover, the advantages of trade including that with capitalist nations were stressed not only by Soviet economists but also by Soviet leaders in the atmosphere of the policy of détente.[3]

The main beneficiary of the change in approach was Soviet trade with Japan, especially Soviet imports of high technology machinery and equipment from Japan. Since the 1960s total Soviet–Japanese trade turnover has grown rapidly, although care must be taken because the data are in current prices and a significant portion of the post-1973 increase is due to price rather than quantity changes. In current value terms it grew from an insignificant level in 1955 of only 3.8 million rubles ($0.9 million at 1955 exchange rates), or less than 1 percent of Soviet trade with Asia, to a level in 1978 of 2,320 million rubles ($3,387 million at 1978 exchange rates), or 57 percent of the total value of Soviet–Asian trade.

At the same time the USSR's trade with Japan was growing, its trade with China was dwindling. The value of Soviet–Chinese trade turnover in 1978 was about one-quarter of its 1955 level despite the increase in prices, and it accounted for only 8 percent of Soviet trade with Asia in 1978 compared with 92 percent in 1955.

The data in table 8.1 suggest a fourfold classification of Soviet trade flows with the Asian countries:

2. See in particular: (a) M. M. Maksimova, *SSSR i mezhdunarodnoe ekonomicheskoe sotrud-nichestvo (The USSR and International Economic Cooperation)* (Moscow: Mysl', 1977) [English translation published in 1979]; (b) E. K. Valkenier, "The USSR and the Third World: New Economic Dimensions," in *The Soviet Union and the World Economy* (New York: Council on Foreign Relations, 1979), pp. 59–80; and (c) I. S. D'yakova, *Vneshnyaya torgovlya raz-vivayushchikhsya stran Azii* (Moscow: Nauka, 1978).

3. See, for example, the speeches of Brezhnev and Kosygin at the last two party congresses.

Table 8.1. Soviet Trade with Selected Countries in Asia, 1955–78 (Millions of foreign-trade rubles)

	1955		1960		1965		1970		1973	
	Ex.	Im.	Ex.	Im.	Ex.	Im.	Ex.	Im.	Ex.	Im.
Japan	2.0	1.6	68.5	55.4	166.5	159.6	341.4	310.9	622.0	372.4
China	673.5	579.2	735.4	763.3	172.5	203.0	22.4	19.5	100.5	100.8
S.E. Asia	43.1	59.6	72.1	216.7	204.0	238.8	388.0	286.7	379.0	276.7
N. Korea	39.7	36.7	35.5	67.2	80.8	79.5	207.0	128.9	224.0	133.3
N. Vietnam/ Vietnam	3.3	0	22.0	20.8	67.4	27.5	166.5	16.7	142.9	36.9
Laos	0	0	0	0	0	1.1	0.3	0	0	0
Cambodia	0	0	0	0	2.6	0.5	2.6	1.4	0	0
Thailand	0	0	0	0	1.6	0	5.5	0.8	2.1	2.4
Singapore	0	0	0	0	2.6	0	1.6	2.9	6.4	3.2
Malaysia	0	19.6	0	100.4	0	101.4	1.6	111.0	0.9	96.7
Indonesia	0.1	3.3	14.6	28.3	49.0	28.8	4.5	25.0	2.7	4.2
Philippines	0	0	0	0	0	0	0	0	0	0
Australia	1.1	6.1	0.4	31.2	1.4	90.7	1.5	60.3	3.2	194.8
New Zealand	0	0	0	0	0.4	7.0	0.7	18.9	1.4	37.3
Total Asia	719.7	646.5	876.4	1,066.6	544.8	699.1	754.0	696.3	1,106.1	982.0
Total World	3,084.0	2,754.5	5,007.3	5,065.0	7,357.2	7,252.5	11,520.1	10,565.1	15,801.7	15,544.0
Asia as Percentage of Total World	23%	23%	18%	21%	7%	10%	7%	7%	7%	6%

Table 8.1. (Continued)

	1974 Ex.	1974 Im.	1975 Ex.	1975 Im.	1976 Ex.	1976 Im.	1977 Ex.	1977 Im.	1978 Ex.	1978 Im.
Japan	905.7	777.5	668.9	1,253.5	748.4	1,372.1[a]	853.4	1,444.4[a]	736.1	1,583.7[a]
China	108.4	105.5	93.1	107.8	179.8	134.6	118.4	130.1	163.8	174.9
S.E. Asia	401.1	423.5	362.2	357.8	454.6	402.1	499.3	567.3	527.6	567.8
N. Korea	194.3	148.9	186.8	151.4	181.8	118.7	164.7	164.0	176.5	201.6
N. Vietnam/ Vietnam	192.3	43.4	158.7	47.8	232.5	63.6	274.2	129.8	305.5	152.3
Laos	0	0	0	0	10.6	0	22.6	0	11.6	0.2
Cambodia	0	0	0	0	0	0	0	0	0	0
Thailand	1.3	9.8	4.0	13.3	7.8	12.4	5.9	2.5	5.7	6.1
Singapore	4.5	13.5	3.8	10.7	11.9	9.1	13.9	12.8	8.8	30.1
Malaysia	0.7	188.0	0.8	101.3	4.2	103.5	8.6	127.8	4.2	121.1
Indonesia	8.0	19.9	7.7	20.9	4.4	27.9	7.6	24.1	8.4	28.0
Philippines	0	0	0.4	12.4	1.4	66.9	1.8	106.3	6.9	28.4
Australia	5.4	178.5	2.1	327.3	3.1	406.6	4.3	324.6	4.6	274.8
New Zealand	2.4	59.4	2.0	30.5	2.4	78.7	3.0	118.6	3.2	42.0
Total Asia	1,423.0	1,544.4	1,128.3	2,076.9	1,388.3	2,394.1	1,478.4	2,585.0	1,435.3	2,643.2
Total World	20,737.8	18,834.4	24,029.6	26,669.2	28,022.2	28,732.8	33,256.3	30,097.0	35,667.8	34,556.6
Asia as Percentage of Total World	7%	8%	5%	8%	5%	8%	4%	9%	4%	4%

Source: Soviet foreign trade statistical yearbooks, various issues.
Notes: In addition Soviet foreign-trade organizations imported 235 million foreign-trade rubles (m.r.) worth of pipe from Japan in 1976, 82.7 m.r. in 1977, and 21.8 m.r. in 1978. These were imports for the Orenburg Gas Pipeline and were made on behalf of the East European countries. (The data are from footnotes to the 1976, 1977, and 1978 import figures. The nature of the transactions is discussed in V. Spandar'ian, "Novyi etap v razvitii Sovetsko–Yaponskoi torgovli" [A New Important Stage in the Development of Soviet–Japanese Trade], *Vneshnyaya torgovlya*, no. 12, Dec. 1977, p. 14.)

Table 8.2. Proportion of Trade with the USSR for Selected Countries in Asia, 1976

	Percentage of country's exports going to the USSR	Percentage of country's imports coming from the USSR
Japan	3.4	1.8
China	2.5	4.0
North Korea	37.2	31.0
Vietnam	37.0	42.0
Thailand	0.4	0.3
Singapore	1.0	0.2
Malaysia	2.2	0.3
Indonesia	0.4	0.3
Philippines	3.4	0.3
Australia	3.7	0.5
New Zealand	3.5	0.4

Sources: For all except China, North Korea, and Vietnam: *Yearbook of International Trade Statistics, 1976* (New York: United Nations Statistical Office, 1977). For China: *Handbook of Economic Statistics, 1978* (Washington, D.C.: CIA, 1978), p. 64; for North Korea: Y. S. Kim, ed., *The Economy of the Korean Democratic People's Republic* (New York: Paragon Book Reprint Corp., 1979); for Vietnam: *Soviet Economy in a Time of Change,* vol. 2, U.S. Congress, Joint Economic Committee (Washington, D.C.: U.S. Government Printing Office, 1979), p. 571.

1. Countries with which USSR imports are far greater than USSR exports (Malaysia, Indonesia, the Philippines, Australia, and New Zealand);
2. Countries for which Soviet exports and imports are roughly the same (North Korea, Vietnam, and China);
3. Countries with which the USSR trades almost nothing (Laos, Cambodia, Thailand, and Singapore);
4. Soviet–Japanese trade, a category to itself in the context of these countries.

For countries in the first category Soviet imports are focused on one or two primary products that are among the traditional exports of the trade partner. The Soviet Union in turn exports virtually nothing to the partners to finance the imports, instead using its hard currency earnings from exports to other countries.

Table 8.3 contains data on the seven most important primary products that the USSR imports from Asia: natural rubber, meat, raw sugar, rice, wheat, wool, and tin. Asia supplies half or more of Soviet imports of natural rubber, wool, and tin (col. 7); in the other cases a lower but

Table 8.3. Data on Key Soviet Primary Product Imports from Selected Countries of Asia, 1975–77

Product	Year	(1) Total Soviet production (thous. tons)	(2) Total Soviet imports (thous. tons)	(3) Total Soviet exports (thous. tons)	(4) Domestic utilization (1)+(2)−(3) (thous. tons)	(5) (2)÷(4)	(6) Imports from Asia Country[a]	(6) Amount	(7) (6)÷(2)	(8) (6)÷(4)	(9) (6)÷(Asian production)
Rubber	1975	1,450	235	na[b]	1,685	.14	M, I	218[c]	.93	.18	M, I .09[d]
Meat	1977	14,800	617	33	15,384	.04	NZ, A	193[e]	.31	.01	NZ, A .05[f]
Raw sugar	1977	13,043	4,287	na	17,330	.25	P	635[g]	.15[g]	.04[g]	P .25
Rice	1977	2,213	460	na	2,673	.17	NK	164	.36	.06	NK nd[h]
Wheat	1977	92,004	6,702[i]	2,118	96,558	.07	A	959[j]	.14[j]	.01[j]	A .10
Wool	1975	467	109	7	569	.19	NZ, A	61[k]	.56	.11	NZ, A .06[l]
Tin	1977	29	10	na	39	.26	M	5	.50	.13	M .08

[a] Country abbreviations: A, Australia, I, Indonesia, M, Malaysia, NK, North Korea, NZ, New Zealand, P, Philippines.

[b] No data are given in the yearbook, which for these products probably indicates very small or zero trade.

[c] Imports from Malaysia = 166, from Indonesia = 52.

[d] Soviet imports from Malaysia are .11 of Malaysian production; Soviet imports from Indonesia are .06 of Indonesian production.

[e] Imports from New Zealand = 105, from Australia = 88.

[f] Soviet imports from New Zealand were .09 of production, from Australia .03 of production.

[g] Imports from Cuba in 1977 were 3,652 thousand tons, which is .85 of all Soviet sugar imports and accounts for .21 of total Soviet sugar utilization.

[h] No data available on the Korean rice crop.

[i] Data are given only in rubles, so this is estimated using the unit value in the Australian data.

[j] Imports from the United States were 2,830 thousand tons, which was .42 of all imports and represented .03 of total utilization.

[k] Imports from New Zealand = 18, from Australia = 43.

[l] Soviet imports from New Zealand and Australia are .06 of each country's production.

Sources: Column 1: CIA, Handbook of Economic Statistics, 1978 (Washington, D.C., 1978); cols. 2, 3, and 6: Soviet foreign-trade statistical yearbooks for 1975 and 1977; and col. 9: Asian production data from same source as for col. 1.

nevertheless significant proportion of Soviet imports of the product originates in Asia. In the case of rubber (natural plus synthetic), wool, and tin, more than 10 percent of Soviet domestic utilization is supplied by imports from Asia (col. 8); the ratios are lower, but still significant, for rice and sugar. Thus the USSR is to some extent dependent on Asia for guaranteeing its supplies of some important primary products and, to a lesser extent, some food products.

On the other hand, the last column of table 8.3 (col. 9) shows that sales to the USSR account for a significant, although mostly not overwhelming, portion of total production of these products in Asia. Because these countries have fairly diversified export structures, these ratios do not mean that the USSR accounts for a large amount of total export from Asia (see table 8.2). But, nevertheless, for these products, which are important sources of export revenues, the USSR is a major customer, and a customer that pays in hard currency.

USSR exports to this first group of countries are in all cases insignificant. In part this reflects the fact that these countries have not been major recipients of Soviet aid and therefore have not had a reason or the wherewithal to purchase Soviet machinery and equipment. But the fundamental problem is that Soviet machinery and equipment are not generally competitive with Western equipment. Because Asian countries receive hard currency for exports to the USSR, they feel no compunction to spend it there unless the Soviets happen to produce the best (for the price) of a particular item desired by an Asian firm, which does not occur very frequently.

To sum up trade with this first group of countries, we can say it is lopsided toward Soviet imports, mainly because the primary and food products involved are important to the Soviets for guaranteeing domestic supplies. But it is also lopsided because Soviet exports are not competitive with their Western counterparts.

The second distinctive group of countries in table 8.1 are the socialist countries of Asia: North Korea, Vietnam, and China. Trade with them is much closer to being bilaterally balanced, and the flow of goods in each direction is much more diverse than in the case of the countries discussed above. Of Soviet exports to Southeast Asia, almost all go to North Korea and Vietnam. In recent years 30–40 percent of these exports have been machinery and equipment, two of the most important groups being aircraft and trucks. The rest comprise primary products and food, in particular petroleum products, rolled ferrous metals, cotton, and grain. Keeping track of imports from these two countries is increasingly difficult because their own data are sparse and because since 1976 Soviet data have grown increasingly less informative on all primary product trade, including imports from these countries. We know that North

Korea exports to the Soviet Union rice, clothing, magnesium granules, and rolled ferrous metals, as well as small amounts of nonferrous metals, and primary and food products. Vietnam has traditionally exported clothing and some food and primary products. Presumably, Vietnamese reunification has shifted the composition of those exports somewhat, for example toward rubber, but the data are not published so one cannot be sure.[4]

There is no hard information on the prices at which the USSR conducts trade with these countries, a crucial area of ignorance. The Soviet terms of trade with Vietnam are *probably* favorable to Vietnam in the same way as are Soviet terms of trade with Cuba.[5] On the other hand the general tenor of Soviet–North Korean relations (which we discuss below) suggests that North Korea's terms of trade with the USSR are probably similar to its terms of trade with the rest of the world.

The richer diversity and closer balance of these trade flows compared to those of the five countries discussed before reflect the power of bilateral trade agreements (and negotiations), as well as Soviet aid, and the strong Soviet political interest in North Korea and Vietnam. Without these elements North Korea and Vietnam might well have been part of the first category of countries.

China also falls into this second category of bilaterally balanced trade, but obviously the politics of the situation make this a much different relationship than that characteristic of Vietnam or North Korea. In recent years about three-quarters of Soviet exports to China have been machinery and equipment, most importantly energy equipment, trucks, and aircraft. Soviet imports from China are dominated by no specific product groups, but the (relatively) most important groups are fruits and berries, and clothing.

The other countries of Southeast Asia—Laos, Cambodia, Thailand, and Singapore—fall into a third group of countries, where Soviet trade is quite small even by the standards of the Soviet Union's modest trade in Asia. Soviet trade with Singapore represents the only significant activity in this group, and much of Soviet imports from Singapore (about one-half in recent years) consists of ship repairs.

---

4. In 1976, the last year for which any data on rubber imports are available, the Soviet Union imported 4.7 million tons of rubber products from Vietnam (there were no imports in 1975, and this is most assuredly the beginning of shipments from former South Vietnam), which was a little more than 7% of Soviet rubber imports that year.

5. See, for example, L. H. Theriot and J. Matheson, "Soviet Economic Relations with Non-European CMEA: Cuba, Vietnam, and Mongolia," in *Soviet Economy in a Time of Change,* compendium of papers submitted to the Joint Economic Committee, Congress of the United States (Washington, D.C.: U.S. Government Printing Office, 1979) [hereafter cited as *JEC-79*), vol. 2, pp. 551–81.

Soviet–Japanese trade is in a category by itself (relative to Soviet trade with other Asian countries) with very strong similarities to Soviet trade with Western Europe. As a resource-poor country, Japan needs many of the primary products that the USSR exports, and as a developed nation, Japan produces manufactures that the USSR wants very much. Approximately three-quarters of export earnings in Japan come from four product groups: coal, petroleum and petroleum products, timber, and cotton. In recent years upwards of one-half of Soviet imports from Japan have been machinery and equipment, especially equipment for chemical plants, automobile factories, and oil refineries. Other significant imports include rolled ferrous metals, pipe, and chemicals.

Surely the most important facts about Japan are its proximity to Siberia and the obvious complementarity of Japan's rapid industrial growth with Siberia's unexploited natural resources. As was pointed out above, Japan already accounts for more than half of all Soviet trade with Asia. And it could well be that in the 1980s, with the completion of the Baikal–Amur Mainline Railroad (BAM) and the development of a number of territorial production complexes in Siberia, Japan will become by far the most important non-East European trade partner of the USSR.

Shipping Services

The Soviet merchant fleet has grown impressively since the early 1960s, quadrupling its size from 1961 to 1978.[6] At the beginning of 1978 it numbered 1,700 ships (with a carrying capacity of 17.2 million tons), and although it was still far behind the fleets of such major shipowning nations as Japan and Great Britain in terms of capacity and quality, it did possess 3 percent of the world's tonnage and ranked ninth in the world, slightly ahead of the United States. The large number of outmoded general-purpose vessels in the Soviet liner fleet are well suited for coastal deliveries to Soviet Far Eastern ports and for trade with many less developed countries. The major role of the Soviet fleet is the delivery of Soviet exports such as oil, coal, and other bulk commodities to Western Europe and Japan. The carriage of Soviet exports accounted for almost three-quarters of the hard currency earnings of the Soviet fleet in 1978, which in turn accounted for 6 percent of total Soviet hard currency earnings, more than the exports of any single manufacturing industry and exceeded only by exports of hydrocarbons, timber, military equipment, and gold. Other activities of the Soviet fleet include participation in cross trades linking foreign ports—for example, the carrying of Phil-

6. Material on the Soviet merchant fleet is drawn from W. Carr, "The Soviet Merchant Fleet: Its Economic Role and Its Impact on Western Shipowners," in *JEC-79*, vol. 2, pp. 663–77.

ippine copra to Western Europe on a backhaul basis after delivering Soviet exports to Southeast Asia. The Soviets have been able to make some inroads in liner services between the United States and Japan by charging rates below those set by the Western-dominated systems of shippers' cartels ("conferences"). In addition the Soviet fleet is active in Asia in the delivery of Soviet economic and military aid cargoes to Vietnam and North Korea and in the support of Soviet armed forces in the Far East.

Another increasingly important form of Soviet shipping service is the Trans-Siberian Landbridge.[7] Starting in 1971 a growing share of freight traffic between Europe and Japan has been carried in container shipments on the Trans-Siberian Railroad at lower rates than all-water routes and in roughly the same time. The 1971 agreement between the Soviet transport agency, Soyuzvneshtrans, and several Japanese and European freight-forwarding agents provided that westbound containerized cargo would be amassed at principal ports in Japan and that vessels, both Japanese and Soviet, would carry them to the Soviet port of Nakhodka, where they would be loaded onto specialized flatcars for the trip across the Soviet Union. At the other end, depending on the destination, the containers would be loaded either onto ships (usually Soviet) or onto European trains for final delivery. Since its inception, traffic has grown rapidly on the landbridge, from about 2,300 containers (in equivalent 20-foot units) in 1971 to almost 80,000 in 1976, representing about 1 million tons of traffic and 25 percent of the Japan-to-Europe container cargo. Its future growth, however, is a matter of debate. Soviet authorities are actively pushing its growth. For example, they are now providing feeder service for the overland route from Singapore, Manila, and Hong Kong. And the expansion of Soviet vessel capacity on the Japan–Nakhodka sea leg of the container route is consistent with Soviet plans to expand their merchant fleet. But opposition is mounting from those shipping interests, members of the Far Eastern Freight Conference, including major Japanese shipping firms, who have heavy investments in deep-sea container carriers and who have been hurt by the Trans-Siberian Landbridge.

Soviet Banking in Asia

Another part of the Soviet Union's economic role in Asia is played by the Singapore branch of the London-based Moscow Narodny Bank (MNB).[8]

7. See E. B. Miller, "The Trans-Siberian Landbridge, A New Trade Route Between Japan and Europe: Issues and Prospects," in *Soviet Geography: Review and Translation*, vol. 19 (Apr. 1978), pp. 223–43; see also *World Business Weekly*, vol. 3, no. 12 (Mar. 31, 1980), pp. 9–10.

8. Based on J. T. Danylyk and S. T. Rabin, "Soviet-Owned Banks in the West," in *JEC-79*, vol. 2, pp. 482–505.

The USSR maintains a network of seven wholly owned banks and three branches located in major financial centers of Europe, the Middle East, and Asia, where they play an active role in local money markets and in facilitating the financing of trade with the Soviet Union and other socialist economies. The USSR State Bank and Foreign Trade Bank are the major shareholders of the Soviet-owned banks abroad, and they determine the banks' policies. That is, they establish policy guidelines for the direction of bank activities, credit plans (including credit ceilings for individual socialist countries), and interest rates on certain loans. In other respects the banks appear to be free to make their own day-to-day operating decisions. Aside from the special attention they give to the financing of trade with socialist countries, the Soviet-owned banks provide the same services as those provided normally by banks in capitalist countries, including making and collecting payments and processing trade documents. They can also, however, provide Moscow with valuable commercial intelligence. Through their credit departments and contacts with their correspondent banks they can obtain credit information on importers and exporters in various countries that would not normally be available to the Foreign Trade Bank and foreign trade organizations in the Soviet Union.

The Singapore branch of the MNB was opened in 1971 in order to provide on-the-spot service to the bank's clients in Southeast Asia. Its main functions were: (1) to help expand Soviet exports to the area by providing credits to Asian importers; (2) to collect information on Asian economic and commercial conditions; and (3) to gain access to the Asian-dollar market and to the interbank market in hard currencies created by the Monetary Authority of Singapore. In the first few years of its existence the branch was highly successful. By 1973 it had grown into one of the three largest foreign-owned banks in Singapore, and by 1974 its assets represented about one-half the total assets of the MNB.

As Soviet hard currency needs mounted in the 1970s, Moscow applied intense pressure on its foreign-based banks to find new ways of generating hard currency earnings. Many of the banks, especially the Singapore branch of the MNB, deemphasized their traditional and relatively risk-free financing of Soviet trade in favor of the far riskier, but potentially highly profitable, financing of real estate, construction, shipping, mining, and other enterprises.[9] When the recession of 1974–75 set in, many of these risky, inadequately secured loans turned sour, leading to a loan write-off of possibly $300 million—almost all by the Singapore branch.

9. As one observer stated: "[The banks] suddenly began engaging in and tolerating reckless operations. They made all the mistakes the capitalists made... [and] they hired banking's black sheep. Greedy for market share, they took capitalist sharks for customers." Quoted in Danylyk and Rabin in *JEC-79*, vol. 2, p. 496.

Furthermore, the rapid growth of the MNB branch in Singapore and its spreading involvement in Southeast Asia raised the concern of business interests in Singapore and in Hong Kong, Malaysia, Thailand, and Indonesia, who were strongly suspicious of Soviet intentions.[10]

Since 1977 the Singapore bank has instituted a number of reforms that it hopes will repair the damage done to its reputation by its previous tactics. Major management and personnel changes were made and banking policy was returned to the more traditional activities associated with the financing of Soviet trade. But repercussions from its earlier ventures, in the form of law suits and investigations by banking commissions, are still being felt.

THE USSR AND JAPAN

The Soviet Union and Japan are the most natural trading partners, and, although their trade with each other has grown substantially, their potential trade flows are surely much higher than actual flows to date. Japan's gross national product (GNP) was $969 billion in 1978, ranking third in the world behind the GNPs of the United States ($2,108 billion) and the USSR ($1,254 billion).[11] But Japan's industrial might is built on imported primary products, and the eastern part of the Soviet Union is one natural source for those materials.

Indeed Japan is now by far the Soviet Union's largest trading partner in Asia, accounting for more than half the USSR's total trade with Asia in 1978. Moreover, Japan is now the Soviet Union's second largest trading partner among all the advanced industrial nations of the West, second only to West Germany in 1977 and 1978.

On the other hand the Soviet Union is the tenth largest trading partner of Japan. Although, as was indicated, the Soviet Union in the mid-1970s purchased only about 3.5 percent of the goods exported by Japan and was responsible for less than 2 percent of the goods imported by Japan, in regard to certain types of goods the Soviet Union is one of Japan's major trading partners.[12] For instance, in 1975 the Soviet Union was the leading supplier of Japanese imports of nonferrous and precious metals; second in Japanese imports of timber, platinum, zinc, potash fertilizers, and cotton; third in the imports of scrap steel, chrome ore, and nickel; and fourth in the imports of coal, fuel oil, and fresh fish. Soviet deliveries (in 1976) accounted for the following percentage shares

10. See, for example, *New York Times*, June 26, 1976, and *Far Eastern Economic Review*, vol. 101, no. 30 (July 28, 1978), pp. 80–87.

11. *Handbook of Economic Statistics, 1979* (Washington, D.C.: CIA, 1979).

12. The data that follow are from V. Spandar'ian, "Novyi vazhnyi etap v razvitii sovetsko-yaponskoi torgovli," *Vneshnyaya torgovlya*, no. 12 (Dec. 1977), p. 16.

of Japanese imports: commercial timber, 18; cotton, 17.5; cotton seeds, 60; potash salts, 24: secondary aluminum, 73; palladium, 35; rhodium, 44; scrap steel, 12; and whale meat, 50. In turn the Soviet Union has become a major purchaser of the products of some of Japan's leading industries, particularly machinery and equipment industries. In 1975 the Soviet Union ranked as follows as a purchaser of Japanese exports: first in the export of mechanical shovels, special motor vehicles, fixtures, pipes of special steel, seamless pipes, artificial silk, woolen yarn, and knitted textiles; second in the export of ready-made clothes and knitted goods, footwear, plastics and resins, tin plate, special steels, hoisting equipment, farm machinery, and heavy-duty trucks; third in the export of steel pipes and cables, cable products, metal-cutting lathes, construction and mining equipment, electric measuring and controlling tools, and rolling stock; and fourth in Japan's export of iron-and-steel products and those of general engineering and textile industries.

These commodity listings reflect one of the two major reasons for the magnitude of Soviet–Japanese economic relations: the fact that they are natural trading partners in terms of the complementarity of their economic needs. Japan produces advanced industrial goods and requires raw materials; the USSR produces raw materials and desires advanced, high technology industrial goods.

The second major motivating force for the growth of Soviet–Japanese economic relations is the locational factor. In terms both of transportation costs and of Soviet plans and ambitions to develop Siberia and the Soviet Far East, extensive Soviet–Japanese trade and Japanese involvement in the development of Siberia, especially its energy resources, appear rational and attractive to both parties.

In addition the locational factor has also led to the development of coastal trade between the Soviet Far East and the northeastern areas of Japan. Beginning in 1963 this trade has grown from a level of about 1.5 million rubles to 43 million rubles in 1976 and it was expected to reach 56 million rubles in 1980.[13] A special Soviet foreign trade organization, Dalintorg, was set up to administer this trade. Dalintorg deals directly with more than one hundred Japanese small- and medium-sized firms, trade cooperatives, and associations. The administration of this trade appears to be quite decentralized. The commodities exported by Dalintorg, which represent the surplus production of Soviet Far Eastern enterprises, include timber and sawed wood, fish, coal, and minerals.[14] Dalintorg uses receipts from these exports to buy consumer goods (in-

13. Ibid., p. 17.
14. B. N. Slavinsky, "Siberia and the Soviet Far East Within the Framework of International Trade and Economic Relations," *Asian Survey*, vol. 17, no. 4 (1977), p. 328.

cluding clothes, radios, and cameras), fishing equipment, and industrial products and equipment to meet the needs of the Far Eastern area.

An important role in the growth of Soviet–Japanese economic relations has been played by government-to-government trade agreements and by credit (both government and private) granted by Japan to the Soviet Union. There have been three official Soviet–Japanese five-year trade agreements covering the periods of the Soviet Eighth, Ninth, and Tenth Five-Year Plans (1966–70, 1971–75, 1976–80).

Trade negotiations between the USSR and Japan are conducted on different levels. On the Soviet side the negotiators are the usual officials of the Ministry of Foreign Trade, relevant foreign-trade organizations, and because of the large technology component, representatives of the State Committee on Science and Technology. It is, in addition worth noting that the current USSR trade representative to Japan, V. Spandar'ian, is a highly respected Soviet authority on foreign trade, formerly chief foreign-trade economist at Gosplan.

The Japanese, on the other hand, delegate much authority to semi-public and private institutions in negotiations, like the Keidanren (Japan's Federation of Economic Organizations), the Japanese Chamber of Commerce and Industry, the Japanese Association for Trade with Socialist Countries of Europe, the Japan International Cooperation Agency, and the Japan Export–Import Bank. Japan's trading houses, Mitsui, Mitsubishi, Sumitomo, Kanematsu, and others, also play a key role in economic relations with the USSR. The official discussions between the Soviet and Japanese political leadership apparently touch only lightly on mutual cooperation. The main task of reaching accords, even for government-sponsored copartnership projects, falls to the Japanese business community operating through various semiofficial channels There is also a Joint Japanese–Soviet Economic Committee that meets in Moscow and Tokyo, alternately each year, to discuss different prospective projects of mutual interest.

By the end of the 1970s Japan was the leading granter of credit to the Soviet Union.[15] Soviet long-term indebtedness to Japan (government and privately held) has been estimated to total about $2 billion in 1977, which represents a little more than 20 percent of the Soviet long-term net hard-currency debt at the time.[16] Furthermore, at the end of 1977 the Soviet Union had a credit line of $2.8 billion from Japan out of a total of $12.8 billion worth of government credit lines then available to

15. *Economist*, vol. 275, no. 7101 (Mar. 15, 1980), p. 37.

16. R. S. Mathieson, *Japan's Role in Soviet Economic Growth* (New York: Praeger, 1979), p. 230; calculations based on P. G. Ericson and R. S. Miller, "Soviet Foreign Economic Behavior: A Balance of Payments Perspective," *JEC-79*, pp. 217, 221–23.

the Soviet Union.[17] The major form of Japanese credit to the Soviet Union is in conjunction with compensation agreements. Under compensation agreements Japan supplies the Soviet Union with credits at low interest rates, with which the Soviet Union purchases machinery, equipment, and plant. Principal and interest are then paid back at a later date in the form of raw materials and semifinished products that are produced with the imported capacity. Such arrangements have features attractive to both countries. The Soviet Union acquires access to sophisticated modern technology with reduced immediate investment costs. Japan obtains future supply commitments to important raw materials that are not produced in Japan and, therefore, avoids the problem of market disruption often present in the United States and Europe in connection with compensation agreements.[18]

Soviet–Japanese economic cooperation developed rapidly in the late 1960s and early 1970s as a number of agreements were signed, most of which involved Siberia and the (Soviet) Far East. In recent years negotiations have slowed considerably as Soviet–Japanese political relations have deteriorated. We discuss here interesting examples of projects completed or in process now and then turn at the end of this section to future prospects.

Civil Engineering

The Soviet Union has insufficient railway and port facilities in Siberia and the Soviet Far East for the economic expansion it wishes to undertake in those areas. With these motivations in mind, the USSR has undertaken some major civil engineering projects in conjunction with the Japanese. One is the construction of a new port at Vostochny on Wrangel Bay, which, with the completion of the BAM, will greatly increase Japanese access to the raw materials forthcoming from their economic cooperation with the USSR in the development of Siberia. The Wrangel Bay project was conceived in 1970 and began its first operations in 1973. At its completion it is intended to be the largest commercial port of the Soviet Far East. Whereas Vladivostok is mainly a military port, the port at Vostochny will help to handle the growing volume of international commercial freight now being generated by Soviet Siberian developments and the Trans-Siberian Landbridge container service between

17. *Economist*, vol. 275, no. 7101 (Mar. 15, 1980). (This article discusses the post-Afghanistan restrictions on Western credit to the Soviet Union.)

18. After the enactment of the Stevenson amendment to the Eximbank Act, which limited the granting of U.S. credit to the USSR, the Soviets were able to negotiate with the Japanese for the construction of four ammonia plants (originally planned for U.S. firms) with financing by the Japanese Export–Import Bank.

Europe and Asia. The joint venture was agreed to at a meeting of the Japan–Soviet Joint Economic Committee in Moscow in 1970. The Japanese government agreed to an investment of $100 million in long-term credits.

Forestry Products

Two Japanese–Soviet Far East Forestry Development Projects were undertaken (1968 and 1974). A third project was discussed in 1977 but nothing came of it. In the first, the Japanese Export–Import Bank granted the Soviet Union $163 million in deferred credits, primarily to cover the costs of machinery purchases from Japan. In return Japan was to receive supplies of lumber and sawed timber through the year 1974. The second entailed a loan of $550 million from the Japanese Export–Import Bank. Under it, timber resources of the Kirenga, Selemdzha, and Amgun river basins were to be opened up for the first time, and paper and pulp mill capacity in Eastern Siberia was to be expanded to a large degree. In addition there was an Industrial Wood Chip and Pulp Development Project in 1971, which entailed credits of $45 million extended by the Japanese for the construction of plant, port loading facilities, and wood chip carriers. The Japanese strongly desired this project because a supply of wood chips would serve to revitalize their paper and pulp industries, which have never recovered from the loss of Sakhalin's paper and pulp industries in World War II.

Coal

In the realm of Soviet coal industries the Japanese have played a major role. Most Japanese coal imports from the USSR now come from the Kuznetsk basin and Sakhalin Island but far greater amounts will be available under new agreements between the USSR and Japan. The Soviets would like to relieve pressures on Kuznetsk coal supplies, and they also desire additional coking coal supplies in the Far Eastern regions in order to support a prospective integrated iron and steel mill in that area. With these goals in mind, a Soviet–Japanese agreement in 1974 provided for coal supplies to Japan from the Chul'man coalfield in South Yakutia, in return for Japanese government-backed credits for the purchase of equipment and machinery to be used in the development of this coalfield. The Chul'man coalfield is one of the largest in the world, with commercially viable reserves of greater than 40 billion tons, mainly in high-quality coking coal. Long-term credits for the development of the Chul'man coalfield were subscribed through a consortium called the South Yakutia Coal Development Cooperation Company in association with the Export–Import Bank of Japan. Under the terms of the agreement Japan will receive coal supplies at prices well below world market prices because production costs for East Siberian coal are very low. There are estimates that Russia's Yakutsk coalfields will, in the future, supply Japan with 10 percent of its coking coal requirements.[19]

Oil

After the discovery of huge reserves of oil and gas in the Tyumen oblast in Western Siberia the Soviets realized that in order to develop the vast amount of resources in this area, they would need foreign financing and technical assistance. In 1974 general accords on joint Japanese–Soviet oil industry development were reached, resulting in cooperation in all sectors of the Soviet oil industry as well as in a contract to export 20 million tons of Soviet crude oil annually. There was talk of a possible deal involving Japan and America to build a pipeline from the Tyumen oilfields to the Pacific, but this arrangement fell through following the withdrawal of American participation and conclusions by the Japanese that the venture would not be sufficiently profitable.

The main thrust of Japanese involvement in Soviet oil industry development shifted in 1975 to the oil and gas deposits of the Sakhalin continental shelf under the Sakhalin Continental Shelf Oil and Gas Cooperative Exploration Project. According to the terms of the agreement concerning this project Japan has granted the Soviets a loan that will be paid back only in the event that oil is discovered. If commercially viable reserves are discovered—and estimates of the reserves of the northeast area of the Sakhalin shelf where Japan is involved place those reserves at 5 billion tons—then Japan will, for ten years, receive 50 percent of the oil discovered in sales from the USSR.

Gas

In 1976 negotiations on the Northern Star Gas Project, involving the gas fields in Tyumen oblast, which had originally involved only the United States and the Soviet Union, became international with the inclusion of Japan and several European countries (West Germany, France, Italy, and Austria). Revised proposals for the project included construction of a pipeline from Orenburg to Uzhgorod and Eastern Europe. The cost of this pipeline is more than one-third of the estimated final cost of $19 billion for the entire project. Japan has thus far granted a loan of $460 million to assist in the construction of the pipeline and other facilities related to the development of the Tyumen fields. Prospects for a near-term conclusion of negotiations on this project are quite poor.

19. *Economist,* vol. 261, no. 6944 (Oct. 2, 1976), p. 92.

Another project, the Yakutia Gas Exploration Project, after two years of stop-and-start negotiations, was concluded in 1976. Under its terms an initial investment of $50 million was arranged, involving equal amounts from American and Japanese investors. Eventual exploration costs are expected to be much higher and the entire project is expected to cost $3.5 billion. From this amount the U.S.–Japanese consortium will build a pipeline, processing facilities, and a fleet to carry the exports of 60,000 tons of liquid natural gas that each country will receive annually for the first twenty-five years of production. Despite the high costs of the Yakutia project the Japanese and their U.S. partners are confident of the viability of the venture.

Chemicals and Petrochemicals

The Japanese have been major contributors to the rapid growth of the Soviet chemical and petrochemical industries. Specifically, Japan has supplied ammonia production plants, ammonia transport vessels, and fertilizer plants. In the field of petrochemical engineering Japanese manufacturers have supplied substantial amounts of equipment and plant that involve many facets of oil refinery and petrochemical technology. In the field of synthetic textiles the Soviet Union is making strides to increase both technology and capacity, and to this end an agreement was reached in 1977 for an exchange of information and researchers in the synthetic fibers field, as well as for the supply of polyester plants and technology to the USSR. Soviet authorities have also contracted with Japanese firms for the supply of equipment and plant in the fields of synthetic resins, plastics, and rubbers. Despite the impact of these efforts on Soviet chemical and petrochemical development the USSR still imports from Japan some very specialized chemical products, mainly of a pharmaceutical and medical nature, and in these areas the Soviet Union relies on Japan as its chief supplier. Japan also continues to provide the Soviet Union with certain products of its heavy petrochemical industries.

Machine Building and Metalworking

The machine-building and metalworking sector is, of course, basic to the development of industry in general, and the Japanese have become intimately involved in the development of the Soviet machine-building and metalworking industries. A great many of Japan's largest engineering companies have entered into cooperation agreements with the Soviet State Committee for Science and Technology. Frequently, these agreements provide for exchange of information on know-how and licensed technologies in many different fields of heavy engineering. Predominantly the flow of knowledge is from Japanese companies to the Soviet

Union, often being embodied in the latest designs of plant and equipment.

In the automotive industries Japan has supplied the Soviet Union with various types of equipment, ranging from vehicles and machinery for construction projects, forestry, and coal mining to machinery for truck and automobile production. The Japanese provided important automotive equipment to the Kama River truck plant. This included transfer machines, grinding machines, broaching machines, program-controlled lathes, and other special purpose machine tools such as crankshaft grinders. The intertwining of technologies involved in the international transfer of technology is clearly illustrated in the fact that the program controllers used on the Japanese machine tools were produced in Japan on a license acquired from an American firm and the crankshaft grinders on a license acquired from a French firm.

Precision Equipment

The Japanese have supplied the USSR with a highly sophisticated satellite communications system, components and plants for television production, and various other high technology electrical equipment. Japanese firms have also supplied medical and hospital equipment and an X-ray film plant.

Computer technology is perhaps the most sensitive area of the precision industries. Under the Coordinating Committee (COCOM) agreement among Western countries the export to the Soviet Union of defense-oriented computers is prohibited. While there have been seemingly innocuous sales of computers for process control in refrigerator compressor manufacturing plants and the sale of television and computer equipment for use in the Olympics, there remains some degree of mystery regarding two other computer sales. In the sale of an NEAC 2200/1200 computer, worth $9.5 million, the report of the sale indicated that the supply of this particular machine was an agreed exception to the COCOM agreement. In another sale of two computers, Mathieson writes, "from their nature, it is thought that these went to a scientific institute rather than a manufacturing plant for process control."[20]

Reverse Technology Transfer

All the preceding has dealt mostly with Japanese exports of producer goods to the USSR and with Soviet exports of raw materials and semi-manufactures to Japan. Although, in fact, nearly all the information available concerns this trade, there is sporadic mention of Soviet exports

20. Mathieson, *Japan's Role*, p. 213.

of finished goods to Japan and of advanced technology, specifically in the metallurgical industries. One example of Soviet exports of metallurgical technology to Japan was the sale to Japan by the Soviet patent agency, Licensintorg, of licenses for Soviet blast-furnace evaporative-cooling technology; 23 of the 40 blast furnaces in the world that have adopted this modern technology are located in Japan. In addition, in 1974 Licensintorg sold a new technology for the dry quenching of coke-oven output to a Japanese firm.

Problems in Soviet–Japanese Economic Relations

Soviet–Japanese economic relations are not without their problems. First of all there are the usual difficulties that arise when a capitalist market economy engages in trade with the Soviet Union. Japanese businessmen complain about long, capricious, and arbitrary negotiating tactics on the part of the Russians.[21] The Soviets complain of fluctuations in Japanese economic conditions, which lead to instability in Japanese purchases of certain Soviet goods, despite fluctuations in world economic conditions.[22]

Besides such common economic problems there are problems of a political nature. One such area of conflict in trade negotiations has been the issue of the South Kurile group of islands, to which both the Soviet Union and Japan stake territorial claims. The Japanese have often tried to enter this political consideration into the negotiations, in an attempt, perhaps, to link economic assistance and credits to a return of the islands to Japan. But efforts to use this as a bargaining lever have failed. The Soviet position is adamant on the matter:

> The ultra-right, ultra-leftist Maoist groups and double-dyed nationalist organizations have decided to place the main emphasis on the so-called territorial questions, under which pretext attempts are being made to take away from the Soviet Union the South Kurile group of islands, which were transferred to the USSR as a result of the military defeat of Japan in accordance with existing international agreements.[23]

Another source of political strain was the 1976 MIG-25 incident and the 1977 fisheries negotiations. What the Japanese considered to be Soviet bullying in both these events heightened Japanese concerns about the advisability of expanding economic relations with the Soviets and of placing too heavy a reliance on them for raw materials and energy supplies.

21. *Far Eastern Economic Review,* vol. 96, no. 22 (June 3, 1977), pp. 9–11.

22. For complaints of this nature, see V. N. Khlynov's review of "Yaponiya v sisteme mirovykh khozyaistvennykh svyazei," *Problemy Dal'nego Vostoka,* no. 11, (Nov. 1, 1971), pp. 188–90.

23. Ibid., Nov. 3, 1978, p. 46.

Soviet authorities address these political tensions, stress the benefits for Japan in expanded economic relations with the Soviet Union, and point out aspects of Japanese discriminatory behavior toward the Soviet Union. For example, in his article on the May 1977 Trade Agreement, Spandar'ian stated:

Of course, the tense atmosphere of Soviet-Japanese relations could not fail to affect our economic ties. It is common knowledge that the Soviet Foreign Trade Minister's visit to Japan was postponed and the agreement of trade turnover and payments for 1976–1980 was signed only in May 1977. The regular meetings of the Soviet-Japanese and the Japanese-Soviet committees on economic cooperation were also postponed. . . .

There is no doubt, for example, that the Soviet Union is capable of developing the richest oil fields in Tyumen', or building the Baikal-Amur Railway Line using its own efforts and resources. Those circles within Japan and outside it which for various reasons have prevented Japanese companies from cooperating on a compensation basis with Soviet organizations in carrying out these projects have damaged Japan's national interests, particularly in the context of the worsening energy, raw materials and general economic crisis in the capitalist world.

In spite of the fact that the attempts of anti-Soviet circles in Japan and their overseas instigators are being rebuffed by ever greater sections of the business, public and political circles in the country, Japan still lags behind other capitalist countries in certain major aspects of economic cooperation with the Soviet Union and this makes Japanese firms less competitive on the Soviet market.[24]

Soviet–Japanese economic-political relations have continued to deteriorate in the last few years, and we see no prospect that the trend will reverse in the near future. In this regard it is striking how inflexible and clumsy the Soviets have been in their dealings with the Japanese. Soviet leaders seem unwilling to make political concessions of any sort, and negotiations on some economic cooperation projects frequently stall over Soviet insistence on very favorable terms. As the quotation from Spandar'ian seems to suggest, it appears that, at least in the past, the Soviets have felt that Siberian resources provided a very strong basis for their negotiations with Japan, a country poorly endowed with natural resources. These Soviet perceptions of their own bargaining position with Japan were probably unrealistic even before Chinese–Japanese economic relations began to develop, and they certainly were unrealistic after those developments. But perceptions change slowly, especially with an aging leadership such as exists in the USSR, and improvements in

---

24. Spandar'ian, "Novyi vazhnyi etap . . ." ("A New Important Stage in the Development of Soviet–Japanese Trade," translation from English-language *Foreign Trade*, vol. 12 [Dec. 1977], pp. 18–19).

Soviet–Japanese economic and political relations will most likely not occur until after the succession in the USSR, if then.

THE USSR AND CHINA

In the 1950s Soviet economic assistance to China involved

one of the largest technology transfers in history. . . . From 1950 to 1959, the
Soviets delivered $1.35 billion worth of equipment and completed 130 projects,
including factories for trucks, machine tools, and generating equipment. In
addition, the Soviets provided massive technical aid in the form of blueprints
and technical information, some 10,000 Soviet technicians and advisers, and
training for 15,000 Chinese in the USSR. Soviet financial aid helped, although
only $430 million of the $1.4 billion in Soviet loans was specifically for economic
development. More important for Peking was the USSR's . . . willingness to accept large amounts of China's raw materials and consumer goods in payment for
Chinese imports.[25]

The abrupt termination of this Soviet economic assistance to China by
Khrushchev in 1960, in the wake of the burgeoning Sino–Soviet ideological and political conflict, brought this period to a sudden end. The
Chinese reacted with a sense of rage to the abrupt withdrawal of all
Soviet advisers and the termination of work on aid projects, leaving
many of them in midstream. Economic relations between the two nations
subsequently deteriorated. Annual trade agreements were suspended in
1967, and apparently all channels of economic cooperation were closed
from 1967 to 1969.[26] Economic relations reached a low point in 1969–
70, at the time of the border clashes on the Ussuri River. The volume of
Soviet–Chinese trade (measured in foreign trade rubles) in 1970 was less
than 3 percent of what it had been ten years earlier.

Trade between Russia and China began to grow again in the 1970s,
with the signing of a trade agreement in November 1970. By 1978
Soviet–Chinese trade turnover was eight times its 1970 level but still less
than one-quarter of the 1960 level. Despite the fact that trade with
Russia accounted for only about 2.5 percent of total Chinese trade turnover in 1977–78, Chinese trade with Russia is not inconsequential. The
Soviet Union is one of China's ten largest trading partners (sixth in 1976,
eighth in 1977), the leading supplier to China of such important items as
aircraft, electric power generating equipment, trucks, timber, and various spare parts, and China's third largest supplier of machinery and

25. R. E. Batsavage and J. L. Davis, "China's International Trade and Finance," in
Chinese Economy Post-Mao, Joint Economic Committee, Congress of the United States
(Washington, D.C.: Government Printing Office, 1978) (hereafter cited as *JEC-78*), p. 710.
26. L. A. Orleans, "Soviet Perceptions of China's Economic Development," in *JEC-78*, p.
133.

transportation equipment, accounting for 11 percent of total Chinese imports of this equipment. China, in turn, is a major supplier to Russia of lead, tungsten, some antimony, and fluorspar and could be its major supplier of tin if sales of this metal were resumed.[27]

Of perhaps more relevance to the issue of Russia's role in Asia than the direct economic relations between the USSR and China are the triangular (and multiangular) relations involving the USSR, China, and Japan. There are two major aspects of this relationship: first the competitiveness of China and Russia for Japanese investment and trade, and second the impact on Japan of the Sino–Soviet conflict.

In 1978 the post-Mao leaders of China embarked upon a massive program to acquire Western machinery and technology in an effort to quickly modernize the Chinese economy. Exuberantly pursuing this program, the Chinese bureaucracy began contacting Western businessmen, signing letters of intent, negotiating and signing contracts. The major objects of interest are iron and steel mills, coal mining equipment, offshore oil exploration equipment, petrochemical and synthetic fiber complexes, nonferrous metals plants, transport equipment, and entire communications systems. The dimensions of the proposed program appear awesome. The first reports were of active Chinese interest in about $40 billion worth of plant, equipment, and technology, with the actual signing of $7 billion worth of contracts by the beginning of 1979.[28] Estimates for the total purchases from the West in the eight-year program (1978–85) ranged between $120 billion and $230 billion.[29]

The Japanese were set to play a leading role in China's development program. The natural complementarities of the two economies were there as they were in the Soviet–Japanese relationship: Japanese equipment and technology for Chinese coal and oil. Japan is already China's largest trading partner, with a trade turnover in 1978 of $5.07 billion.[30] In February 1978 the two countries signed an eight-year trade agreement calling for a trade turnover of $20 billion and laying out a concrete purchasing schedule for the first five years, 1978–82. The bond between China and Japan was strengthened by their signing of a Treaty of Peace and Friendship in August 1978, which gave further impetus to their economic relations.

By the beginning of 1979 the Chinese leadership began to realize that it had been expanding its purchases abroad in an unrealistic way and it started to cut back. It suspended 29 contracts, worth $2.6 billion, signed

27. *China Business Review*, vol. 5, no. 3 (May–June 1978), pp. 21–24.

28. *China: Post-Mao Search for Civilian Industrial Technology* (Washington, D.C.: Central Intelligence Agency, 1979), p. iii.

29. *Economist*, vol. 270, no. 7068 (Feb. 17, 1979), p. 91.

30. *Japan Economic Yearbook, 1979–80* (Tokyo: Oriental Economist, 1980), p. 215.

with Japanese companies in late 1978, and it ordered a moratorium on major new contract signings. But fairly quickly, after it was able to put its foreign exchange position back on a more solid footing, it reinstated all but one of the contracts (the one still in doubt was for only $76 million out of the original $2.6 billion).[31] Economic discussions resumed, and at the end of the year China and Japan announced the signing of a low-interest loan agreement providing for Japanese aid of $1.5 billion over a five- to eight-year period. An initial loan of $200 million (in yen) was provided in 1980 to be used for a series of hydroelectric-power, railway, and harbor projects. These sums, to be provided on a government-to-government basis, are in addition to credits of $4 billion already furnished to China by Japanese banks.[32]

The economic relations between Japan and China are very similar in substance (i.e., credits for primary products) to those between Japan and the USSR. The two relationships are potentially competitive and there are signs that some Japanese business interests would prefer the Chinese connection to the Soviet one, but there are no signs yet that Japan is giving up one for the other. Action continues to move ahead on both fronts. The existence of the triangle is advantageous to the Japanese in that it puts them in a better economic bargaining position with each of the others.

The ASEAN nations are reportedly watching the expansion of Japanese–Chinese relations with mixed emotions. On the one hand they are concerned that increased Japanese aid and trade to China will mean less to them. But on the other hand they are not averse to the economic growth of China, because they see it as a protection against the domination of Asia by Japan. Indeed, the argument is made that they are also not opposed to the increased involvement of the Soviet Union in Asia for the same reasons.[33]

The second aspect of the triangular Soviet–Chinese–Japanese relationship concerns the impact of Sino–Soviet hostility on Japan. This shows up in the economic wooing of Japan by China to get Japan to agree to the anti-hegemonism clause in the Treaty of Peace and Friendship.[34] It also shows up in the increase of Soviet troops in fall 1979 on some of the South Kurile Islands as a reminder to Japan that better relations with China must mean worse relations with the Soviet Union.[35] And it has shown up in Chinese objections to some of the projects and

31. *China Business Review*, vol. 6, no. 5 (Sept.–Oct. 1979), pp. 58–60.

32. *New York Times*, Dec. 5, 6, and 9, 1979.

33. *Asia 1979 Yearbook* (Hong Kong: Far Eastern Economic Review, 1979), p. 21.

34. G. W. Choudhury, "New International Patterns in Asia," *Problems of Communism*, vol. 28, no. 2 (Mar.–Apr. 1979), p. 16.

35. *Economist*, vol. 273, no. 7101 (Oct. 6, 1979), p. 69.

proposed projects between Japan and the Soviet Union. The leading example of this is the strong Chinese objections that direct Japanese assistance in the construction of the BAM would strengthen both the economic and military position of the Soviet Union in the Far East. In response to these objections the Japanese withdrew from their direct involvement in the construction of the BAM.

THE USSR AND VIETNAM AND NORTH KOREA

Russia's economic relations with the other two communist countries in Asia—Vietnam and North Korea—are much different from its relations with China. In its economic relations with Vietnam and North Korea it appears to be pursuing a policy of courting and coercing each of them into a position of dependency. It seems to have been fairly successful with Vietnam but not (yet) so with North Korea.

Prior to 1975 Vietnam was able to get support and economic assistance from both the USSR and China without pledging allegiance to either. After 1975, with the reunification of the country accomplished and the United States out of the picture, the struggle between Russia and China for influence over Vietnam intensified. With their more advanced level of economic development the Soviets were at an advantage. They extended substantial economic assistance to Vietnam, giving it most-favored-nation status and credits with which to purchase machinery and equipment, oil, food, and raw materials, often at subsidized prices below world levels (and with oil, even below CMEA levels).[36]

Vietnam, however, appeared unwilling to become dependent on any one nation. It tried to establish relations with any nation that could help it rebuild its economy—Western nations, including the United States, and the ASEAN nations. It joined the International Monetary Fund, the World Bank, the UN, and the Asian Development Bank and enacted a very liberal code for foreign investment. It expanded its trade with noncommunist countries, which grew from 11 percent of its total trade in 1970–75 to 43 percent in 1977.[37] At one point in mid-1978 the Vietnamese reportedly made a private inquiry about the possibility of joining ASEAN.[38] But these attempts did not enable it to maintain its independence. By 1977 Vietnam's economy clearly was in deep trouble, especially in terms of food shortages. Its relations with Cambodia and China were deteriorating. And when its decision in March 1978 to fully nationalize the commercial sector in the South led to a mass exodus of

36. Theriot and Matheson, "Soviet Economic Relations," pp. 569, 575.
37. Ibid., pp. 570–71.
38. *Asia 1979 Yearbook*, pp. 316–23.

Chinese from Vietnam, a complete Sino–Vietnamese split resulted and China terminated its $300 million aid program.

In 1978 Vietnam made several moves that formally and completely allied it with the Soviet Union, the two most important being the announcement in June of full Vietnamese membership in CMEA and the signing of a twenty-five-year Soviet–Vietnamese Friendship and Cooperation Treaty in November of the same year. These moves were prompted in large part by Vietnam's inability to resolve successfully its domestic economic problems and by its inability to attract sufficient Western capital to make a substantial contribution to recovery. Membership in CMEA holds for Vietnam the promise that the CMEA members will carry through on all the projects abandoned by the Chinese, and the prospect that Eastern Europe will join in a strengthened Soviet effort to subsidize Vietnam directly through loans and aid and indirectly through trade at very advantageous prices. The Soviets probably required these public signs of allegiance as a quid pro quo for more substantial Soviet and East European aid. The Soviets get an Asian ally out of this, and from the economic point of view they can use Vietnam's formal CMEA membership to more effectively spread the costs of aid to Vietnam among all CMEA members. This is apparently the way Cuba's membership in CMEA has worked, and there seems little reason to believe that the Soviets will deal with Vietnam differently.[39]

Over the longer term economic relations with Vietnam may hold significant benefits for the USSR. Vietnam does have a good deal of relatively cheap skilled labor and moderately good infrastructure in the form of roads, harbor facilities, and so forth.[40] It also has several primary products, for example, rubber and especially oil, that the Soviets need. Now that the Soviets are growing cognizant of the full extent of their problem with energy, it is not at all out of the question that they will somehow try to obtain some of the oil in Vietnam's rich continental shelf. Indeed in July 1980 the Soviets and the Vietnamese signed an agreement on the exploration and extraction of oil and gas from the continental shelf.[41]

39. All the evidence that the USSR pressured Vietnam into joining CMEA and signing the friendship and cooperation treaty is circumstantial. For the most detailed case see ibid., pp. 321–22. A comparison of Vietnamese and Cuban membership in CMEA is given in Theriot and Matheson, "Soviet Economic Relations." For the status of that country in CMEA, see Edward A. Hewett, "Cuba's membership in the CMEA," in *Revolutionary Cuba in the World Arena*, ed. Martin Weinstein (Philadelphia: Institute for the Study of Human Issues, 1979), pp. 51–76.

40. For a discussion of this in the somewhat different, but related, context of Vietnam's prospects for attracting Western capital, see Alec Gordon, "Viet-Nam after April 1975," in *The Far East and Australasia* (London: Europe Publications, 1978), p. 1114.

41. Ngyen Khyu Mai, "Vsestoronnee sotrudnichestvo," *Ekonomicheskaya Gazeta*, no. 29 (July 1980), p. 19.

Soviet relations with North Korea are marked by the stubbornness and determination of the North Korean leader Kim Il Sung to maintain his independence from both Russia and China. Under the leadership of Kim, North Korea is a tough communist society that spends 20 percent of its GNP on defense (the highest share in the world except for Israel), maintains the fifth largest army in the world, and is struggling economically. It has steadfastly refused to join CMEA; about 40 percent of its trade is with noncommunist countries. Because of Kim's unwillingness to make a strong commitment to the Soviet Union, North Korea has been unable to attract Soviet economic or military aid in quantities sufficient to meet its needs.[42]

Despite Kim's policy of self-reliance North Korea inaugurated in 1972 a large-scale program of importing machinery from Western Europe and Japan on credit, to be repaid through increased exports to these suppliers. But the program was unsuccessful in stimulating sufficient exports to pay for the hard-currency debts incurred. Furthermore, the increase in OPEC oil prices, followed by the 1975 recession and the drop in metals prices (important exports for North Korea), combined to create a severe balance-of-payments crisis in North Korea. The Soviets were unwilling to give more credits to North Korea although they did agree to decrease interest payments and postpone principal payments on the $700 million that North Korea owed them. Soviet–North Korean trade from that point on was on a cash-only basis, and therefore turnover fell from $1.3 billion in 1974 to $0.3 billion in 1975. Because the Soviets would not do more than this, North Korea was forced to default on some of its $2.4 billion hard-currency debt that came due in 1975.[43]

The attitude of the Soviet Union toward North Korea appears now to be one of maintaining a foothold relationship, and no more, and waiting for North Korea's policies (or leaders) to change. The North Koreans have swung back and forth between the Soviet Union and China. At the end of the 1970s they were swinging in China's direction. But that may not last long. Certainly the current economic reformist and anti-Maoist policies of the present Chinese leaders do not give Kim Il Sung a secure feeling. This uneasy balance will probably last until the end of the Brezhnev era. The new post-Brezhnev leadership in the Kremlin might, however, decide to pursue a more vigorous policy, attempting to bring North Korea into CMEA and more under Soviet influence.

42. For a general discussion of the Korean economy, including recent developments in Korean–Soviet relations, see "Korea-North," *Asia 1979 Yearbook*, pp. 216–19. A useful overview of the history of Korean–Soviet relations is given in Donald S. Zagoria, "Korea's Future: Moscow's Perspective," *Asian Survey*, vol. 17, no. 11 (Nov. 1977), pp. 1103–12.

43. For a discussion of this, see T. M. Burley, "Economic Survey of North Korea," in *The Far East and Australasia*, pp. 619–623, and "Korea-North."

9

Prospects for Siberian Economic Development

ROBERT W. CAMPBELL

It is often suggested that there is an intimate relationship between Soviet policies and actions toward developing the economy of Siberia and the strategic and foreign policy role that the USSR will play in the affairs of the Pacific Basin. The general line of argument is that Siberia is one of the few remaining significant storehouses of energy resources and raw materials in a world hungering for those ingredients of growth and that there will be great economic temptation to develop them. It is further argued that the development of those resources is closely linked to foreign policy actions because they constitute a basis for expanded foreign trade with countries of the Pacific and because the developmental problems are so difficult that economic help and cooperation from other countries will be required to overcome them.

The purpose of this chapter is first to offer a brief survey of Soviet experience in trying to develop Siberia economically, and to place these efforts in the context of general Soviet economic policy. That will be followed by a survey of the current status of developmental policies in the area, illustrated heavily with two of the major current efforts, that is, energy production and the BAM. This will lay a foundation for then turning to the basic questions of current concern, that is, the degree to which Siberian development is a domestic affair versus an externally oriented program, and to what extent it can be handled by the Russians themselves without inviting outside help.

Before I go further, I should explain how I interpret the concept of *Siberia,* a term used in the literature with considerable variation in meaning. When the focus is interaction with the Pacific Basin the area intended by analysts is often what Paul Dibb calls "Pacific Siberia," that is, the regions the Russians call Eastern Siberia and the Far East. This concept excludes a large part of what Siberia means in most other discussions, that is, it excludes the region the Russians call Western Siberia, which is where much of the "Siberian resources" that motivate the concerns underlying this book are located. Once we admit Western Siberia into the discussion, we almost need to include Kazakhstan, the northern part of which in terms of resources and developmental problems has a

229

great deal in common with Western Siberia. Central Asia (the Uzbek, Tadzhik, Turkmen, and Kirgiz SSRs) also has some features in common with "Siberia" (especially in terms of its mineral wealth) and a competitive/complementary relationship with Siberia in relation to development prospects. Thus, for certain purposes it will be appropriate to talk about all the area east of the Ural Mountains. Once we have enlarged the geographic scope in this way to embrace the whole area that shares common problems in development and in resources, we have also introduced a great deal of heterogeneity. Nevertheless, that seems fully appropriate because I consider that one of my major tasks is to deal with the difficulties this heterogeneity poses for trying to give simple answers to how the issues of Siberian economic development are related to Soviet policy in the Pacific Basin. To avoid ambiguity in what follows I will use standard Soviet regional terminology, in which the East as a whole is made up of Siberia, East and West, the Far East, Kazakhstan, and Central Asia.

PAST POLICY AND EXPERIENCE

Soviet doctrine on regional development has always proceeded from the basic premise that economic development in the czarist period was uneven and that socialist planning would raise the economic level of the backward, colonial, peripheral areas up to that of the European areas, where the industrialization of the Russian empire began.

This effort would include among other areas the Muslim lands that became the Central Asian republics and Kazakhstan and Siberia. In practice, of course, the Soviet planners come up against the dilemma that the best way to get rapid growth of GNP as a whole is to concentrate development efforts in the areas already developed because that is where the availability of skilled labor, infrastructure, markets, and economies of scale through agglomeration maximize the payoff to additional resources. The backward areas usually return smaller increments of output to any given amount of investment.

These underdeveloped areas were usually underdeveloped because of discouraging objective factors, and this is certainly true for the areas east of the Ural region. The area as a whole was held back by its remoteness from the more populous and developed areas west of the Ural Mountains and the associated transport barrier to integration. Much of the area is simply not attractive for economic activity, because it is located too far north, is characterized by mountainous terrain, is climatically inhospitable, and has other defects. In particular, agricultural resources are poor, making it difficult to support a large population with local food production. But the size of the area creates many exceptions to these generalizations.

The northern parts display in exaggerated form the resource problems we have described, but those problems are much more manageable as we look at more southerly parts of the territory. The problem of remoteness from the more developed regions of the country is much greater for Eastern Siberia and the Far East than it is for Western Siberia, Kazakhstan, and Central Asia. The point about population is really only applicable to the Siberias and the Far East. Central Asia and, to a somewhat smaller degree, Kazakhstan have adequate and indeed rapidly growing population resources although these are not always suitable for purposes of economic development.

In any case, despite their announced intentions to bring these areas up to a development level comparable to that of the European USSR and despite significant successes in developing these areas, the Soviet planners have succeeded but slightly in altering the basic proportions between economic activity in the East and in the rest of the country.

Consider first the input side. The priority and emphasis given to the East are reflected in the regional allocation of investment shown in table 9.1. The share of Siberia, Kazakhstan, and Central Asia in total investment was stable until just before World War II, when the Russians began to prepare for war by accelerated investment in the East. Then during the war, evacuation of plants from the West led to a sharp shift in investment to the East. After the war, however, there was a sharp rever-

Table 9.1. Share of Siberia and the East in Total Investment (Percent)

	All eastern regions	Trans-Ural RSFSR only
First Five-Year Plan (FYP) (1928–32)	21.4	13.4
Second FYP (1933–37)	20.5	13.3
Third FYP (1938–41)	22.4	15.1
War years (1941–45)	26.7	18.0
Fourth FYP (1946–50)	21.4	13.5
Fifth FYP (1951–55)	24.2	15.6
Seven-Year Plan (1959–65)	28.7	16.3
Eighth FYP (1966–70)	29.8	16.3
Ninth FYP (1971–75)	28.8	16.1

Sources: Calculated from data in standard Soviet handbooks. These investment data are presented in a variety of definitions and price bases, but with care it is possible to maintain comparability for the various regions in any given period.

sal as investment was devoted to rebuilding the war-damaged European areas. There has since been a slow upward movement but remarkably little change in the two decades since 1959. The work force also has not grown any faster in the East than in the West of the country, and its share also reflects the wartime shock, the postwar lag, then again a slight relative growth in the two decades since 1960.

Similarly, on the output side, except for the war period, the East has not shown any favorable differential in growth. During the war both Siberias and the Far East experienced faster industrial growth than the rest of the USSR, and this was especially true of Western Siberia, where output rose 2.7 times compared to an actual decline for the USSR as a whole (see table 9.2). Since 1945, however, only Eastern Siberia has managed to maintain a growth of industry more or less equal to that for the country as a whole (mostly as a result of a big spurt at the end of the 1950s), and the other two regions have fallen well behind—between 1945 and 1975 their rates of industrial growth were about 8.5 percent compared to 10.2 percent claimed for the USSR as a whole. Kazakhstan also got a special boost from the evacuation eastward during World War II and its industry has managed to keep growing at about the all-Union rate. The other Central Asian republics (except for tiny Kirgiz), however, have seen an erosion of their relative standing in industrial output.

To keep the current level of development of these regions in perspective, remember that in 1970 Western Siberia accounted for 5.1 percent of total industrial production in the USSR, Eastern Siberia for 3.2 percent, and the Far East for 2.7 percent.[1] Central Asia and Kazakhstan accounted for 7.2 percent.[2]

For the other major component of total output—agriculture—it is more difficult to document just what happened to the Eastern RSFSR's share. Looking at the handbooks, one gets the impression that the Soviet statistical office considers agricultural output statistics for regions within the RSFSR more or less worthless before about 1958. It will be remembered that under Stalin agricultural statistics became hopelessly out of touch with reality, and most official data were subsequently totally redone. It was apparently not considered worth the effort to do so on a regional basis for the early postwar years. In any case revised data for these years have never been published. But if we judge by sown area and by livestock numbers, it appears that Siberia and the Far East did manage an increase in their share of crop output in the 1950s, especially as a

---

1. These figures are based on data in Siberian Division, Academy of Sciences of the USSR (SO AN SSSR), B. P. Orlov, ed., *Ekonomicheskie problemy razvitiya Sibiri* (Novosibirsk: Nauka, 1974), pp. 36–40.

2. S. I. Divilov, *Chislennost' i struktura zanyatykh v narodnom khozyaistve* (Moscow: Ekonomika, 1976), p. 77.

Table 9.2. Soviet Indexes of Industrial Output

	1940	1945	1950	1960	1970	1975
All USSR	58	53	100	304	691	988
West Siberia	32	86	100	283	640	971
East Siberia	51	62	100	294	752	1,130
Far East	61	70	100	244	578	811
Kazakhstan	43	59	100	316	807	1,146
Uzbek SSR	55	58	100	230	466	704
Tadzhik SSR	66	49	100	285	658	914
Kirgiz SSR	47	57	100	288	888	1,350
Turkmen SSR	70	61	100	235	472	727

Sources: Standard statistical handbooks.

result of the Virgin Lands program in Western Siberia. However, since 1960 (the period for which more or less official data on the gross output of agriculture are available in the standard statistical handbooks) the share of these three regions in all-Union gross agricultural output has stayed essentially constant at 9–10 percent. But there is an imbalance in the region. If we consider the area combining the Eastern RSFSR and Kazakhstan (the northern part of Kazakhstan is essentially integrated with Western Siberia), we find that Kazakhstan and Western Siberia today have about 65 percent of the population in the area, but 75 percent of the gross value of agricultural output.[3]

The Central Asian areas have enjoyed a favorable growth differential in agriculture and have increased their share in all-Union gross agricultural output from about 8.3 percent in 1950 to almost 15 percent in 1976.

There are two significant implications in this discussion. First, economic development in the East has been very expensive in terms of capital investment. It is a region that soaks up investment resources far in excess of its proportion of population, labor force, industrial output, and agricultural output while giving a barely perceptible differential in overall growth performance. This has always been the basic issue in contention between the "Siberians," who advocate special efforts to develop Siberia, and the "Europeans."

By standard Soviet calculations most investments in Siberia appear to be uneconomic compared to competing alternatives in the European part of the country. To soften this reality somewhat the Gosplan and

3. Central Statistical Bureau of the USSR (TsSU SSSR), *Narodnoe khozyaistvo SSSR v 1975* (Moscow: Statistika, 1976), p. 336.

Gosstroy officially sanction a lower standard rate of return to be used in evaluating projects in many areas of Siberia and the Far East.[4]

Second, there seem to be very powerful inertial mechanisms at work that preclude any strong differential emphasis on developing Siberia or the East. The only thing that has ever overcome this inertia was the shock of World War II, and that was followed by a relapse. This seems to remain true even today. One might have expected the BAM and the huge effort to develop Siberian oil and gas to cause a rise in the East's share of investment and to induce a spurt in its industrial development above that of the rest of the country, but there are as yet no such changes detectable in the standard aggregate measures found in the handbooks. It is to an examination of the obstacles and difficulties that stand in the way of accelerated Siberian development that we now turn.

OBSTACLES TO DEVELOPMENT

Predictions concerning the great growth potential of Siberia, whether made by the "Siberians" in the context of Soviet regional planning debates, by Soviet spokesmen holding out the temptation of trade increases to Pacific Basin nations, or by foreign policy analysts forecasting the role of the Soviet Union in Asia, are based on the extraordinary mineral, energy, and timber resources of the area. Those resources are indeed impressive but they have often been described elsewhere and I do not need to elaborate on them here. With respect to other resources, however, the East is rather *badly* served, and this is both the explanation for the past failure of the East to grow more rapidly than the rest of the country and one of the major considerations that will determine whether the great potential predicted by some analysts for the East will be realized. First, the area is for the most part poorly supplied with human resources. Second, the infrastructural base of the region is weak: it lacks transportation facilities, housing and urban amenities, power supplies, and other kinds of supporting industries and inputs. Third, it has a poor resource base for agriculture. There are some exceptions but huge portions of the area can never be agriculturally productive because of short growing season, inadequate or excessive rainfall, deficiencies of soil and terrain, and so on. The principal areas suitable for reasonable agricultural operations are in Western Siberia and Northern Kazakhstan but even there the limited prospects for significant expansion were demonstrated by the experience of the Virgin Lands program. This great expansion of sown acreage in the late 1950s moved the margin of cultivation beyond what was feasible in this semiarid area, and much of that

4. "Kompleksnoe razvitie proizvoditel'nykh sil Zapadnoi Sibiri v tsentre vnimaniya uchenykh i prakticheskikh rabotnikov," *Planovoe Khozyaistvo*, no. 9 (1978), p. 102.

land has dropped back out of cultivation. All these debilities are inter-connected and mutually reinforcing. Low population densities and low densities of economic activity mean that infrastructural costs per unit of output must be high, and this disadvantage is further exacerbated by the high unit cost of constructing any kind of infrastructural facilities. On the other hand it is difficult to attract people because of the primitive character and inadequate provision of such infrastructural elements as housing, urban services, and commercial and cultural facilities. The pov-erty and localized nature of agricultural resources interfere with the provision of an adequate and a varied food supply, and this is another factor that makes it difficult to attract labor. The enticement of signifi-cant wage differentials for moving into the areas is little compensation if money wages cannot be turned into real income.

The Population Problem

These problems find a kind of summary expression in the difficulty of expanding the labor force in the area. The population and labor force situation vary somewhat among the different subregions of the East. What was said above applies mainly to the two Siberias and the Far East. The four republics of Central Asia proper have rapid rates of popula-tion growth and plenty of population resources to support economic development. Kazakhstan is more difficult to characterize because its northern areas have more in common with Western Siberia than with its southern part, where conditions are similar to those in Central Asia. Hence we need to talk about these areas separately.

1. Siberia and the Far East

If the Eastern RSFSR is to grow faster than the national economy as a whole, it must succeed in attracting population and labor force differen-tially. In this region death and birth rates follow fairly closely those in the rest of the USSR, so that its population can grow faster than the all-Union rate only by migration into the area. Unfortunately, it seems virtually impossible to achieve any significant net inflow of population. In the intercensal period 1959–70 there was a net *outmigration* of about 783,000 persons. However, individual regions had different experi-ences; West and East Siberia lost population by emigration, the Far East gained.[5] The *urban* population of the three regions taken together grew by much more than the natural increase, implying very large rural–urban migration. This has significant implications for the agricultural problem. One of the great obstacles to growth in the area is that it is not

5. M. V. Kurman, *Aktual'nye voprosy demografii* (Moscow: Statistika, 1976), p. 134.

self-sufficient with respect to food. Its agricultural base needs to be expanded but this is difficult to achieve when rural areas are losing population at a rapid rate.

We can get a clearer idea of these patterns from looking at some more complete data for 1973.[6] During 1973 the growth of the population by natural increase was 248,000, but the population total grew by 296 persons over the year, implying net immigration of about 48,000 persons. Net migration into *urban* places, however, was almost 268,000, implying that the rural population declined by about 220,000 persons. Other data in the volume corroborate the presumptions above as to interregional migration within the areas. Urban places in Western Siberia gained 48,000 persons from Eastern Siberia and the Far East but lost 51,000 to urban areas in those regions. Eastern Siberia lost 56,000 and gained 51,000. The net gainer was the Far East, gaining 47,000 and losing only 40,000. (These data refer only to migrants arriving in urban places, but given the strong rural–urban cast to the migration movement as a whole, it seems unlikely that there was enough interregional rural–rural or urban–rural movement to affect the pattern of regional flows shown by migrants into urban areas.) The necessary data for similar calculations for the period since 1973 are unavailable but some extrapolations and use of the 1979 census totals suggest that the USSR has been able to get significant migration into the area since 1975 and most notably has reversed the emigration flow from Western Siberia. If we project the populations of the three regions at the rates of natural increase exhibited in 1973 and compare these with the actual growth in each region, the implication is that between January 1, 1974, and January 1, 1979, Western Siberia received a migration of about 460,000 people, East Siberia may have lost as many as 70,000, and the Far East received almost 100,000.[7]

2. Kazakhstan

It is very difficult to estimate migration in northern Kazakhstan because most available information relates only to the Kazakh SSR as a whole. But we know that during the 1959–70 period about 735,000 persons, net, migrated into the area.[8] Most of this immigration must have been to the northern areas in connection with both the Virgin Lands program and the growth of the industrial labor force.

6. TsSU SSSR, *Naselenie SSSR, 1973* (Moscow: Statistika, 1975), pp. 16–19.

7. These estimates are based on ibid. and the preliminary census figures for population by oblast reported in *Ekonomicheskaya Gazeta*, no. 18 (1979), pp. 15–16.

8. Kurman, *Aktual'nye Voprosy demografii*, p. 135.

3. Central Asia

As already mentioned, Central Asia has a quickly growing population. Between 1959 and 1970 this area added about 9 million people, compared to the 2.8 million people added in Siberia and the Far East. From 1970 to 1979 it added another 7.4 million, compared to 2.9 million in Siberia and the Far East. Contrary to what is often suggested, the area seems to be fairly successfully absorbing what has usually been thought of as surplus labor. In 1959–70 the growth rate of people of working age at 2.0 percent per year fell considerably behind the growth of the state labor force at 5.96 percent per year during this period. But given that in 1970 the state labor force still accounted for only 53 percent of the working age population in Central Asia, there no doubt remains a large population "surplus" that finds it difficult to find adequate employment opportunities.

It might seem that the solution to the population problem of the rest of Eastern RSFSR would be to move people out of Central Asia to the areas of population deficit. Unfortunately, these people have strong ethnic identification, are very unwilling to migrate, even from rural areas to the cities in their own republics, and are but little interested in acquiring the skills and education needed (including the Russian language) for them to provide the labor needed to sustain growth in Siberia. It appears that people from this Soviet variant of the sunbelt do not like the harsh climatic conditions of Siberia and the Far East any more than do citizens of the European USSR.

Within Kazakhstan there seems to be very little migration from the rural areas or from the southern areas of the republic into the largely Russian and urban industrial areas of the north. A look at ethnic changes in the intercensal period shows that most of the population growth in the urban areas of the north was made up of peoples other than Kazakhs or Central Asians. The total growth of the urban population in the northern tier of oblasts in the period was 1,354,000 persons, 80 percent of whom were accounted for by the increase in persons who identified themselves as belonging to one of the European nationalities. (In fact this is probably an underestimate because not all the Europeans are enumerated. Especially important is the fact that Germans were treated as nonpersons in the 1959 census, so that we cannot tell what contribution they made to the growth of the urban population.)

Similarly, there is very little migration of Central Asian ethnics into the Siberian areas. With the exception of Kazakhs in some regions there are too few of the Central Asian nationalities to have merited separate listing in the nationality tables of either the 1959 or 1970 census reports, and so we cannot tell how much their numbers have increased. But if we look at the migration data in the 1973 handbook or in the 1970 census, it seems that there was very little migration of Central Asian ethnics into the two Siberias and the Far East. Of the total of 1,631,000 persons who moved into urban places in the three-region area in 1973, only 71,000 came from Central Asia and Kazakhstan, and 40,000 of those were from Kazakhstan, presumably mostly from its northern tier of oblasts which are essentially an extension of Western Siberia. These numbers are small enough that most of those who move from those areas are more likely to be Europeans than members of the Central Asian nationalities.

In short, although the manpower pool available in the East as a whole is growing rapidly, the increments are in the wrong place to meet the needs of development in the Eastern RSFSR and Northern Kazakhstan and there is little prospect of persuading the Central Asian surplus to migrate. And this area of growing manpower supplies competes with Siberia, the Far East, and Northern Kazakhstan for the investment funds needed for development. Note in table 9.1 that while there was a rise in the East's share of all USSR investment after the Fifth Five-Year Plan, all the increment was accounted for by Central Asia and Kazakhstan.

THE PROBLEM OF INTEGRATED REGIONAL DEVELOPMENT

A second important obstacle to the development of the isolated regions of the East is the weakness of the Soviet economic system in generating development integrated at the regional level. From the perspective of a "pioneer" region, as the Russians characterize much of the Siberian area, there is an intricate problem of coordinating the various interdependent activities both sequentially in opening it up and in terms of mutual interdependence once production facilities have been built. Provision of transport is necessary before extensive construction can begin. Workers cannot be attracted without building housing and urban service facilities. Development projects such as creation of a gas province, a steel mill, or a paper processing complex involve large masses of construction materials and equipment that must be assembled, warehoused, repaired, and serviced, requiring an elaborate structure of supply and service bases. Once facilities are in production there are heavy transport requirements to move the outputs out and the inputs in for what are usually isolated facilities. If there is an attempt to create more than isolated lines of production, complexes of interrelated plants and branches need to be brought into production more or less simultaneously, involving both forward and backward linkages. Because it is expensive to bring in supporting inputs, industries to produce such inputs for the big projects ought to be developed at the same time. In the other direction, because the demand for energy, steel, minerals, and other Siberian-produced resources is now mostly in the west, there is a need to create downstream users locally to save transport costs.

Unfortunately, however, the Soviet administrative structure does not seem to lend itself very well to interbranch coordination at the territorial level. It is strongly branch oriented and centralized in its administrative structure, and decisions about all these interrelated activities tend to be made from separate ministerial headquarters in Moscow. The perspective of these bodies is not much oriented toward coordination with other branches generally, let alone on a regional level. The ministry responsible for building an individual element in a regional development project—cement plants, power stations, chemical plants, or whatever—may find it expedient to focus its energies and resources on a higher priority task elsewhere, leaving other elements of the project without customers or without crucial inputs. Huge stocks of equipment are amassed but are of little use because the supporting repair and service facilities are not provided at the proper time or because no provision is made for spare parts and fuel to operate them. A notorious example in Siberian development was the creation of very large and expensive hydropower capacities that stood idle because the plants that were intended to use their output were not built or because the transmission lines that would have taken their power to centers of existing demand did not get built.[9]

As one element in the set of reform measures introduced in July 1979, the Gosplan has been directed to examine the plans and their fulfillment for the territorial complexes around which Siberian development is now to be organized.[10] As the decree makes clear, Gosplan in the past followed the development of individual units of the complexes only in the context of separate ministerial plans. It is probably unrealistic to expect that the new decree will have much effect.

In addition to the branch bias that comes out of the basic Soviet administrative structure, responsibility is also split between levels, with little provision for coordinating the financing, the timing, and the scale of locally provided facilities (especially housing and such urban services as food supply, health care, and eating establishments) with the needs of the central development projects that depend on these related activities. The administrative structure lacks territorial nodes where responsibility and authority for the overall development of a region could coalesce. Even where there are regional bodies, they suffer from a double weakness: their territorial jurisdiction is not coincident with the process they

9. This seemed to be happening all over again with the Zeya hydropower station (see *Pravda*, Jan. 28, 1979, p. 3).

10. Ibid., July 29, 1979, p. 2.

are trying to cope with, and in general they lack political clout either to push or to control development activities in their territory. Some of the most persuasive illustrations of these problems come from the experience of developing the oil and gas resources of Western Siberia. There is an endless flow of stories in the Soviet press about the absence of any comprehensive or balanced approach to growth in this area. Oil and gas wells stand idle because there are no lines to gather and transport their output. Associated gas is flared because the plants to process it are not being built along with the oil fields. Pipelines cannot operate at capacity because the compressors and gas cleaning equipment that are needed for them do not get produced and delivered. Housing, power, and transport are never provided soon enough and these bottlenecks throttle the attainment of the other targets. Each separate administrative body, if it is to achieve its goals, must provide its own infrastructure at the cost of great duplication, underutilization, and uneconomic operation of warehouse, supply, and service facilities. For an especially revealing and concentrated dose of examples see the reports from a conference held in Tyumen in 1978 aimed at airing and trying to find solutions for some of these problems.[11]

These problems of coordination appear in any kind of pioneering regional development effort (the Alaska pipeline is an example from U.S. experience), but one irony of the Soviet case is that a planned economy supposedly uniquely designed to ensure thorough execution and full coordination in advance seems in practice much less able to handle this problem than Western economies because of its structure. This makes development in these pioneer regions expensive, slower than it ought to be, and a very great obstacle to solving the problem of attracting population discussed earlier.

ALTERNATIVE DEVELOPMENT PATTERNS FOR THE EAST

Against this background, how should we think about the potential for Siberia to develop into a powerful force in the economic life of the Pacific Basin countries? Perhaps the easiest way to think about the issues involved is to set up a framework of three possible extreme development patterns for Siberia. (1) One would be expansion along autonomous regional lines. The Siberian economy would grow from its own resources in an integrated way. Increases in energy output would cover the growing needs of energy-using industries such as chemicals, aluminum, and others, and their outputs would be consumed in the developing machinery industries

11. "Kompleksnoe razvitie," in *Planovoe Khozyaistvo*, no. 9 (1978), pp. 97–114, and "Osnovnye problemy kompleksnogo razvitiya Zapadnoi Sibiri," in *Voprosy ekonomiki*, no. 8 (1978), pp. 15–37.

(which would provide the investment goods required for investment programs), in the fertilizer industries, and so on. The fertilizer would be used to help expand agricultural output, which would grow fast enough to provide raw materials for light industry and feed the growing population, which would be supplying the labor force to make it all happen.

A totally different approach would be to direct development along highly specialized lines and then engage in extensive trade with other regions. Given the nature of Siberia's resources, it might focus on the production of minerals, energy, and timber and on the industries closely related to these branches, exchanging the outputs with other regions for products it could not produce so easily. This specialization pattern could be effected along two quite different lines, to make up the total package of three possible patterns. (2) One would be to choose as the trading partner other regions of the USSR. (3) The other would be to conduct this trade with the world outside the USSR as the trading partner.

In each of these strategies the relationship with the outside could be looked at in terms not only of goods but also in terms of investment, population, and technology. That is, the region would have this three-way choice separately on the issues of whether or from what region to accept an inflow of labor, a net inflow of goods to permit its capital stock to grow faster than its own savings, or a net inflow of technical skills to contribute to growth by raising productivity.

None of these alternatives is likely to be realized in pure form. It is uneconomic for any nation, let alone a single region, to be completely autonomous, so that there is always some specialization and trade. And as for the choice of trading partner under a specialization strategy, there is no reason that trade must be exclusively domestic or with foreign nations. The usual outcome would be some kind of split between the two. Moreover, in this split there is no requirement for bilateral balancing. Siberia could export only to other regions of the USSR while obtaining all its imports from outside the country, with exports from the other parts of the USSR to the world market paying for the imports to Siberia. But by envisaging these polar strategies our attention may be usefully directed to the questions we want to ask.

On the specialization/autonomy issue, Siberia seems to have leaned heavily toward the specialization pole. This point is generally accepted by students of the matter and I confine myself here to only a few examples.[12]

First, the structure of industrial output is quite different from that of

12. Excellent description and interpretation of this reality are found in the work of SO AN SSSR. Two of their volumes that not only document this point but also constitute extremely useful surveys of the status of the Siberian economy and the issues involved in its further development are Orlov, ed., *Ekonomicheskie problemy,* and M. K. Bandman, ed., *Razvitie narodnogo khozyaistva Sibiri* (Novosibirsk: Nauka, 1978).

the rest of the country as shown in table 9.3. Note the heavy emphasis on
the energy industries, which would be still greater if we were looking at
1978 and oil and gas were included.[13] There is also strong specialization
in timber and wood processing. The branches that are seriously underdeveloped in the area are the consumer goods industries (light industry
and food processing), which means these goods must be imported to
maintain the population. The apparent exception (the great importance
of the food-processing industry in the output of the Far East region)
reflects the predominant position of the fishing industry (accounting for
20% of the Far East's total industrial output), and most of the output of
that industry is exported from the region. Western Siberia is strongly
specialized in machinery, coal, and timber, and the chemical industries
associated with the last two, and very high fractions of the output of
these industries are exported. The heavy concentration on machinery is
a legacy of the wartime evacuation from the western USSR. This industry still serves national markets and is poorly adapted to local needs. As
one author says: "The mix of machines and equipment produced does
not correspond to the profile of the regional economy . . . only 26.5
percent of the output of the machine-building industry is used within
the eastern zone, and almost three-fourths of it is exported. . . . On the
other hand because of its narrow specialization the flow of machinery
and equipment into Siberia from the western regions grows steadily."[14]
Similar assertions are often made about the product mix of the Siberian
steel industry.

Such data as are available on commodity flows in and out of Siberia
and the Far East confirm this outward orientation. In 1970 Western
Siberia exported 62.28 million tons of coal and coke, 16.75 million tons
of petroleum and petroleum products,[15] and 8.66 million tons of timber
products. Much of the rest of its total exports of 107.45 million tons
must have been ferrous metals, machinery, and grain. Other very large
outshipments were 10.51 million tons of ores and concentrates and 25.3
million tons of timber and products from Eastern Siberia. Eastern Siberia had to import 5.7 million tons of petroleum and products, and the
Far East 10.32 million tons. Almost all these shipments moved by rail,
with only small amounts of river (and in the case of the Far East, ocean)
shipments.

13. By 1975 the share of electric power and fuel in the industrial output of Siberia had
risen from the 13.5–14% shown here for 1970 to 19.2% (T. B. Baranov, "Osnovnye
pokazateli razvitiya promyshlennosti Sibiri v sedmoi–devyatoi pyatiletkakh," *Izvestiya SO
AN SSSR, Seriya obshchestvennykh nauk,* no. 1 [1979], p. 32).

14. Bandman, ed., *Razvitiya narodnogo khozyaistva Sibiri,* pp. 215–16.

15. This does not include any pipeline shipments, because it is one of the peculiarities of
Soviet statistical practice to exclude pipeline shipments from most transportation statistics.

Table 9.3. Structure of Gross Output of Industry, 1970 (Percent of total)

	West Siberia	East Siberia	Far East	All USSR
Ferrous metallurgy	7.1	1.1	1.1	6.6
Nonferrous metallurgy	2.5	14.9	9.4	na[a]
Coal	10.2	5.5	4.2	1.7
Electric power	3.3	8.5	2.3	2.9
Machine building and metalworking	26.2	15.0	20.0	23.0
Chemicals and petrochemicals	8.1	4.5	1.1	6.0
Lumber and wood processing	5.3	15.0	10.5	5.2
Construction materials	3.6	5.6	7.0	4.1
Light industry	9.8	14.2	5.7	17.0
Food processing	18.0	14.7	34.4	21.2

Source: SO AN SSSR, B. P. Orlov, ed., *Ekonomicheskie problemy razvitiya Sibiri* (Novosibirsk: Nauka, 1974), p. 38.
[a]Not applicable.

It is true that there is some reluctance to continue to develop Siberia as a staple-export region, and a hope for more integrated development. As one author says:

The tasks of further development of the Soviet economy require a substantial change of territorial proportions in production. Otherwise beyond 1980 there will be a sharp growth in the socially necessary expenditures for the transport of raw materials, energy and semifinished goods from the East to the West, and of finished production for productive and personal use in the reverse direction.[16]

But I do not see how the planners can evade the forces that have induced this specialized role for Siberia and the Far East. The existing pattern is easily explainable by the fact that the East does have a distinctive resource base and distinctive scarcity relationships. Most of its industrial specialization is based on its abundant mineral, timber, and energy wealth, with some anomalies inherited from the exigencies of wartime relocation. It is short on population so that conditions are discouraging for labor-intensive lines of production. Its agricultural resources, especially in the eastern regions, are extremely poor, so that it cannot feed itself, and this validates and perpetuates the weakness in population resources. These peculiarities of resource mix constitute long-range, stable, economic forces that are not likely to be easily changed or evaded.

Western skepticism about the prospects for integrated development in the East is summed up by one author as follows:

16. "Osnovnye problemy," *Voprosy ekonomiki,* no. 8 (1978), p. 24.

Unless Siberia . . . can resolve its chronic shortages of labor and moderate its seemingly insatiable demands for investment capital, it appears to be destined to remain a highly specialized exporter of energy and other forms of natural wealth with an industrial structure dominated by the early stages of the production process.[17]

Soviet planners are apparently coming more and more to share this view. In today's discussions advocating an attempt to shift from isolated projects to the creation of territorial production complexes, there is a realization that it is undesirable to try to develop fully rounded integrated regional economies. There is fairly widely accepted acknowledgment that these territorial production agglomerations will be "truncated" complexes combining only a relatively few branches of production.

One observer has commented that a review of the regional development ideas implicit in successive five-year plans shows that behind the current one there seems to be "a growing commitment to specialized (as opposed to balanced) development in remote and environmentally harsh areas . . . [and] . . . a growing acceptance of a classic core-periphery relationship between the European part of the country and Siberia."[18]

Because Siberia seems forever committed to a specialized role based on its natural resources, the question that arises from our earlier characterizations of the possible development patterns is how Siberia is likely to divide its trade and other external connections between the rest of the USSR and countries outside the USSR. That is a very big question, of course, but we can approach it by looking at a couple of illustrative examples and issues.

SIBERIAN ENERGY RESOURCES

One good way to pursue the question of whether Siberian outputs are best traded to the rest of the USSR or to countries outside the USSR is to ask how badly they are needed for internal use in the USSR. To answer this question comprehensively is an undertaking far beyond the author's capacities. Indeed the Association of American Geographers is spending several hundred thousand dollars to examine the subject for only a few commodities. But one can attain a good perspective on this trade question and can establish a framework for thinking about it by considering Siberian energy, especially oil and gas. Quantitatively this case over-

17. Robert Taaffe, "Soviet Regional Development," in Stephen Cohen, Alexander Rabinowitch, and Robert Sharlet, eds., *The Soviet Union Since Stalin* (Bloomington: Indiana University Press, 1980), pp. 172–73.

18. Robert Jensen, "Soviet Regional Development Policy and the Tenth Five Year Plan," *Soviet Geography: Review and Translation*, vol. 19 (Mar. 1978), p. 198.

shadows all the others in terms of its drain on investment outlays in the East, in terms of the value of Siberian oil and gas relative to other natural wealth in Siberia, and in terms of the contribution that energy resources are making or could make to exports. Soviet energy exports in 1976 accounted for about 34 percent of the value of all exports and probably more than half all hard currency earnings.

It is true that there are large energy resources in the East, especially in Siberia. Eighty-two percent of the total hydroelectric potential of the USSR is east of the Urals (66% without Kazakhstan and Central Asia). These areas account for an even higher share of the *undeveloped* potential.[19] The fullest and most authoritative survey of coal resources to date shows that 75 percent of reserves in the A + B + C_1 class and as much as 93 percent of the geological reserves are in the East.[20] These are scattered all over the region, but worth special note in connection with export questions are the coking coals in Southern Yakutia in the Far East. The coking coals of Western Siberia and the low quality, but cheaply mined, lignites of the Kansk–Achinsk Basin (which is mostly in Western Siberia with a small spillover into Eastern Siberia) are most likely only of domestic significance. In the case of gas reserves, 81 percent of the reserves in the A + B + C_1 categories are east of the Urals.[21] The preponderance of this huge total for gas (several times the proved reserves of the United States) is in the giant fields of the northern areas of Tyumen oblast, but there are also significant amounts scattered across the map to the east as well—in Tomsk and Irkutsk oblasts, Krasnoyarsk *krai,* and the Yakutsk ASSR. Although the Soviet Union does not publish reserve information for oil, oil reserves are similarly lopsided in their regional distribution, with the East being the area where most additional oil is likely to be found.

These huge energy resources are often cited as the basis for the expectation that it will be possible to develop Siberia along the lines of export-led growth into a significant element in the economy of the Pacific Basin. In my opinion, however, this outcome is highly improbable.

First, the production potential for oil and gas is going to be committed almost exclusively to the domestic needs of the USSR itself and to exports to areas other than the Pacific Basin. The Soviet Union is the second largest consumer of energy in the world after the United States. As in the United States, economic growth in the USSR has been paral-

19. A. M. Nekrasov and M. G. Pervukhin, eds., *Energetika SSSR v 1976–1980 godakh* (Moscow: Energiya, 1977), p. 129.

20. N. V. Mel'nikov, ed., *Toplivno-energeticheskie resursy* (Moscow: Nauka, 1968), pp. 64–65.

21. A. D. Brents et al., *Ekonomika gazodobyvayushchei promyshlennosti* (Moscow: Nedra, 1975), p. 25.

leled by a rapid expansion of energy production. The USSR has energy
resources in sufficient abundance that it has been able to expand energy
output not only to meet its own growing energy needs but also to expand
energy exports. From being a net energy importer in the 1950s the
USSR has become a significant energy exporter, releasing about one-
fourth of its oil production and a significant amount of coal and gas. It
has plans to increase rapidly the export of gas and nuclear-based electric
power. Energy exports are split roughly half and half between the other
socialist countries and the capitalist countries.

Exports to the socialist countries make up for a scarcity of indigenous
energy resources in those countries and provide an essential ingredient
for their growth. In 1977 the group of East European countries consist-
ing of Poland, East Germany, Czechoslovakia, Hungary, and Bulgaria
obtained about 22 percent of their total primary energy consumption in
the form of oil and gas from the USSR.[22] Cuba, too, was deeply dependent on Soviet oil to meet its energy requirements. Unless the USSR is
willing to impose a very heavy drag on the economic performance of
these countries, it must continue to deliver oil and gas to them at approximately the current levels. Exports to capitalist countries permit large
hard currency earnings that are used to import foreign technology.
These technological imports are a major feature of current Soviet development strategy aimed at stimulating productivity growth and enhancing Soviet competitiveness in the world market. At the end of the 1970s
Soviet oil and gas exports accounted for about half all Soviet hard currency earnings. Oil has thus been an indispensable pillar of the technology transfer strategy, both to finance imports directly and to provide the
debt-servicing capacity that has emboldened the Western countries to
extend large credits.

This energy-exploiting policy has been possible because of an abundance of relatively cheap oil and gas resources. Between 1960 and 1980
about 85 percent of the total increment in Soviet primary energy output
came from oil and gas production. It was great good fortune for Soviet
planners that they found these oil and gas resources because it would not
have been possible to achieve with coal alone the realized growth and
export performance. At first these increments of oil and gas supply
came almost exclusively from areas in the European USSR but many of

22. The calculation of this figure is complicated and somewhat imprecise because there
are some gaps and inconsistencies in the energy data available for the East European
countries and because beginning in 1977 the USSR ceased to publish the physical amounts
by country for its trade in energy products. But total energy consumption in these five
countries was about 560 million tons of standard fuel, while imports of Soviet oil were
about 105 million tons of standard fuel and imports of Soviet gas about 19 million tons of
standard fuel.

those resources have now been depleted, and to continue the policy line of the past it is necessary to turn to the energy resources of the East.

Virtually all the increment of primary energy output in the period 1976–80 has been from the East. Indeed, in the case of oil the output increase in the East exceeds the total national increment because Siberian additions must make up for losses in the declining fields of the West. The depletion of resources in the West and the corollary necessity of making up deficits from the East are already worse than the planners predicted for the Tenth Five-Year Plan (1976–80) and will be still more serious in the period beyond 1980.

This shift of hydrocarbon production from West to East is an extremely expensive proposition and raises great technological problems not easy to solve. These costs and difficulties have directed much attention to coal, nuclear, and hydroelectric power sources as alternatives. They are also likely to slow oil and gas expansion sufficiently to check the growth of energy exports and probably reduce them in absolute terms, even if serious efforts are made to free oil by substituting other energy sources in internal consumption. The problem is especially acute with respect to oil, and the Soviet planners are hoping to make up for loss of oil exports to some extent by substituting gas exports. But whatever the magnitude of energy exports turns out to be in the 1980s, they are very likely to move almost exclusively westward rather than to the Pacific Basin. This outcome is conditioned by two facts: much of the total will be committed to the East European countries, and, to the extent that energy export consists of gas, considerations of location and transport require that it go west rather than east.

The most convincing evidence for skepticism about significant oil exports to the Pacific Basin is what happened to the promise of Tyumen oil for Japan. The Russians originally talked of selling to Japan as much as 40 million tons per year but later cut this to 25 million tons per year, supposedly because it turned out that the reserves at Tyumen were not large enough. It does not make sense to say there were not enough reserves—after all this is the source that now accounts for half of Soviet oil output! The deal finally collapsed altogether and no more has been heard of it recently.

There are two main exceptions to the bleak prospects for energy exports to the Pacific Basin. The first is coal. The Russians already have a compensation agreement with the Japanese for the development of coking coal resources in Southern Yakutia. The Japanese will provide financing and equipment to be repaid in shipments of coking coal. Shipments are to start in 1983 and extend over a period of twenty years to aggregate more than 100 million tons. The other is an agreement on a project in which both the United States and Japan are to participate for the export of liquified natural gas from the Vilyui Basin in Yakutia. An agreement was reached in 1974 and this project has been moving fitfully forward since then. The Stevenson amendment prohibited use of Export–Import Bank credits for Soviet energy projects, making it impossible for U.S. financing to be provided on the scale originally intended, but exploration and evaluation of reserves have been carried out with financing provided by Japan and a group of U.S. banks, and the American partners (El Paso Natural Gas Company and Occidental Petroleum) still expect that the project will eventually be carried out. If it is, it would generate exports of 20 billion cubic meters of gas per year over a twenty-five-year period, half to the Japanese and half to the United States.[23]

A third cooperative project with the Japanese, an effort to find oil on the Sakhalin shelf, might also be considered export oriented. This deal, which is actively proceeding, involves the Japanese provision of rigs and management. Any oil found is to be split between the Soviet Union and the Western partners. Current evaluations are that this effort is unlikely to generate much new production. If these exploration efforts or independent Soviet efforts do open up significant new reserves on the continental shelf, it is far from certain that much of it will be available for export. Eastern Siberia and the Far East are both deficit regions with respect to petroleum products. In 1970 Eastern Siberia had to import 10.3 million tons of oil and products and the Far East 5.47 million tons.[24] Any oil found off Sakhalin will probably find its best use in freeing these regions from the burden of an extremely long and expensive rail haul for oil.

The supply conditions for other Siberian resources are more favorable for export expansion. The timber resources of the East, especially in Eastern Siberia and the Far East, are far in excess of domestic needs and could support regional exports well beyond the amounts that will be needed for the USSR itself. There is already a large-scale Soviet–Japanese deal under which the Japanese are providing great amounts of investment and consumption goods, on credit, to be repaid with round-wood and sawed timber. The amounts promised are 17.5 million cubic meters of roundwood plus .9 million cubic meters of sawed lumber over a five-year period. These are not terribly large amounts in relation to current annual production: 25.9 million cubic meters of roundwood in the Far East and 57.3 million cubic meters in Eastern Siberia and 23.9 billion cubic meters of sawed lumber in the two regions. (These are 1975 data, the most recent available.) Furthermore, the amounts of round-

23. Jonathan Stern, *Soviet Natural Gas to 1990* (Lexington, Mass.: Lexington Books, 1980), pp. 204–06.

24. TsSU SSSR, *Transport i svyaz' SSSR* (Moscow: Statistika, 1972), p. 75.

wood already committed under this deal are not terribly large in relation to the 8 million cubic meters already going to Japan in 1976, although the sawed lumber will represent a considerable expansion beyond the 1976 level of about .1 million cubic meters.

For ferrous metals the situation is not so clear. One of the big developments to be facilitated by the BAM is an expansion of steel production capacity in the Far East, on the basis of the iron ore and coking coal of the Aldan region. Some Soviet authors speak as if there will be enough extra production to make possible exports of steel and allied products. The growth of production and consumption of steel in the USSR have not moved smoothly together in the last decade. Soviet net exports of steel have been as high as 11 million tons but in one year there was actually a net import (see Soviet foreign trade handbooks). But a plant in the Far East producing 9 million tons of rolled product output might be insulated enough by distance to be immune from these vagaries and to generate a stable flow of exports.

And of course all the other minerals that are so frequently spoken of (copper, lead, zinc, tin, asbestos, sulfur, and so on) are still there, awaiting development and potential foreign purchasers. Many of those resources are still far from fully explored and evaluated. The conditions for their exploitation are still being studied. For many of them exploitation is likely to cause very expensive and dangerous environmental disruption, and there is still a great deal of research to be done to generate and evaluate technologies and approaches to exploitation that will minimize these dangers. When there exist already fairly well-defined targets for particular capacity increments, the economic and technical studies that will determine their scale, location, and associations are still to be carried out. In short, the lead times for generating much of the output for export are likely to involve a decade or more. How extensive such exports will be depends not only on completion of the Baikal–Amur railway, but also on Soviet ability to compete in the world market with other potential suppliers of these commodities. Because other chapters in this volume are more directly concerned with the BAM and with the external demand side, I will not discuss these aspects of the problem in detail. But it may be appropriate to look briefly at the Baikal–Amur line to appreciate the timetable involved, its resource demands, and the competition these demands create with other investment programs.

THE BAIKAL–AMUR MAINLINE RAILROAD (BAM)

The BAM is a very large and expensive undertaking. Early estimates were that the railroad itself would cost aroung 6 billion rubles by the time it was finished. A later source suggests that if such ancillary facilities as feeder lines and stations are included, the total cost would be more like 11 billion rubles.[25]

Given the usual Soviet overoptimism about costs, one would guess that all figures cited so far are likely to be serious underestimates. But if we spread a total of 11 billion rubles over the eight years in which most of the expenditure is to take place (1976–83, i.e., the Tenth Five-Year Plan and continuing through completion of the route in 1983), the resulting 1.4 billion rubles per year would amount to 7 percent of total investment allocated to the Eastern RSFSR in 1975.

Furthermore, this project must look to the Soviet controllers of resource use more and more like a costly white elephant. The original justification of the BAM envisaged heavy utilization of its capacity for hauling oil exports. Of the 35 million tons of freight expected to flow eastward in the early years after completion, 25 million tons was to be accounted for by the export of Tyumen oil to Japan.[26] As argued above, that is unlikely to happen and so the BAM is likely to be very lightly used in its early years. Such an experience has to strengthen the argument for slowdowns and diversions of investment resources to competing projects with higher and faster payoffs. There is an interesting article in a recent Soviet economic journal in which the author says that "when the BAM is opened for operation the return on capital investment will be considerably less than presented by the effectiveness norms."[27] The main theme of his article is to present noneconomic benefits that would justify the Eastern investments against this kind of charge.

Aggregate investment targets are traditionally overambitious in the Soviet economy, and in execution some projects are dropped or delayed. The general tone of the pronouncements about the BAM in the late 1970s is that it is on schedule, but even if all sections are completed and linked to permit through traffic by 1983 as planned, I suspect that it will be far from really ready to carry out the intended function of giving access to the whole area in which these fabulous resources lie.

One major use of it will probably be as a landbridge route from the Far East to Europe. The Russians are already well under way on a program of trying to win away a significant share of ocean transport by offering container service via the Trans-Siberian Railroad. There would also be some movement in the other direction. The amounts of these flows have grown fairly rapidly in the 1970s, from 2,314 twenty-foot

25. Theodore Shabad and Victor L. Mote, *Gateway to Siberian Resources* (Washington, D.C.: Scripta Publishing Co., 1977), p. 67.

26. P. Bunich, "Economic Impact of the BAM," in ibid., p. 136.

27. G. Tarasov, "Kompleksnoe razvitie Dal'nego Vostoka," *Planovoe Khozyaistvo*, no. 11 (1978), pp. 46–53.

containers (capable of containing about 50,000 tons of freight¸ in 1971 to 80,000 containers (equivalent to about 150,000 tons of freight) in 1976. It is predicted that this traffic could grow to as much as a million tons in the near future.[28] But a large share of that total is westward movement, the direction in which the BAM was to be underutilized anyway, and does not help much in achieving full utilization in the eastward direction.

But the important point is the fact that the railroad itself will not produce any exportable commodities. Other big investment projects must be completed first to generate the output that the BAM is intended to transport to export destinations. This is going to be an expensive program—one Soviet official has estimated that the investments in the development of the ancillary facilities may require three to four times as much investment as the railroad itself.[29] As already explained, most of these production facilities are still a long way from realization, and much investment will have to be diverted to them before they are ready to contribute exports. I believe that it is very unlikely that the decisionmaking mechanisms of Soviet planning will permit any significant change in the regional proportions of investment.[30] The huge investment in the BAM itself and the demands of the oil and gas program in Western Siberia, which surely will have the highest possible priority, are likely to starve the other projects so that they will be a very long time in coming into operation. This situation is very likely to enhance the Soviet interest in drawing other countries into the process of financing and equipping these projects on the basis of compensation agreements. That campaign is somewhat in abeyance now because of the level of Soviet indebtedness, and because of wariness on the part of the Japanese as they assess past troubles with the Russians and contemplate the possibilities of China as an alternative partner. But the Russians are likely sooner or later to reevaluate the situation and to initiate a new campaign for expansion of Western ties on all the traditional points—credits, most-favored-nation tariff treatment, compensation agreements—and to do their best to woo potential partners away from their fascination with China.

28. Elisa B. Miller, "The Trans-Siberian Landbridge," *Soviet Geography: Review and Translation*, vol. 19 (Apr. 1978), pp. 224, 233.

29. Yu. Sobolev, "Narodnokhozyaistvennaya programma osvoeniya zony BAM," *Planovoe Khozyaistvo*, no. 7 (1978), p. 77.

30. In addition to the general inertia of the system and the competing demands of the established regions, one new force working in this direction today is a policy of emphasizing replacement and modernization of existing capital. Because most of the existing production facilities are located in the older areas, the higher the share of total investment funds used for replacement and modernization, the lower the share available for greenfield facilities in pioneer areas.

IN CONCLUSION

The thesis of this chapter has been that there are powerful economic
and institutional forces working against a dramatic takeoff in economic
development in Siberia predicated on its undisputed wealth of mineral,
timber, and energy resources. The resource base is extremely weak in
the complementary elements necessary to create the conditions for and
to sustain all-around economic development. For most of the area there
is remarkably little in the way of agricultural resources, and the weakness of the food base combines with adverse climate to make it difficult
and expensive to attract and retain the population resources indispensable for development. Sheer space itself exerts a malign influence.
There is so much of it in relation to the resources that the density of
economic activity is extremely low, which means that the infrastructural
investments needed to tie the region together are very costly per unit of
output, and that economies of agglomeration are elusive. If the great
expanse of the Soviet East makes parts of it economically more suited for
integration with the Pacific Basin than with the economic heartland of
the USSR, this huge expanse also interposes a formidable distance barrier between much of the East and any external partners in the Pacific
area. Institutionally, the Soviet system is probably on balance inimical to
the emergence of strong independent regional development. Decisions
are made in Moscow, and to the extent that the system responds to
regional pressures, the political weight of established regions limits
marked changes in the regional allocation of investment resources. The
branch focus of operational economic decisionmaking often puts branch
considerations ahead of comprehensive regional development.

Admittedly there are significant new elements in the situation today—
notably a strong concern on the part of the USSR to strengthen the
economic basis for projecting its influence in Asia, especially against
China, and a growing urgency in both the USSR and the world as a
whole to find replacements for the established mineral and energy resources that are being rapidly depleted. It is not the purpose of this
chapter to predict how these opposing forces will be resolved, and it
would be foolhardy to offer a forecast of how fast Soviet trade with the
Pacific will grow or how fast and in what directions Siberian output will
grow. Rather, the most useful thing I can do is to review some critical
variables that we should be monitoring, as Siberian development
proceeds.

1. One important consideration will be what happens with respect to
the current Soviet national development strategy with its emphasis on
expanded trade and technology transfer from the advanced countries as

vital stimulants to growth and productivity change. It is my view that this strategy is firmly enough based on compelling economic logic that it will survive a leadership change. With this strategy the task will be to find items to export to pay for current imports and to service debt already accumulated. In particular, some replacements must be found for the oil exports that recently have played so important a role in this strategy. The Soviet planners would like to expand the exports of finished goods for this purpose, but there are very many obstacles to any such expansion in their trade with the developed capitalist countries from which the technology imports come. The best prospects for Soviet exports are likely to remain minerals, raw materials, and semifinished products rather than highly fabricated goods. Siberia is where those potential resources are located, and the Soviet leaders will be compelled to follow through with Siberian development despite the obstacles and discouragements described in this chapter.

2. However, those exports, especially if they are going to the Pacific Basin, will have to be other than energy because of problems of availability and location of the energy resources. Of course, the nonenergy exports may well be energy-intensive products—chemicals, ores, and primary metals, especially aluminum—in which eastern hydro and coal resources give the Russians an advantage. As one moves away from energy commodities proper, however, the question of the USSR's competitive position vis-à-vis other potential suppliers becomes more important in predicting export potential. I believe that there may be some problems here. There are alternative sources for iron ore, coal, and timber. Any exports of steel from the Far East must compete with the very modern and efficient Japanese steel industry, and the world market for copper is characterized by large price swings. The greatest potential customer for many of these commodities, Japan, is strongly attracted for political reasons to the USSR's potentially strongest competitor in supplying these primary products, i.e., China. The Soviet pricing system is such that the Russians can always manipulate the price to meet foreign competition, but they may have to reevaluate the gains from Siberian development projects if price competition reduces the foreign-exchange earnings. Such uncertainties may also make potential foreign partners reluctant to become involved in long-term participatory deals with price guarantees if they think that other alternatives are likely to prove cheaper. After all, this kind of consideration has been instrumental in dampening enthusiasm for the Yakutian liquified natural gas deal.

3. The argument for Siberian development oriented toward the Pacific Basin is largely based on simple spatial logic, but an economist would point out that this need not govern all aspects of Siberia's external

relations. There is likely to be a substantial amount of multilateralism in Siberia's external relations. Even as exports go to markets in the Pacific Basin, much of the financing, technology imports, and outside participation in development may still have to come from other countries, particularly Western Europe. These are the countries that have established trading ties with the Russians, and they have probably not completely exhausted their lending potential. A very large share of the technological imports that have so far gone into Siberian development have come from those countries instead of from Japan, the United States, or other Pacific Basin countries. This is true for the line pipe and compressors, for example, used in Siberian gas development. And even when the goods have come from the United States (some pipeline compressors or submersible pumps), they have not been paid for by corresponding energy exports to the United States. The importance of this point is that Siberian exports can probably grow without necessarily requiring the development of comprehensive economic ties with partner countries in the Pacific Basin that might spill over into political and strategic interdependence.

4. It seems very likely that as Siberian development proceeds, the investment stringency will become more and more acute. Soviet investment strategy must be overextended, with resources spread over too many projects delaying the payoff to the program that will come only when it is complete. In this situation the Soviet Union is likely to greatly intensify its efforts over the next decade to find foreign partners to provide economic and technical assistance. One of the most challenging and probably frustrating tasks of Western countries will be to sustain an awareness of the great bargaining power they have in this relationship and to find ways to exercise it.

10

Soviet Military Power in Asia

PAUL F. LANGER

In recent years, the growth of Soviet power in Asia has generated increasing concern among the countries of the region and, to a lesser extent, in the United States as well. In this chapter I focus on the military dimension of the Soviet position in Asia. The following discussion addresses within that context three major issues: (1) Soviet security perspectives and concerns in Asia, (2) the present Soviet military position in the region and the resulting state of the regional military balance, and (3) important problems created for the Asian nations and for the United States by the continuing buildup of Soviet military power.

The discussion is based on information gathered from a range of public documentary materials, governmental and nongovernmental, including Soviet, U.S., Japanese, and Chinese sources. Admittedly, Soviet documentation is sparse insofar as specific data on military matters are concerned. Its value lies primarily in assisting us in the identification of major themes in Soviet policy relevant to Asia. The reiteration of such themes must of course be interpreted against the background of actual Soviet behavior. No attempt has been made to adduce evidence for every statement I make, as the focus of my analysis is on the larger and longer range security trends in Asia rather than on the details of the present military situation in that region. While the emphasis of the discussion is on Northeast Asia, where Soviet military power is concentrated and where the major actors—China, the Soviet Union, the United States, and Japan—converge, I also give some attention to Southeast and South Asia when this seems relevant to Soviet Asian strategy and security concerns.

SOVIET SECURITY PERSPECTIVES AND CONCERNS IN ASIA

During the past decade Soviet military power capable of employment in Asian conflict situations has grown conspicuously. The quantitative increase in Soviet ground, air, and naval forces earmarked for Asia has

The views expressed in this chapter are mine alone. They do not necessarily reflect the views of The Rand Corporation, with which I am affiliated, or of that organization's governmental and other research sponsors.

255

been accompanied by qualitative improvements, including the gradual development during the 1970s of a potential for projecting military force into areas distant from Soviet territory. This development is viewed in Asia with concern and even with alarm. The resulting mood of uneasiness has been reinforced by certain official U.S. statements, plans, and decisions (for example, the announcement of American troop withdrawals from Korea or the transfer of Seventh Fleet units from the Pacific to the Indian Ocean), which have created the impression that the United States is seeking to reduce its Asian security commitments. Quite naturally, the question has been asked, What prompts the continued Soviet military buildup in Asia at a time when there is no sign of a corresponding American military effort in the area or of substantial increases in the military potential of the countries of the region capable of posing a threat to Soviet national security?

When viewed from the perspective of the Asian nations directly affected, the steady growth of Soviet military might in the region gives the impression that Soviet military strategy and resource allocation have shifted toward an increased emphasis on the Asian theater, where the proliferation of sources of internal and external conflict creates obvious opportunities for Soviet intervention. Massive Soviet force deployments along the Sino–Soviet frontier, the recent garrisoning of Soviet ground forces on the northern islands claimed by Japan, and the continued Soviet assistance offered to Vietnam in its military confrontation with China could be taken as supporting evidence for such an interpretation, especially when viewed against the background of Soviet military intervention in Afghanistan.

However, when we examine Soviet behavior in other parts of the non-Western world (Africa or the Middle East, for example) or compare the military buildup in the Soviet Far East with that on the European front, we find no convincing evidence for the contention that Asia during the 1970s has *suddenly* and dramatically gained special prominence at the expense of other areas where the Soviet Union has an important stake. In other words, the growth of Soviet military capabilities directed toward Asia on the ground, in the air, and on the sea has proceeded during the past decade not markedly faster than in other theaters. To date, the bulk of Soviet forces remains deployed against NATO; the most advanced Soviet military equipment and weapon systems (for example, the Backfire of SALT II fame or the latest missile systems) are assigned to the Soviet Far East only after minimum needs in the European theater have been met.

It appears then that the Soviet military buildup in Asia is in essence part of a worldwide, relentless process transforming the USSR into a truly global power, while not long ago it qualified as a superpower only on the strategic, nuclear plane. If Soviet military priorities have not been basically altered by the events of the past decade and if the focus of Soviet security concerns remains as before on Europe, Soviet statements and behavior do suggest two important conclusions regarding present Soviet perspectives on Asia. We find (1) an enhanced capacity and readiness on the part of the Soviet Union to exploit opportunities in—and intervene militarily into—the turbulent Asian arena, and (2) growing Soviet concern about a regional security threat that centers on China and its developing ties with the United States and Japan as the focus. Soviet attention to Southeast Asia (Indochina) must be viewed primarily in those terms: it provides pressure points on both China and Japan.[1]

The record of past Soviet actions suggests the centrality of military power in Soviet political strategy. This power is not necessarily employed directly, for Soviet behavior is characterized by a great deal of caution whenever there is the risk of military confrontation with the United States. Frequently, Soviet military power is brought to bear in an indirect way through a display of force or through arms aid. That is certainly true in Asia, where the psychological-political impact of the growing Soviet military presence has its important function and where Soviet military assistance to actual or potential adversaries of the United States and China constitutes a major means of exercising leverage. (Such arms aid also has the advantage of being capable of fine tuning. Thus, we know that since 1973 Pyongyang has been removed from the select list of recipients of advanced Soviet military equipment, thereby signaling Moscow's dissatisfaction with North Korea's tilt toward Beijing and indicating also the Soviet desire to restrain Kim Il Sung from reckless military ventures.)

Emphasis on the use of military power as an instrument of Soviet policy is attributed to the historical experience and geopolitical position of the Soviet Union, both markedly different from the American condition; to the chronic weakness of the Soviet economy; and to the decline of Soviet ideological appeal abroad. The heightened, worldwide visibility

---

1. Re Japan it is instructive to quote the views of Dr. I. I. Kovalenko, a Japan expert who heads the Central Committee's section concerned with Japan and is responsible for the issuing of the USSR Academy of Sciences Yearbooks on Japan. Summarizing his analysis, N. Vladimirov reviews Japan's situation in an article originally published in *Problemy Dal'nego Vostoka*, no. 4 (1979), pp. 38–51, and later translated in the Academy's publication *Far Eastern Affairs*, no. 1 (1980), pp. 26–37, under the title "Japan Faces the 1980s." Here is what he has to say on Southeast Asia's importance to Japan: "Southeast Asia is of vast importance from the angle of military strategy. Located here are the main centres of supply and it is through its sealanes that Japan ships in most of the raw materials it needs. In the final analysis Japan's snag-free economic activity depends on the situation in this part of the world" (p. 32).

of Soviet military power is, of course, not unrelated to the fact that the
Soviet Union is challenging U.S. influence across the globe. That contest
is played out in several geographic arenas, including Asia, and on several
military levels, not the least being the strategic one.

It is true that Soviet ground-based strategic weapon systems need not
be positioned in the Asian territories of the USSR to be militarily effective. But the dispersal of such weapons and their basing in the Asian–
Pacific region offer economic and military, as well as political-
psychological, benefits. Moreover, a portion of the Soviet posture in Asia
has a dual function, strategic and regional, in the sense that it provides
added security for Soviet theater forces. Further, as the dividing line
between strategic and theater-oriented advanced weapon systems has
become increasingly blurred, it is no longer always obvious whether
certain elements of Soviet military power located in Asia should be labeled *strategic* or *regional*. Even though a major part of the Soviet nuclear
military posture in the Far East appears to be designed for essentially
nonregional missions (such as the Yankee and Delta SSBN ballistic mis-
sile-equipped submarines), it nevertheless adds to the political impact of
the Soviet military presence in Asia, thereby influencing Asian perceptions of the regional U.S.–Soviet military balance.

The China Threat

As in other parts of the world, American power constitutes the principal
external obstacle to Soviet domination of the Asian–Pacific region. Much
of the Soviet military posture in the Far East is therefore designed to
constrain the U.S. military presence in Asia. Nevertheless, judging by
the Soviet force posture in the Far East, by Soviet official statements, and
by other, nonmilitary indicators, the Soviet Union since the outbreak of
conflict with China perceives itself as being also faced with specifically
Asian security challenges. As yet these challenges are of a *potential* nature, but they are becoming more pressing because of their formal or
informal linkages to American military power and because of the Soviet
Union's geopolitical vulnerabilities.

China and Japan interpose a barrier against the expansion of Soviet
influence in Asia, especially when acting in common with and backed by
the military-technological-economic might of the United States. The
emergence of a Sino–American–Japanese coalition has been a specter
haunting Soviet policymakers and strategists at least since the early
1970s, when the United States and Japan took the first steps toward
normalizing relations with the PRC. The prevention of such a tripartite
anti-Soviet front has been at the core of Soviet political strategy toward
Asia for the past decade. Soviet policy statements are evidence that the

growing rapprochement among the three powers in the economic and political spheres is viewed in Moscow as merely the formative stage of an anti-Soviet alliance in Asia. Clearly, the Soviets fear, not entirely without justification, that such trilateral cooperation will gradually extend to the military dimension, thereby markedly changing, to the detriment of the Soviet power position, the conditions for managing local military conflicts and Chinese involvement in them. (Thus, it can be argued that Soviet caution during the Chinese "punitive expedition" into Vietnam was in part dictated by concern about the U.S. response to direct Soviet military involvement and about the subsequent effect of such a development on U.S.–Soviet relations.)

China would, at any rate, constitute a serious Soviet security problem even without American political-military support for Beijing. This has been especially true since the rift between the two major communist powers about two decades ago. The Soviet security perspective in Asia and worldwide thus bears the imprint of years of confrontation with the world's most populous, and Asia's largest, nation. The two countries share a border that stretches for more than 4,000 miles across Asia. Bitter ideological-political and territorial conflicts rooted in history going back to czarist times have envenomed the two nations' relationship. They continue to vie for leadership in the Third World, especially in Asia, where time and all but the purely military assets appear to be on China's side. But Chinese military inferiority and technological backwardness are to some extent compensated for by China's enormous manpower resources, its proved tenacity in resisting foreign invaders, and the vastness of the country, where invading armies tend to bog down, as did those of the Japanese in the 1930s and early 1940s. To make matters worse, the creation in recent years of a Chinese nuclear arsenal, modest though it may be by superpower standards, carries the risk of making any major Soviet military operation against China a costly one. Moreover, the recent opening of China to the United States, Japan, and the West has created favorable conditions for Chinese military modernization. Therefore, it has been argued that, time being on the Chinese side, the Soviet Union is faced with the need for acting militarily now if it is to act militarily against China at all. Yet Soviet strategy against China has exhibited great caution. It is doubtful whether, now that conditions for direct military intervention in China appear less favorable than ever, the Soviet Union would consider reversing its past policies short of a major Chinese act of provocation. After all, other options remain open to Moscow.

Moscow's strategy has long been characterized by an attempt to develop a security glacis along the periphery of the Soviet Union. The attempt appeared to have largely succeeded in Eastern Europe until the emergence of a threat to Soviet control in Poland early in 1981. To a much lesser extent has it been successful in the Near and Middle East, where the process—witness Afghanistan—is still under way and its outcome remains uncertain. In Asia, after a modest beginning with the creation of a Mongolian People's Republic (1924), no further progress was registered. North Korea, a potential candidate for Soviet domination, continues to guard jealously its independence while China's physical dimensions, international prestige, and proved spirit of national resistance discourage Soviet intervention along the lines of the Afghan incursion.

Soviet strategy against China has aimed, therefore, at encircling China politically and militarily or at the very least operating a pincer movement from the north and south. (Brezhnev's proposal of an Asian collective security pact, originally advanced in 1969, was an early, well-advertised move toward wholesale implementation of that strategy in Asia.) Large contingents of Soviet forces have been deployed along China's borders. Meanwhile, Soviet policy has sought to create a belt of nations—from Afghanistan and India to Indochina—linked to the Soviet Union through friendship pacts and military assistance programs. Whether this strategy will have the effect of easing the Soviet security problem in Asia is doubtful. It might well lead instead to a further geographic extension of the Soviet confrontation with the PRC, producing new and onerous Soviet military commitments in areas distant from Soviet sources of power. Meanwhile, the Soviets face the unenviable security dilemma of having to plan for a two-front war on the widely separated European and Asian fronts. The emerging Sino–American–Japanese coalition has further aggravated this Soviet dilemma. So far, however, the Soviet leaders have been unwilling to make the major concessions that an accommodation with Beijing would require. Instead, they have continued to strengthen their military power along the entire Sino–Soviet frontier in order to exert pressure on the Chinese. However, military analysts agree that the present Soviet force deployments along the Sino–Soviet frontier may be adequate for a quick seizure of contiguous Chinese territory but do not appear appropriate for a full-scale military invasion of China and a prolonged occupation of that country.

Japan's Threat Potential

An analysis of Soviet policy statements, writings on Asian affairs, and behavior in Asia suggests that Japan is perceived in Moscow as a potential security threat. Several elements appear to enter importantly into the Soviet perspective on the role of Japan: (1) the legacy of past military confrontations with Japan, (2) the American–Japanese military tie, (3) the threatening implications of Japan's sustained growth in economic power and technological sophistication, and (4) the special Sino–Japanese relationship.

As in their perceptions of a residual German security threat to the Soviet Union, Soviet leaders are sensitized to the potential Japanese menace by still vivid memories of past hostile military encounters with Japan.[2] The two powers have faced each other on the Korean peninsula, on Chinese territory, and in areas traditionally included in the Chinese zone of influence. They have clashed repeatedly in enormously costly and bloody land and sea battles: in the Russo–Japanese War, in confrontations triggered by the spread of the Bolshevik Revolution into the Far East and leading to the Japanese armies' attempted occupation of Siberia, in the large-scale Soviet–Japanese tank battles of the 1930s, and in the sudden thrust of Soviet armed forces into Japanese-occupied Manchuria during the closing days of World War II, a military operation that led to the capture and abduction of hundreds of thousands of Japanese into Siberian labor camps.

It is true that Japan's wartime defeat vastly changed the balance of military power in Northeast Asia to the Soviet advantage. Postwar Japan's national strategy in Asia now relies on economic influence rather than on military force. Nevertheless, history has left in both nations a residue of psychological attitudes that can be described only as dark suspicions of the neighbor's intentions.

Militarily, Japan today is puny compared with the USSR. Despite frequent Soviet statements regarding the alleged remilitarization of Japan,[3]

2. In that connection one might recall how Stalin gloated over Japan's defeat in World War II and the forced return of territories that Imperial Russia had lost to Japan as a result of military defeat. More recently, to cite another example, Secretary General Brezhnev alluded to the Soviet–Japanese military confrontations of the 1930s: ". . . Nor do we forget the heroic epos of Khalkhin-Gol when with a crushing blow the Soviet and Mongolian forces repelled the Japanese militarists attempting to encroach on Mongolian land" (*Problemy Dal'nego Vostoka*, no. 3 [1979], p. 64.) In November 1978 Soviet Ambassador Polyansky, speaking to a Japanese reporter in Tokyo, reminded him of Japan's role in the Soviet Far East and the destruction caused by the Japanese armies, pointing out that these events can never be removed from the pages of Japanese–Soviet relations (*Mainichi Daily News*, Nov. 25, 1978, p. 1). Many other examples from Soviet statements could be cited.

3. An endless number of Soviet broadcasts, articles, statements, and book-length analyses of the alleged "remilitarization" of contemporary Japan have been pouring forth from Moscow in the past decade. For some typical samples of such interpretations, see the articles by I. I. Ivkov (reportedly a penname of the previously mentioned Dr. Kovalenko) that appeared in *Problemy Dal'nego Vostoka*, no. 3 (1978), pp. 46–60, translated into English in JPRS 72621 (Jan. 15, 1979), pp. 52–69, under the title "Japanese Militarism Rears Its Head," or V. Viktorov's analysis, "Militarizatsiya Yaponii," in *Mezhdunarodnaya Zhizn'*, no. 1 (1979), pp. 120–21. More recent examples are the articles by S. Modenov, "On a War Footing," in *International Affairs* (Moscow), no. 2 (1980), pp. 78–83, and by V. Dalnev, "Impediments to Soviet–Japanese Relations," in *International Affairs* (Moscow), no. 2

this evident fact is presumably fully understood in Moscow. Yet Japan's strategic location and symbiotic military relationship with the United States make its potential military role in the region a matter of long-range concern to Moscow. Even in the present circumstances of Japanese military weakness, American–Japanese cooperation has a powerfully negative effect on the Soviet Union's ability to exploit its military superiority over Japan. While the U.S.–Japanese security pact enhances the American military position in the region, the American nuclear umbrella over Japan constrains the employment of Soviet military power in Northeast Asia and weakens its political-psychological impact.

There is evidence that after Japan's wartime defeat the Soviet Union hoped to gain a foothold in Hokkaido so as to minimize American influence in the military occupation of Japan. Determined U.S. opposition frustrated Soviet attempts to carve out a Soviet occupation zone on the large northern island. The incorporation into the USSR of the small Kurile Islands, to the north of Hokkaido, could not compensate, politically or strategically, for that Soviet failure. Nevertheless, until the outbreak of the Korean War Soviet policymakers could still hope for the emergence of a neutral Japan after the expected withdrawal of the American military occupation forces. But, as in so many other respects, the Korean War also ushered in a new era with regard to the status of Japan. Reemerging as a sovereign nation, Japan concluded a security treaty with the United States (1951) and under American auspices embarked on a slow but steady rebuilding of indigenous defensive military capabilities. Since that time, Soviet strategists have been forced to include in their calculations the presence of American forces in and around Japan. Bases in Japan allow the United States to project military power at short notice into adjacent areas and to use the advanced industrial and repair facilities of Japan. Over time a division of labor between these U.S. forces and the growing Japanese Air, Naval, and Ground Self-Defense Forces has evolved—a process that to Soviet dismay has quickened in the past two years.

This American military presence in Northeast Asia has also prevented the Soviet Union from gaining much leverage over Japanese policy.[4] As long as Japan's political and economic orientation toward America and noncommunist Asia remains fixed, Soviet bargaining power will at any

---

(1981), pp. 49–53. It should be noted, however, that whereas these Soviet accusations against Japan are hardly justified under present circumstances, when Japan's forces are essentially of a defensive nature, concern about future Japanese defense policies is shared more widely in and around Japan.

4. The current strength of U.S. forces in Japan is about 46,000 men, primarily marines and air force personnel. American strength in Korea, mostly army and air force, now stands at about 40,000.

rate be limited, especially if in the years ahead Japan economically should become more deeply involved with China.[5] That leaves the Soviet Union with military power as the primary instrument for leverage in Japan. But Soviet threats against Japan meant to discourage the conclusion of a Sino–Japanese peace treaty proved Soviet military power to be of limited use in dealing with Japan because of Japanese faith in American protection. This will continue to be the case as long as the American security guarantee is credible and the military balance in the region does not clearly tilt toward Soviet supremacy. The American military presence in Japan also reinforces Japan's ability to seal off the three major straits vital to Soviet naval forces for access to the open seas. Finally, American military bases on Japanese soil allow the United States to intervene on short notice in critical situations in nearby areas such as the Korean peninsula—or in northeast China, for that matter—thus deterring Soviet use of military power in the region. Hence, even without a massive military instrument of its own, Japan is making a substantial contribution to the maintenance of a regional military balance.

Logically, Soviet strategy toward Japan aims at eroding the American–Japanese military relationship. Yet it is questionable that the Soviet Union would gain much even if such a policy were really successful. Presumably, it is understood in Moscow that as long as the American security tie remains strong, it will discourage Japan from remilitarizing itself. A substantial weakening of the American guarantee for Japan, or of its credibility as perceived by the Japanese, could propel that country toward the development of an independent military force with its own nuclear weapons, thereby profoundly affecting the regional military balance—a prospect that cannot be welcomed in Moscow. Under these circumstances Soviet objectives in Northeast Asia may be better served (although far from satisfactorily) by a loose and weakened U.S.–Japanese security tie than by its complete rupture.

The astounding growth of the Japanese economy since World War II will no doubt be recorded as one of the salient developments of the late

5. In fact it can be argued (and is, in fact, argued in Tokyo) that economically Japan is more indispensable to the Soviet Union than the other way around. Nevertheless, actual economic exchanges between the two countries (in 1980 amounting to about $4.6 billion, of which 2.8 billion represented Japanese exports to the USSR) and anticipated levels for the future are sufficiently important to Japanese business circles that they are reluctant to participate in any anti-Soviet economic boycott. Thus, in 1980 the Japanese requested that the U.S. government exclude from its economic sanctions against the Soviet Union's military incursion into Afghanistan the joint venture between Japan and the Soviet Union to develop oil and gas resources off Sakhalin (U.S. firms were to have been involved through technological assistance). Although a limited embargo on trade with the USSR remained in force during 1981, a gradual relaxation of these Japanese economic sanctions was under way until the Polish crisis brought the process to a halt.

twentieth century. In 1982 Japan with a gross national product exceeding a trillion dollars has drawn even with the Soviet Union in economic power. The effect is being felt worldwide but especially in Asia. Japanese investments and trade in the Asian–Pacific region have grown to the point where Asia is being transformed into a Japan-dominated economic zone that reaches to the borders of India and may soon include Australia and New Zealand. This impressive spread of the economic-technological influence of a Japan aligned with the United States and now moving closer to the PRC tends to reduce Soviet leverage in Asia. Understandably, it is a matter for Soviet concern, particularly as it also has military implications. The Soviet analyst I. I. Ivkov acknowledged this recently when he stated: "It is well known that it is primarily a country's industrial base and the existence of skilled manpower which constitute the foundation of military industry. Both these factors are present in Japan."[6]

An Anti-Soviet Triple Alliance in Asia?

Soviet pressure on China has compelled the Beijing leaders to seek an opening to the United States. The result has been a dramatic change in great-power relationships in Asia and globally. Quite apart from the political benefits to the United States from the rapprochement with China, there has been a payoff in the military sphere. The Soviet Union now, like the United States earlier, finds itself having to plan for simultaneous military conflict in Europe and Asia.

A fundamental consequence of this reconfiguration in Asia has been the Sino–Japanese rapprochement. The drawing together of China and Japan, both of them in a larger sense allies of the United States in its competition with the Soviet Union, must be considered a major Soviet defeat. It is not clear how Soviet policy can escape the resulting political-military cost except by compromising with at least one of the parties concerned or by increasing its military investments in the area. Apparently, Soviet efforts are now under way on both fronts. On the one hand there is the confirmed Soviet military buildup in East Asia around China and Japan; on the other, the Soviets are attempting to mute the conflict with China and to improve relations with Japan by holding out economic incentives. It may be too early to judge whether this combination of stick and carrot will improve the Soviet position in Asia but in the past this same strategy has proved singularly unsuccessful.

Soviet statements and behavior suggest strong concern about the future course of the Sino–Japanese relationship, about American support for a Beijing–Tokyo rapprochement, and about what are perceived in Moscow as indications that Sino–Japanese ties are assuming a military

6. Ivkov, "Japanese Militarism."

coloration. Soviet suspicions are fed by the coming and going between Beijing and Tokyo of men who are known to have influence in Tokyo and Beijing in military matters.[7] China's leaders have consciously deepened Soviet suspicions through their well-advertised words and actions. Thus, Deng Xiaoping in an interview published in *Time* early in 1979 urged Japan and the United States to work together with China "to place curbs on the polar bear," suggesting that "the only realistic thing for us is to unite."[8]

The Japanese government, on the other hand, has repeatedly stressed that cooperation with China will not reach into the military sphere, that arms exports to China are excluded from Japanese plans, and that Japan's security will continue to rest wholly on the American guarantee supplemented by an indigenous, although modest and purely defensive, military effort. Yet there are undeniably ambiguities in the present state of the Sino–Japanese relationship. The Beijing leaders are clearly determined to promote at least quasi-military ties with Japan[9] or, failing that, to encourage Soviet doubts about the nature of the Sino–Japanese tie and the extent to which Sino–Japanese cooperation with the United States will involve security issues.

Ever since the Chinese opening to the United States, Moscow has feared that American advanced weapons technology and weapon systems might make their appearance in China, transforming a potential Chinese threat to Soviet security into an actuality. American denials of such intentions have not dispelled Soviet apprehensions. The suspicion remains strong in Moscow that the United States is encouraging its European partners to provide China with military matériel. Soviet fears regarding a similar role for Japan are as yet less pronounced owing to the

7. The first active Japanese military figure to visit China in decades was Colonel Shima of the Japanese Self-Defense Forces, who went to China in March 1978 by invitation. He was followed by a number of retired (but still influential) Japanese generals as well as by civilian officials from the Defense Agency and the National Defense Council. Apart from Deng Xiaoping (whom Soviet commentators, not without some justification, describe as essentially a military man), Japan has been visited by such eminent Chinese military leaders as Vice-Minister of Defense Su Yu, who in May 1979 called on the Director General of the Defense Agency, alluding to the threat posed to Japan by the Soviet military buildup in the Far East and the use of Cam Ranh Bay. He was preceded by Zhang Caijian, Deputy Chief of the General Staff. The Chinese military visitors made it a point to meet with Japanese retired officers to discuss the strategic situation and to warn against Soviet hegemony. They also invited their Japanese counterparts and other Japanese with influence in military decisions to visit Beijing.

8. *Time*, vol. 113, no. 7 (Feb. 12, 1979), p. 12.

9. Two Japanese faculty members of the National Defense College who met in March 1980 with Vice-Defense Minister Su Yu in Beijing were reportedly asked by him to promote an exchange of students between the two countries' military academies (Kyodo news dispatch, Mar. 14, 1980, reported in the *Japan Times*, Mar. 15, 1980, p. 4).

reassuring effect of Japanese domestic constraints on arms transfers and repeated Japanese official pledges of restraint in this and other matters related to export policy. Nevertheless, the Soviets are conscious of the high level of Japanese technology and of the danger that it might be applied to military ends. Thus, *Pravda*, in commenting on the visit to Japan of the Chinese Deputy Chief of Staff Zhang Caijian, highlighted his inspection of industrial plants capable of producing the latest automatic missile guidance systems, which according to the Soviet commentator are coveted by the Chinese.[10] Even if Japanese technological cooperation should remain outside the military sector, it could produce a quantum jump in Chinese industrial-military capabilities. Premier Kosygin's warning that Japanese economic cooperation with Beijing may encourage the latter's "aggressive intentions" should be viewed in that context.[11]

THE SOVIET MILITARY POSITION
AND THE REGIONAL MILITARY BALANCE

How to assess regional military balances has always been a hazardous task. Conventional assessments tend by necessity to become inventory comparisons of putative adversaries' forces and weapon systems; they generally ignore all but the most obvious disparities in performance characteristics and neglect other contextual, nonquantifiable, or non-military factors. In the case of Asia, assessments are complicated by a lack of consensus as to the logical boundaries of *Asia* as well as by the instability of the internal political situation and of international alignments. Here, in contrast to Europe, there are no overarching alliance systems. Whatever alliances do exist are mostly bilateral ones, the actors tend to behave more unpredictably than in the West, and the context in which military power is brought to bear is more fluid. Thus, ten years ago U.S. forces were massively involved in fighting in Vietnam, which had the support of China and the Soviet Union. Today, the United States no longer plays a direct military role in Indochina. Instead one witnesses a military confrontation pitting China against Vietnam, with the latter enjoying the open support of the Soviet Union and China the tacit encouragement of the United States.

The nature of modern weapons adds to the complexity of assessing the regional military balance, raising the question of what portion of which weapon systems at which locations should be considered at a time

10. *Pravda*, Oct. 15, 1978.
11. Interview of Premier Kosygin with the Japanese political leader Yohei Kono, as reported by Kyodo on November 24, 1978 (Foreign Broadcast Information Service [FBIS], *Daily Report: Soviet Union*, Nov. 27, 1978 [Washington, D.C.: FBIS], p. M1).

when strategic weapons exist side by side with theater-oriented forces and when the latter may have dual functions. Moreover, technology has rendered the mission of theater forces more flexible; missiles can be retargeted, ships and planes redirected, and armed forces moved over great distances from area to area in a relatively short time.

Soviet Military Capabilities in the Asian Theater

While keeping these caveats in mind, it may nevertheless be useful for an assessment of the regional military balance to provide a rough estimate of Soviet military assets in the Asian theater.[12] A substantial portion of all Soviet nonstrategic military power is currently assigned for action in Asia: from about one-fourth of total Soviet military capacity for ground and air forces to about one-third of Soviet naval tonnage for the Pacific Fleet. The bulk of all these forces is directed against China and against U.S. forces based in the Asian region.

Soviet ground forces in Asia are almost entirely China oriented. The Soviet military buildup along the Sino–Soviet frontier has been proceeding in parallel with the deterioration of Soviet relations with the PRC. In 1965 (i.e., prior to the border clashes of the late 1960s) the Soviets maintained 20 combat divisions in the Sino–Soviet border areas and the Mongolian People's Republic. By 1979 these forces had grown to 45 combat divisions (in addition to elite border troops). Although half the units are below full strength, the total of these ground forces reportedly exceeds 400,000 men. It should be noted that this buildup was not undertaken at the expense of Soviet military capabilities on the Western front. The desired manpower level had apparently been reached by the early 1970s. Since then the Soviet effort against China has shifted its emphasis from quantitative to qualitative improvements in military ca-

12. The factual information provided hereinafter was distilled from a number of public sources that agree on essential points though not necessarily on details. These variations are accounted for by the different methods used in arriving at force estimates. They also relate to definitional differences, varying geographic coverage, and several other factors, including the timing of the particular estimate. Figures cited should therefore be regarded as approximations. (For the most convenient and comprehensive listings of elements of the Soviet force posture relevant to Asia, see *The Military Balance*, the annual report issued by the International Institute for Strategic Studies [London]. Slightly revised versions of these yearly tabulations appear also in the annual reports of the Japanese Defense Agency.)

Major sources used include the official annual reports of the U.S. Secretary of Defense and the Chiefs of Staff, the White Papers (*Boei Hakusho*) of the Japanese Defense Agency, and the studies and reports of the International Institute for Strategic Studies, the Research Institute for Peace and Security (Tokyo), and The Rand Corporation (Santa Monica, Calif.). This reliance on non-Soviet sources is necessitated by the virtually total absence of published Soviet data on military matters. Whatever Soviet information is available tends to be nonspecific.

pabilities. The massive anti-China ground forces are currently supported by four tactical air armies and one long-range aviation division. Upgrading of the ground forces along the frontier has led to the introduction of advanced equipment, including tactical nuclear rockets and T-62 tanks as well as SA-6 and SA-9 surface-to-air missiles. Electronic intelligence maintains continuous surveillance of Chinese territory (as well as of militarily significant areas of non-Chinese Asia).

Although the 3.5-million-strong Chinese ground forces remain numerically vastly superior to the Soviet armies stationed along China's borders, the wide qualitative gap in military equipment, communications technology, and air support leaves no doubt about the Soviet ability to win a border war. Military experts agree that, although the Soviet positions are essentially defensive, they would allow the Soviet forces to make rapid and successful penetrations into Chinese territory. Particularly vulnerable is China's northeast (Manchuria), which is threatened by the bulk of Soviet ground forces. It is too early to know whether the lapse, effective in April 1980, of the Sino–Soviet Treaty of Friendship and Mutual Assistance will prompt the Soviet Union to beef up further its China-oriented force. Such a need seems unlikely to arise, for China's capacity to project military power beyond its borders remains extremely limited. The planned military modernization will take many years. At the same time, the Soviet Union is faced with constraints growing from demands on its military resources in Afghanistan, while military requirements in Eastern Europe, Vietnam, and elsewhere show no sign of decreasing.

A recent development (1978–81) has placed a Soviet force, reportedly of division strength, on the approaches to Japan. This garrison force on the small northern islands occupied by the Soviets after World War II but still claimed by Japan has caused alarm and puzzlement in Tokyo. Some Japanese analysts see a connection between this Soviet military encroachment on Japan and growing Soviet amphibious capabilities; it suggests to them a threat of Soviet landings on Hokkaido. It is difficult to share this view, as the Japanese Ground Self-Defense Forces maintain four full divisions with air support on the island, four times the present strength of the Soviet contingents they face. More likely the Soviet advance toward Japan is prompted by a desire to secure the Sea of Okhotsk, from which Soviet submarines can launch ballistic missiles against the continental United States. Uneasiness generated in Tokyo by this Soviet move might also fit in with the objectives of the intermittently revived Soviet hard-line strategy against Japan, a strategy that in the long run may prove to be counterproductive for Soviet interests, as it tends to spur Japanese rearmament.

The Soviet air force in the Far Eastern territories of the USSR, which is capable of immediate intervention in any Asian contingency, has grown even more quickly than the ground forces. Fighter aircraft alone increased sixfold (from 210 to about 1,200) between 1965 and 1979. Total Soviet air strength in the Far East is currently estimated at 2,400 combat aircraft, including 800 air defense fighters, 1,200 strike aircraft, and 350 bombers. These forces have received advanced combat aircraft, such as the Foxbat and Flogger fighters, the Forger naval fighter, and the Fencer fighter-bomber—not to mention the dual-capability Backfire. To these must be added the availability of long-range aviation, para-troop, and air mobile forces and long-distance transports (such as the AN-12 with its 6,000 mile range). The numerically impressive (5,000 units?) Chinese air force with its antiquated aircraft is clearly no match for the modern Soviet aviation deployed in the Far East. Japan's air force, on the other hand, has more recent American aircraft in its in-ventory but it numbers fewer than 400 combat aircraft.

Judged by the siting of Soviet Far Eastern air bases and the range of the aircraft stationed there, the primary target for these air forces must be the PRC. But other contingencies could be met from the same bases as well. The lengthening reach of these forces and the addition of a substantial although indeterminate number of long-range transports are now providing the Soviet military with the means of intervening prac-tically anywhere in Asia. The appearance of the Backfire weapon system is indicative of the trend; when flown from Soviet bases in the Far East, this aircraft can reach virtually all of Southeast Asia without refueling.

The most striking and widely noted change in the Far Eastern military situation insofar as the Soviet posture is concerned involves the modern-ization and growth of the Soviet Pacific Fleet. Although the tonnage figures often given—1.5 million tons for the Soviet Pacific Fleet against 700,000 tons for the U.S. Seventh Fleet—tend to distort the relative strength of the two naval forces (in the Pacific and Indian oceans) by including large numbers of very small and very old Soviet naval craft, here too the trend is unmistakable: The Soviet Union is steadily pro-ceeding to transform what once was essentially a coastal navy into a modern oceangoing fleet rivaling its American counterpart.

A recent inventory of Soviet Pacific Fleet strength, limited to comba-tant units and omitting older ships, shows 105 submarines, 32 of them with ballistic missiles; 352 surface ships (among them 1 carrier, 11 cruis-ers, 31 destroyers, and 73 amphibious craft); and about 400 naval air-craft. Another tabulation, restricted to major modern combatants, places their number on the Soviet side at 70 as against 79 for the United States. In addition it reports the number of Soviet submarines in the Pacific/Indian Ocean area under Pacific Fleet command at 100 as against 79 for the United States. In 1979 the Pacific Fleet added its first, but well-advertised, V/STOL aircraft carrier, the 40,000-ton *Minsk*, together with two guided missile craft. Clearly, the Soviet naval command is bent on bridging the gap between the Pacific and Seventh fleets. Although this program is advancing at the rate of nearly 100,000 tons annually, the Soviet side will be at a disadvantage for at least the next decade. Its single carrier faces several larger U.S. aircraft carriers normally assigned to the Seventh Fleet, which also commands substantial superiority in naval aircraft and amphibious potential. As a result the Soviet navy remains heavily dependent on land-based support. This gap between the two Pacific navies is likely to diminish considerably during the coming decade as the Soviet naval construction program steadily removes existing inadequacies. In fact the gap has been substantially reduced by the drawdown of major units from the Seventh Fleet in line with the U.S. attempt to strengthen intervention capabilities in the Middle East at a time when local conflicts there may otherwise offer opportunities for the Soviet Union to expand its influence in the region. Meanwhile, the Pacific Fleet could be effective in a wide range of functions from disruption of essential shipping in the Pacific Ocean area to political-military employment of naval craft in local Asian conflicts.

All of Asia is, of course, exposed to the central strategic nuclear forces of the USSR but it is also vulnerable to a growing nuclear force specifically assigned for use in the Asian theater. This force includes bombers capable of carrying nuclear weapons. The Soviet Far East has also received the SS-20, a land-based intermediate-range ballistic missile until recently reserved for use on the NATO front. Thus, whatever the various elements in the Soviet military posture in Asia in whatever numbers, there appears to be an unmistakable trend toward building Soviet military power throughout the spectrum of military preparedness. Although many reasons, all plausible, can be given for this disturbing phenomenon, Soviet goals behind the trend remain unclear.

Apart from the bureaucratic momentum that tends to propel a military program once it is under way, several considerations leave little ground for optimism with regard to a slowing of the Soviet military effort. The worldwide confrontation between the USSR and the United States is not likely to ease suddenly. This is particularly true in Asia, where deep-rooted Sino–Soviet antagonism promotes the drawing together of China, Japan, and the United States into a coalition hostile to Soviet influence. There is also little prospect that the Soviet entanglement in Vietnam and Afghanistan will soon end. Meanwhile, internal conflicts in the Middle East, South Asia, and elsewhere in the Third World will continue to invite Soviet intervention. Moreover, competition over resources will keep international tensions at a high level.

In the absence of a better outlook for the Soviet economy than exists today and in view of the unlikelihood of a reversal of the decline in the

Soviet Union's political-ideological appeal, military power and its political uses seem destined to remain the preferred and virtually the sole instrument of Soviet policy abroad. Soviet military might in Asia must then be expected to continue its steady growth in the years ahead. Whether this expanding Soviet military power will adversely affect the stability of Asia will not depend, of course, on the military factor alone.

Asian Military Contingencies: Soviet Strengths and Vulnerabilities

What we know about Soviet military capabilities and force design in the Soviet Far East suggests certain conclusions regarding the strengths and vulnerabilities of Soviet forces for defensive or offensive action in the region. These may be summarized as follows. (1) The Soviet military buildup relevant to Asia has created over time a military position adequate for defense against offensive actions by any Asian nation, or combination of nations, operating without the direct and massive military support of the United States. (2) Soviet military capabilities in the Asian theater are such that today—and even more surely by the mid-1980s— these assets could be used effectively for offensive action (i.e., for intervention along the Soviet periphery) should this prove politically or militarily expedient. (3) Certain deficiencies inherent in the Soviet military posture could be mitigated during the coming decade but not entirely removed. They would render difficult any *large-scale, sustained* Soviet military action in Asian areas away from the Soviet periphery. (4) Although these deficiencies also impose limits on Soviet assistance to allies in a prolonged conventional war, Soviet military capabilities in the Asian theater are sufficient to provide substantial support once "wars of liberation" or other forms of low-level regional conflict are underway. (5) Soviet attainment of essential strategic parity with the United States is leaving its mark on the perceptions of the Asian nations allied to the United States. However, Soviet theater forces do not as yet appear to be capable—or to be perceived as capable—of sustaining a conventional conflict with U.S. theater forces in the air and on the seas, at least in arenas away from the Soviet periphery.

Chinese Main Force units in the two northeastern military regions alone are estimated at 50–60 divisions. Despite this Chinese numerical superiority, Chinese hit-and-run operations aside, the Soviets would have no difficulty defending their territory against conventional Chinese attacks. In view of the slow pace of China's military modernization process, the Soviet defensive position along the Sino–Soviet border is therefore expected to remain secure through the 1980s and well beyond.[13]

13. The possible use by China of its modest nuclear arsenal would, of course, create an entirely new situation—one outside the scope of this discussion. The same is true of the possible Soviet employment of nuclear weapons in Asian contingencies.

Military analysts conclude that the present Soviet force posture would allow the Soviet Union to undertake short-term "punitive actions" across the border against China, although here logistic shortcomings could create difficulties should the action turn into a protracted operation requiring a sustained flow of supplies. The Soviet military problem in Asia has always been and still is one of logistics. The major enemies are the Russian climate and the enormous distances separating the Soviet Far East from the centers of industrial production in the western regions of the USSR. These obstacles can be partly overcome through the on-going economic development of Asian Russia, the improvement of the West–East transportation network, the expansion of ocean shipping, and the prepositioning of military and other needed supplies. But these measures, all now underway, will require substantial time as well as economic and human resources, thus competing with other demands on the far from affluent Soviet economy.

If these constraints on sustained Soviet military action are likely to discourage large-scale military involvement in China or in a distant Asian–Pacific theater, they are much less inhibiting with regard to limited military intervention along the Soviet periphery. Soviet force deployments against China are generally viewed as evidence of an essentially defensive Soviet strategy. Yet U.S. Secretary of Defense Harold Brown in his *Annual Report for Fiscal Year 1981* concluded that "Soviet forces in the Far East are geographically positioned, exercised, and apparently designed for offensive operations."[14] In explanation of this apparent contradiction it might be said that although Soviet forces along the Chinese border are in a defensive posture, even without receiving reinforcements from the European center they are capable of quick offensive actions against China in pursuit of limited military objectives. Such objectives could include a rapid blow against the industrialized portion of the Chinese northeast (Manchuria), perhaps followed by a temporary occupation. Despite the Chinese advantage in manpower few military experts doubt the outcome in view of the substantial Soviet superiority in military hardware and mobility. Even U.S. support on the level of conventional weapons is not considered likely to alter the balance of forces favoring the Soviet Union,[15] so long as the conflict remains geographically limited and of short duration—admittedly, large "if's."

Korea constitutes another potential target for Soviet military intervention. The Soviet Union can hardly afford to be indifferent to the political

14. *Report of Secretary of Defense* (Washington, D.C., Jan. 1980), p. 4.

15. On this point see, for example, Admiral (ret.) Noel Gayler, former commander-in-chief, U.S. Pacific Forces, "Security Implications of the Soviet Military Presence in Asia," in Richard H. Solomon, ed., *Asian Security in the 1980s: Problems and Policies for a Time of Transition* (R-2492-ISA) (Santa Monica: The Rand Corporation, Nov. 1979), pp. 54–68.

alignments on the neighboring peninsula, given its strategic location with regard to the Soviet Far East (Vladivostok, the Pacific Fleet's home port, is close to the Korean border), to Japan, and to China. At this point it seems idle to speculate on the outcome of Soviet military intervention in Korea in connection with a local conflict there because the prerequisite for such a Soviet action would be major changes in the military balance in Korea adversely affecting Soviet interests. It needs to be stressed, however, that the Soviet Union has developed a military posture on the approaches to Korea that would allow it to intervene on the peninsula rapidly and with considerable force, should its interest in maintaining a nonhostile Korean regime on its borders be threatened.

Whereas military operations along the Soviet periphery could be supplied relatively easily, Soviet intervention in force on a sustained level and at great distance from Soviet territory is likely to remain difficult at least for the next decade. This is true despite the recent precedents of Soviet military operations in Africa and the Middle East and despite the growing number of long-range transport aircraft that are entering the Soviet inventory. The reasons are largely inherent in the logistical constraints from which the Soviet military position in Asia suffers.

The vast distances that separate the major industrial and population centers of European Russia from the less developed territories of the Soviet Far East are currently bridged only by the tenuous steel ribbon of the Trans-Siberian Railroad with its few feeder lines. That vulnerability will be somewhat lessened when the 2,000-mile Baikal–Amur Mainline Railroad, now under construction, becomes fully operational sometime in the 1980s. Completion of that added link with the Far East will augment the present inadequate capacity for the West–East movement of men and equipment by land. Being situated farther from the Chinese border, the railroad will also reduce the vulnerability of trans-Siberian traffic to disruption by Chinese attacks. Meanwhile, the northern sea route to the Far East is not expected to offer an attractive fast alternative to the Trans-Siberian Railroad. Although the Soviets have made much progress over the years in keeping the Arctic sea-lane to the Soviet Far Eastern territories open, use of that route for supply of the coastal areas (such as the naval base of Vladivostok) remains time-consuming, very costly, and unreliable.

These internal logistical difficulties are compounded when massive military power projection into Asian areas away from the Sino–Soviet frontier is concerned. In the first place, any larger Soviet military operation in land areas beyond China (such as in Indochina) would have to be conducted by skirting China. But Soviet port capacity in Siberia remains inadequate for such purposes. Severe weather conditions prevail much of the year around the two principal bases on which Soviet naval forces will have to rely during the 1980s, Vladivostok and Petropavlovsk. Vladivostok suffers from another shortcoming. Despite its awesome name ("Rule the East!"), it has no direct access to the open sea; naval craft based there must pass through one of three narrow straits (Tsushima, Tsugaru, or Soya) to gain entry into the Pacific. These choke points are not under exclusive Soviet control. They could be mined and sealed off by Japan, especially if assisted in such an operation by the United States Navy. Petropavlovsk has other deficiencies. Isolated at the southern tip of the Kamchatka Peninsula, it faces the open sea but it is situated far north and cannot be supplied by land from Soviet territory.[16]

Understandably, the Soviets are seeking to overcome these handicaps. The extent to which their planners are prepared to invest during the 1980s in such a costly task will provide an indicator of the seriousness of Soviet security concerns in the region or, in the absence of a growing Sino–American–Japanese threat to Soviet security, will testify to the force of the expansionist momentum in Soviet strategy in Asia.

The Soviets have long been actively searching for more suitable bases or for means of making the existing ones more operational.[17] Warmwater ports with access to the open sea are a military imperative for Soviet strategy in Asia. It is not surprising, then, that under the terms of the Soviet–Vietnamese Friendship Treaty Soviet naval and air force elements have obtained permission to use the former U.S. bases of Cam Ranh Bay and Danang. Should this arrangement with Vietnam become permanent, some Soviet communications and supply problems would be solved. However, analysts of Soviet military affairs point out that even if the Soviet base problem in the Far East should be mitigated during the coming decade, there is still considerable doubt about the warfighting capabilities of the Pacific Fleet. At present, the fleet lacks air cover away from the shore; suitable long-range combat aircraft (the Backfire?) would have to be transferred to the Pacific in greater numbers to reduce

16. Japanese analysts have suggested that the Soviets might decide to construct a link to Petropavlovsk in connection with the building of the BAM. So far there is no indication that such a major project is being contemplated. It would, however, fit in with Soviet efforts to seal off the Sea of Okhotsk through fortification of the Kurile Islands, including also the four islands that Japan still claims but that Moscow considers Soviet territory and is keeping militarily occupied. The Sea of Okhotsk could then provide a safe haven for Soviet ballistic missile submarines capable of attacking the United States from sheltered positions.

17. Reports have been circulating in Japan that (possibly as a quid pro quo for Soviet advanced arms) North Korea has allowed the Soviet Union to expand port facilities at Najin in the northernmost part of Korea, south of Vladivostok, and that military use by the Soviets may eventually become feasible. The strained Soviet–North Korean relationship and the Pyongyang regime's stress on independence from outside powers make the realization of such a scheme highly improbable.

that vulnerability. The Pacific Fleet also remains vulnerable to sub-marine attacks and is as yet ill equipped for larger amphibious opera-tions. In all these respects it remains inferior to the U.S. Seventh Fleet.

The contingencies discussed above involve, in various settings, a Soviet military role (whether through arms supplies or through direct interven-tion) in conflict with Asian powers. They assume no direct military role for the United States. The war between China and Vietnam in 1979 might serve as an example of such a situation. It is certainly likely that other political or territorial conflicts could arise in various parts of Asia during the 1980s in which the United States would prefer not to play a direct role. Similarly, as in the recent fighting in Indochina, the Soviet Union may continue to exercise great caution and shun direct military involvement. As noted, there are military (quite apart from political) reasons for the Soviet Union to limit its military role to advice and arms supplies: a shortage of sea-based tactical air power, an inability to sustain forces at sea for long periods, and the absence of naval allies. As a U.S. expert in this field concluded in 1979, "At the moment, the Soviet Uni-on's capabilities for distant combat remain embryonic."[18] The world-wide Soviet–American battle may thus be conducted in Asia primarily on the political-psychological plane and through proxies.[19]

The Soviet role in the ongoing Sino–Vietnamese conflict seems to support the contention that in Asia at least, Soviet strategy seeks to avoid military commitments and direct involvement in areas remote from the Soviet borders. Soviet behavior in the Hanoi–Beijing confrontation points up the strengths as well as the limitations of the Soviet military posture in the Far East. A display of Soviet military might in the South China Sea accompanied the Sino–Vietnamese hostilities in 1979—a dozen or so Soviet naval vessels were cruising off the coast and long-range Soviet aircraft were patrolling the same ocean areas, thus warning the Chinese leaders not to go too far and leaving them uncertain of Soviet reactions. Although making occasional use of the former Ameri-can bases of Danang and Cam Ranh Bay, the Soviets have so far care-fully avoided any military confrontation with Chinese forces. At the same time, they have effectively stiffened Vietnamese resolve through

18. Andrew Marshall, Director of Net Assessment in the Pentagon at this writing, in "Sources of Soviet Power: The Military Potential in the 1980s," *Prospects of Soviet Power in the 1980s* (London: International Institute for Strategic Studies, 1979), part II, p. 13.

19. It is sometimes suggested that Soviet naval forces are designed with a view to their political impact—their ability to demonstrate Soviet military strength with high visibility—as much as to their military utility. In this connection it is asserted that the Soviet Union has been building large, 32,000-ton cruisers with very large guns, no longer being installed on modern U.S. naval ships, but that these same cruisers are also equipped with the latest surface-to-surface and surface-to-air missiles.

economic assistance, the provision of military supplies, and political propaganda support.

We do not know whether or at what point the Soviet leaders would have been prepared to enter the conflict militarily on the Vietnamese side should the Chinese forces have carried the war more deeply into Vietnam. The question naturally arises as to the Soviet reaction should China attempt to teach the Vietnamese another lesson by invading their territory a second time. If, as we assume, Soviet concern is primarily with finding means of weakening the PRC—the major external obstacle to the spread of Soviet influence throughout Asia—it must be assumed that the Soviets would once more lend the DRV their support. What form might such support take?

It is highly unlikely that the Soviets would choose to become embroiled on China's southern flank, far from Soviet bases and territory. The Soviet Union has more convenient pressure points against China along its own borders. Logistic difficulties in supporting protracted and large-scale military operations (of the kind the United States conducted in the Vietnam War) will no doubt continue to militate for some time to come against such a strategy—not to speak of the political disadvantages connected with the presence of substantial Soviet forces in Vietnam and Cambodia. It seems likely then that Soviet assistance would be offered, as in the past, through stepped-up economic and military supply efforts. Political pressures could be applied to protect this operation from interference by other powers and if possible to obtain their cooperation for gaining overflight rights to circumvent Chinese territory (for example, by passing through India). As is already the case at present, the Soviet Union, both for economic and for political reasons, would surely seek to enlist contributions from its own zone of influence in Eastern Europe and if feasible from elsewhere. The absence of firm Soviet allies in Asia would render such efforts less effective than might be similar attempts on the part of the United States, a fact that points up the disparity that characterizes the U.S. and Soviet positions in Asia.

It is conceivable that Chinese military pressures would be too strong for Vietnam to contain without direct outside military support. But as long as the Sino–Soviet conflict continues, the Soviet Union could ill afford to let Vietnam be defeated. Vietnam is too valuable a Soviet ally in Asia, politically and strategically. Still it is difficult to envisage the dispatch of large contingents of Soviet ground forces into Southeast Asia. More likely in such a contingency would be a massive Soviet anti-China effort from the air, or possibly a naval blockade, should there be no danger of a U.S. reaction.

A much more probable military contingency than direct Soviet involvement in war with China (or than a confrontation with the U.S. navy in the Pacific) is a Soviet role in Asian civil wars ("wars of liberation"). Considering the character of the Vietnamese regime and its perspectives on the outside world, it is doubtful that the Vietnamese will ever be willing or capable of serving Soviet interests by playing the role of "Asian Cubans." However, this judgment does not rule out the possibility that in certain circumstances Vietnamese and Soviet objectives could suffi- ciently coincide to allow for military cooperation (for example, with regard to Cambodia's Thai neighbor). At any rate there exist ample opportunities for Soviet involvement in "wars of liberation" in the vast and unstable zone stretching from Southeast Asia to the Middle East. It is not likely that in such a contingency Soviet ground forces drawn from those stationed along the Sino–Soviet frontier would be utilized. As indi- cated above, logistical problems would create major obstacles since Chi- nese territory interposes itself between the USSR and the landmass of continental Asia. It has also been argued that these China-oriented forces might play a role in the case of Soviet military involvement in the Middle East—Iran or the Persian Gulf. However, there would be some risk for the Soviets in denuding their frontier with the PRC of even a portion of the military contingents assigned to the Soviet defense against China. These forces are probably viewed as a reservoir to be drawn on for use other than against China only in real national emergencies else- where. Moreover, logistically the employment of the anti-China forces in Middle Eastern crises cannot look attractive for the Soviet Union. They would have to be moved westward over thousands of miles into regions of the USSR where military forces earmarked for Middle East action are readily available. It can be argued therefore that the many divisions now deployed by the Soviets along the borders with China will have to be maintained in that position for use against the PRC (or possibly for Northeast Asian contingencies) at least as long as the Sino–Soviet tension continues at its present high level. If geographic and military considera- tions thus limit the capacity of the Soviet ground forces in Asia to be mobilized for intervention in civil wars, this is not meant to denigrate Soviet capacity to play a military role in such conflicts. The ongoing buildup of Soviet paratroop, air mobile, and amphibious forces has reached a level where capacities for massive and rapid Soviet interven- tion anywhere in the Third World already are a reality.

Nevertheless, in the appraisal of plausible Soviet military actions in Asia, the form that these might take and their consequences, the U.S. factor would have to be taken into account, as well as the responses of U.S. allies in the region. Despite its military eclipse in Indochina the United States maintains security pacts with Japan, the Republic of Ko- rea, and other Asian nations; it has indicated its stake in the integrity of China; and it continues to deploy large contingents (totaling about

180,000 men) of naval, air, and ground forces in the Western Pacific, Korea, the Philippines, and Japan. In the eyes of American allies in Asia, the Seventh Fleet remains at once a symbol of the American commitment to the security of the region and a tangible guarantee that this commitment can be sustained.

On the other hand the past decade has seen the Soviet Union display a military presence in Asia that is perceived as rivaling that of the United States.[20] The Soviet Pacific Fleet has been built up to a point where its combat units now outstrip, in numbers although not in military potential, those of the Seventh Fleet. An Asia-oriented nuclear force of intermediate-range ballistic missiles has been deployed in the region. So have about 2,000 combat aircraft, including many equipped to carry nuclear weapons. This impressive Soviet military panoply operates against a background of Soviet strategic weapon systems on land and sea, ranging from missiles to long-range strategic bombers deployed throughout the Soviet Far East and on submarines cruising the Pacific Ocean.

The impression has thus been created that the Soviet Pacific Fleet is now in a position to interdict the flow of vital U.S. and Asian allied resources. This impression has been reinforced by the U.S. decision in 1980 to detach key units of the Seventh Fleet to the Indian Ocean and the Middle East to protect vital U.S. and allied interests there. Many Japanese appreciate the United States Navy's need for the adoption of a swing strategy and a strengthening of the U.S. position in the Persian Gulf, where Japan's oil lifeline might otherwise be threatened. Yet, the drawdown of the Seventh Fleet came as a shock and suggested a weakening of the U.S. ability to counter Soviet pressures in the Pacific region. The issue of the perceived changing naval balance is particularly worrisome for nations such as Japan and Korea, whose industries and economic viability depend on a massive inflow of raw materials, especially oil.[21] For Japan and Korea the ability to maintain minimum import

20. According to the Department of Defense's *Annual Report—Fiscal Year 1981* (p. 112), roughly half the United States Navy's larger combat units were typically deployed in the Western Pacific—before the crises in Iran and Afghanistan.

21. A study that appeared in a Japanese-language journal on defense affairs in January 1980 concluded that in 1985 the absolute minimum level of Japanese raw material imports, in terms of 1976 import levels, would be as follows: oil, 61%; iron ore, 36%; coal, 22%; and food, 56%. See Takashi Baba, "1985-nen goro ni okeru waga kuni shuyo shigen no saitei shoyo yunyu-ryo ni tsuite" ("Regarding Japan's Minimum Required Import Quantities of Major Resources in 1985"), *Shin Boei Ronshu,* vol. 7, no. 3 (1980), p. 86. The magnitude of the problem of supplying Japan in time of war can be gauged also by the data submitted in the spring of 1980 to the Japanese Diet by a high-ranking official of the Japanese Defense Agency. He stated that each year Japan would require a minimum import of 190 million tons of oil, food, and other essential supplies (oil from the Persian Gulf, food from Aus-

levels of natural resources is widely acknowledged to be a matter of life
and death. Any serious indication that these levels cannot be assured
because of a weakening of American military power must inevitably lead
to a reappraisal of national policy and defense strategy.

Although concerns on this score in recent years have set in motion a
review of Japanese national security programs for the 1980s, the problem of Soviet interdiction of American and allied sea lines of communication appears to be a danger anticipated rather for the mid- or late
1980s than for the immediate future. Thus, the U.S. Secretary of Defense has stated that the United States together with its allies could close
down the main Soviet fleet exits from the Sea of Okhotsk into the Pacific.
At the same time, he had to admit that

it could take as long as three months to bring the Soviet submarine threat under
control in the Atlantic and Pacific. During those months, if typical estimates are
valid, we could lose a significant percentage of U.S. and allied reinforcement and
resupply shipping, while the Soviets could lose a very large number of their
submarines. [Nonetheless,] essential supplies, under these conditions, would get
through.

Yet, these mildly reassuring conclusions were followed by remarks
largely offsetting their effect. The secretary said:

Although these estimates could be conservative, they give us no grounds for
comfort. With the appearance of the Backfire [airplane] Soviet land-based naval
aviation may expand in size and will certainly grow in capability, especially as
techniques for ocean surveillance and long-range air-to-air surface missiles are
linked with this aircraft. Indeed, the Backfire is likely soon to become a greater
threat to our naval forces and sea lines of communication than Soviet submarines. In part, this is because we invested so many resources in so few surface
combatants during the late 1960s and early 1970s. But it is also because we lack
an adequate defense against massed bomber and missile attacks. How well we
can now counter the threat with land-based and carrier-based aircraft and
AEGIS-equipped ships remains to be seen.[22]

The Soviet military position, on the other hand, remains highly vulnerable (as noted) because of logistical difficulties and the constricted
nature of its base structure. Soviet naval and supply operations would
have to cope with interruptions through actions of the Seventh Fleet and
with the possibility that the Pacific Fleet would find itself bottled up in its
isolated Siberian bases through joint actions by the United States and

---

tralia and the United States). To transport these enormous quantities would in turn require 400 large cargo ships. But, he added, the Maritime Self-Defense Force could at best
give protection to half of these; for the remainder it would have to rely on the United
States.

22. U.S. Department of Defense, *Annual Report—Fiscal Year 1981*, p. 114.

Japan. There appears to exist at present a rough equilibrium of mutual risk in any nonnuclear direct confrontation in Asia between the Soviet Union and the United States. It is doubtful that either superpower would want to risk such a confrontation in Asia unless a conflict had already broken out in the Middle East or in Europe. In that eventuality the regional military balance would probably no longer be relevant because the Pacific region would have become part of a larger, global military confrontation. By then it would presumably have reached the strategic level. Short of such a cataclysm, it seems probable that the battle of U.S.–Soviet military presences in Asia will continue at least during the 1980s to be conducted through proxies and arms aid, as well as on the political-psychological plane. Even under such conditions, of course, the policy decisions of key U.S. allies in Asia will continue to reflect their perception of the trends of the regional as well as of the global military balance. Indications are that these nations' reading of that *trend* currently reflects a reduced faith in American staying power. If allowed to persist, this perception could over time pose important problems for the United States and its Asian allies as well.

SOME KEY POLICY ISSUES

The principal result of the growth of Soviet military power in the region has been a drawing together of the United States, China, and Japan in recognition of a common danger. Desirable as this new relationship may be, it also raises the question of the limits that should be set to the rapprochement and the dangers that could be generated by going too far too fast.

These dangers are most obvious in regard to U.S. cooperation with China. Chinese policies toward the Soviet Union appear to be cast in concrete—or at least that is the view of most experts. As the Chinese approach to Vietnam has clearly demonstrated, the Beijing leaders are willing to take the risk of military confrontation with the Soviets. The new relationship with Washington is likely to have been an important factor in this. But it is by no means certain that the larger U.S. interests in its global dealings with the Soviet Union are served by indirectly encouraging such a Chinese risk-taking attitude. The consequence may be that the United States will be drawn into the Sino–Soviet conflict against its will.

A greater degree of military cooperation between the United States and its Japanese ally offers many advantages to the United States. The growth of Soviet military power and of the Soviet military presence around Japan creates anxieties there. But with limited resources and faced with growing demands also in the Middle East and elsewhere, the

United States may be tempted to press Japan beyond what the Japanese political situation can tolerate to step up dramatically its military contributions. Such eagerness to push Japan into assuming a larger share of the common defense could in turn encourage the Japanese to review reluctantly their national security strategy. Interpreting U.S. policy as testifying to weakness of will or resources available for the guarantee of Japan's security, the Japanese may then decide to take the road to full-fledged rearmament. The international repercussions of such a move would be enormous.

There can be little doubt that at least some of our Asian allies need reassurances about the state of the theater military balance. The Japanese and the Koreans particularly have an overriding stake in the security of their sea lines of communications. Their perspective on the issues can best be illustrated by a few quotations from Japan's Defense White Papers:

The improvements in the Soviet Union's military capability since the 1960s have not only eased the national security position of the Soviet side, despite this containment policy, but also altered the military balance between the United States and the Soviet Union as well as its structure to some extent.[23]

The Soviet Union has expanded its nuclear deterrent capability against the United States and at the same time has reinforced its military posture in Europe and the Far East. This has been accomplished through improved air defense capability at home, modernization of ground forces and tactical air power, strengthening of naval power and the expansion into the outer oceans. The Soviet force strength, in particular, surpasses that of the United States, and the safety of the sea and air lanes from the U.S. mainland is being jeopardized. (ibid.)

The "blue water" expansion of Soviet naval power into the outer oceans also is a matter of concern to the national security of Japan which is situated along passage strait routes to the outer oceans. . . . (ibid., pp. 24–25)

. . . the fleet [Seventh Fleet] has a sufficient anti-submarine capability for its own defense. However, there is reason to conclude that it lacks sufficient capabilities for the protection of large numbers of merchant vessels. It will therefore be difficult to counter completely the Soviet capabilities for severing the sea lines of communication.[24]

The official U.S. statements on the question of Soviet interdiction of the Pacific sea lines of communication have already been cited. They can be received only with mixed feelings in Japan. Ways will have to be found

---

23. Japanese Defense Agency, *Defense of Japan* (White Paper) (Tokyo, 1977), p. 14.
24. Boeicho (Defense Agency), *Nihon no Boei* (Defense of Japan) (Tokyo, July 1978), p. 39. This is the writer's translation from the original Japanese-language White Paper; no official English translation was available.

of reassuring the Japanese that if the problem cannot be completely solved, it can at least be mitigated through U.S. efforts coupled with Japanese assistance.

Finally, there is the key issue of how to reduce the danger of direct military confrontation with the Soviet Union in Asia and yet safeguard the interests of U.S. allies. The growth of Soviet military power in the region, as noted, has been steady although essentially unspectacular. There is no reason to believe that its momentum will be lost during the coming years so long as the Sino–Soviet conflict poses a security problem for the Soviet Union and Soviet involvement in Indochina continues. Yet on the whole Soviet military power in Asia has not been translated into commensurate political influence. Whether Moscow shares that interpretation is of course unclear. At any rate other instruments are not currently available to the Soviet Union to bolster its position in Asia and they are not likely to become available in the near future. Under these circumstances the United States may have no choice but to restore and maintain an equilibrium of military forces in the Asian–Pacific region. It should be effective also on the political-psychological plane.

Nevertheless, all friendly Asian nations except China would probably support any U.S. move that might bring a halt to the military buildup in the Asian region. Effective regional arms control measures (for example, a neutralization of Indochina or mutual force reductions in the two Koreas) may be completely out of the question for a long time to come. However, growing U.S. attention to the restoration of a military equilibrium in the region, coupled with a costly stalemate in Indochina, may eventually create conditions offering more attractive opportunities for arms limitations than exist today.

11

Coalition Building or Condominium? The Soviet Presence in Asia and American Policy Alternatives

RICHARD H. SOLOMON

Since World War II Asia has been a region of shifting alignments in the ongoing global rivalry between the Soviet Union and the United States. In Europe the pattern of alliances between East and West, between the NATO states and the Warsaw Pact, has remained relatively stable for more than thirty years, and until recently much of the developing world has been at the margins of Soviet–American competition. In Asia, however, the postwar years have been characterized by major periodic alterations in the pattern of great power relationships as they affect the Soviet–American competition. The Sino–Soviet alliance of the 1950s gave way to political feuding in the 1960s and a military confrontation in the 1970s. China's unsuccessful efforts of the 1960s to organize a third international center around the "newly emerging forces" of the developing world, symbolized by Indonesia's Sukarno, gave way in the 1970s to openings toward the noncommunist states of Japan, the United States, and Western Europe as Beijing sought protection against Soviet political and military pressures and access to advanced technology and development capital. At the same time, India has shifted from balanced relations between East and West to near alignment with the Soviet Union.

The primary forces animating these changes, and regional developments related to them, have been the state of Sino–Soviet relations and the Soviet–American competition. The bipolar regional alignments of the 1950s reflected the Sino–Soviet alliance and the Soviet–American cold war. The fluidity of the subsequent decade was stimulated by the eruption of the Moscow–Beijing feud. And the 1970s brought to Asia a renewed trend toward polarization along the faultline of the Sino–Soviet military confrontation, reinforced by the breakdown of Soviet–American détente at mid-decade.

The United States, the Soviet Union, and the major and minor states

The views expressed in this analysis are my own and do not necessarily reflect those of The Rand Corporation, with which I am affiliated, or any of its sponsors.

of Asia are now faced with choices about how far they should proceed in
building coalitions or formal alliances with which to contain the influence of adversaries and their allies. Can a stable balance of relationships
be achieved among the major powers, or will continuing rivalries again
drive Asia toward confrontation?

The ominous worldwide growth of Soviet military power, and particularly its projection into Asia, is the primary factor shaping the emerging
pattern of alignments in the region. Does Moscow intend to engage in
coercive diplomacy through military pressures to gain greater influence
in Asia? Will the Soviets seek to work out a great power "deal" (as they
have proposed to the United States in various forums since the late
1960s) to guarantee access to Asia and to inhibit the formation of a
coalition of major and regional states against them?

It is highly unlikely that the great powers can negotiate an understanding about future alignments in Asia. A condominium of the major
states would gain no general acceptance, just as "spheres of influence"
politics has been outdated by the global reach of Soviet and American
power and the increasing fluidity of the international system. Moreover,
the predominantly military character of the Soviet presence is likely to
be unsettling rather than stabilizing, especially as Moscow seeks to
strengthen its position in Asia and related regions, such as the Middle
East, by involving itself in local disputes and political instabilities.

The United States must formulate an Asia policy that responds to
growing Soviet involvement by maintaining a stabilizing presence that
will protect its own interests and those of its allies. America must establish the *capability* to mobilize a countervailing coalition in response to
Soviet pressures, yet without gratuitously provoking Moscow's concerns
about "encirclement." The policy the United States adopts must be designed to prevent an action–reaction cycle of Soviet and American initiatives in Asia (as elsewhere) that would unnecessarily polarize the region
and increase the risks of military confrontation.

KREMLIN STRATEGIES FOR SECURING THE USSR'S ASIAN FRONTIER

Contemporary Soviet concerns about the security of the USSR's Asian
frontier are rooted in the history of the Mongol invasion of Russia in the
twelfth and thirteenth centuries and the more recent experience in the
1900s of major Asian countries allying themselves with imperial states of
the West. The colonial European powers that gained spheres of influence in China during the nineteenth century did not constitute a direct
military threat to czarist Russia, but Moscow's defeat at the hands of the
Japanese imperial navy in 1905 clearly threatened Russian security.

Soviet fears of a two-front military threat, which were aroused by

Western intervention against the newly founded Bolshevik state at Arkhangel and Vladivostok in 1919, were fully realized in the German–Japanese axis of the 1940s. From that time to the present, Moscow's Asian security problem has been to prevent the two-front challenge of a modernizing Asian country allying itself with a hostile power of the West.

A United Front of Socialist and Anticolonial States

The post-World War II era in Asia began positively for the Soviet Union. Moscow's establishment in late 1949 of an alliance with the newly victorious Chinese communists, and the concomitant diminution of Western influence in China and the decolonized states of the region, seemed the beginning of a golden age for Soviet interests. The USSR's eastern frontier was secured through the alliance with China, and Moscow's influence was projected widely through vigorous communist movements in North Korea, Malaya, and Indochina and anticolonial governments in Burma, Indonesia, and India.

Through these developments, in combination with prior Soviet initiatives in Eastern Europe, Moscow established a two-front security challenge to which the Truman and Eisenhower administrations responded by establishing the North Atlantic Treaty Organization (NATO) alliance in Europe and the Central Treaty Organization (CENTO) in the Middle East and by negotiating bilateral and multilateral security treaties with the Philippines (1952); the Republic of Korea (1954); the Republic of China on Taiwan (1954); Japan (1960); the ANZUS states of Australia and New Zealand (1951); and Australia, New Zealand, Pakistan, the Philippines, Thailand, and European allies with interests in Asia (the SEATO treaty of 1955).

Moscow's golden age was short-lived, however. Beijing did not support Soviet participation in the 1955 Bandung Conference of Asian and African states and later fully expressed opposition to Soviet influence in Asia in the polemics of the 1960s. The Chinese leadership openly resisted Moscow's participation in the Second African–Asian Conference of 1964 on the grounds that the USSR was not an Asian country.[1] The

---

1. See "Statement of the Government of the People's Republic of China on the Soviet Government's Statement Concerning the Preparatory Meeting for the Second Asian–African Conference," *Peking Review*, no. 23 (June 5, 1964), p. 7. Analysts of Sino–Soviet relations have noted the origins of Beijing's challenge to Soviet influence in Asia and other Third World areas in statements by Mao Zedong's colleague (later to be purged) Liu Shaoqi. In 1946 Liu told Anna Louise Strong that Mao had developed an Asiatic form of Marxism that would influence other developing countries in Asia, a perspective that Liu repeated in November 1949 at a Trade Union Conference of Asian and Australasian Countries in Beijing. See Donald S. Zagoria, *The Sino–Soviet Conflict 1956–1961* (Princeton: Princeton University Press, 1962), pp. 14–15.

concurrent breakdown of the Moscow–Beijing security relationship, which resulted from Chinese and Soviet differences over the PRC's fledgling nuclear weapons program, its defense and foreign policies, and its initiative in the Taiwan Strait crisis of 1958, led Moscow to initiate political and military measures to contain the expansion of Chinese influence in Asia.

In the mid-1950s Khrushchev and Bulganin sought to develop ties with India, Burma, and Indonesia. And during the last years of the Khrushchev era the Soviet leadership attempted to build political pressures against the Chinese and their anticipated detonation of nuclear weapons by signing a limited nuclear test ban treaty with the United States.[2] Prior to China's first atomic bomb detonation in 1964, American and Soviet leaders even mused about the possibility of joint or tacitly coordinated Soviet–American military action against China's nuclear facilities.[3]

A Military Buildup and Asian Collective Security

Khrushchev's successors took the Chinese challenge no less seriously. After failing to reestablish a positive relationship with the Chinese following Khrushchev's ouster, Brezhnev and Kosygin initiated a military buildup along the Sino–Soviet frontier in 1965, increasing the initial deployment of 17 Soviet divisions to more than 45 (3 of which were stationed in the Mongolian People's Republic) by 1975. And although this buildup has grown only slowly since the late 1970s, continuing qualitative improvements in weaponry and associated equipment are heightening the combat capabilities of the Soviet forces.[4] At the same time, Moscow continues to increase its air and naval deployments in the Soviet Far East targeted on Japan and U.S. forces in Asia.

Despite the venom of Chinese political attacks on the United States during the 1960s, American leaders came to warn Soviet leaders of the adverse consequences of military action against the Chinese, much as they rejected Jiang Jieshi's (Chiang Kai-shek's) appeals for American support of Taiwan-based military action against the south China coast during 1962–63 at the time of the collapse of Beijing's Great Leap Forward.[5] Moscow, however, has sought to reinforce its military response to

2. Theodore C. Sorenson, *Kennedy* (New York: Harper & Row, 1965), pp. 724–25; Arthur M. Schlesinger, Jr., *A Thousand Days: John F. Kennedy in the White House* (Boston: Houghton Mifflin, 1956), p. 915.

3. Schlesinger, *Thousand Days*, p. 904.

4. *The Military Balance, 1981–1982* (London: International Institute for Strategic Studies, 1981).

5. For the Kennedy administration's position, see Henry A. Kissinger, *White House Years* (Boston: Little, Brown, 1979), pp. 183–86.

what it views as a growing Chinese political and military challenge by the
creation of a political coalition that would isolate Beijing within the international communist movement, in the Third World, and in Asia. In
1969, after the first of a series of serious military clashes along the
Sino–Soviet frontier, Soviet Communist Party General Secretary Brezhnev called for the establishment of a "system of collective security" in
Asia as an alternative to balance-of-power politics and as a replacement
for "existing military-political groupings."[6] This vague concept was read
by almost all observers, however, as constituting the basis for a new, anti-
China coalition.[7]

Despite widespread distrust of Chinese intentions throughout the region, the Soviets found virtually no takers for their proposal. Although
India and Indonesia viewed China as their major security challenge,
they failed to endorse the Brezhnev initiative, as did North Vietnam and
North Korea, socialist states seeking to balance themselves between the
contending powers. Only the Mongolian People's Republic and Iran
spoke out in favor of the idea.[8]

Brezhnev's attempt to form an Asian collective security system reinforced the impact of related developments, impelling China's leaders to
undertake their third major departure in foreign policy since the founding of the PRC in 1949—an opening to the West. Mao Zedong and Zhou
Enlai read Brezhnev's proposal as part of his earlier assertion that "proletarian internationalism" justified "support for progressive forces in all
countries," a policy of limited sovereignty for socialist states that was
used to rationalize the Soviet military intervention into Czechoslovakia
in the summer of 1968.[9] The Sino–Soviet border clashes of the following
year dramatized to the Chinese the significance of the Soviet military
buildup along their northern frontier, signaling to the world that the
Moscow–Beijing feud had become a direct and an immediate threat to
China's security.[10]

6. L. I. Brezhnev, "For Strengthening the Solidarity of Communists, for a New Up-
swing in the Anti-Imperialist Struggle" (June 7, 1969), as translated in *Current Digest of the
Soviet Press* (*CDSP*), vol. 21, no. 23 (July 2, 1969), p. 16.

7. See Bernard Gwertzman, "Moscow May Seek Asian Defense Pact," *New York Times*,
June 14, 1969, and Kissinger, *White House Years*, pp. 178, 180.

8. Arnold L. Horelick, *The Soviet Union's "Asian Collective Security" Proposal: A Club in
Search of Members* (Santa Monica: The Rand Corporation, Mar. 1974), P-5195.

9. See Brezhnev's speech to the Fifth Congress of the Polish United Workers' Party
(Nov. 12, 1968), as translated in *CDSP*, vol. 20, no. 46 (1968), pp. 3–5; see also the
Brezhnev speech cited in n. 6 above.

10. For differing interpretations of the origins of the Sino–Soviet border clashes of
1969, see Roger G. Brown, "Chinese Politics and American Foreign Policy: A New Look at
the Triangle," *Foreign Policy*, no. 23 (Summer 1976), pp. 3–23, and Thomas W. Robinson,
"The Sino–Soviet Border Dispute: Background, Development, and the March 1969
Clashes," *American Political Science Review*, vol. 67, no. 4 (Dec. 1972), pp. 1175–202.

The Evolution of an Anti-Hegemony Countercoalition,
and Moscow's West Asian Breakout

Awareness of China's vulnerability to the growing Soviet military presence in Asia stimulated PRC leaders to repair their country's tenuous
links to the international community—links that had been strained by
the years of Cultural Revolution turmoil. During the 1970s Zhou Enlai's
artful diplomacy achieved China's admission to the United Nations, the
establishment of diplomatic relations with the states of Western Europe,
and ultimately the normalization of relations with Japan and the United
States. The objective of this reactivated Chinese foreign policy was to
build a coalition of states united on the theme of anti-hegemony, opposed to Soviet expansionism and Moscow's efforts to create collective
security arrangements in Asia and bilateral defense relationships
throughout the Third World.

Moscow's initial reaction to the PRC's shift in foreign policy was to
accelerate efforts to reduce tensions with the United States through the
diplomacy of détente—even as programs to modernize and expand Soviet strategic and conventional weaponry proceeded apace. For the first
half of the decade the Soviets competed with the Chinese to improve
relations with the United States and Europe, a situation that facilitated
the negotiation of agreements on Berlin and the prevention of acciden-
tal nuclear war, and the first strategic arms limitation treaty.[11]

During the brief years of détente the Soviets first attempted to preclude, and then to draw the United States away from, its formative
relationship with the Chinese and establish the appearance, if not the
reality, of a Soviet–American condominium in global affairs. Soviet proposals for the treaty on the prevention of nuclear war initially included
language that would have justified joint Soviet–American military action
against China in the event of some Chinese provocation—an implication
repeatedly rejected by the United States.[12] And senior Soviet leaders
sought to convince the Nixon and Ford administrations that détente
could be sustained only on the basis of an end to the process of normalizing Sino–American relations.[13]

By the mid-1970s the Soviet leadership seems to have concluded that
détente was not moving events in a direction favorable to Soviet interests.[14] The new Soviet relationship with the United States had limited

11. Kissinger, *White House Years*, pp. 766, 835–40.
12. Ibid., pp. 545, 548–50, 554, 708, 1146, 1152, 1208.
13. Ibid., p. 1251; Richard M. Nixon, *RN: The Memoirs of Richard Nixon* (New York, Grosset and Dunlap, 1978), p. 1030.
14. This interpretation is developed at length in William G. Hyland, *Soviet–American Relations: A New Cold War?* (Santa Monica: The Rand Corporation, May 1981), R-2763-FF/RC.

economic payoffs (as a result of congressional resistance to trade concessions for the USSR embodied in the Jackson–Vanik and Stevenson
amendments), and Soviet leaders distrusted America's purposes in its
Middle East diplomacy and its slowly evolving China connection. Moreover, in view of the uncertain benefits of détente, Moscow probably felt
that Soviet interests could be pursued most effectively through the use
of military assets: arms sales, military assistance, support of proxy military interventions in Third World countries, and, in the extreme, the
direct use of Soviet armed forces.

In the latter half of the 1970s the Soviets resorted to various military
initiatives to counter what they saw as an evolving anti-Soviet coalition of
China, Japan, the United States, and Western Europe. The impact of
their actions, however, was to accelerate the process of coalescence,
speeding the full normalization of Beijing's relations with Japan and the
United States and, after the invasion of Afghanistan, justifying the evolution of Sino–American relations into areas of low-level defense cooperation. To be sure, such developments were implicit in the events of the
early 1970s, but Soviet actions accelerated political initiatives that otherwise might have taken many more years to play out, if they would have
been realized at all.

Much of the Soviet action between 1975 and 1979 took place in Africa
and the Persian Gulf: the intervention, along with Cuban proxies, in the
Angolan civil war; involvement in the Ethiopian Marxist revolution
against Emperor Haile Selassie in 1977; the shift of support from Somalia to Ethiopia and the development of port facilities at Massawa and
Dahlak; involvement in South Yemen and the development of naval and
air facilities at Aden and on the island of Socotra; and the invasion of
Afghanistan in late 1979.

These initiatives did much to degrade confidence in Soviet intentions
and enhanced the American political reaction against détente. They also
heightened public awareness of the linkage between the economic security of Western Europe, Japan, and other industrializing states of East
Asia and access to Middle Eastern energy supplies. The security of Asia
could not be reckoned in regional terms alone, and an ability to defend
the sea-lanes and maintain access to distant oil resources would be critical to a sense of confidence in the future.

By 1978, however, events began to have a more direct impact on
alignments in East Asia. Sino–Japanese negotiations over a peace and
friendship treaty, which had languished for several years, gained renewed momentum. Despite Soviet threats about the effects of such a
treaty on Russo–Japanese relations, the negotiations were successfully
concluded during the summer of 1978. Vice-Premier Deng Xiaoping
traveled to Tokyo in September for the official signing ceremony. He

carried warnings about the Soviet threat to world peace that rendered Japanese denials that the anti-hegemony clause of the treaty was specifically directed against the Soviet Union ritualistic and implausible.

Sino–Vietnamese tensions were accelerating dramatically in the wake of clashes along the Vietnamese–Cambodian frontier initiated by Cambodia's brutal and xenophobic Pol Pot government, which was closely tied to the Chinese. Hanoi's forced expulsion of hundreds of thousands of ethnic Chinese, either over Vietnam's northern border into the PRC or out to sea as "boat people," burdened the states of Southeast Asia with a flood of refugees. In response the Chinese abruptly cut off all economic assistance to the Vietnamese.

The Soviets wasted little time in involving themselves in the feud, initially by admitting the Vietnamese to CMEA (the Moscow-based Council of Mutual Economic Assistance) in the record time of two days and by accelerating deliveries of military equipment to Hanoi. In the fall, as Vietnamese troops prepared to invade Cambodia, Moscow and Hanoi signed a treaty of peace and friendship that included the obligation to consult in the event of threats to the security of either party. And Russian ships and aircraft began appearing regularly at the American-built naval and air facilities at Danang and Cam Ranh Bay.

During this same period the Sino–American normalization negotiations took on new life. Following the visit to Beijing of national security adviser Zbigniew Brzezinski in May 1978, China expressed heightened interest in acquiring American scientific training and industrial technology, and Beijing helped to accelerate the negotiations over a normalization agreement in the fall. Just ten days before Vietnamese troops crossed the border into Cambodia on December 25, Premier Hua Guofeng and President Carter announced an agreement to complete the normalization of U.S.–PRC relations by January 1, 1979. And the now peripatetic Deng Xiaoping visited Washington in late January to celebrate normalization, amidst warnings that China would have to "teach the Vietnamese a lesson" for their military action against the Pol Pot government.

The Chinese must have calculated that full normalization with Washington would give them some added margin of protection against Soviet pressures should they take military action against Hanoi—which they did within a month of Deng's return to Beijing. Although the Russians maintained a small naval presence in the South China Sea during the month-long border war, they did not directly enter the fray or take countermeasures along China's northern frontier. Subsequent assessments of the conflict either lauded the Soviets for their restraint or questioned their reliability as an ally; yet all evaluations raised public awareness of the connection between the conflicts of the great powers and the feuds of the region.

The events in Indochina were paralleled by other Soviet military moves in Northeast Asia. Moscow's troop buildup along the Sino–Soviet frontier from 1965 to 1975 was oriented primarily against the Chinese. Beginning in mid-decade, however, Soviet military capabilities in Asia were expanded to pose an increased threat to American and Japanese naval and air forces. The Soviet Far East Fleet, headquartered at Vladivostok, was significantly expanded. The antisubmarine cruiser *Minsk* and the amphibious assault ship *Ivan Rogov* were deployed to the region in 1979, and SS-20 intermediate range missiles were deployed to the Soviet Far East. The stationing of the antiship version of the Tu-26 "Backfire" bomber and MIG-25 "Foxbat" interceptors in the Soviet Far East heightened the threat of long-range satellite-directed air attack on ships of the U.S. Seventh Fleet and aircraft of the strategic airlift. And in the fall of 1978 Soviet ground forces began to garrison the contested northern islands off Japan's Hokkaido, raising the threat of airborne and amphibious attack on Japan across the narrow Soya and Nemuro straits.

Coping with the Asian Front of a Multifront Strategic Challenge

Moscow faces an increasingly complex security problem in East Asia. The coalition of China, Japan, the United States, and American allies in Southeast Asia and Western Europe constitutes a multifront strategic challenge, and the Soviet Far East is no longer buffered by a friendly China. In Southeast Asia the USSR's Vietnamese allies are caught between Chinese military pressures and the political opposition of the ASEAN states (two of which—the Philippines and Thailand—are directly allied to the United States); yet Soviet political influence in the region is minimal, with its potential for growth limited to Indonesia and Malaysia, that is, the countries that fear Beijing's possible influence over large ethnic Chinese minorities.

Only in West Asia and the Middle East does the situation show greater—if uncertain—promise for Soviet interests. India, concerned about China's growing ties to the West, actively supports Soviet diplomacy and is a major recipient of Soviet military assistance.[15] Afghanistan is likely to be a base for more active Soviet involvement in Southwest Asia and

15. In May 1980 India signed a major arms sales agreement with the Soviet Union (see Dusko Doder, "Soviets and India Set $1.6 Billion Arms Agreement," *Washington Post*, May 29, 1980), and in July of the same year, New Delhi shifted its Indochina policy in support of Soviet interests by establishing diplomatic relations with the Vietnam-installed Cambodian government of Heng Samrin. Soviet leader Brezhnev visited New Delhi in December 1980, at the time of the arrival of new Soviet aircraft deliveries, to discuss Indian reactions to the Soviet invasion of Afghanistan with Prime Minister Indira Gandhi. In an address to the Indian parliament, Brezhnev called for an agreement among the great powers not to intervene in the Persian Gulf area.

the Persian Gulf, despite continuing political instability and insecurity within the country and the international political costs to Moscow of its military intervention. And heightened tensions among Iran, Syria, Jordan, and the other Arab states resulting from the Iraq–Iran war of late 1980 may provide opportunities to project Soviet influence in the Middle East.

More significantly, perhaps, those states where American and Chinese influence have been strong are increasingly weak or in turmoil. Pakistan, faced with Soviet and Arab pressures, has been reluctant to accept American military assistance in the absence of a comprehensive U.S. security guarantee. Iran is in chaos and rabidly anti-American. Egypt, Saudi Arabia, Oman, and Turkey are politically vulnerable and/or reluctant to permit the stationing of American forces on their soil. Furthermore, the uncertain prospect for progress in the Arab–Israeli peace negotiations over the Palestinian issue implies the further erosion of American influence in the Middle East.

At the same time, Soviet access to the region is facilitated by geographical proximity to the southern provinces of the USSR and the use of bases at Massawa in Ethiopia on the Red Sea, Aden in South Yemen, and the island of Socotra.[16] This combination of regional political instability, geographical proximity to the USSR's southern frontier, and limited American presence in an area of strategic significance because of its oil resources has been the basis for what has been characterized as a Soviet effort to attain a strategic "breakout in the Arc of Crisis."[17]

For East Asia, however, Moscow's policies must be designed to deal with an increasingly active coalition of China and Japan allied to the United States and the NATO states. The question for the future, and the issue that will shape American policies toward the region, is how Moscow intends to cope with this trend.

Current Soviet strategy toward East Asia seems designed to neutralize the military potential of this formative coalition and then to pursue political and economic initiatives in coordination with military pressures to break it up. Moscow approaches this challenge with a coalition of its own based on treaty relationships with the Mongolian People's Republic, North Korea, Vietnam, India, Afghanistan, South Yemen, and Ethiopia. It also has military assistance agreements with Bangladesh, Sri Lanka,

16. See Albert Wohlstetter, "Half-Wars and Half-Policies in the Persian Gulf," in W. Scott Thomson, ed., *National Security in the 1980s: From Weakness to Strength* (San Francisco: Institute for Contemporary Studies, 1980), pp. 139–47.

17. William G. Hyland, "The Sino–Soviet Conflict: A Search for New Security Strategies," in Richard H. Solomon, ed., *Asian Security in the 1980s: Problems and Policies for a Time of Transition* (Cambridge, Mass: Oelgeschlager, Gunn, and Hain, 1980), pp. 49–50.

and a range of other states in the Middle East and Africa.[18] Using its home-based military capabilities and naval and air facilities in Vietnam, South Yemen, and Ethiopia, Moscow is creating a structure of bases and deployments designed to (1) guard the Soviet Far East against attack and to secure sea-deployed strategic missile forces in the Sea of Okhotsk and elsewhere in the Pacific; (2) develop a significant military threat that will inhibit initiatives by China, the United States, Japan, and allied states; (3) deploy a military capability to counter the American Seventh Fleet and U.S. bases in the Pacific; and (4) develop naval and air forces capable of protecting Soviet sea and air transport and challenging the security of the sea-lanes of communication between the United States and its Asian allies, and from the Middle East and the Persian Gulf to the Western Pacific.

The USSR's military capabilities are substantial enough to deter any attack on Russian territory. Recent increases in naval forces and ground deployments on Japan's Northern Territories seem designed to counter an American and Japanese capability to control the strategic maritime passages through which Soviet naval forces must transit to reach the open sea (or which hostile submarines must use to challenge Soviet bases and naval units in the Sea of Okhotsk).

The increasingly offensive Soviet air, naval, and theater nuclear threat to America's Pacific bases and naval presence seems designed to challenge the cohesion of the coalition sustained by U.S. military forces and allied economic strength. American strategy for the security of its Pacific allies, as with NATO, is to combine a nuclear umbrella with light deployments of conventional forces that can hold off nonnuclear attack long enough for reinforcements from the United States to arrive by air or sea lift. The growth in numbers and accuracy of Soviet strategic rocket forces has largely neutralized the inhibiting effect of American ICBMs and bombers, and doubts among our own Asian allies about American willingness to use nuclear weapons on their behalf have now been significantly enhanced by Moscow's attainment of rough strategic parity.

If, in addition, the security of American bases and air- and sea-lift capabilities that constitute the reinforcement structure linking the United States to its allies can be threatened by Soviet theater nuclear forces and antiair and antiship capabilities, the Soviet Union will have substantially countered the defense strategy that sustains America's ties to its allies and to friendly states. And if Soviet naval and air threats to the

18. A complete listing of Soviet treaty relationships and military assistance agreements throughout the world will be found in *The Military Balance, 1979–1980*. The ones noted here are those most relevant to the security of Asia.

security of the sea-lanes were combined with Soviet control over Middle East oil supplies, the USSR would hold the critical resource that sustains the economies of Western Europe, Japan, and—to a lesser degree—the United States.[19]

It is impossible to know if this is an accurate assessment of Moscow's strategy for countering a multifront challenge. Soviet writings do not describe in such bald terms the USSR's strategic intentions although Soviet officials do not shrink from asserting their right to involve themselves in all global affairs of concern to the USSR, and senior military officers openly describe their intention to use sea power to "counter the Oceanic strategy of imperialism."[20]

Whether Moscow's actions since the mid-1970s reflect a Soviet "grand design" is debatable, but they certainly demonstrate an intention to build capabilities that can be used to pursue Soviet state interests, and a willingness to do so when opportunities or challenges arise (and when the risks of action are minimal or the costs of inaction great).

Moscow's Asian Agenda for the 1980s

Perhaps the only reliable assessment of Soviet intentions toward Asia will be a post hoc evaluation of Moscow's actual use of the capabilities and relationships now being established. If my interpretation is correct, however, a number of lines of initiative from Moscow are likely in the coming decade. First, the Soviets will probably continue to strengthen their military presence in the region, emphasizing further increases in both the number and quality of naval and air deployments designed to counter American and allied military assets, and a strengthening of air- and sea-transport capabilities for supporting military assistance programs and interventions on behalf of regional allies.

Politically, Moscow is likely to sustain efforts to establish bilateral political alliances to counter Chinese influence and reinforce its military base structure in Asia (which is now limited to the use of naval and air facilities in Vietnam). Moscow may seek to strengthen relations with the key states of North Korea and Indonesia.

There is considerable distrust in Soviet–North Korean relations, and Pyongyang has tended to tilt toward the Chinese; however, Moscow's position in Northeast Asia would be improved substantially by closer ties

19. For a more elaborate description of the effects of such a development on the United States and its allies, see Walter J. Levy, "Oil and the Decline of the West," *Foreign Affairs*, vol. 58, no. 5 (Summer 1980), pp. 999–1015.

20. See statements by Soviet Admiral Gorshkov and Foreign Minister Gromyko, as quoted in Admiral (ret.) Noel Gayler, "Security Implications of the Soviet Military Presence in Asia," in Solomon, ed., *Asian Security in the 1980s*, pp. 56, 65.

to North Korea. Military and political pressures on China, Japan, and U.S. bases in the area would be significantly compounded by Soviet access to port facilities in North Korea, which are not subject to winter icing (unlike those at Petropavlovsk, for example). The anticipated succession to Kim Il Sung in the 1980s, and evidence of tensions between North Korean military leaders and civilian politicians over Kim's efforts to pass on political control to his son, may give Moscow opportunities for intervention. Analysts of Soviet–North Korean relations have noted evidence of Soviet efforts in recent years to improve relations with Pyongyang.

Greater Soviet influence in Indonesia would similarly give Moscow access to a critical geographical location astride the strategic Straits of Malacca, thus reinforcing the encirclement of China and the creation of a string of maritime and air bases that would give the USSR substantial control of the sea-lanes that are essential to the American presence in Asia. Growing Chinese influence in Southeast Asia may induce Jakarta to build a closer relationship with Moscow (or at least Hanoi) as a counter to feared PRC pressures. And political instability resulting from a contested succession to President Suharto's leadership may also give Moscow opportunities for intervention in Indonesian affairs.

Moscow can be expected to pursue a two-track, pressures-and-incentives approach to the Chinese and Japanese in an effort to constrain them without closing the door to an improvement in relations. The Soviets can anticipate a change in leadership in Beijing in the 1980s, and they remain hopeful that a new PRC leadership will seek to lower tensions if not to improve significantly relations with the USSR.

To date, however, Moscow has been unwilling to initiate significant reductions in its military deployments along the Sino–Soviet frontier, to withdraw troops from Mongolia, or to lower its level of assistance to Vietnam. But the Soviets probably take a relatively long-term view, assuming that it will take some years for Beijing's dealings with the United States to generate the kind of anti-Western reaction in China that will give the USSR a new opening with a successor leadership to Deng Xiaoping.

Similarly, the Soviets will probably strengthen their military deployments targeted against the Japanese, even as they calculate that Tokyo's needs for the energy and industrial resources of Siberia—timber, iron ore, coal, gas, and fish—will eventually lead the Japanese to seek closer ties with them. However, Moscow's leaders seem unable to assess the degree to which their current military pressures on the Japanese and Chinese are actually driving Tokyo and Beijing toward more coordination of foreign and defense policies with the United States. The anticipated Soviet leadership succession in the 1980s conceivably could bring to power new leaders less inclined to approach Asia in military terms than were Brezhnev and Kosygin, but it is more likely that the military will have enhanced influence in a post-Brezhnev leadership, especially in view of the uncertain prospects for U.S.–Soviet détente and future strategic arms limitation negotiations, possible challenges to Soviet control in Eastern Europe, the ongoing turmoil in the Middle East and Persian Gulf, and Moscow's concerns about the future growth of Chinese and Japanese military strength.

THE SOVIET ASIAN PRESENCE AND AMERICAN POLICY CHOICES

The present decade is likely to see the loose coalition of the United States, its Asian treaty allies, and friendly states of the region, including China, evolve more in reaction to further Soviet initiatives than as a result of a strong a priori policy orientation or sense of common strategy. (China alone appears to have a clear strategic view, pressing for a "united front" to counter Soviet "hegemony.") But to the degree that policy can be shaped to reflect the longer term challenges of an era, and in anticipation of major developments, this analysis attempts to establish a basis for identifying America's major policy choices.

American and allied policy must take into account four major characteristics of the Soviet Union's current involvement in Asia.

1. *Soviet influence in Asia is largely military in character.* Moscow's efforts to shape events in Asia have relied most heavily on military capabilities. Its political influence in Asia is minimal and is largely restricted to states seeking great power support and protection as they pursue their own local objectives.

Moscow's economic influence in Asia is even more restricted. The raw materials of the Soviet Far East are available to the countries of the Pacific Basin from other suppliers, and Moscow cannot accelerate the development of Siberia without foreign capital and technology. As table 11.1 indicates, trade with the Soviet Union constitutes less than 3 percent of the imports or exports of all the states of the region, excluding Moscow's treaty allies (India, North Korea, Vietnam, and Mongolia). In contrast, America is a major trading partner of ten states that collectively account for almost 90 percent of total Asian GNP. Moreover, one of the USSR's major potential trading partners in Asia, Japan, has begun to shift from balanced economic relations with China and the Soviet Union to a tilt toward the PRC (see figs. 11.1 and 11.2).

The unidimensional aspect of Moscow's involvement in Asia in one sense minimizes the complexity of an American response; yet it accents the ominous quality of the USSR's presence and limits Moscow's ability to influence events through diplomacy and trade.

2. *The USSR will approach Asia in the 1980s from a position of rough*

Table 11.1. Soviet and American Trade with Asian Countries, 1979 (Figures expressed as percentage of the total imports and exports of the individual trading partner)

Country	Soviet Union		United States	
	Percent of partner's total imports	Percent of partner's total exports	Percent of partner's total imports	Percent of partner's total exports
Australia	0.39	3.01	21.83	12.77
Burma	0.42	0.24	4.48	3.11
China, People's Republic of[a]	1.29	1.23	11.69	4.40
India	6.13	10.71	10.01	13.48
Indonesia	0.17	0.35	13.57	25.19
Japan	1.57	2.39	16.00	27.53
Malaysia	0.11	2.20	12.32	20.39
Mongolia	85.00 (two way)		0.0	0.0
New Zealand	0.15	4.17	11.63	16.90
North Korea	45.82 (1977)[b]	61.33 (1977)[b]	0.0	0.0
Philippines	0.12	1.81	23.92	36.01
Singapore	0.12	1.26	13.03	11.41
South Korea	0.02	0.01	20.63	28.86
Taiwan	0.0	0.0	22.90[c]	35.00[c]
Thailand	0.11	0.62	13.33	12.22
Vietnam	49.90 (1978)[d]	74.63 (1978)[d]	0.11	0.33

Sources: Unless otherwise noted, all figures have been computed from data in *Direction of Trade Year Book, 1980* (Washington, D.C.: International Monetary Fund, 1980).

[a]*China: International Trade Quarterly Review*, Fourth Quarter 1979, CIA, NFAC, ER-CIT, 80-003, May 1980, pp. 10, 12.

[b]*Present State of DPRK Economy, Foreign Trade*, Korean Affairs Report, no. 73, JPRS no. 75438, Apr. 4, 1980, pp. 31, 33.

[c]*Review of Relations with Taiwan*, statement by Richard Holbrooke before the Subcommittee on Asian and Pacific Affairs of the House Committee on Foreign Affairs, June 11, 1980, as published in Department of State Bulletin, Aug. 1980, p. 53. Washington, D.C.: *Industry of Free China*, vol. 54, no. 4, Oct. 1980, p. 147, Taiwan: Economic Construction Commission, Executive Yuan.

[d]*National Basic Intelligence Fact Book*, Jan. 1980, CIA, GC-BIF, 79-001, pp. 210, 133; *USSR Foreign Trade in 1978*, Statistical Handbook (Moscow, 1979), pp. 200, 203, 223, 230. Dollar-ruble commercial exchange rate of 1.47 (1978) and 1.36 (1977) was computed by A. Becker.

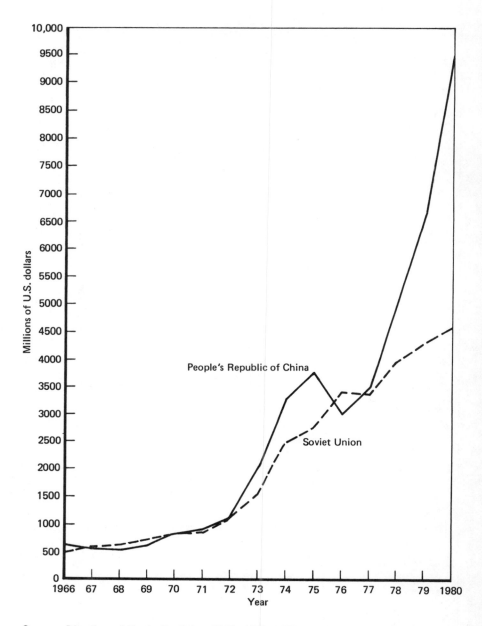

Source: *Direction of Trade Statistics,* 1981, 1980, 1979, 1970–76, and 1966–70 (Washington D.C.: International Monetary Fund).

Fig. 11.1. Japan's two-way trade with People's Republic of China and Soviet Union, 1966–80 (in millions of U.S. dollars).

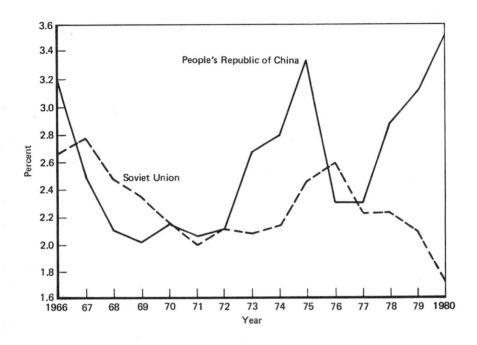

Source: Direction of Trade Statistics, 1981, 1980, 1979, 1970–76, and 1966–70 (Washington D.C.: International Monetary Fund).

Fig. 11.2. Japan's two-way trade with People's Republic of China and Soviet Union, 1966– 80, as a percentage of Japan's total foreign trade.

strategic parity and with increasing superiority relative to the United States and its allies in theater nuclear and conventional military forces. After well over a decade of 3 to 5 percent per year increases in defense spending, the Soviet Union has now achieved a position of rough strategic parity with the United States.[21] Concurrently, recent Soviet deployments of theater nuclear weapons to Asia evince an intention to counter American and allied forces with a limited nuclear threat (and therefore a somewhat more credible one). Growing deployments of Soviet conventional forces indicate an attempt to challenge the security of sea and air communica-

21. Some analysts see this development as more ominous than the creation of a stable "balance" in U.S. and Soviet strategic forces, in view of improvements in the accuracy of Soviet missiles that, in theory at least, place in jeopardy the security of America's land-based strategic retaliatory force of Minuteman missiles. However, approximately one-third of the U.S. strategic missiles, carrying many more than half the warheads targeted on the Soviet Union, are carried on sea-based submarines or on bombers.

tion routes, American and allied bases and their associated forces, and Chinese ground forces. And development of Soviet long-range sea- and air-transport capabilities and naval intervention forces reveals an intention to support local allies (as when the Soviets provided military assistance to Vietnam in advance of its conflicts with Cambodia and China in 1978 and 1979).

This altered military context holds a number of implications. Past American strategic superiority presented the USSR with an implicit, and at times explicit, threat that the United States would escalate local and conventional conflicts to the nuclear level, where it enjoyed supremacy. But such threats are no longer credible except in extreme cases where fundamental state interests are involved. Local and conventional force balances increasingly dominate calculations of risk in regional conflicts, and Moscow appears determined to build a preponderance of such forces in Asia, as it has done in Europe and the Middle East.

The Soviets have been cautious and prudent in initiating military action in past Asian conflicts but, when important state goals are involved and risks are seen as minimal, Soviet leaders have not hesitated to use force (as in Afghanistan in 1980). Indeed, the establishment of alliances or "peace and friendship" treaties with the USSR has become a reliable harbinger of war, judging from the experiences of India, Vietnam, and Afghanistan. This situation can imply only enhanced prospects for Soviet "coercive diplomacy" in Asia.

3. *The evolution of the Soviet presence in Asia appears to fit into a global pattern of military expansion.* As noted earlier, there is an apparent geopolitical pattern to recent Soviet initiatives. Moscow is creating a worldwide system of regional yet mutually supporting military capabilities. A threat to the security of Middle East oil imperils Japan's economic future, just as Soviet bases in the Persian Gulf and Indochina facilitate naval and air movements from region to region.

As a result, American policy planning for Asia cannot be regional in scope or random in character. Defense planning must consider Soviet capabilities and initiatives in other areas of the world, Moscow's strategic capabilities as well as regional force deployments, and global economic patterns as well as those unique to Asia.

Similarly, while Soviet access and assistance to its client states may be facilitated by the parochial conflicts of those states, such support has had substantial effects on regional and global security. Moscow's acquisition of base rights and the exacerbation of refugee problems in Indochina, Ethiopia, and Afghanistan strain the resources and political stability of neighboring states in a way that has a significant impact on regional security. Also, Soviet support for proxy forces—most notably Cuban, East German, and Vietnamese—has made possible actions by small re-

gional states that have served Moscow's purposes. Yet the initiatives of
these proxies have buffered the Soviets from the possibility of direct
conflict with the United States and its allies.

4. *Random* and extraregional developments *will significantly affect circumstances in East Asia.* Whether it be the impact of the health of the
American economy on Asian trading patterns, or the effect of NATO's
military strength on Moscow's ability to redeploy its Europe-oriented
forces to the Far East, events beyond Asia will have a significant effect on
Asian affairs. Thus, America's policies for Asia must be cast in a global
framework.

Similarly, random events not under Moscow's influence or control can
create circumstances that the Soviets, or their clients, will be quick to
exploit in the absence of some countervailing presence. Thus, U.S. policy must also take account of the possibility of such unexpected events.

An American Policy Dilemma: How to Cope
with the Soviet Challenge?

Formulation of an American policy response to Moscow's growing military presence in Asia is complicated by the absence of a national consensus on how to cope with the global Soviet challenge. In the 1980s there
are no concepts like *containment* or *détente* that evoke sufficient domestic
political support to structure dealings with the USSR or make possible
arms control negotiations. Can the United States and its allies undertake
a major effort to build up Western defenses? Is arms control a workable
process for constraining a global arms race? Should the United States
cooperate with the Soviet Union in economic and cultural affairs at a
time when Moscow is assertively involving itself in the internal affairs
and regional conflicts of other states? Is it possible, or desirable, to
negotiate an arrangement with Moscow that would stabilize the U.S.–
Soviet competition in Asia? Will American efforts to strengthen Japan
and China as counterweights to Soviet pressures set in motion forces that
will facilitate the unfavorable emergence of major new competitive
power centers?

A policy for managing the ongoing competitive relationship with the
Soviet Union must involve elements of cooperation as well as the expectation of continuing geopolitical rivalry and possible military confrontation. But such a complex perspective on U.S.–Soviet relations lacks the
symbolic clarity needed to rally public support or to build a consensus
for action among contentious congressmen or disparate allies.

Should the United States view Moscow's military buildup in Asia as a
defensive response to the Sino–Soviet feud and to past decades of American military superiority? Such concepts as *offense* and *defense* have little

relevance to Soviet military doctrine, which stresses offensive capability
as the basis for effective defense, a preponderance of power over a
balance, and the development of a war-fighting capability rather than
maintenance of deterrent or retaliatory forces.

Should America view the USSR as a legitimate presence in Asian
affairs or as a power to be contained and, where possible, excluded from
the region? And can the United States counter Russian military capabilities while at the same time accepting Moscow's economic and political involvement in regional affairs? Can economic ties be separated from
their security implications when matters of energy dependence or the
industrialization of the Soviet Far East (embodying unresolved territorial conflicts with China and Japan) are involved?

The United States is in a period in which it must strengthen its military
defenses and alliance relationships while at the same time sustaining
efforts to negotiate a framework for coexistence with Moscow. Prospects
for economic or political cooperation with the USSR should be linked to
Soviet restraint in military matters. To be credible, however, this approach requires not only enhanced American military capabilities but
also a broad coalition of states whose interests and capabilities are sufficiently congruent to make possible coordinated responses to the global
Soviet challenge.

The Problem of American Credibility

American actions in Asia in the 1970s seriously eroded the credibility of
U.S. regional defense and political leadership, leaving a legacy that
could weaken the "loose Oceanic alliance" of relationships with treaty
partners and friendly states. Despite official statements that the U.S.
Vietnam trauma is over, Asians still doubt America's ability to sustain a
coherent foreign policy and to act in support of its own interests, not to
mention those of its allies. The Carter administration's 1977 decision to
withdraw U.S. ground forces from South Korea and its subsequent reversal of that decision raised questions about America's intentions to
remain active in Asian security affairs; the withdrawal of American support for the government of the Republic of China on Taiwan and for the
besieged Shah of Iran raised doubts about the constancy of U.S. support
for allied governments; and the failure of the mission to rescue the
American hostages in Tehran led many Asians to question the technological and organizational capability of the United States to conduct
complex military operations.

The uncertain American response to the Vietnamese invasion of Cambodia, combined with declining regional programs of security assistance,
limited sales of military equipment, and curtailed training programs for

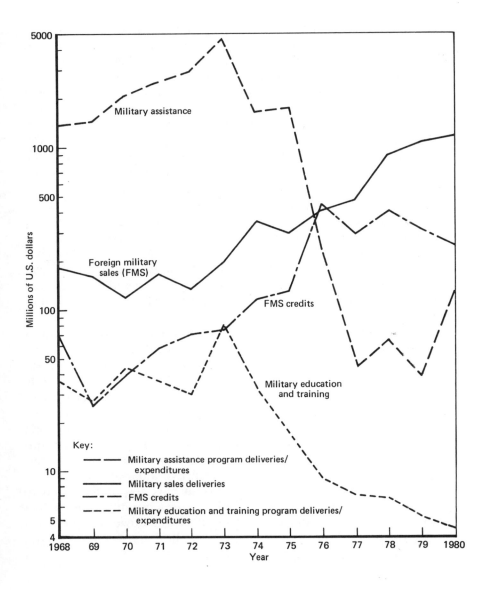

Source: Foreign Military Sales and Military Assistance Facts, Dec. 1977, Dec. 1979, and Dec. 1980 (Washington D.C.: Security Assistance Agency, Department of Defense).

Fig. 11.3. U.S. military sales, FMS credits, military assistance, and military training program deliveries to East Asia and the Pacific, 1968–80.

foreign military officers (see fig. 11.3), reinforces the sense of a declining American role in Asian security affairs. This has been compounded
by the belief that U.S. military resources are stretched thin between
treaty obligations in Northeast Asia and the operational requirements of
responding to the Soviet challenge and regional turmoil in Southwest
Asia and the Persian Gulf.

Some Asian leaders, fearful that the United States is seeking to compensate for its own weaknesses by encouraging a greater regional defense role for Japan or by establishing a "division of labor" with the
Chinese, are appealing to the United States to give them a third alternative to accommodation with the Soviets and their proxies or with a major
Asian power. They give only limited recognition to the U.S. stabilization
of access to the Philippine bases; the reversal of the Korean troop withdrawal decision; upgraded defense cooperation with Japan; completion
of normalization of relations with the PRC and initiation of low-level
security cooperation; the increased defense presence in the Persian
Gulf, which protects Asian access to energy resources; and the upgraded
military capabilities of the Seventh Fleet and other forces in the Western
Pacific.

These attitudes are significant, for, if reinforced, they could set in
motion departures from current foreign policies that would erode the
presently favorable pattern of American treaty relationships and working ties with most of the states of Asia. Should the Japanese conclude
that the United States is not a credible guarantor of their security interests, they could embark on a more independent and nationalistic
course or accommodate to growing Soviet military pressures and economic enticements. The Chinese could conclude that the American connection has such uncertain benefits that a coalition with Japan or reconciliation with Moscow might become attractive alternatives.

Similarly, the ASEAN states which thus far have responded firmly to
the growing Vietnamese and Soviet military presence in Southeast Asia
could seek accommodation with Hanoi, if not its Soviet backer. Such
developments may not occur, however, for the United States can still
influence the perceptions and policy choices of its allies and friends—as
well as its adversaries.

To Accommodate, Restrict, or Balance the Soviet Presence in Asia?

In developing a policy orientation toward Soviet involvement in Asia,
the United States can either seek to conduct a policy of balance of power
or one of forming a united front against the Soviets and their allies.[22]

22. Robert A. Scalapino, "Approaches to Peace and Security in Asia: The Uncertainty
Surrounding American Strategic Principles," *Current Scene* (Hong Kong: U.S. Consulate

This choice will be less clear in formulating operational policies than in this conceptual analysis because American power to influence events and to shape the policies of other states is limited, and because many specific policy choices will not be obviously restrictive or balancing in effect. Unless the United States should choose to reduce to a minimal level its involvement in regional affairs or should come to view the Soviet presence in Asia as so benign as to be worthy of support and facilitation (highly unlikely alternatives), the American presence in Asia is likely to reflect both containment and counterweight. Aggressive Soviet initiatives will provoke a containment mindset among American and Asian policymakers; a relaxation of tensions and increased confidence in Moscow's intentions will encourage less restrictive policies of accommodation and balance.

American policies should thus be designed to restrain the Soviet Union's expansionist and aggressive impulses while holding open the possibility of accommodation. The United States must be able to mobilize counterpressures when Moscow's initiatives prove threatening, without *anticipating* Soviet actions in a way that only provokes the undesired initiative or undercuts domestic or foreign political support.

Whatever the intentions of U.S. policymakers, however, the Soviets have a disturbing tendency to impose their own interpretations on the purposes of others. Self-imposed restraint may be viewed as weakness or indecisiveness, or Soviet leaders may impute hostile intentions to their competitors and in anticipation of the actions of others take initiatives that have the effect of bringing about their worst imaginings.

Much of Soviet behavior in the 1970s had the quality of a self-fulfilling prophecy, imputing intentions to act against the USSR when, in fact, the situation was far more open than Soviet leaders probably assumed. Such presumptive behavior can be minimized only by clearly communicating American intentions to Soviet leaders and by sustaining coherent policy programs. Given Moscow's determination to play a superpower role in world affairs, the fundamental distrust underlying the U.S.–Soviet rivalry, and the uncertainties of the American policymaking process, it is doubtful that either major swings of policy or the preemptive behavior that drives the competition can be completely eliminated from the relationship. Yet effective diplomacy can minimize misunderstandings.

Soviet leaders assert that the United States upon occasion has misled the USSR about its own intentions to react to Soviet initiatives or to play

General, 1978), vol. 16, nos. 8 and 9, Aug.–Sept., 1978. The author rejects the third alternative of a major reduction in U.S. forces in Asia based on the argument that our military presence does not contribute to regional security. He does not consider a U.S.–Soviet deal or condominium in matters of Asian security, presumably because of the implausibility of such an arrangement.

a role in local security situations—most notably in 1949, when Secretary of State Acheson stated publicly that Korea was beyond the U.S. Asian defense perimeter. Thus, clarity of intention and constancy of purpose are important to the credibility of American dealings with the Soviets, in Asia as elsewhere.

The United States will be confronted with a range of decisions affecting Asian security in the 1980s:

- How substantial a military buildup should the United States undertake in Asia with its own resources and through the encouragement of its allies and friends? Should America consciously seek to create a major Asian strategic front to complicate global Soviet military planning, or should it limit its defense planning to the security of its traditional allies and to the maintenance of a sea-deployed strategic retaliatory force?

- How far should the United States develop its relationship with China? Should it rest content with having normalized political relations with Beijing, or should it develop a coordinated defense program to strengthen China's military capabilities, giving the Chinese greater protection against Soviet pressures and the capacity to constrain Soviet initiatives in the region?

- Should the United States accede to Moscow's expanded military presence in Indochina and to the Vietnamese invasion of Cambodia, or should it actively build forces of resistance against the Vietnamese to increase the costs of expansionist military initiatives? Or can America weaken Moscow's Asian coalition by drawing the Vietnamese (as well as the Indians and North Koreans) into a more neutral international position?

- Should the United States encourage ASEAN to become a regional defense coalition with strengthened ties to the West, or should it merely backstop with American military resources what remains largely a political and an economic association?

Choosing among these alternatives will require both a clear view of American objectives in Asia and a sense of strategy toward the Soviet Union. The United States is in a position of defending the Asian status quo, for its relations with the region are basically sound and extensive. America no longer faces a hostile coalition of states dominating the Asian mainland which are determined to spread their influence to the island nations of the Pacific through violent revolutions. The breakdown of the Sino–Soviet alliance and the normalization of U.S.–PRC relations eliminated the major source of tension in U.S. dealings with Asia and gave it greater access to the region. The United States wants to preserve this access for political, commercial, and cultural purposes through strengthened ties with its traditional allies, stable dealings with China, and commercial and cultural ties with Taiwan. America has good relations with Singapore, Malaysia, and Indonesia, and even friendly if minimal contacts with reclusive Burma. Only Vietnam, with its client states of Laos and Cambodia, and North Korea present problems of security and political normalization for the United States and its allies.

The United States must, however, maintain a secure environment in which its economic vitality and the access it gives the states of the region to its markets, technology, and capital can be fully realized. Nevertheless, it is in this context that the Soviet Asian presence challenges the American inclination to limit its regional role to commerce, culture, and politics. U.S. access is contingent not only upon the degree of security it provides individually to its allies but also upon its contribution to the collective sense of regional stability—and to the effectiveness of its security role in areas beyond Asia that affect the interests of its allies.

A coherent American policy program for Asia must serve the complex purposes of pursuing U.S. interests and meeting the needs of its allies, while being flexible enough to both constrain Soviet military pressures and respond to signs of Soviet restraint. Much of the American presence in Asia will have little to do with the Soviet Union. U.S. economic ties to the region, in particular, must be managed effectively in a time when trade imbalances, protectionist pressures, and North–South economic tensions will strain otherwise productive trading relationships.

American policy toward the Soviet Union must be composed of (1) defense programs designed to counter Soviet capabilities both at the strategic level and in the Asian (and Middle East) region; (2) political, economic, and military coalition activities with allied and friendly states; and (3) cooperative actions with the Soviet Union itself to minimize the disruptive impact of the U.S.–Soviet competition.[23]

The American Military Role

American policy should make the most effective use of its economic, political, and cultural ties; yet it cannot avoid dealing with Moscow's predominantly military efforts to extend Soviet influence.

23. These three areas of activity cannot be pursued simultaneously without creating serious political dilemmas. For example, heightened cooperation with China may create anxieties in smaller states that fear PRC pressures, and negotiations with Moscow on matters of regional security may create fears of a U.S.–Soviet condominium that will undercut America's ability to create a regional coalition.

The gradual erosion of the credibility of the American military presence in Asia during the 1970s now threatens to undermine its links to allied and friendly states. The perception in Japan, China, and elsewhere that the Soviets have attained equivalence if not a measure of advantage in strategic weaponry and concern that the United States will be reluctant to take risks on behalf of the security of its allies where the threat of nuclear confrontation with the Soviet Union is involved lead many Asians to view the United States as an uncertain guarantor of regional stability and security. This perception can only be reinforced by unfavorable conventional military balances, the evident American caution about Vietnam-type involvements in the internal security of regional states, and U.S. reluctance to be a supplier of arms.

If such perceptions are not corrected, highly adverse situations could well develop in the coming decade. Trends toward rearmament, including nuclear proliferation, can already be seen. Doubts about the American commitment to maintain an active security presence—when combined with enhanced indigenous military capabilities or heightened Soviet military pressures—can readily lead to the dissolution of coordinated responses to security threats. Or, as demonstrated by Pakistan's reluctance in 1979 to accept limited American military assistance, a tendency to accommodate to real or presumed Soviet threats may emerge. Failure to correct current trends in the U.S.–Soviet military balance through American initiatives could result in the formation of new security coalitions (such as China and Japan), further accommodation to the Soviets (the "Finlandization" of Japan or Sino–Soviet rapprochement), or the breakout of regional violence.

The United States faces four interrelated military tasks if it is to deal with these unfavorable trends.

1. The integrity of American strategic retaliatory forces must be reaffirmed, as it presumably will be through some combination of the MX missile, manned strategic bomber, cruise missile, and Trident submarine programs. This development is fundamental to reassuring allies that the United States will be prepared to respond to Soviet initiatives and that America's "nuclear umbrella" is credible enough to enable the United States to compete effectively with the Soviet Union at lower levels of the spectrum of force.

2. In view of the deployment of Soviet SS-20 IRBMs to the Far East, the United States must maintain sufficient theater nuclear systems of its own in Asia to neutralize Moscow's ability to threaten U.S. bases on allied soil. The deployment of submarine-launched cruise missiles and the maintenance of nuclear-capable aircraft carriers in the Pacific will be especially important in that they establish a countervailing force to Soviet deployments but without the need for land basing. This will minimize

the sense of vulnerability of U.S. allies in maintaining other forms of security cooperation with it while conveying a willingness to challenge Soviet military initiatives in Asia without having to escalate conflict to the level of strategic nuclear war.

3. Conventional force deployments in Asia are likely to require strengthened naval and air capabilities. There is an evident need to increase the American naval presence in Asian waters to assure the security of sea transport lanes. Without such assurance the ability of the United States to sustain a defense strategy for Korea and Japan based on limited tripwire forces that can be reinforced in time of conflict will be increasingly called into question. One or two additional aircraft carriers assigned to the Seventh Fleet would do much to sustain security of the sea-lanes, and carriers have the advantages of mobility while minimizing political sensitivities and the related complexities of land bases. The decision of the Reagan administration to build a fifteen-carrier navy, if realized, will do much to counter the impression of an overtaxed and a declining American military presence in Asia—an impression that will be reinforced if, as rumored, the Soviets deploy their first aircraft carrier to Asia late in the 1980s.

4. The development of new naval basing facilities in Southeast Asia would help to ease fears that the United States will be unable to counter the presence of Soviet or Vietnamese forces or is abandoning its regional security role to the play of the Sino–Soviet rivalry.

Asian air defense will become increasingly problematic in the 1980s as the Soviets deploy more long-range naval attack aircraft, interceptors, reconnaissance aircraft, and airborne assault units to their Far East provinces. An effective countervailing force will require the cooperation of allies, especially Japan and potentially China. One of the major issues the United States must face, particularly in an era of constrained defense budgets, is how far to develop an integrated regional air (and naval) defense system with other states.

Similarly, if the United States intends to limit its ground force deployments in Asia to the current infantry division in South Korea and the marine amphibious unit and battalion landing team in Okinawa, there is a clear need to strengthen allied ground forces. The United States will not be able to maintain effective working relations with regional allies unless the continuing cutbacks in U.S. military assistance and training programs and in credits for foreign military sales (see fig. 11.3) are reversed, and it will not be possible to maintain the strength of indigenous forces that constitute the first line of defense against Soviet proxy initiatives.

The modest American responses to the Soviet invasion of Afghanistan and the Vietnamese military takeover of Cambodia emphasize the probability that local conflicts into which the Soviets or their clients inject themselves will be the major threats to regional security. Without a countervailing American or allied presence, such initiatives will be seen as relatively risk-free and advantageous to the extension of Soviet influence.

Coalition Activities with Allied and Friendly States

There is irony in the fact that the less favorable the American military position is relative to the Soviet Union, the more the United States requires the support of its allies; yet the greater the lack of confidence in American defense capabilities, the less willing are allies to collaborate with the United States because of their greater vulnerability to Soviet pressures. Unless the United States strengthens its own defense capabilities, allies may be reluctant to cooperate in security matters, just when such collaboration is especially needed.

This dilemma will be compounded in the 1980s by the growing defense capabilities of states that can strengthen their own military systems with substantial domestic scientific and industrial capabilities (e.g., Japan, China, and South Korea). If the United States mismanages its evolving relationships with the countries of Asia, it may face new security coalitions in the next several decades that could weaken American access to the region, heighten military threats resulting from the proliferation of sophisticated weaponry, and enhance Soviet involvement resulting from a perception that Moscow might serve as a counterweight to increased Chinese or Japanese military capabilities. The United States is now in a critical period when its own actions can shape the evolution of Asian defense relationships. The costs of a continuing decline in its involvement in such affairs could well be increased great-power rivalry, greater conflict among regional states, and the eventual emergence of geopolitical patterns that will limit America's welcome.

Japan. There is broad consensus in the United States that political, economic, and security ties to Japan are the core of America's involvement in Asia. Japan's economic strength has grown out of all proportion to its role in political and security affairs. A major question for the 1980s is how to develop the U.S.–Japanese defense relationship so that it reflects a greater balance among Japanese industrial capabilities, security concerns, and new aspirations for leadership in regional and world affairs. Continuing economic tensions between the two countries must be carefully managed to avoid adverse effects on political relations, and the Japanese will have to be sensitive to American concerns that they are getting a free ride in security matters. At the same time, U.S. hectoring of the Japanese to spend more on defense without a well-defined concept of security planning will erode political support in Tokyo. American defense officials must give greater consideration to Japanese notions of "comprehensive security."

There is a clear sense among Asian specialists that the Soviets have seriously mishandled their relations with the Japanese, adopting rigid and counterproductive policies on sensitive issues such as the contested northern territories and the development of relations with China. Indeed, following Moscow's garrisoning of the northern islands in 1978, the Japanese have formally identified the Soviet Union as their primary security problem.

As a consequence, Japanese policy—with some support from the United States—is moving away from "equidistance" between the two communist states toward a pro-China tilt. The Sino–Japanese treaty of peace and friendship is not balanced by a treaty of good neighborly relations with the Soviet Union, and Japan's foreign trade increasingly favors the Chinese at the expense of the Soviets (see figs. 11.1 and 11.2).[24] While the United States has not encouraged Japanese contacts with China on matters of security, both American and Chinese officials urge the Japanese to increase their defense spending and to play a more active role in securing the home islands and their surrounding waters.

This policy evolution is sustained by broad support in the United States and Japan for strengthening Japanese–American cooperation in defense. After three decades of a predominant American role in implementing the Mutual Security Treaty, there is recognition that the defense relationship must reflect Japan's economic strength, the new public mood of acceptance of defense responsibilities, and the pressures on American military resources. A genuine partnership based on active consultation and joint planning must be created in the 1980s, with Japan assuming greater responsibilities in air defense and antisubmarine warfare. The sensitive issues in this process concern the extent of Japan's defense perimeter beyond the home islands (in view of lingering fears in East and Southeast Asia about Japan's past imperial ambitions) and the relative weight of efforts among the three military services, where the ground forces—of reduced significance for Japan's contemporary security challenges—traditionally have exercised major political influence.

American officials, responding to congressional pressure, have urged Japan to use its economic strength to carry a greater share of the defense burden almost irrespective of the uses to which enhanced Japanese mili-

---

24. This shift is encouraged by the United States to the degree that American officials and private investors are reluctant to support coinvestment projects in the Soviet Far East, such as the Yakutia gas project.

tary capabilities will be put. A shared conception of security roles and
missions must emerge in the 1980s if the Mutual Security Treaty is to
remain the framework for defense cooperation between Japan and the
United States. This will no doubt involve expansion of Japanese military
capabilities; yet it may be more productive for Japan, with its economic
vitality and lingering resistance to rearmament, to provide economic
assistance to stabilize countries critical to the alliance, such as Turkey, or
to provide states such as India and Pakistan with alternatives to Soviet or
American aid.[25]

There is also a growing awareness that America's role in securing Japan's access to Middle East energy resources and in protecting the sea-
lanes will play a major role in sustaining the U.S.–Japanese relationship.
Should the United States fail to provide for Japan's energy security or to
reorganize the workings of the defense relationship, the Japanese could
consider such alternatives as "autonomous defense" or the need to accede to Soviet military and economic pressures.

These possibilities sharpen the sense of choice about U.S. policies
affecting Asia. Should America encourage the Japanese to maintain balanced relations between Moscow and Beijing, or should it support Japan's current move toward closer relations with China and seek to create
a U.S.–PRC–Japan coalition? It is almost certainly beyond American
capabilities, if not contrary to U.S. interests, to convince the Soviets that
by being more accommodating to Japanese interests America can sustain
a less threatening regional balance in Asia. Moscow's inflexibility on the
northern territory issue reflects fears of what concessions would mean
for the Soviet position in Eastern Europe or the Sino–Soviet border
negotiations. And reversal of the trend toward Soviet militarization of
the Far East would very likely require a comprehensive settlement of
security issues involving China and Japan as well as the American defense strategy in the Western Pacific. Such a settlement is beyond America's capacity to encourage, and negotiations with the Soviets on such
fundamental issues affecting the basic interests of so many major states
would convey the impression of a Soviet–American condominium if
relations with U.S. allies and friends were not handled effectively.

American interests will clearly be served by strengthening the security
relationship and economic dealings with Japan. Such bilateral ties will
not prejudice the development of balanced relations among the other
major powers of the region, and the degree of U.S. encouragement for
Tokyo to develop closer ties with the Chinese or the Soviets should be a
function of Chinese, or Soviet, actions. Because the USSR is the one

25. See Takuya Kubo, "Security in Northeast Asia," in Solomon, ed., *Asian Security in the
1980s,* p. 107.

power with the military resources to threaten Japanese security, Moscow must bear the burden of consequences of its policies in Asia. Continuing military pressures against Japan, China, and the United States will only stimulate increased security cooperation among the three powers, while greater Soviet flexibility on such issues as the status of the northern territories would provide the basis for increased cooperation. American policies in Northeast Asia should hold open the possibility of such accommodation while taking as a baseline the current reality of Moscow's presence and policies in the region.

The United States does, however, have some potential leverage in defining the future character of security and economic relations in Asia. It could use its own resources to encourage greater Japanese investment in Siberian development and it could foster greater collaboration between Tokyo and Beijing in matters of regional security. The problem is to convince the Soviets that they have some influence over American policies and to develop a dialogue with Beijing and Tokyo that will prevent any approach to Moscow concerning Asian security from undermining U.S. relations with these major Asian states.

China. There is a great division of opinion in the U.S. official community on how to develop ties with the PRC.[26] Whereas political normalization was widely accepted, the question of whether to make America's relationship with China one element in a set of policies designed to cope with the global Soviet challenge has generated considerable debate, as reflected in the controversy surrounding such media phrases as "playing the China card" and "arms sales to China."

The arguments for and against security cooperation with China indicate the complexity of the issues involved in formulating a policy that will gain public and political consensus. Some argue that U.S.–PRC security cooperation would caution or deter the Soviet Union from taking actions threatening to American and Chinese interests. Others say that such cooperation would be a provocation to Moscow and would undermine the possibility of future improvements in U.S.–Soviet relations. Some advocate American military assistance to China as a way of complicating Soviet planning and enabling the Chinese to resist pressures

26. Recent public opinion data reveal, however, what has been termed a "colossal shift of opinion in American views about the People's Republic of China" from a strongly unfavorable view to a highly positive one. In 1977 only 11% of a national opinion sample thought the United States should assist "mainland China" in building up its military strength against the USSR, while in 1980, 47% believed it should. (See William Watts, *Americans Look at Asia: A Need for Understanding* [Washington, D.C.: Potomac Associates, 1980], pp. 7, 51.) Despite this shift, official and academic specialists on national security, the Soviet Union, and Asia remain strongly divided on the issue of security cooperation with the PRC.

from Moscow. Others assert that such U.S. assistance would only incite Moscow to take preemptive military action against the PRC.

Some argue that U.S.–PRC military cooperation will help to maintain a balance of power by securing a major state with the capacity to play an important role in Asia and in global affairs. Others argue that such cooperation will damage the prospect of creating a regional balance by stimulating other states to maneuver in the context of the Sino–Soviet rivalry. States fearful of the growth of Chinese power would seek ways of countering pressures from a strengthened Beijing, perhaps by establishing closer ties with the Soviet Union.

Some argue that it will be difficult to sustain a U.S.–PRC relationship without a measure of security cooperation, inasmuch as China's concern with Soviet hegemony has been the primary motivation for Beijing's effort to normalize relations with the United States. Others assert that as China becomes stronger, it will inevitably go its own way or will double-cross the United States by improving relations with the Soviet Union. Some argue that political instability in Beijing will make the Chinese unable to pursue a constant foreign policy based on normal relations with the United States.

Some say that in a period when the United States is at least temporarily vulnerable to the Soviet global challenge, it needs all the support it can get from allies and friendly states. Others say that Beijing, long committed to a policy of "self-reliance," will be reluctant to coordinate policies with the United States, and that America should strengthen its own capabilities rather than seek unreliable relationships to compensate for its own short-term deficiencies.

What kind of a policy framework can be constructed from this welter of arguments? Although no one policy could possibly reconcile all these purposes and concerns, the United States can at least establish a baseline for policy in the benefits of having achieved political normalization with the PRC. The United States no longer faces a two-front strategic challenge from a China either allied to the Soviet Union or determined to work against both American and Soviet interests in Asia. Normalization has eliminated a major strain in U.S. dealings with Japan, and the Chinese have been supportive of American ties to NATO and U.S. diplomacy in the Middle East, the Persian Gulf, Africa, and South Asia.

Normalization has even, for a time at least, defused the virulence of Beijing's confrontation with Taiwan. PRC media no longer speak of "liberating" Taiwan, and there is no evidence of Chinese efforts to build the specialized military capability needed to invade the island. However, PRC leaders do assert the objective of "reunifying" the island with the mainland in the 1980s, and Chinese pressures on the United States to terminate all arms sales to Taiwan indicate the intention to use at least political pressures to resolve the island's future. But for the moment tensions have been significantly reduced in the Taiwan Strait.

Normalization gained broad support in the United States and China, although the issue of Taiwan's future threatens the further growth of U.S.–PRC relations. If this issue can be managed effectively by Beijing and Washington, the *indirect* strategic advantages that have accrued to the United States and the PRC will presumably be reinforced by parallel but mutually supporting foreign and security policies where Chinese and American interests converge. And within the limits of China's ability to finance trade, educational exchanges, and cultural contacts, the United States is likely to make some contribution—along with Japan and Western Europe—to China's economic and social modernization.

This normal and cooperative bilateral relationship is the essential foundation upon which other forms of cooperation might grow. It is important to develop this relationship in its own right, for the flexibility it gives U.S. foreign policy and for the reassurance it gives China's leaders that America takes seriously their efforts to improve the lives of their vast population.

Soviet officials warn against any U.S.–China cooperation, citing their own experience as an example of how the Chinese can turn against those who have helped them. It seems unlikely, however, that this argument will influence American policymakers who are convinced of the advantages of a normal and friendly bilateral relationship with the PRC. Attempting to keep China in a dependent or backward state, as the Chinese say the Soviets tried to do in the 1950s, will guarantee Chinese hostility and an end to a cooperative relationship. Although some Chinese interests and objectives are undoubtedly in potential conflict with American purposes in Asia, the PRC is decades away from acquiring the range of national capabilities needed to pursue any latent imperialistic ambitions. Beijing's freedom of action will be constrained for many decades by the presence in Asia of the Soviet Union, Japan, and the United States.

The most divisive issue in U.S. China policy, apart from the Taiwan question, is how to formulate a relationship with the PRC in the context of the ongoing U.S.–Soviet competition and the Sino–Soviet conflict. Advocates of a policy of "evenhandedness" or balance between the Soviets and Chinese would have the United States adopt a posture of strict noninvolvement in Chinese political or security actions that impinge on Soviet interests or involve military modernization; or, to borrow a phrase from the Chinese themselves, we should "sit on the mountain and watch the tigers fight."

This approach is difficult to sustain because of the disparities in power between China and the USSR and because the Soviets have both the capabilities and the record of initiatives to threaten American, and Chinese, interests. Avoidance of consideration of a U.S. relationship with China in an effort to cope with the Soviet challenge ignores the fact that even normalized U.S.–PRC political relations are viewed by Moscow as harmful to Soviet interests, and it presumes that the United States can deal with the Soviet challenge with only its own resources and the cooperation of traditional allies.

A second approach assumes that the United States is so menaced by an imminent Soviet threat that it should develop an active security relationship with Beijing as part of a global political-military coalition to contain the USSR's hegemonic ambitions. This position would involve substantial sales of defense-related technology and military equipment to China in order to strengthen the country and build a multifront challenge to the Soviet Union.

But American capabilities are not generally judged to be so inferior to those of the USSR, and a security relationship with China is viewed as a dangerous substitute for the strengthening of America's own defenses. It is also assumed that such an approach would be gratuitously provocative to Moscow and might well undermine U.S. ties to key allies, polarize relationships in Asia, and create longer term problems for American involvement in the region.

A third position would establish a more flexible set of alternatives. It assumes that the China relationship holds certain benefits for U.S. and PRC efforts to deal with the Soviet challenge but that mismanagement of this relationship through excessive manipulation could either provoke Moscow, degrade U.S.–PRC relations, or threaten the interests of our allies. This view holds that a durable bilateral relationship with the Chinese will maximize the indirect strategic benefits of political normalization for the United States. But it also attempts to establish the possibility of active national security collaboration with Beijing and to communicate to Soviet leaders that threats to American and Chinese interests will provoke a collective response. The intent of this position is to caution Moscow without being provocative and to give Soviet decisionmakers a sense that their actions will influence the pace and direction in which U.S.–PRC security cooperation evolves.

However, as noted earlier, the Soviets may assume the worst about American and Chinese purposes and take preemptive actions that provoke a Sino–American response. Also, once security cooperation has been initiated, it may be difficult to modulate the level of activity, to find an appropriate stopping point. The Chinese may resent the fact that we are less than fully forthcoming in helping them strengthen their defenses. They may feel "used" inasmuch as American assistance to them will be a function, in some measure, of Soviet actions. And traditional

U.S. allies or states with which it wants to maintain friendly relations may react to U.S.–PRC cooperation with actions that would upset regional security arrangements or give the Soviets political access they otherwise might not have.

Such a *conditional* and modulated approach to Sino–American security cooperation is preferable, however, to alternatives that are either heedless of the risks of unrestrained collaboration with the Chinese or so limited that they forgo opportunities to caution Moscow, strengthen the U.S.–China tie, and establish a stabilizing balance of relationships in Asia. Moreover, such a policy formalizes the pattern of U.S.–PRC security cooperation of the past decade, reflecting both the constraints on such activities and the pressures for them.

There are a number of conceptual and practical issues involved in implementing a policy of conditional U.S.–PRC security cooperation. How should the two sides respond to threatening Soviet actions? Prior to Moscow's invasion of Afghanistan, contacts between Washington and Beijing were largely political. Sino–American actions proceeded in parallel, with a modest degree of coordination achieved through the high-level leadership dialogue initiated in 1971. The United States said it would be "evenhanded" in making sales of sensitive technologies to China and the USSR and it ruled out direct sales of military equipment to either party. After the Afghan crisis the Carter administration modified its policy by permitting limited sales to China of dual-use technology and nonlethal military equipment such as communications gear and transport aircraft. A dialogue between senior defense officials was accelerated, and military delegations from the two sides exchanged visits.[27] Following the election of Ronald Reagan to the presidency in 1980, Reagan's secretary of state, Alexander Haig, visited China in June 1981 and announced that the United States would consider selling lethal arms to China on a case-by-case basis.

In a sense, China and the United States have now ascended the first low steps of a "stairway" to a fully developed security relationship. These steps have established high-level official contacts for exchanges of views on political and defense issues and have created an institutional framework for communications: the exchange of military attachés and limited sales of technology and equipment that will eventually strengthen China's industrial base and its military infrastructure. The United States is only beginning to consider the sale of advanced technologies (such as avionics), lethal but clearly defensive military hardware (such as antitank rockets), or weaponry with an ambiguous "defensive–offensive" capability (air-to-

27. See Philip Taubman, "U.S. and China Forging Close Ties; Critics Fear That Pace Is Too Swift," *New York Times*, Dec. 8, 1980.

air missiles and short-range fighters or ground-attack aircraft). Clearly offensive weapons systems (long-range fighter-bombers) or institutional measures for taking coordinated actions (such as joint military staff planning) are at present beyond the thinking of policy planners in Washington and Beijing—as much because of China's limited ability to pay for and absorb such weaponry as because of complex foreign policy considerations and tensions over Taiwan.

Decisions to take further steps toward security cooperation will be influenced above all by Soviet actions. Higher levels of Sino–American cooperation would become politically acceptable in the United States (and probably in China as well) only in the event of a heightened and imminent Soviet threat. As former Secretary of Defense Harold Brown phrased it during a visit to Beijing in early 1980, the United States and China currently prefer to be friends rather than formal allies. A Soviet invasion of Poland or intervention in Iran or Pakistan, however, would very likely promote higher levels of Sino–American security cooperation.

The idea of a Sino–American security relationship remains sufficiently novel that only limited thought has been given to the practical measures each side might take should they decide to collaborate more actively. Some areas where Chinese and American military planners would find their interests served by closer collaboration are already evident, however. For example, certain Soviet military activities relevant to SALT verification and research and development of new weapons systems are more observable from China's borders than from anywhere else. Also, by interdicting the Trans-Siberian and BAM railroads, the Chinese could tie down the Soviet divisions arrayed along the Sino–Soviet frontier so that Moscow could not swing them into action westward in the event of a military contingency in the Middle East or Europe. Similarly, the Chinese have made it evident that they want a strong NATO to hinder redeployment of Soviet forces from Eastern Europe and the western USSR to the Sino–Soviet frontier in the event of a military conflict with China. (For this reason, Beijing has expressed strong reservations about the Mutual and Balanced Force Reduction negotiations, and concern about the weakening of NATO.)

The buildup of Soviet air power in the Far East, especially at the numerous air bases near Vladivostok, raises the possibility of joint U.S., Chinese, and Japanese air defense planning. Similarly, the growth of the Soviet Far East Fleet and Moscow's use of naval and air bases in Indochina raise the possibility of collaborative sea-lane and air defense in order to countervail the growing Soviet threat. Soviet interventions in certain Third World countries could be more effectively resisted through joint Sino–American efforts, as in Indochina or Afghanistan.

This discussion has proceeded on the assumption that Sino–Soviet tensions and Moscow's military challenge will increase rather than diminish in the 1980s. We should not totally rule out, however, the alternative of a diminution in Soviet–American tensions or Sino–Soviet hostility. American policy toward the Soviet Union should retain sufficient flexibility to be able to respond to signs of a less assertive mood in Moscow. And the United States should not assume that Sino–Soviet hostility is any more immutable than was its own lengthy confrontation with the Chinese. Some PRC leaders appear to favor seeking an improvement in relations with the USSR. In the abstract a reduction in Sino–Soviet tensions would serve China's interest in concentrating on economic development, and Moscow has expressed the desire for such an evolution. Yet to date Soviet leaders have been unwillng or unable to offer Beijing a credible inducement for a relaxation in the two-decade-long Sino–Soviet confrontation.

Although there are thus substantial impediments to the reestablishment of a *friendly* relationship between Beijing and Moscow, some diminution in Sino–Soviet hostility is not beyond all possibility. It seems to be in China's long-term interest to establish a more neutral position between the United States and the Soviet Union, especially as China's defenses are modernized and can provide greater protection against Soviet pressures. The impact of such an eventual development for U.S. interests will be a function of whether the United States has established the basis for stable friendly relations with the Chinese, the health of its formal alliance relationships in Asia (particularly with Japan), and the state of America's own military defenses.

America's China policy must thus be grounded on its own defense capabilities and on a strong bilateral relationship. At the same time, it must be sufficiently flexible in matters of security cooperation to be able to caution Moscow without foreclosing the possibility of improved Soviet–American relations or being caught off balance by an unexpected shift in China's political alignment.

The Regional Conflicts: Korea and Indochina. Much of the Soviet Union's ability to influence events in Asia is related to the state of regional conflicts, especially in Korea and Indochina. The Sino–Soviet rivalry in these areas is the principal factor tending to polarize the region. American policy toward these conflicts must be designed to dampen great-power rivalry by providing a stabilizing presence that will preempt other major powers from intervening or to balance an established Soviet presence.

For three decades the Korean peninsula has been divided in a tense but stable military confrontation between the communist North and capitalist South. The military confrontation across the DMZ has been sustained in a balance reinforced by the American security commitment to the Republic of Korea (ROK) and by limited Soviet and Chinese military assistance and political support for the Democratic People's Republic of Korea.

In the 1970s this stable pattern began to change as China normalized relations with the United States and South Korea's economic vitality gave the ROK new resources for managing its own defenses. American grant aid to the South Korean military ended in 1976 although the U.S. troop presence remains.

The 1980s will probably see further alterations in the factors that have sustained the division of the peninsula. A gradual crossover in power relationships and possibly an alteration in the military balance between North and South are likely to result from the social and economic dynamism of the South. Leadership changes, already accomplished in Seoul and anticipated in Pyongyang, will introduce an element of unpredictability into current policies and prospects for political stability.

In anticipation of these changes, the major powers have begun to explore alternatives to the "communist–capitalist" confrontation of the past. The United States fitfully envisions ways of engaging the North without undercutting its ally in the South; Japan is slowly developing official working-level contacts with the ROK and modest trade with the North; and the two major communist powers cautiously explore new openings in both Pyongyang and Seoul.

Although Kim Il Sung has long sought to maintain a balance in relations between China and the Soviet Union, Moscow's dealings with North Korea have never been close. Perhaps as a way of pressuring Kim, the Soviets have periodically established contacts with South Korean officials and private groups. Although the Chinese have staunchly espoused Kim Il Sung's cause, according him recognition as the "sole legitimate government" of Korea and supporting his call for the "independent and peaceful reunification" of the peninsula (with perhaps more stress on the word *peaceful* than Kim would prefer), Beijing's contemporary concern with Soviet interventions has led Chinese leaders to stress the need for stability on the peninsula. Although it seems unlikely that the Chinese will establish official contacts with Seoul, low-level and indirect trade has been developing between the PRC and South Korea, further blurring the sharp line of confrontation.

As suggested earlier, Moscow's interests would be served by establishing a closer relationship with North Korea, which would undercut Chinese influence and strengthen an outflanking presence in Northeast Asia that would support Soviet military deployments. The North Koreans appear to keep the Soviets at arm's length, presumably to limit Moscow's ability to intervene in their internal affairs. Nevertheless, it seems likely that the Soviets—and the Chinese—will try to influence the expected succession to Kim Il Sung. In anticipation of this and other changes, both Moscow and Beijing will continue to test the evolving balance on the peninsula and will explore the potential for influence resulting from strains in America's relations with the ROK and greater South Korean autonomy.

Korea's keystone location at the intersection of Soviet, Chinese, Japanese, and American interests in Asia makes it critical for the United States to maintain a credible presence on the peninsula throughout the 1980s. Withdrawal of the American military would undermine the present balance between North and South, stimulate trends toward nuclear proliferation, and tempt various parties to engage in potentially destructive military and political maneuvering. An uncertain American role in Korean security would also undermine Japanese confidence in the U.S. security relationship at a time when Tokyo is accelerating its defense modernization.

America's approach to South Korea must thus be designed to sustain close ties at a time when the ROK's enhanced economic and military capabilities will further reduce its dependence on the United States and when its leadership transition will very likely create strains in the relationship. At the same time, possibilities for American contact with North Korea—a potentially important new element for stabilizing relations between North and South—may further erode South Korean confidence in the United States if they are not handled properly.

Indochina is another feature on the Asian political landscape where great power interests intersect. Since World War II Indochina has endured almost ceaseless violence and shifting political alignments. At the present time a unified Vietnam seeks to consolidate control over Laos and Cambodia, while Beijing and Hanoi—only five years ago allies in a communist victory—are locked in a bitter military confrontation. Vietnam, which sought for many years to balance its relations between Moscow and Beijing, is almost totally dependent on Soviet military and economic assistance. Thus, the United States ironically finds itself aligned with China in an effort to preserve the security of Thailand against Vietnamese military pressures and to prevent the Soviet Union from establishing permanent military facilities in Indochina.

American and Chinese interests thus substantially converge regarding the Soviet presence in Southeast Asia although the Chinese seek an accommodating Vietnam and independent, friendly states in Laos and Cambodia, whereas America's allies and friendly ASEAN states would prefer to have the present conflict result in balanced relations between the Chinese and the Indochina states.

American and ASEAN approaches to the conflict in Indochina differ from that of the Chinese in the degree to which military pressures should be sustained on Vietnam and on Hanoi's expeditionary forces in Cambodia. China seeks support for the remnant forces of the Pol Pot government along the Thai border as a way of preventing the consolidation of Vietnamese control over Cambodia, while also maintaining military pressures along the Sino–Vietnamese and Sino–Lao borders. For the United States and most of the ASEAN states this policy only sustains Vietnam's dependence on the Soviet Union, gives Moscow a pretext for maintaining its use of military facilities at Danang and Cam Ranh Bay, and holds the dangers of insurgent warfare in Cambodia destroying the ravaged Cambodians and spilling over into Thailand. Malaysia and Indonesia evince increasing discomfort at the growth of Chinese influence in Southeast Asia through Beijing's active ties to Thailand and the United States.

American policy toward Indochina must thus maneuver between conflicting objectives and shifting relationships. We must strengthen our military presence to reassure allies and friends that we can inhibit Vietnamese and Soviet intervention and reinforce their own security, yet we must preserve sufficient political flexibility to support possible trends toward a neutralization of Cambodia or a more independent evolution in Hanoi's policies. The strength of the American military position in Southeast Asia is a fundamental asset in dampening the rivalry of the great communist powers and ensuring the security of our allies. Failure to strengthen the U.S. presence will most likely bring greater violence and instability to Southeast Asia.

Specific U.S. objectives in the 1980s must be to contain the conflict in Indochina and ensure the security of Thailand while using American military, economic, and political resources to sustain the vitality of ASEAN. This task could be seriously complicated by political instability and leadership crises in the Philippines and Indonesia; and the Soviet Union, with Vietnam, can be expected to try to break up ASEAN by playing on Indonesian and Malaysian fears of Chinese influence in Southeast Asia. American diplomacy must be flexible enough to support the genuine autonomy of ASEAN (and, if necessary, its growth into a security coalition) and to counterbalance Soviet and Chinese influence if their rivalry threatens to engulf the region.

Direct American Dealings with the Soviets in Asia

A third set of policy choices for the United States concerns direct contacts with the Soviet Union. Areas of direct involvement are not extensive because of the predominantly military quality of the Soviet presence in Asia and because Moscow's actions in the region have tended to be competitive with or in opposition to American purposes. But Moscow and Washington share an interest in limiting the potential for direct clashes of interest, especially where they might lead to military confrontations; and opportunities for mutually beneficial political or economic initiatives do arise.

A Soviet–American Deal on Asia?   On several occasions during the 1970s senior Soviet leaders have privately hinted to American officials interest in some form of "deal" on policies toward Asia, or they have made formal proposals that would have amounted to Soviet–American collusion on regional security matters. All these tentative feelers have implied some understanding about relations with the Chinese: a tradeoff of U.S.–Soviet détente for Sino–American normalization or coordinated efforts to contain the PRC through military pressures. A similar notion was embodied in the 1969 Brezhnev proposal for an Asian Collective Security arrangement: a multinational forum that would contain Chinese influence and give the Soviet Union a context for influencing events in Asia that was not provided by its own limited presence in the region.

The United States faces a basic dilemma in dealing with the Soviet Union on Asian matters. The USSR is unwelcome in almost all capitals of the region; yet it has the military power to intervene in local disputes where one party seeks assistance or to directly threaten the security of even major states such as China or Japan. The United States cannot ignore the interests and concerns of the Soviets in Asia, but a dialogue with Moscow on regional issues would erode the trust of friendly states which fear Soviet influence and would recoil from the prospect of a Soviet–American condominium on regional affairs. A Yalta-type general settlement or great power understanding for Asia would be unworkable today, and the appearance of even an attempt to establish such an understanding could seriously undercut America's relations with virtually all the countries of the region.

This is not to say, however, that there cannot be direct understanding between Washington and Moscow about Asian developments. It is probably more important than ever that the U.S. communicate clearly to Moscow its intentions and its determination to strengthen a coalition of allied and friendly states in reaction to further Soviet challenges. Yet such discussions between American and Soviet officials are likely to be restricted to matters of bilateral import or to involve issues in which allies of the two sides or other interested parties would have a role in formulating policy. In other words, international relationships in Asia are most likely to reflect the play of coalitions of states sharing common interests and coping with shared threats, not highly structured alliances or spheres of influence predetermined by the superpowers.

Regional Arms Control.   Soviet and American interests do converge in the desire to limit conflict situations that could lead to a direct U.S.–Soviet military confrontation. Asia has not been the focus of post-World War II arms control negotiations although tacit efforts have been made to limit local arms races and maintain a stable military balance. In Korea, for example, both sides have exercised self-restraint in supplying weapons to their respective allies in order to prevent renewed warfare on the peninsula.

There will be new opportunities for such tacit arrangements in Asia in the coming decade, above all in Korea. Nevertheless, Moscow could attempt to establish a closer relationship with Pyongyang by supplying new weaponry—especially more advanced aircraft. And South Korea is likely to seek from the United States, or build for itself, new and more sophisticated weapons systems. If the stability of the confrontation on the Korean peninsula is to be maintained, both Moscow and Washington will have to monitor the evolving military balance and show continuing restraint in their arms sales policies.

Tacit or explicit understandings about great power involvement and weapons supply arrangements could also help to stabilize local conflicts in Indochina. It is unlikely that Soviet leaders, intent upon developing a military presence on China's southern frontier and establishing regional basing arrangements in Vietnam, will be interested in restraint, but to the degree that the United States becomes more active in military assistance programs and develops plans for increasing regional deployment of American naval and air forces, Moscow may become interested in regional arms control arrangements.

Such opportunities are likely to be limited, however, owing to distrust among the great powers and peculiarities of geography and alliance relationships. As the United States discovered in its exploration of Soviet–American naval limitations in the Indian Ocean during the late 1970s, arms control arrangements could not maintain a stable balance in South and Southwest Asia because the Soviet Union's Central Asian frontier provinces give Moscow ready access to the region. Naval limitations would only restrict American and allied forces, not those of the USSR.

In addition the growth of regional arms production capabilities and complex international alignments will make arms control issues in the 1980s more than just a matter for U.S.–Soviet negotiation. Any negotiations on theater or strategic nuclear forces will probably involve Soviet concerns about Chinese (and European) weapons systems as well as PRC worries about Moscow's SS-20 threat and the weakening of the NATO deterrent. The United States should not reach agreements with Moscow without the involvement of its allies and friends. Similarly, the United States is unlikely to accept limitations to its own weaponry that assume nonexistent coordinated defense arrangements with other states—for example, with China.

In sum, an arms control approach to lowering the risks of direct U.S.–Soviet confrontation would not supplant the need for the United States to maintain stabilizing military balances in Asia, either through its own forces or through sales of equipment and assistance to allies and friends. At the same time, the proliferation of regional weapons production capabilities and more complex patterns of international alignment will make bilateral Soviet–American agreements less effective in stabilizing regional force balances.

Economic Relations.   Moscow has repeatedly sought U.S. and allied cooperation in the development of trading relations and investments of technology and capital for the exploitation of energy and natural resources in the Soviet Far East. Economic analysts observe that resource development in the Far Eastern provinces of the USSR is largely dependent on foreign capital because Moscow has concentrated its scarce investment resources in Western Siberia and the European USSR. Moreover, if Moscow is to continue to accelerate its economic development through importation of foreign technology, it must pay for such imports through foreign sales of the largely unexploited resources of its Asian provinces.

What would appear to be the basis for significant cooperation, however, is complicated by the pattern of Soviet control of exports and delayed return on investments and by Moscow's currently strained political relations with Washington and Tokyo. Although the Soviets cannot accelerate the exploitation of Siberia's resources without foreign investment, Moscow controls the pace at which foreign investors are compensated, regardless of contractual arrangements upon which the investments may be based. And without a significantly higher level of confidence in Soviet purposes in Asia and elsewhere than exists at present, the United States and Japan are unlikely to give Moscow such reverse economic leverage. Besides, there are significant opportunity costs to making such investments in the USSR since many of the resources of Siberia are available elsewhere.

Investment opportunities that would increase Soviet production of oil, gas, and coal present particularly difficult choices for Washington and Tokyo. Although Moscow uses its energy exports to pay for imports of Western capital goods, a Soviet energy deficit is anticipated in the late 1980s, and Moscow is not likely to want to export major quantities of energy supplies, especially petroleum. Although imports of Siberian gas could meet up to 20 percent of Japan's energy needs, there are strong disincentives to becoming energy dependent on the USSR or investing in a resource that the Soviets might not want to export.

An even more complex problem, especially for the United States, will arise if the energy deficit impels Moscow to intervene in the Middle East and Persian Gulf to establish control over petroleum resources. At the least, future Soviet energy needs could put even greater demands on an already strained international oil market. Thus, in the abstract, the United States has an incentive to facilitate Moscow's exploitation of domestic energy sources in order to reduce Soviet pressures to buy or control foreign supplies.

In practice, however, politics and public mood will significantly affect the willingness of foreign investors to promote Moscow's economic development. While American or Japanese investment in Siberian development projects could help to improve East–West relations, such events as the Soviet invasion of Afghanistan and the garrisoning of Japan's northern territories undermine the political basis and the public confidence that would support such investment decisions. Thus, American willingness to foster Siberian economic development or to encourage coinvestment involving the Soviet economy will remain dependent on the state of U.S.–Soviet relations.

CONCLUSION

America's Asia policy cannot be exclusively a matter of dealing with the Soviet challenge, and its Soviet policy must be global in scope and based on its own resources. Asia and the Soviet challenge now intersect in a fundamental way because of the worldwide reach of Soviet power and the significance of U.S. relations with major Asian states and key regional allies in developing responses to Moscow's growing military capabilities and interventions in third countries. American efforts to constrain the imperialistic impulses of the Soviet Union will require various forms of collaboration with a broad range of countries.

In the three decades since World War II, the Soviet Union has attempted to secure its Asian frontier through the establishment of bilateral alliances and regional military deployments that would counter the American presence in Asia and constrain the growth of other power centers—especially in Japan and China. The great failures of Moscow's Asian diplomacy have been the "loss" of China, an inability to establish an effective working relationship with Japan, and the expulsion of the Soviets from Indonesia in 1965. At the beginning of the 1980s Moscow faces the difficult task of resisting the formation of a coalition of states opposed to the expansion of Soviet influence in Asia: China, Japan, and the United States, which are in turn linked to America's allies in ASEAN, ANZUS, and NATO. The Soviets have responded with additional increases in their military dispositions in Asia and with efforts to strengthen their own coalition of supporters based on bilateral treaties with Mongolia, North Korea, Vietnam, India, and Afghanistan.

The coming decade thus holds the ominous prospect of a further polarization of alignments in Asia and increasing militarization as each side seeks to strengthen its position, weaken the opposing coalition, or anticipate the initiatives of its adversary. America's Asia policy must thus manage the game of coalition and countercoalition without unnecessarily polarizing Asian affairs. It must counter Moscow's growing military presence in the region without compounding a cycle of action and reaction that would destroy prospects for attaining a stable regional balance.

The U.S. response to the Soviet presence in Asia must be composed of three related elements that also affect the political, economic, and military dimensions of its bilateral relations with its allies and with the friendly states of the region.

A strengthened American military presence in the Western Pacific and a more active program of military assistance to U.S. allies are essential to counter Soviet capabilities and sustain regional confidence in U.S. security guarantees. American access to Asia for commercial, cultural, and political affairs will vary in proportion to the vitality of its regional security role. The United States faces a major challenge in reestablishing the credibility of its defense commitments in Asia. If it fails to do so, the economic dynamism of the region will be gradually translated into indigenous military capabilities and new patterns of security cooperation that might eventually exclude American influence and access.

The strength of the Soviet challenge requires an effective entente of alliance relationships and cooperative ties to friendly, if nonaligned states. Basic U.S. associations in Asia will remain with Japan, the Republic of Korea, the Philippines, Thailand, Australia, and New Zealand. American support for ASEAN will become increasingly important if and as the Soviets establish themselves as a permanent military presence in Indochina. And while U.S. economic ties to Asia will develop on a bilateral basis, the 1980s may well see the emergence of a "Pacific Basin Community" as a framework for managing the strains of economic growth and trade imbalances.[28] This and other forms of economic or political regionalism could strengthen a coalition of friendly states that will stabilize Asia in the face of the challenges of the 1980s and beyond.

28. See *An Asian–Pacific Regional Economic Organization: An Exploratory Concept Paper*, Committee on Foreign Relations, U.S. Senate, July 1979; Lawrence B. Krause and Sueo Sekiguchi, *Economic Interactions in the Pacific Basin* (Washington, D.C.: Brookings Institution, 1980); and Lawrence B. Krause, "The Pacific Economy in an Interdependent World," in Kermit W. Hanson and Thomas W. Roche, eds., *The United States and the Pacific Economy in the 1980s* (New York: Bobbs-Merrill, 1980).

United States relations with China will be the dynamic—and most controversial—element in our response to Soviet initiatives. American policy toward security cooperation with the Chinese must strike a balance between indifference toward China's defenses and gratuitous provocation of Soviet concerns about encirclement or the creation of threats to the interests of U.S. allies. Washington and Beijing must caution Moscow with the possibility of significant collaborative responses to Soviet threats while remaining sensitive to the concerns of states like India, Vietnam, and Indonesia, whose policies could enhance or limit Soviet access to the region.

American policy must also retain the flexibility to respond to changing circumstances in Korea, Indochina, and South Asia. Although development of normal U.S. relations with North Korea, or Vietnam, is neither likely nor appropriate in terms of the contemporary policies of Hanoi and Pyongyang, normalization could eventually help to minimize regional polarization and deal with the most immediate sources of regional instability. We should also remain alert to the possibilities of European allies establishing stronger relations with countries such as India and Vietnam, which would also minimize the trend toward regional polarization.

Direct Soviet–American dealings will be at the margin of U.S. policy in Asia, given the predominantly military character of Moscow's presence in the region and conflicting Soviet and American foreign policy objectives. Yet Asian security issues could well become an element in arms control discussions in the 1980s—a prospect that will require genuine American consultation with allies and friends if the appearance of a Soviet–American condominium is not to damage confidence in the U.S. security role. And finally, economic cooperation between the United States and the USSR, or American facilitation of Japanese investment in the development of the Soviet Far East, must remain linked to the overall state of the Soviet–American relationship.

Contributors

Seweryn Bialer is Ruggles Professor of Political Science and director of the Research Institute on International Change at Columbia University. He is the editor of a three-volume study of *Radicalism in the Contemporary Age* (1977). Among his other publications are *Stalin and His Generals* (1969) and *Stalin's Successors* (1980). He is now engaged in a book-length study of Soviet foreign policy during the Brezhnev era and its prospects during the 1980s.

Robert W. Campbell is professor and chairman of economics, Indiana University, Bloomington. His principal research interests are Soviet and East European energy problems and questions of technological progress and innovation in the Soviet economy. These two interests are combined in his recent book, *Soviet Energy Technologies*, published by Indiana University Press, 1980.

Ralph N. Clough is a research fellow at the Washington Center of the Asia Society. He is a former member of the State Department's Policy Planning Council and Director, Office of Chinese Affairs, and is the author of *East Asia and U.S. Security, Island China*, and *Deterrence and Defense in Korea: The Role of U.S. Forces*.

Ed. A. Hewett is a senior fellow at the Brookings Institution. Prior to going to Brookings in 1981 he was an associate professor of economics at the University of Texas at Austin. He is the author of a book entitled *Foreign Trade Prices in the Council for Mutual Economic Assistance*, and he has written articles on Soviet and East European foreign trade and the Hungarian economy. He has traveled throughout the Soviet Union and Eastern Europe and has done research in the Soviet Union and Hungary. He is currently working on a book entitled *Energy, Economics, and Foreign Policy in the USSR*.

Fuji Kamiya is one of the most prominent political scientists in Japan. A Tokyo University graduate, he is now professor of international relations at Keio University and serves as a member of the board of directors of the Japan Association of International Relations, Japan Association of International Law, Japan Institute of International Affairs, and Research Institute for Peace and Security. He also was a visiting professor at Columbia University from 1977 to 1979.

329

Paul F. Langer has written extensively on the international relations of the Far East and on the Soviet role in Asia. He is currently a consultant to The Rand Corporation.

Herbert S. Levine is a professor of economics at the University of Pennsylvania and senior consultant to Wharton Centrally Planned Economies Projects. He has written extensively on the Soviet economy, economic planning, and the econometric modeling of centrally planned economies. He is coeditor of the forthcoming volume *The Soviet Economy to the Year 2000.*

Robert A. Scalapino is Robson Research Professor of Government and director of the Institute of East Asian Studies at the University of California at Berkeley. He is also editor of *Asian Survey,* a scholarly monthly publication. His recent books include *Elites in the People's Republic of China, Asia and the Road Ahead,* and *The Foreign Policy of Modern Japan.*

Sheldon W. Simon is professor of political science and director of the Center for Asian Studies at Arizona State University, Phoenix. He is the author of five books and some forty scholarly articles and book chapters dealing with Asian security matters. He has taught at the University of Hawaii, George Washington University, the University of British Columbia, Carleton University (Ottawa), and the University of Kentucky. His Ph.D. is from the University of Minnesota.

Richard H. Solomon is director of The Rand Corporation's research program on International Security Policy and heads Rand's Political Science Department. From 1971 to 1976 he served as Senior Staff Member for Asian Affairs on the National Security Council, having previously been professor of political science at the University of Michigan. Dr. Solomon received his Ph.D. from the Massachusetts Institute of Technology in 1966, specializing in political science and Chinese politics. Apart from numerous written contributions to professional journals, he has published four books: *Mao's Revolution and The Chinese Political Culture* (1971); *A Revolution Is Not a Dinner Party* (1976); *Asian Security In The 1980s* (1979); and *The China Factor: Sino–American Relations and The Global Scene* (1981).

John J. Stephan is professor of history at the University of Hawaii. Educated at Harvard and the University of London, he is a specialist in Russo–Japanese relations and in the history of Siberia and the Soviet Far East. Among his works are *Sakhalin: A History* (1971); *The Kuril Islands: Russo–Japanese Frontier in the Pacific* (1975); and *The Russian Fascists: Tragedy and Farce in Exile, 1925–1945* (1978).

Donald S. Zagoria is a professor of government at Hunter College and the Graduate Center of the City University of New York. He is also a fellow at the Research Institute on International Change at Columbia University. In recent years Professor Zagoria served as a consultant to both the National Security Council and the East Asia Bureau of the Department of State. He has written two books, *The Sino–Soviet Conflict* and *Vietnam Triangle,* as well as many articles on Soviet and Chinese foreign policy.

Index

Acheson, Dean, 306
Aden, Soviet military facility at, 289, 292
Adenauer, Konrad, 129
Afghanistan, 56, 64, 80; communist takeover of, 1, 33, 50; friendship treaty with
  USSR, 292, 300, 327; as link in Soviet
  encirclement of China, 73, 260; rebels
  aided by China, 74; as Soviet base of
  operations, 291–92
Afghanistan, Soviet invasion of, 1, 43, 54,
  62, 86, 92, 135, 150, 256; as brake on
  possible new Soviet ventures, 157; Japanese sanctions against USSR, 8, 51,
  150, 263n; military drain on USSR,
  268; North Korean reaction to, 189–90,
  192; political image costs to USSR, 36,
  45, 87, 156, 170, 292, 326; Soviet perspective of, 33, 41, 44; strain on intra-
  Western relations, 39, 55; U.S. reaction,
  41, 55, 84, 135, 309, 317
Africa, 41, 314; Soviet expansionist policy
  in, 1, 80, 135, 289, 293
African–Asian conferences, 285 and n
Aigun, Treaty of (1858), 37
aircraft carriers: Soviet vs. U.S. Pacific
  fleets, 270, 309; U.S. need, 308, 309
air defense, U.S., 293, 308, 309; joint
  U.S.–Japanese–Chinese planning, 318
airplanes, Soviet exports of, 208; to
  China, 209, 223
Alaska, 34; pipeline, 240
Albania, 69, 187
Aldan region, plans for steel plant in,
  249
Algeria, Soviet arms supplies to, 185n
"American card" of China, 104
Amgun River basin, timber resources of,
  216
ammonia production plants, Soviet, 216n,
  219
Angola, 1, 7, 50, 135, 289

anticolonial movements, 5, 37, 38. See also
  "national liberation movements"
anti-hegemony clause: in Sino–Japanese
  peace treaty, 48, 70, 100 and n,
  137–38, 144, 145–46, 159, 177n, 225,
  290; in U.S.–PRC joint communiqué of
  1978, 177n–178n
anti-hegemony countercoalition, 288–91
anti-Maoism, 104, 106. See also China,
  demaofication
AN-12 aircraft, 269
ANZUS Pact, 5, 156–57, 285, 326
Aquino, Benigno, 16
Arab–Israeli peace negotiations, 292
Arab world, Soviet influence in, 3, 292.
  See also Middle East
Arctic sea-lanes, 273
Arita, Keisuke, 146
Arkhangel, 285
arms control, 282; lack of commitment of
  Reagan administration, 26, 113; regional, 324–25; U.S.–USSR negotiations,
  26, 288, 318, 324–25, 328
arms race, 109–10, 301, 308; between two
  Koreas, 197, 198–99, 324
arms supplies and military aid, 62, 324,
  325; Chinese, to Afghan rebels, 74;
  Chinese, to North Korea, 185, 320; Chinese, to Pol Pot guerrillas in Cambodia,
  160, 167; European, to China, 77, 98,
  265; Soviet, 2, 89, 257, 260, 275, 289,
  292–93; Soviet, to India, 185, 291 and
  n; Soviet, to North Korea, 68, 178, 179,
  185–86, 198–99, 257, 320, 324; Soviet,
  to Vietnam, 83, 159–60, 163, 276, 290;
  U.S., 302, 303 (chart), 304, 309, 327;
  U.S., to China, 23–24, 47, 55, 77, 78,
  313–14, 316, 317–18; U.S., to Pakistan,
  10, 44, 80, 84, 292, 310; U.S., to South
  Korea, 198–99, 320, 324; U.S., to Taiwan, 20, 90, 314; U.S., to Thailand, 10,

333

arms supplies (*continued*)
77; U.S. and Western, to ASEAN, 4,
154–55, 168, 172
ASEAN (Association of Southeast Asian
Nations), 3, 6, 10, 17, 168–73, 326;
attitude toward Soviet–Chinese–Japanese economic triangle, 225; and
Cambodian issue, 10, 158, 160, 161–62,
166, 167, 172, 321–22; character and
direction of countries, 156, 168; Chinese minorities resented, 25, 154, 155,
161; Chinese rapprochement, 160, 170;
Concord and Treaty of Amity and Cooperation, 10; courted by China, 6, 7,
73, 160; economic growth and orientation, 12, 156, 162, 168, 172; foreign
policy options for, 304, 322; implications of Soviet–Vietnamese treaty for,
161–62; international trade, 12, 27, 51,
162, 168–70, 169 (table); Japan's relations with, 8, 42, 156, 173; members,
10; opposition to Soviet-backed Vietnamese expansion, 166–67, 172, 322;
reaction to Afghanistan invasion, 156,
170; relations with U.S., 25, 27, 41,
79–80, 84, 155, 156, 162, 170, 172–73,
291, 322; reliance on U.S. and Western
arms supplies, 4, 154–55, 168, 172; Soviet contacts with, 43, 44, 51, 79–80, 84,
88, 169–71; Soviet port call privileges
denied by, 155, 162; Soviet pressure on,
79–80, 84, 154, 155; Soviet prospects
minimal, 84, 156, 157–58, 291; Soviet
standing diminished due to its backing
of Hanoi, 20, 42, 43, 79, 165, 170;
Soviet vs. U.S. trade with, 169 (table);
Soviet wooing of, 6, 43, 84, 88, 156,
291, 322; split perspectives on China
and Vietnam, 19–20, 73, 79, 158,
161–62, 291; suspicions of China, 25,
79, 90, 155, 168, 322; suspicions of
Vietnam, 51–52, 73, 79, 322; UN resolution on withdrawal of foreign troops
from Indochina, 160; U.S. policy options toward, 172–73, 306, 322, 327;
Vietnam's inquiry for membership in,
226
Asian Collective Security System proposal
of USSR, 45, 56, 87, 98 and n, 155,
260, 287, 323
Asian Development Bank, 226

Association of American Geographers,
244
Association of Southeast Asian Nations.
See ASEAN
Attlee, Clement, 126
Australia, 2, 128, 264; alliances, 4, 8, 154,
155, 285, 327; Soviet trade with, 206
(table), 206, 207 (table); Soviet vs. U.S.
trade with, 297 (table); trade with
ASEAN, 12
Austria, 218; *1955* peace treaty, 129
automotive industry, Japanese: equipment
and know-how exports to USSR, 220;
international trade inroads and imbalances, 18–19

Backfire bombers, 18, 256, 269, 274, 279,
291
Baikal–Amur Mainline Railroad (BAM),
32, 110, 210, 216, 222, 226, 229,
249–51, 273, 274n; possible Chinese interdiction, 318
"balance of power" policies, 287; U.S., 60,
304–05
"balancing centers of power" policy, U.S.,
50
Bali, ASEAN summit conference at
(*1976*), 10
ballistic missiles, Soviet, 278, 293, 299;
against China, 97, 268; on cruisers,
275n; ICBMs, 40; on *Minsk*, 270; priority of European over Asian targets,
257; SA-9, 268; SA-7, 185; SA-6, 185,
268; SS-N-18, 40; SS-20 (IRBM), 97,
270, 291, 308, 324; on submarines, 258,
268, 269; against U.S., 40, 268, 299
ballistic missiles, U.S., 40; cruise, 308;
ICBMs, 293; Minuteman, 299n; MX,
308; Pershing, in Europe, 41; Trident,
40, 308
Bandung Conference (*1955*), 285
Bangladesh, 74; Soviet military aid to, 292
banks, Soviet-owned foreign, 211–13
Barishnykov, V. N., 47
Beijing, Treaty of (*1860*), 37
Belgrade conference of nonaligned nations (*1978*), 181
Bhutan, 74
Bialer, Seweryn, 21, 23
bipolarism, 58, 62, 283
boat people, 290

Bolshevik Revolution, 35; European intervention, 285; Siberian Intervention by Japan, 32, 261
Bonin Islands (Ogasawara), 121
Bradley, General Omar, 121
Brandt, Willy, 140
"breakout in the Arc of Crisis," 292
Brezhnev, Leonid, 203n, 261n, 296; anti-hegemony clause objections, 177n; and China, 44, 55–56, 95, 286–87; Collective Security System proposed by, 45, 56, 98n, 260, 287, 323; Indian policy of, 291n; and negotiations with Japan, 136–37, 138, 139, 141, 144, 149; and North Korean relations, 180–81, 191; principles of equality, sovereignty, non-interference, and non-use of force espoused, 94n, 98n
Brezhnev Doctrine, 94; and Czechoslovakia, 287
Brezhnev regime, 2, 21, 95, 118
Brown, Harold, 19, 77, 272, 318
Brzezinski, Zbigniew, 46, 48, 50, 82, 145, 290
Bulganin, Nikolai, 286
Bulgaria, 68, 85, 246
Burma, 87, 88; Soviet influence in, 285, 286; Soviet vs. U.S. trade with, 169 (table), 297 (table); U.S. contacts with, 307

Cairo Declaration (1943), 125, 133
Cambodia, 226, 307; Chinese arms for Pol Pot guerrillas, 160, 167; Chinese–Vietnamese rivalry in, 5, 51, 72, 73, 321–22; exiles in Pyongyang, 45; Heng Samrin government, 150, 160, 166–67, 291n; Pol Pot regime, 68, 71, 72, 158–59, 188, 290, 322; Soviet influence in, 1, 3, 42, 44, 71, 84, 154, 165; Soviet trade with, 204–05 (table), 206, 209; Soviet–Vietnamese rivalry in, 164–65; Vietnamese domination of, 42, 71–73, 84, 87, 161–62, 163, 164–65, 321–22; Vietnamese invasion of, 8, 20, 42, 43, 51, 156, 157, 158–59, 160, 166–67, 290; Vietnamese invasion response of U.S. called uncertain, 302, 309–10; Vietnamese troop strength in, 165, 166; Vietnamese withdrawal demanded, 157, 166

Cambodian issue, 166–68; ASEAN and, 10, 158, 160, 161–62; and danger of Thai–Vietnam war, 167–68, 322; North Korean stance, 45, 68, 188, 190, 192; UN resolution, 51, 160; U.S. policy options, 172, 173, 306, 322; U.S. position in, 166, 167
Cambodian refugees, 167
Cam Ranh Bay, Vietnam, Soviet base at, 42, 51, 71, 79, 265n, 274, 275, 290, 322
Canada, 12
capitalism: centers of, 53; Chinese trade relations, 100n, 105; "crisis" of, 44; production devices used by Chinese, 4; vs. socialism, 54, 203; Soviet acceptance of trade relations with, 203, 206, 222, 246; Soviet denouncement of Chinese convergence with, 102–03, 105–06
Carter, James Earl, 41, 145, 177n, 290
Carter administration, 50, 199; arms control negotiations, 26; and China, 77, 317; loss of credibility, 302; and South Korea, 4, 9, 302; and Thailand, 79; unraveling of détente, 113
Ceauşescu, Nicolae, 181
CENTO (Central Treaty Organization), 285
Central Asia, Soviet, 32, 37, 57; agricultural growth, 233; development of, 37, 63, 230; development potential, 230–31, 245; industrial output growth, 232, 233 (table); investments, 231; military installations in, 97; population growth, 235; strategic value, 63; U.S. missile threat to, 40
Central Asian ethnics, 237–38; Muslims, 36
chemical products: Siberian vs. total USSR output of, 242, 243 (table); Soviet imports from Japan, 142, 210, 215, 219
Chenpao Island, Sino–Soviet border clashes near, 94
Chiang Kai-shek. See Jiang Jieshi.
China, People's Republic of (PRC): admission to UN, 288; adversaries on borders of, 6, 21–22, 71, 72, 97, 160, 163, 260, 267–68; aid to Afghan rebels, 74; air force of, 269; anti-hegemony foreign policy of, 100 and n, 137–38, 159, 288, 289–90, 296; anti-Maoist movement, in Soviet view, 104, 106; armaments and

China, People's Republic of (*continued*)
armed forces of, 23–24, 47, 55, 72, 78;
armed forces strength, 268, 271; arms
supplies to North Korea, 185, 320;
ASEAN courted by, 6, 7, 73, 160;
ASEAN split perspectives on, 19–20,
73, 79, 158, 161–62; ASEAN suspicions
of, 25, 79, 90, 155, 168, 322; and Cambodian issue, 160, 166–67, 290,
321–22; communist victory of *1949*, 38,
58; credit extended by Japan and West,
100n; Cultural Revolution, 47, 68, 104,
179, 288; demaofication, 4, 6–7, 14, 48,
64–65, 96 and n, 101–07, 111; divergent U.S. views on, 313–14; ethnic minorities, 67; European arms sales to, 77,
98, 265; European diplomatic relations
restored, 288; foreign policy options of,
304, 308; Four Modernizations, 47, 48,
100, 106; future direction uncertain,
14, 16, 17, 52; future neo-Stalinist repression possible, 16, 26; Great Leap
Forward, 103, 104, 286; implications of
Soviet–Vietnamese treaty for, 160–61;
and India, 72, 74, 291; Indochina policy goals of, 321; international trade (*see*
trade, international); Japan and (*see*
Sino–Japanese relations); and Korea,
11, 177, 199, 319–20; and Kurile Islands dispute, 48, 122, 133, 138–39;
leadership split presumed possible, 47,
99 and n, 100–01, 106–07; military and
economic expenditures, 105 and n; military modernization, 23, 105, 268, 271,
315–16; modernization programs, 7,
13, 14, 15, 23, 47, 100, 103, 104–06,
224; modernization projects, 225; and
Mongolian People's Republic, 65, 66;
nationalism, 64, 104, 107; NATO supported by, 7, 314, 318, 324; and North
Korea, 11, 25, 43, 45, 67–69, 176, 179,
183–93 passim, 228, 320; nuclear capability of, 39, 108, 259, 271n, 286,
324; and Pakistan, 73, 74; its socialism
questioned by Soviets, 44, 94, 105–06;
socioeconomic problems, 14–16; Southeast Asian relations, 19–20, 25, 71–73,
89–90, 153, 154, 155, 158, 160–61,
295, 321–22; and South Korea, 194,
195, 320; South Korean trade alleged,
192 and n, 320; Soviet relations (*see*

Sino–Soviet relations); strategic indigestibility of, 23, 66–67, 88, 259, 260;
and Taiwan, 20, 90, 314–15; ties to
Thailand, 158, 160, 161, 321, 322; turn
to market socialism, 105–06; turn to the
West, 6–7, 13–14, 39, 40, 45, 100 and
n, 104, 287, 288; U.S. relations (*see*
Sino–U.S. relations); and Vietnam, 5–6,
43, 47, 71–73, 154, 226–27, 275,
321–22; Vietnam attack as "punishment," 72, 89, 192–93, 259, 290; Vietnam attacked by, 7, 42, 50, 51, 63,
94–95, 155, 157, 159, 275; Vietnamese
ethnic and geopolitical rivalry, 5, 7, 72;
Vietnamese–Soviet treaty as threat to,
156, 158, 160–61. *See also* Sino–Japanese–American entente; triangle, strategic, Soviet–American–Chinese
"China card," American, 46, 111, 313
Chinese Communist Party (CCP), 16, 58,
87, 100, 101, 106
Chinese ethnics, in Southeast Asia, 17, 25,
154, 155, 161, 291
Chinese Nationalists, 58. *See also* Taiwan
Chul'man coalfield, development of,
217
Chun Tu Hwan, 81
Churchill, Sir Winston, 125
class struggle, 103
clothing, Soviet imports of, 209, 214
CMEA. *See* COMECON
coal: Siberian resources and development,
217–18, 245, 247, 325; Siberian vs. total
USSR output of, 242, 243 (table); Soviet
exports, 246; Soviet exports to Japan,
142, 210, 213, 214, 217–18, 247
COCOM (Coordinating Committee), 219
cold war, 59, 283; renewal of, 135; rhetoric of USSR media, 76; as state of
affairs between Asian communist neighbors, 43–44
Collective Security System proposal of
USSR, 45, 56, 87, 98 and n, 155, 260,
287, 323
colonialism, 35, 54, 135; in Asia, 5, 59,
284; present-day Soviet equivalent, 135
COMECON (Council for Mutual Economic Assistance, *also* CMEA), 61, 227;
shunned by North Korea, 187, 228;
Vietnamese membership, 71, 159, 163,
227 and n, 290

communism, Soviet-style, failure as a
model, 4, 86, 91
communist ideology, 5–6, 30, 44; nationalism in, 6
communist parties: Asian, limited Soviet
influence, 61, 87, 88; Asian guerrilla,
ties to Chinese communists, 87, 88;
Asian parliamentary, ties to CPSU, 61,
87; Asian post-World War II movements, 285; attraction of Chinese communism for, 100, 111; of China (CCP),
16, 58, 87, 100, 101, 106; excom-
munication of China attempted by
USSR, 98 and n, 100, 287; of India
(CPI), 74, 87; international conference
of 1976 in East Berlin, 98n; of Japan,
48 and n; Philippine guerrillas, 16, 88;
pro-Soviet, recent power seizures by, 1;
shift of influence toward China, 111; of
South Asia, 1950s growth, 61; of Southeast Asia, 4, 25, 71, 88, 161, 162, 168;
of Sri Lanka (SLCP), 87; Western European, 53, 98n, 111
Communist Party of the Soviet Union
(CPSU), 61, 87, 108; 20th Congress, 38,
178; 24th Congress, 94n; 25th Congress, 94 and n, 138, 180; 26th Congress, 44, 56
communist states: new cold war between,
in Asia, 5–6, 43–44, 59–60; 1980 Sofia
meeting of Soviet bloc, 189
compensation agreements, 216, 251
computer technology, 220
construction materials production, Siberian vs. total USSR, 243 (table)
consumer goods: Soviet imports from Japan, 214–15; underproduced in Siberia, 242, 243 (table)
containerized cargo, Trans-Siberian Landbridge, 211, 216, 250–51
containment policies: Soviet, 89; Soviet,
vis-à-vis China, 40, 66–67, 74, 82, 95,
153, 154, 286, 323; U.S., 59, 305
contradictions, 46, 49; global, Asia as zone
of, 39, 53; revisions by Chinese, 103;
Soviet analysis and exploitation of, 54–55
"correlation of forces," 46, 53
cotton, Soviet exports of, 208; to Japan,
142, 210, 213–14
Council for Mutual Economic Assistance.
See COMECON

counterrevolutionism, Soviet charge
against China, 102
credit arrangements, international: compensation agreements, 216, 251; Japan
to China, 225; Japan to USSR, 215–16
and n, 217, 218, 219; West to USSR,
246
Crimean War, 37
cruise missile, U.S., 308
Cuba, 181; CMEA membership, 227 and
n; missile crisis, 122, 178; proxy forces
for USSR, 2, 7, 289, 300; Soviet combat
brigade in, 41; Soviet energy exports to,
246; Soviet trade with, 207 (table), 209
Cultural Revolution, 47, 68, 104, 179, 288
Czechoslovakia, 192, 246; Soviet military
intervention of 1968, 287

Dahlak, Soviet military facility at, 289
Dalintorg, 214
Dallin, Alexander, 29
Danang, Vietnam, Soviet base at, 42, 51,
71, 79, 274, 275, 290, 322
defense: "division of labor," Japan and
U.S., 262; "division of labor," possible
U.S. and China, 304; Soviet strategy,
293–94, 299–300; Soviet view of,
301–02; U.S. planning of, 300, 306;
U.S. strategy, 293; Western sharing of
burden and integration needed, 19,
281, 304, 309–12. See also military
strength; regional security
Delta SSBN submarines, 258
Democratic People's Republic of Korea.
See North Korea
Democratic Republic of Vietnam. See
Vietnam
Deng Xiaoping, 14, 15, 82, 96n, 182, 191,
265 and n, 289, 290, 295
détente, 134, 135, 288–89; breakdown of,
13, 40, 98, 135, 283; factors in breakdown of, 2, 13, 101, 111–12, 113, 135,
288–89; as "objective" trend in Soviet
perception, 46, 54; in setting of
Sino–Soviet conflict and Sino–U.S. rapprochement, 50, 59–60, 98, 99, 111,
288; Soviet condition of ending
Sino–U.S. rapprochement ignored, 99,
288; value for Soviet Union, 113
developing nations, 53. See also Third
World

development strategies, 240–41, 244, 252–53
Dhanabalan, Supphiah, 171
Dibb, Paul, 229
Dostoyevsky, Feodor, 35

East China Sea, 155
East Germany, 194, 246, 300
EC-121 incident, 187
economic diplomacy: Japanese role, 8–9, 261, 264; Soviet failure, 2, 42–43, 61, 169; U.S., 307, 327. *See also* trade, international
economic growth: in East Asia, 11–12; Soviet vs. Western model, 91. *See also* industrial production
Egypt, 166, 292
Eisenhower administration, 285
electric power, in USSR: nuclear based, 246; Siberian vs. total USSR output, 242 and n, 243 (table). *See also* hydroelectric power
electronic equipment, USSR imports of, 20
El Paso Natural Gas Company, 248
energy: Japanese needs, 9, 15, 52, 70, 221, 278 and n, 312, 325; Sakhalin exploration, 70, 218, 248; Siberian output, 242 and n, 243 (table); Siberian resources, 229, 234, 243, 244–45, 247–48, 325; Soviet consumption, 245; Soviet exports, 210, 245, 246–48; Soviet production, 245–46; Soviet resources, 246, 325; Soviet shortage predicted, 118, 227, 325–26. *See also* coal; gas, natural; hydroelectric power; oil
energy equipment, Soviet exports of: to China, 209, 223; nuclear technology, 246
equality, principle of, in international affairs, 87, 94n, 98n
equipment: Siberian production, 242; Soviet exports of, 208, 221, 226, 246; Soviet exports to China, 209, 223–24; Soviet imports from Japan, 206, 210, 214, 215, 217, 219–20; Soviet products not competitive with Western quality, 208
Ethiopia, 50, 289, 300; Soviet influence in, 1, 3, 135; Soviet military facilities in, 18, 289, 292, 293; Soviet treaty with, 292

Etorofu, 121, 123 (map), 124, 125, 126, 127, 128, 131, 146
Europe: Helsinki accords, 140, 148; military contingencies, 318; Soviet historical view of, 35; Soviet military buildup in, 256–57; stable pattern of alliances, 283; as traditional Russian priority, 37, 38, 57–58, 111
Europe, Eastern, 312; CMEA (COMECON) contributions, 227; nationalism, 61; post-World War II borders legitimized, 140; Soviet energy exports to, 246 and n, 247; Soviet sphere of influence, 58, 89, 259, 285
Europe, Western: arms control interests, 26, 324; arms sales to China, 77, 98, 265; Asian relations, 328; attitude toward Soviets, 2; communist parties of, 53, 98n, 111; diplomatic relations with China restored, 288; nuclear weapons, 324; Soviet policy in, 20, 55, 58, 98, 129, 140; as Soviet policy priority, 41, 111, 112; Soviet rhetoric, 35, 40; Soviet trade with, 143, 210, 218, 254; ties with China, 39, 40, 45, 77, 98; trade with North Korea, 228; as U.S. priority, 76. *See also* NATO
European Economic Community (EEC, Common Market), 53; Japanese trade imbalances with, 19
European ethnics, USSR, 63, 109, 237–38
Eximbank Act, Stevenson Amendment to, 216n, 248, 289
Export–Import Bank (Japan), 215, 216n, 217
Export–Import Bank (U.S.), 248

Far East, Soviet: agricultural growth, 232; air power buildup, 268–69, 286, 291, 318; coal production, 217, 243 (table), 247; coal resources of, 245, 247; development potential, 231, 296; economic development of, 37, 42, 51, 110, 325; electric power output, 243 (table); energy deficit of, 242, 248; fishing industry, 242, 243 (table); foreign investment and participation in development, 51, 216–19, 247–48, 325–26; in-and-out commodity flow, 242–43; industrial output, 242, 243 (table); industrial output growth, 232, 233 (table); military deployments, 18, 97, 256; naval bases, 44, 273–74, 286, 291; nomenclature, 229, 230; population problem, 235–36, 237–38, 243; steel industry expansion plans, 217, 249; timber production, 243 (table), 248–49; timber resources, 243, 248; U.S. missile threat to, 40. *See also* Sakhalin; Yakutia

Far Eastern Freight Conference, 170, 211

Far East Forestry Development Projects, 217

Fencer fighter-bomber, 269

ferrous metallurgy, 249; Siberian vs. total USSR output, 242, 243 (table); Soviet technology transfer to Japan, 221. *See also* rolled ferrous metals; steel

fertilizer: Japanese export of plants to USSR, 218; Soviet exports to Japan, 213–14

"Finlandization," 308

fish, Soviet exports of, 242; to Japan, 213, 214

fishing rights, Soviet–Japanese dispute, 69, 131, 134; *1977* negotiations, 141–42, 221

Five-Power Defense Pact, 4, 155

Flogger fighter aircraft, 269

food processing industry, Siberia, 242, 243 (table)

food products: Soviet exports of, 207 (table), 208, 213; Soviet imports of, 206, 207 (table), 208, 209

Ford administration, 50, 288

foreign military sales: U.S., 302, 303 (chart), 304, 309; USSR, 210

Foreign Trade Bank (USSR), 212

forestry development projects, Soviet–Japanese, 217

Forger naval fighter aircraft, 269

Four Modernizations, China, 47, 48, 100, 106

Foxbat combat aircraft, 269, 291

France, 33, 37, 218; China and, 100n; Indochina war, 72; Japanese auto imports, 19

free trade, international, threat to, 19

friendship treaties, Soviet, 1, 2, 260, 292–93; as harbingers of war, 300

F-16 aircraft, to South Korea, 199

Fukuda, Takeo, 144

Gandhi, Indira, 44, 291n

Gang of Four (former Chinese leaders), 14, 15, 47, 103, 106

Gang of Four (South Korea, Singapore, Taiwan, Hong Kong), 12

gas, natural: Sakhalin exploration, 70, 218; Siberian resources, 218, 244–45; Soviet exports of, 246, 247–48; Tyumen project, 218, 240, 245; U.S. and Japanese development participation, 218–19, 247–48, 311n, 325; Western European development participation, 218, 254; Yakutia resources and project, 219, 245, 248, 253, 311n

GATT (General Agreement on Tariffs and Trade), 10

German Democratic Republic (East Germany), 194, 246, 300

German–Japanese axis of *1940*s, 285

Germany, 37, 261; Hitler, 2, 33, 37–38

Germany, Federal Republic of (West Germany), 33; antinuclear and neutralist sentiment, 20; China and, 100n, 102; "Ostpolitik," and renunciation of eastern territories, 140; Soviet recognition of, 129; Soviet treaty of goodwill with (*1970*), 140; trade with USSR, 70, 143, 213, 218

"global contradictions," Asia as zone of, 39, 53

GNP comparison, Japan–U.S.–USSR, 213

Gorshkov, Admiral Sergei G., 294n

Gosplan, 215, 233, 239

Gosstroy, 234

grain: Siberian, 242; Soviet exports of, 208; wheat imports, 206, 207 (table)

Great Britain, 4, 33, 37, 128; China and, 100n; Five-Power Defense Pact member, 155

"Great Han" chauvinism, 32, 49, 102

Great Leap Forward, 103, 104, 286

Grishin, V., 192

Gromyko, Andrei, 1, 180–81n, 294n; in negotiations with Japan, 132, 137–38, 139, 141, 146

Gromyko–Matsumoto letter, 132

ground forces, in Asia: Chinese, 268, 271; Soviet, 267–68, 291, 293; U.S., 302, 309

Guam Declaration, 79

Guatemala, 50

guerrilla communists, 87, 88
Gu Mu, 15

Habomais, 121, 123 (map), 124, 125, 126, 127, 128; brief Soviet offer of return to Japan, 130–31, 147, 149
Haig, Alexander, 23, 77, 317
Haile Selassie, Emperor, 289
Haiphong, U.S. mining of, 34
Hatoyama, Ichiro, 129, 131–32, 135, 147
Havana, Cuba: conference of nonaligned nations at, 51; World Festival of Youth (1978), 181
hegemonism: Chinese charges against U.S., 20; Chinese charges against USSR, 20, 40, 296, 314; Soviet charges against China, 40, 47, 103, 105, 107; Soviet proposals against, 65, 87; UN resolution, 65. See also anti-hegemony clause
Helsinki Conference on Security and Co-operation in Europe (1975), 140, 148
Heng Samrin government, Cambodia, 150, 160, 166–67, 291n
Himalayan states, 73
Hitler, Adolf, 2, 33, 37
Ho Chi Minh, 165
Hodge, Lieutenant General John R., 175n
Hokkaido, 38, 121, 134, 138, 140; alleged Soviet occupation attempt, 262; Soviet military threat to, 18, 268, 291
Honecker, Erich, 180
Hong Kong, 213; GNP growth, 12
Ho Tam, 181
Hua Guofeng, 181, 182, 290
human rights issues, 26
Hungary, 192, 246
Hunter, Holland, 117n
hydroelectric power, USSR, 239 and n, 245, 247
Hyland, William G., 95
Hyon Chung Kuk, 189

ICBMs: Soviet, 40; U.S., 293
Ikeda, Hayato, 132–33
imperialism: Chinese convergence denounced by Soviets, 102–03, 105; Soviet, 5, 135; Soviet rhetoric against, 35, 44, 46, 54
India, 84–85, 264, 312; China's relations with, 72, 74, 291; Communist Party of, 74; disinterest in Brezhnev's collective security proposal, 287; as link in Soviet encirclement of China, 73, 260; recognition of Cambodian Heng Samrin regime by, 160, 291n; Soviet arms supplies to, 185, 291 and n; Soviet relations with, 38, 44, 45, 73, 80, 84–85, 90, 283, 285, 286, 291 and n; Soviet support for, against Pakistan, 3; Soviet treaty with, 292, 327; Soviet vs. U.S. trade with, 296, 297 (table); U.S. relations with, 74, 80, 84, 306, 328
Indian Ocean, 84; naval power limitations in, 324; Soviet position in, 3, 13, 18, 32, 97, 153, 162, 163, 269, 324; strategic ballistic weapons in, 40; U.S. buildup in, 9, 27, 40, 76, 80, 256, 278
Indochina, 50, 71–73; as Asian trouble spot, 25, 321–22; as link in Soviet encirclement of China, 71, 72, 260, 324; post–World War II Soviet influence in, 285; procommunist "empire," 3, 71, 72, 154, 155, 163, 166; refugees, 158, 226–27, 290, 300; regional arms control in, 324; security concerns, 319, 321–22; shift in India's policy toward, 291n; Sino–Soviet rivalry in, 42, 43, 51, 71–73, 89–90, 153, 160–61, 319, 321–22; Sino–U.S. convergence and divergence of interests, 321–22; Soviet position in, 3, 42, 43, 44, 51, 71, 72–73, 79, 164–65, 257 (see also Soviet–Vietnamese relations); U.S. policy options in, 322, 324, 328; U.S. withdrawal gap filled by USSR and Vietnam, 44, 83, 153, 266. See also Southeast Asia
Indonesia, 16, 168, 213, 283, 322; ASEAN member, 10; and Cambodian issue, 161–62; Chinese minority resented, 17, 25, 155, 161, 291; Chinese ties of 1960s, 283; Chinese trade resumed, 158; communist coup of 1965, 161, 171; communist party decline, 4; disinterest in Brezhnev's collective security proposal, 287; Malacca Straits claimed by, 153; post–World War II Soviet influence in, 285, 286; power potential of, 27; relations with U.S., 27, 307, 322, 328; reliance on U.S. arms supplies, 4; Soviet relations with, 38, 45, 171, 291, 295, 326; Soviet trade with, 203, 206 (table), 206, 207 (table); Soviet

vs. U.S. trade with, 169 (table); 297
(table); stance toward China vs. Vietnam, 19–20, 158, 161–62, 291, 295;
suspicions of China, 25, 158, 161, 171,
295, 322
industrial production: global, share of
"socialist camp" in, 45 and n; USSR,
243 (table); USSR Eastern regions, 232,
233 (table), 243 (table)
Industrial Wood Chip and Pulp Development Project, 217
inner-core strategy, Soviet, 58–59, 61
Institute of International Relations
(USSR), 31
Institute of Oriental Studies (USSR), 39
Institute of the Far East (USSR), 30, 47
Institute of the USA and Canada (USSR),
31
Institute of World Economy and International Relations (USSR), 30
International Ice Hockey Federation, 194
International Monetary Fund (IMF), 7,
226
International Political Science Association,
194
International Press Service, 194
International Shooting Union's Administrative Council, 194
investment, in Eastern USSR regions,
230–32, 231 (table), 233–34, 244, 250,
251, 254, 325; Japanese, 216–19,
247–48, 325–26; U.S., 51, 218–19,
247–48, 311n, 325–26; Western European, 218, 254
Iran, 11, 277, 292, 318; changes in U.S.
policy direction after collapse, 50, 56,
80, 84; crisis as strain on intra-Western
relations, 39, 55; hostage crisis, 63;
hostage rescue mission failure, 302; and
Soviet collective security proposal, 287;
Soviet perspective and goals, 41, 43, 44;
unpredictability of situation, 55; U.S.
abandonment of Shah, 302
Iraq–Iran war, 292
IRBMs, Soviet, 97, 270, 291, 308
Irkutsk oblast, gas resources of, 245
Islam, 36, 43; Philippine rebels, 87; tide
of revivalism, 36, 90
Israel, 3, 228; peace negotiations, 292
Italy: communist party, 98n; trade with
USSR, 143, 218

Ivan Rogov, the, 147, 291
Ivkov, I. I. (pen name). See Kovalenko,
Ivan
Izvestiya, 144

Jackson–Vanik amendment, 51, 289
Japan: and ASEAN, 8, 42, 156, 173; capitalism, 53; China and (see Sino–Japanese relations); communist party of,
relations with CPSU, 48 and n; defense
spending by, 8, 9, 19, 42, 78, 122, 148,
281, 309, 310–12; economic influence,
8–9, 261, 264; economic strength, 7,
8–9, 11–12, 42, 148, 263–64, 310, 311;
energy needs of, 9, 15, 52, 70, 220, 278
and n, 312, 325; foreign policy of, 90;
foreign policy alternatives of, 304, 308,
310, 312; GNP, 213, 264; history of
claim to Northern Territories, 124–28;
impact of Sino–Soviet hostility on,
137–38, 145, 146, 224, 225–26; importance of Southeast Asia to, 257n; inroads in Southeast Asia, 8, 42, 156, 173;
international trade (see trade, international) and Korea, 176, 177; Korean
cross-recognition proposed by, 195,
199; Liberal Democratic party of, 48,
131–32, 137, 139, 148; lingering resistance to rearmament, 311–12; militarism fears misplaced, 7–8, 9, 122,
261–62 and n, 265; militarism in answer to security gap possible, 263, 281;
nationalism, 81; North Korea and, 190;
North Korean trade and debt, 184, 228,
320; notion of "comprehensive security," 311; raw material needs, statistics, 278 and n; reassertion in
international affairs, 7–9; sanctions
against Vietnam, 8; Socialist party, 133;
and South Korea, 8, 42, 77, 176, 320;
Soviet relations (see Northern Territories dispute; Soviet–Japanese economic
ties and trade; Soviet–Japanese relations); U.S. and (see U.S.–Japanese relations); World War II, 24, 35, 38, 173;
World War II surrender and territorial
losses, 126–28, 147, 149, 261 and n. See
also Sino–Japanese–American entente
"Japan card," Soviet, 42, 55
Japanese Association for Trade with Socialist Countries of Europe, 215

Japanese Chamber of Commerce and Industry, 215
Japanese Defense Agency, 146, 265n, 267n, 278n, 281
Japanese Federation of Economic Organizations (Keidanren), 215
Japanese fishing rights, 69, 131, 134, 141–42
Japanese internees in USSR, 130, 131, 261
Japanese Self-Defense Forces, 122, 148, 262, 265n; Air, 269; branch rivalry, 311; Ground, 268, 311; Naval, 18, 279n
Japan Export–Import Bank, 215, 216n, 217
Japan International Cooperation Agency, 215
Japan–Soviet Trade Treaty of *1957*, 142
Jiang Jieshi (Chiang Kai-shek), 38, 125, 286
Joint Japanese–Soviet Economic Committee, 215, 217
Jordan, 292

Kama River truck plant, 220
Kamiya, Fuji, 21
Kamm, Henry, 12
Kanematsu, 215
Kansk–Achinsk Basin, coal resources of, 245
Kapitsa, Mikhail, 31
Karen people, 87
Karmal, Babrak, 189
Kaysone, Phomvihan, 165
Kazakhs, 57, 67, 237–38
Kazakh SSR, 229–30; agricultural output of, 233, 234; development potential, 230–31, 245; industrial output growth, 232, 233 (table); investments, 231; population imbalance, 235, 236, 237; Virgin Lands program, 234, 236
Kazakhstanskaya Pravda, 194
Keidanren, 215
Khabarovsk conference, 34
Khmer Rouge, 72
Khrushchev, Nikita, 116, 122; anti-China polemics, 95; anti-China stance, 286; economic aid to China cut off, 223; memoirs of, 99n; in negotiations with Japan, 132–33; and North Korea, 68, 178–79; at 20th Party Congress (*1956*), 38

Kim Chung Il, 187, 191
Kim Il Sung, 43, 68–69, 81–82, 178–79, 182, 190–93, 196, 197, 198, 199, 257, 320–21; calls for Korean reunification, 69, 81, 176, 177, 180, 320; dynastic ambitions for son's succession, 187, 191, 295; personality cult, 68, 178, 186; policy of self-reliance, 176, 179, 185, 187, 228; principles of nonintervention and independence advocated in nonaligned movement, 181, 187 and n, 189; Soviet distrust of, 68, 82, 186–87
Kim Yong Nam, 69
Kirenga River basin, timber resources of, 217
Kirgiz SSR, 230; industrial output growth, 232, 233 (table)
Kissinger, Henry, 50
Kono, Yohei, 266n
Korean peninsula: Acheson statement of *1949*, 306; arms race in, 197, 198–99, 324; concept of cross-recognition of two Koreas, 195, 197, 199; German-model coexistence suggested by USSR, 69, 177, 180, 196–97, 198, 199; reunification question, 11, 69, 81, 176, 177–78, 180, 188, 195, 196, 197; Soviet capability for limited military intervention in, 272–73; Soviet concerns, 11, 43, 69, 81–82, 175 and n, 176–78, 180, 195, 273; Soviet policy options, 196–99, 320–21; security concerns, 319–21; standoff between two Koreas, 5, 10–11, 67–69, 195, 197, 319–20, 321; as trouble spot, 25, 54, 56, 59, 198, 319, 320; UN representation question, 193, 199; U.S. policy options, 197–99, 306, 319–21, 324. *See also* North Korea; South Korea
Korean War, 35, 38, 68, 121, 178, 188, 262
Korean Workers' Party (KWP), 69, 187n; Sixth Congress of (*1980*), 191, 192
Kosaka, Zentaro, 141
Kosygin, Alexei, 134, 144, 179, 181, 205n, 266 and n, 286, 296
Kovalenko, Ivan (I. I. Ivkov), 31, 49, 51, 178n, 257n, 264
Krasnaya zvezda, 46
Krasnoyarsk krai, gas resources of, 245
Kunashiri, 121, 123 (map), 124, 125, 126, 127, 128, 131, 146

Kunayev, D. A., 182
Kurile Islands (Chishima), 8, 21, 32, 38, 42, 48, 52, 121, 123 (map), 262; Japanese claim based on treaties of *1855* and *1875*, 124, 125, 127; Japanese claim negated in *1945* and *1951*, 125–27, 220; in *1955–56* peace negotiations, 130–31; official Japanese interpretation of term, 128, 147; Soviet bases on, 18, 146–47, 225, 291; within Soviet 200-mile zone, 141. *See also* Northern Territories dispute
Kuznetsk basin, coal resources of, 217

Lande, Carl, 16
Laos, 307; Chinese–Vietnamese rivalry in, 72, 321; Soviet influence in, 1, 3, 44, 71, 84, 154, 165; Soviet trade with, 204–05 (table), 206, 209; Soviet vs. U.S. trade with, 169 (table); Soviet–Vietnamese rivalry in, 164–65; Vietnamese domination of, 42, 71–72, 87, 164–65, 321; Vietnamese troop strength in, 165
Latin America, 41
Lenin, Vladimir Ilich (Ulyanov), 35, 37
"liberation movements." *See* "national liberation movements"
Libya, Soviet arms supplies to, 185n, 186n
Licensintorg, 221
Lieberthal, Kenneth G., 95, 96
limited military intervention, possible Soviet targets, 272–73, 289
limited nuclear threat, 299
Lin Biao, 99n
Liu Shaoqi, 285n
Li Xiannian, 192
Lockheed bribery scandal, 139

MacArthur, General Douglas, 121
McCarthy, Joseph, 33
machinery: Siberian vs. total USSR output, 242, 243 (table); Soviet exports of, 208, 221, 226; Soviet exports to China, 209, 223; Soviet imports from Japan, 142, 203, 210, 214, 217, 219–20; Soviet products not competitive with Western quality, 208
Malacca Straits, 153, 295
Malaya, post-World War II Soviet influence in, 285
Malaysia, 6, 43, 88, 213, 322; ASEAN member, 10; and Cambodian issue,

161–62; Chinese minority resented, 25, 155, 161, 291; communists of, 4, 161; Five-Power Defense Pact member, 4, 155; Malacca Straits claimed by, 153; relations with Soviets, 79, 171, 291; Soviet trade with, 202, 204–06 (tables), 206, 207 (table); Soviet vs. U.S. trade with, 169 (table), 297 (table); stance toward China vs. Vietnam, 19–20, 158, 161–62, 291; suspicions of China, 25, 158, 322; U.S. relations with, 307
Malik, Yakov, 130
Manchu Empire of China, 5, 34
Manchuria, 67; Russo–Japanese encounters, 32, 261; Soviet occupation of, 38, 261; vulnerability to Soviet attack, 268, 272
Manila Pact, 4, 154
manned strategic bomber, 308
manufactured goods: Siberian vs. total USSR output, 242, 243 (table); Soviet exports of, 208, 220–21; Soviet exports to China, 209, 223–24; Soviet imports from Japan, 142, 203, 210, 214, 215, 216, 219
Maoism, 47, 49, 64, 87; revision, 103–05, 107
Mao Zedong, 4, 6, 15, 35, 68, 140, 192; Asian form of Marxism of, 285n; conflict with USSR, 95, 133, 287
Marcos, Ferdinand, 16, 17, 168
market socialism, Chinese, 105–06
Marshall, Andrew, 275n
Marxism: in East Asia, 4; Mao's Asian form of, 285n
Marxism-Leninism, 44, 54; rhetoric as the surviving aspect of, 86; role in Soviet view of Asia, 29–30
Massawa, Soviet military facility at, 289, 292
Matchanov, N. M., 182
Mathieson, R. S., 220
Matsumoto, Shunichi, 130 and n, 131, 132
Mazurov, Kirill T., 182
meat, Soviet imports of, 205, 207 (table)
merchant fleet, Soviet, 210–11; ship repair, 169, 209
metallurgy, Soviet, 249; Siberian vs. total USSR output, 242, 243 (table); technology transfer to Japan, 221

metals: Soviet exports of, 142, 208, 213–14; Soviet imports of, 209, 210, 224

metalworking industry, Soviet, 219–20; Siberian vs. total USSR output, 243 (table)

Middle East, 52, 84, 314; CENTO, 285; Islamic revival, 36; oil, 42, 52, 278, 289, 294, 326; security concerns, 270, 278, 312, 318; Soviet arms supplies to, 185 and n, 293; Soviet position in, 1, 3, 33, 41, 260, 277, 291–92; U.S. influence eroding, 292

MIG-25 aircraft, 291; defection incident of *1976*, 140–41, 221; supplied to Syria, Libya, Algeria, 185n

MIG-21 aircraft, 186n

MIG-23 aircraft, 185, 186 and n

Miki, Takeo, 134, 137, 139, 149

military equipment sales. *See* arms supplies and military aid; foreign military sales

military intervention, limited, possible Soviet targets, 272–73, 289

military involvement, indirect, 62, 63–64, 88, 91, 275, 280, 289, 300–01

military strength: political-psychological use of, 275, 280, 282; rationale and purpose, 89, 91; Soviet–U.S. comparisons, 1, 18, 40, 62, 274–75, 278, 279–80, 293–94, 308; Soviet–U.S. regional comparisons, 18, 258, 266–70, 299, 308; Soviet–U.S. strategic parity, 18, 109, 135, 271, 293, 299 and n, 308; U.S. need of buildup, 307–10. *See also* Soviet Union, military power of

minerals, Soviet resources, 230, 234, 243, 249

Minsk, the, 147, 270, 291

Minuteman missiles, 299n

Mitsubishi, 215

Mitsui, 215

Miyazawa, Kiichi, 137, 138–39

Mizo tribe, 74

Mobutu, General Sese Seko, 7

Mondale, Walter, 77

Monetary Authority of Singapore, 212

Mongolia, Inner, 66

Mongolian People's Republic (MPR, Outer Mongolia), 43, 58, 89; independence of, 35, 66; Soviet dominance, 61, 65, 66, 176, 260; and Soviet proposal for collective security system, 287; Soviet trade with, 296, 297 (table); Soviet troops in, 267, 286; Treaty of Friendship and Defense with USSR, 97 and n, 292, 327

Mongol population of China, 66

Mongol threat to Russia, 32, 37, 284

Montgomery, Field Marshal Bernard, 23

Moscow Narodny Bank (MNB), 211, 212–13

most-favored-nation status, 251; U.S.–China, 51; USSR–Japan, 142; USSR–Vietnam, 226

multipolarism, 62

Muslims: nationalism of, 45; Soviet Central Asian, 36. *See also* Islam

Mutual and Balanced Force Reduction, 318

MX missile, 308

Naga tribe, 74

Najin, North Korea, 185, 274n

Nakhodka, 211

nationalism: of China, 64, 104, 107; in East and Southeast Asia, 5–6, 86, 156; in Eastern Europe, 61; as element of communist ideology, 6; of Japan, 81; of Muslims, 45; of Vietnamese communists, 79, 156, 161, 166

"national liberation movements," 5, 50, 58–59, 86

NATO (North Atlantic Treaty Organization), 6, 32, 39, 40, 78, 256, 283, 285, 326; Chinese support for, 7, 314, 318, 324; disarray of, 20; Pershing missile deployment, 41; priority over Asia for Soviet military deployment, 97, 256, 270; in U.S. defense strategy, 293

naval exercises, joint U.S.–Australian–Japanese, 4, 8

naval power: Japanese, 18, 279n; limitation problems in Indian Ocean, 324; Soviet, in Asian waters, 3, 4, 18, 155, 267, 269–70, 293 (*see also* Soviet Pacific Fleet); Soviet facilities in Red Sea region, 18, 289, 292, 293; Soviet facilities in Vietnam, 13, 18, 153, 154, 155, 162, 166, 293, 318; Soviet support bases in Far East, 18, 44, 273–74, 286, 291; Soviet threat of interdiction of sealanes, 279, 281–82, 293–94, 309, 318;

U.S., 9, 293 (*see also* U.S. Seventh Fleet);
    U.S. strengthening required, 309; West-
    ern joint maneuvers, 4, 8
NEAC 2200/1200 computer, 220
Nemuro (Habomais) Straits, 130, 291
Nepal, 74
Nerchinsk, Treaty of (*1689*), 34
New China News Agency, 139, 181n
"newly emerging forces" movement, 283
New York Times, 12
New Zealand, 264; alliances, 4, 154, 155,
    285, 327; Soviet trade with, 206 (table),
    206, 207 (table); Soviet vs. U.S. trade,
    297 (table)
Nianlong Han, 137
"*1941* complex," 33
Nixon, Richard M., 50, 55, 288
Nodong Sinmun, 182, 188, 190, 191
nonaligned movement: Belgrade con-
    ference (*1978*), 181; Havana meeting
    of, 51; North Korean espousal of prin-
    ciple of nonintervention by big powers,
    181, 189
nonferrous metals, 249; Siberian vs. total
    USSR output, 243 (table); Soviet ex-
    ports to Japan, 213–14; Soviet imports
    of, 209
noninterference in other nations' affairs,
    principle of, 87, 94n, 98n; North
    Korean espousal of, 181, 189; Soviet
    circumvention in Czechoslovakia, 287
non-use of force principle, 87, 94n, 98n
Northeast Asia: as area of tension, 41, 54,
    69, 75, 78–79, 81, 255, 312–13; Soviet
    military buildup in, 78–79, 291, 293;
    Soviet stake in, 38, 41, 43, 58, 60–61;
    U.S. policy options, 312–13; U.S. strate-
    gic position in, 54, 77, 78–79, 262 and
    n, 279
Northern Star Gas Project, 218
Northern Territories (Kurile Islands) dis-
    pute, 8, 69, 121–51, 311; Chinese role
    and stance in, 48, 70, 122, 133, 138–39;
    history of Russo–Japanese treaties,
    124–25; history of World War II and
    peace agreements, 125–28; Japanese
    claim, 32, 42, 122, 124–25, 128,
    138–39, 147–48, 221; Japanese claim
    weakened in fishing rights negotiations,
    141–42; Japanese popular opinion on,
    148; Japanese sentiment seen fading by

Soviets, 52; in peace negotiations of
    1955–56, 129–32, 147; peace treaty
    made contingent on solution of, 55,
    131–36, 138, 144, 147–48, 149; Soviet
    fortification and strategic use of islands,
    18, 21, 78, 145, 146–47, 150, 225, 256,
    274n, 291, 293; Soviet "interim mea-
    sure" proposal, 134, 149; Soviet intran-
    sigence in, 81, 121–22, 129, 138,
    141–42, 144, 151, 312–13, 326; Soviet
    occupancy of islands, 38, 142
North Korea (DPRK), 10–11, 17, 35, 42,
    58, 61, 175–93, 319–20; armaments,
    185–86, 324; Cambodian issue stance
    of, 45, 68, 188, 190, 192; China not
    criticized by, for attack on Vietnam,
    188–89, 192–93; China tilt of, 176,
    187–88, 192, 228, 257, 294; Chinese
    anti-Maoism opposed, 192, 228; Chi-
    nese arms aid to, 185, 320; default on
    debt, 69, 183, 184 and n, 228; defense
    budget, 228; economic problems,
    183–85, 228; espousal of principle of
    nonintervention within nonaligned
    movement, 181, 189; international
    trade, 182–84, 297 (table); Kim person-
    ality cult, 68, 178, 186; leadership suc-
    cession issue, 187, 191, 295, 321;
    orientation in Sino–Soviet conflict, 25,
    45, 67–69, 82, 176, 179, 181–82, 184
    and n, 187–93, 320; reaction to
    Afghanistan invasion, 189–90, 192; re-
    action to Sino–Japanese treaty of *1978*,
    190; recent disenchantment with China,
    69, 190–91, 192; refusal to join CMEA,
    187, 228; and Soviet Union (*see* Soviet–
    North Korean relations); suspicious of
    U.S.–Japanese ties, 190, 191; trade with
    Japan, 184, 228, 320; U.S. and, 306,
    307, 320, 321, 328; U.S. informal rela-
    tionship desired by, 82. See *also* Korean
    peninsula
North Vietnam, 72. See *also* Vietnam
North Yemen, 3
nuclear facilities of China, Soviet consid-
    eration of preemptive strike on, 108
nuclear power, 247; Soviet technology ex-
    ports, 246
nuclear submarines, Soviet, 97, 258
nuclear test ban treaty, limited
    U.S.–USSR, 286

nuclear weapons: arms control negotiations on, 324; of China, 39, 259, 271n,
286; limited theater threat, 299; proliferation of, 308; regional deployment
by USSR in Asia, 66, 109, 268, 270,
278, 293, 299; strategic, Soviet, 18, 40,
258, 270, 278, 293; strategic, Soviet–
U.S. parity, 18, 109, 135, 271, 293, 299
and n; strategic, U.S., 39–40, 299n,
308; U.S. theater deployment needed,
308; U.S. umbrella, 262, 293, 308

"objective trends," 46, 54
Occidental Petroleum Company, 248
Oder–Neisse border line, 140
OECD (Organization for Economic Cooperation and Development), 143
Ohira, Masayoshi, 136
oil: Chinese shipments to Japan, 15, 52;
Mideast, 289, 294, 326; Mideast, Japanese dependence on, 42, 52, 278 and
n, 326; Sakhalin, 70, 218, 248; Siberian
output, 242; Siberian resources and development, 52, 110, 143, 218, 240,
244–45, 247, 325; Soviet exports, 246,
247, 253; Soviet shipments to Japan, 70,
142, 210, 213, 218; Soviet shortage predicted, 118, 227, 325–26; Tyumen project, 143, 218, 222, 240, 247
Okhotsk, Sea of, 21, 40, 268, 274n; passages to, 279, 293
Okinawa, 121, 134, 177, 309
oligarchies, 17
Oman, 292
one-man political systems, 17
OPEC (Organization of Petroleum Ex-
porting Countries), 52
Outer Mongolia, 58, 61. See also
Mongolian People's Republic

Pacific Basin, Soviet economic interaction
with, 229, 234, 253–54; oil exports
doubted, 247, 253
"Pacific Community," need discussed, 12,
327
Pacific Ocean: sharing of Western defense
burden in, 19, 281, 304, 309; Soviet
position in, 3, 4, 13, 18, 32, 40, 44,
62–63, 78, 147, 150, 269–70, 278, 293;
Soviet–U.S. fleet comparison, 18,
269–70, 274–75, 278; strategic ballistic
weapons in, 40; threat of Soviet inter-

diction of sea-lanes, 279, 281–82,
293–94, 309, 318; U.S. contingent
strength in, 278; U.S. defense strategy
in, 293; U.S. weapons buildup in, 40,
76, 304. See also Soviet Pacific Fleet;
U.S. Seventh Fleet
Pakistan, 312, 318; China and, 3, 73, 74,
84–85; Japanese aid to, 9; SEATO
member, 285; U.S. aid to, 10, 44, 80,
84, 292, 308
Pak Song Chol, 182
paper and pulp mill development projects, Soviet–Japanese, 217
Paracel Islands, 73
Park Chung Hee, 17, 43, 193
parliamentarianism, 86
peaceful coexistence, principle of, 87, 94
and n
Peng Dehuai, 99n
Pen Sovan, 165
Peoples' Daily (Korea), 190
People's Republic of China (PRC). See
China
Pershing missiles, 41
Persian Gulf, 33, 56, 277, 292, 314, 326;
Brezhnev nonintervention proposal,
291n; increased U.S. presence in, 278,
292
Peter the Great, Czar, 34
petrochemicals: Siberian vs. total USSR
output of, 243 (table); Soviet–Japanese
trade, 219
petroleum products: Siberian output, 242;
Soviet exports of, 208, 210. See also oil
Petropavlovsk, 18, 274, 295
Petrov, Dmitrii V., 39
pharmaceutical products, 219
Philippines, 6, 43; ASEAN member, 10;
bilateral shipping arrangements with
USSR, 170; and Cambodian issue,
161–62; communist guerrillas of, 88,
168; internal instability, 16, 17, 322;
Islamic rebels, 87, 168; Soviet trade
with, 206 (table), 206, 207 (table); Soviet
vs. U.S. trade with, 169 (table), 297
(table); U.S. ally, 4, 49, 154, 278, 285,
291, 327; U.S. bases in, 4, 16, 76, 79,
154, 177, 304
pipe, Soviet imports from Japan, 210, 213
pipeline projects, Siberian, 218–19, 240,
242n, 254
Podgornyi, Nikolai V., 107–08

Poland, 37, 246; border accepted by Germany, 140; crisis of *1981,* 1–2, 41, 53, 64, 113, 119, 157, 260, 263n; Soviet invasion threat, 318

polarization, danger of, 283, 284, 319, 327, 328

Politburo, Soviet, 54

"politics of strength," 50

Pol Pot regime, Cambodia, 71, 72, 158–59, 167, 290, 322; Chinese supplies for guerrillas, 160, 167; North Korean support for, 68, 188

Polyansky, Dimitri S., 150–51, 261n

population, world, "socialist camp" share of, 45

port call privileges: Soviet, in Vietnam, 153, 154, 166; Soviet vs. U.S. fleets, in ASEAN ports, 155, 162

port facilities, Soviet, 18, 175, 216, 273–74; Red Sea region bases, 289, 292, 293; Vietnam bases, 13, 155, 162, 293, 318. *See also* Vladivostok

Portsmouth, Treaty of (*1905*), 124–25, 127

potash fertilizers, Soviet exports to Japan, 213–14

Potsdam agreement of *1945,* 58, 126, 133

Pravda, 31, 32n, 139, 195, 266

precious metals, Soviet exports of, 210; to Japan, 142, 213

precision equipment, Japanese exports to USSR, 220

prevention of nuclear war, treaty negotiations, 288

Primakov, E. M., 39

primary products and raw materials: Soviet exports of, 208, 253; Soviet exports to Japan, 142, 210, 213–14, 216; Soviet imports of, 206, 207 (table), 208, 209, 227

"progressive forces," 30, 44, 50, 53

proxy military involvements, 56, 62, 63–64, 88, 91, 275, 280, 289, 300–01

Prybyla, Jan, 15

Pueblo incident, 187

Rand Corporation, The, 95, 255n, 267n

raw materials. *See* primary products and raw materials

"reactionary forces," 30; Chinese abetment charged by Soviets, 102

Reagan, Ronald, 20, 317

Reagan administration, 55, 119; aid to Pakistan, 80; aircraft carrier program of, 309; American "drift" in Asia reversed, 4, 9–10, 60; and arms control, 26, 113; China policy of, 20, 77, 317–18; confrontational stance toward USSR, 113; foreign policy goals of, 60; F-16 aircraft sales to South Korea, 199; and human rights issues, 26; Indian Ocean buildup, 9, 27; lack of subtlety in foreign affairs, 86; and Taiwan, 14, 20

Red Sea, Soviet bases, 289, 292

regional development integration, Siberia, 238–41, 244

regional security, 291–94, 300; arms control, 324–25; China, 258–60, 313–19; Indochina, 319, 321–22; Japan, 260–64, 310–13; Korea, 319–21; regional arms production capabilities growing, 324, 325; U.S. role in Asia as sine qua non of stability, 307–10, 319, 327; U.S.–USSR strength comparisons, 18, 258, 266–70, 299, 308

religious-fundamentalist rebels, 87, 88. *See also* Islam

Republic of China. *See* Taiwan

Republic of Korea. *See* South Korea

revolutionaries, Asian, 86–87. *See also* "national liberation movements"

rhetoric, Soviet, 29, 30, 35, 40, 44–46, 54, 58, 76

rice: Soviet exports to Vietnam, 159; Soviet imports of, 205, 207 (table), 208, 209

rolled ferrous metals: Soviet exports of, 208, 249; Soviet imports of, 209, 210

Romania, 7, 100n, 181; communist party of, 98n; stance toward Afghanistan, 189

Roosevelt, Franklin D., 125–26

Roosevelt, Theodore, 124, 127

RSFSR (Russian Soviet Federated Socialist Republic): agricultural growth, 232, 233; Eastern, investment, 231 (table), 250; Eastern, population problem, 235–36. *See also* Siberia

rubber, Soviet imports of, 203, 206, 207 (table), 208, 209 and n, 227; synthetic, 208, 219

Russia, czarist, 33–34; foreign policy of, 37, 60; geopolitical vulnerability, 32; history of Northern Territories dispute with Japan, 124–25, invasions of, 32, 284

Russians, ethnic, 63; and China policy, 109
Russo–Japanese Treaty of *1925*, 125
Russo–Japanese War (*1904–05*), 124, 261, 284

SA-9 surface-to-air missile, 268
SA-7 surface-to-air missile, 185
SA-6 surface-to-air missile, 185, 268
Sakhalin (Karafuto), 38, 217; conceded to Russia in *1875* treaty, 124, 127; divided by Treaty of Portsmouth (*1905*), 124, 125, 127; Japanese occupation of north (*1918*), 125; in *1955–56* peace negotiations, 130–31; oil and gas, 70, 218, 248, 263n; southern, Japanese claim negated in *1945*, 125–27; strategic importance to USSR, 147
Sakhalin Continental Shelf Oil and Gas Cooperative Exploration Project, 218
SALT (Strategic Arms Limitation Treaty): SALT I, 288; SALT II, 41, 55; verification, 318
San Francisco Peace Treaty (*1951*), 126–28, 133, 147
Sato, Eisako, 134
Saudi Arabia, 292
sea-lanes, threat of Soviet interdiction of, 279, 281–82, 293–94, 309, 318
SEATO (Southeast Asia Treaty Organization), 44, 84, 285
Second African–Asian Conference (*1964*), 285 and n
security: Soviet concept of, 32n, 110, 259; Soviet concerns, 255–58; traditional Russian search for, 32; U.S. concerns, 22, 304–10, 327. *See also* defense; military strength; regional security
Selemdzha River basin, timber resources, 216
Semichastov, I. F., 147
Senkaku Islands, 70
separatist movements, Asian, 87
Shaba crisis (*1978*), 7
Shigemitsu, Akira, 137–38
Shigemitsu, Mamoru, 131
Shiina, Etsusaburo, 137
Shikotan, 121, 123 (map), 124, 125, 126, 127, 128, 147; brief Soviet offer of return to Japan, 130–31, 147, 149
Shima, Colonel, 265n

shipping, Soviet, 210–11; USSR–ASEAN bilateral companies, 169–70
ship repair, in Soviet–Singapore trade, 169, 209
Shtikov, Colonel General T. F., 175n
Siberia, 32, 37, 42, 53, 175; agricultural growth, 232–33; agricultural problems, 234–35, 243; American investments, 51, 218–19, 247–48, 263n, 325–26; branch bias of development decision-making, 239, 252; coal output, 242, 243 (table); coal resources and development, 217–18, 245, 247; development obstacles, 234–40, 252; development potential, 110, 230–31, 234; Eastern, energy deficit of, 242, 248; Eastern and Western, nomenclature, 229–30; energy industry, 229, 234, 242 and n, 243 (table), 325; exports from, 217–18, 242, 245–49, 253–54, 325; forestry development projects with Japan, 217, 248; hydroelectric power potential, 245; in-and-out commodity flow, 242–43; industrial output, 242, 243 (table); industrial output growth, 232, 233 (table); investment, 231, 233–34, 244, 250, 251, 254, 311n, 325–26; Japanese development participation sought, 21, 55, 81, 143, 146–47, 295; Japanese interests in development, 9, 52, 70, 143, 214; Japanese participation and investment, 210, 216–19, 247–48, 325; Japanese reluctance in development participation, 51, 143, 148, 325–26; as Japan's quid pro quo for Northern Territories and peace treaty, 136, 148; labor shortages, 234, 235, 237, 243–44; lack of regional development coordination, 239–40, 252; military installations, 78, 97; mineral resources, 230, 234, 243, 249; natural gas resources and projects, 218–19, 240, 244–45, 248, 254; oil output, 242, 247; oil resources and development, 52, 110, 143, 218, 240, 244–45, 247; population problem, 235–36, 237–38, 240, 243; specialized nature of development, 241–44; strategic value, 63; timber production, 242, 243 (table), 248–49; timber resources, 217, 234, 243, 248; Tyumen oil and gas project, 143, 218, 240, 247; U.S. missile threat to, 40;

Virgin Lands program, 233, 234–35; wartime relocation of industries to, 38, 231, 234; weak infrastructure as development obstacle, 234–35, 238, 240

Siberian Intervention (1918–22), 32, 261

Sihanouk, Prince Norodom, 68

Singapore: ASEAN member, 10; bilateral shipping arrangements with USSR, 169–70; and Cambodian issue, 161–62; economy of, 12; Five-Power Defense Pact member, 4, 155; MNB branch in, 211, 212–13; relations with Soviets, 170, 171; repair of Soviet shipping, 169, 171, 209; Soviet trade with, 204–06 (tables), 206, 209. Soviet vs. U.S. trade with, 169 (table), 297 (table); stance toward Vietnam vs. China, 20, 158, 161–62; U.S. relations with, 307

Sino–Japanese–American entente, 2, 7, 13, 14, 46, 264–66, 312, 326; attraction for a united Korea, 177–78; effect on Sino–Soviet relations, 7, 74–75, 258–59, 260, 264; effect on Soviet–Japanese relations, 70, 81, 135, 147, 150, 264; as reaction to Soviet military buildup and behavior, 54, 150, 280, 289; Soviet perception and fear of, 39, 47–48, 70, 75, 78, 135, 257, 258–59, 289

Sino–Japanese relations, 74, 134–35, 225–26, 288, 289; competition in Southeast Asia, 53; credits to China, 225; oil shipments to Japan, 15, 52; trade, 12, 50, 70, 100n, 142, 143 (table), 224–25, 296, 298–99 (charts), 311; trade agreement of 1978, 224; trade complementarities, 224; trade contracts, 224–25; transfer of technologies to China, 224, 266; U.S. encouragement of, 145, 311 and n, 312; USSR analysis and apprehension of, 3, 39, 42, 45, 46, 47–48, 53, 70, 98, 100, 102, 135, 136–39, 144, 145–46, 177 and n, 225, 263, 264–66, 311; viewed as nonmilitary by Japan, quasi-military by China, 265 and n

Sino–Japanese Treaty of Peace and Friendship (1978), 7, 8, 47–48, 70, 100 and n, 144, 145–46, 177, 224, 263, 289–90, 311; anti-hegemony clause of, 48, 70, 100 and n, 137–38, 144, 145,

159, 177n, 225, 290; Korean reaction, 190; U.S. and, 48, 145, 177n

Sino–Soviet relations, 43–44, 64–69, 74–75, 90, 93–114, 119, 166; accommodation incentives and scenarios, 21–22, 26, 52, 82, 112, 119, 295, 308; Afghan rebels aided by China, 74; as basic force in Asian political changes, 283; border, 21–22, 24–25, 259, 260; border clashes of late 1960s (Chenpao), 94, 267, 287 and n; border concessions by Soviets, 96 and n; border defense, Soviet, 18, 66, 71, 78, 97, 256, 260, 267–68, 271, 272, 277, 287; border units, Chinese, 268, 271; China's inflexibility, 280, 282; Chinese "expansionism" charged, 35, 47, 82, 102; Chinese "militarization" charged, 103, 105, 106; Chinese military threat potential to USSR, 258–60, 265, 271; Chinese polemics, 96n, 139, 285; conflict, 5–6, 43, 50, 59–60, 61, 65, 94, 95, 107, 223, 258–59, 283, 286, 306; conflict of interests rationalized in ideological terms, 94, 103–04; counterrevolutionism charged by Soviets, 102; effect on allegiance of communist parties, 111; future prospects for, 112–14, 119, 304, 313–14, 319; hegemonism allegations by China against USSR, 20, 40, 296, 314; hegemonism allegations by USSR against China, 40, 47, 103, 105, 107; historical and geopolitical differences, 5, 35, 36, 100, 259; impact on Japan, 137–38, 145, 146, 225–26; implications for South Korea, 195; implications of Sino–Japanese–American entente for, 7, 74–75, 258–59, 260, 264; intermittent negotiations, 65–66, 83, 87, 88, 96 and n, 99, 312; as irritant on Soviet behavior toward West, 109–10; Khrushchev polemics vs. Brezhnev "stick," 95; mutual fear, 6, 7; mutual questioning of their socialism, 44, 94, 105–06, 181; in the 1950s, 38, 58–59, 283, 285–86, 315; in the 1970s, 94–101, 283; in the 1960s, 107, 133, 283, 285; nonaggression treaty proposal, 96 and n; North Korean orientation in, 25, 45, 67–69, 82, 176, 179, 181–82, 184 and n, 187–93, 320; preemptive Soviet mili-

Sino–Soviet relations (continued)
tary action feared, 314, 316; preemptive strike against Chinese nuclear facilities considered, 108, 259; racial and nationalistic feelings, 21, 65, 109; rivalry in Indochina, 42, 43, 51, 71–73, 89–90, 153, 160–61, 319, 321–22; rivalry in South Asia, 73–74, 314; rivalry in Third World, 7, 98, 102, 111, 259, 287; rivalry in Vietnam, 71–73, 225; Sino–Japanese rapprochement as sore point in, 3, 47–48, 98, 100, 135, 136–39, 264–65, 311; Soviet anti-China military action designs rebuked by U.S., 286, 288; Soviet economic aid of 1950s, 223; Soviet fear of modern China, 2–3, 33, 40–41, 103–06; Soviet goals, 55–56, 64–67, 74, 82–83, 95, 99, 264, 286–87, 295; Soviet leadership's thinking on China deemed unified, 108–09; Soviet military threat to China, 260, 267–68, 272, 276, 286, 295, 313; Soviet normalization efforts, 55–56, 65, 82, 95–99, 107, 319; Soviet perception and rhetoric, 35, 40–41, 44, 46–48, 52, 82, 101–07; Soviet polemics, 95, 96 and n, 98, 139; Soviet policy failure analyzed, 99–101; Soviet policy of "carrot and stick," 95–99, 264, 295; Soviet policy of containment of China, 40, 66–67, 74, 82, 95, 153, 154, 286, 323; Soviet stance during Chinese attack on Vietnam, 42, 51, 72, 94, 155, 157, 171, 259; Soviet "Vietnam connection" as irritant, 157; strategic indigestibility of China, 23, 66–67, 88, 259–60; subversion efforts by Soviet intelligence, 99 and n; trade, 43, 96, 202, 203, 204–06 (tables), 206, 208, 209, 223–24, 296, 297 (table); trade agreements, 223; traded products, 223–24; U.S. as determining factor in, 112, 113, 280, 313–14, 315–16; and U.S.–Soviet détente, 50, 59–60, 98, 99, 111, 283, 288–89

Sino–Soviet Treaty of Friendship and Mutual Assistance (1950), 283, 285; abrogated by China, 65, 95, 268

Sino–U.S. relations: as basic force in Asian political change, 283; Chinese motives for normalization, 112, 119; Chinese venomous attacks of 1960s,

286; diplomatic relations, 7; limits on, 25–27, 52, 280, 307n; most-favored-nation status, 51; normalization, 4, 13, 34, 39, 45, 46, 47, 264, 288, 306, 314–15; normalization agreement of 1978, 177n–78n, 290; security cooperation explored, 99, 289, 304, 306, 313–19, 328; Southeast Asian interests' convergences and divergences, 321–22; Soviet perception of, 34, 39, 45, 46, 47, 49, 50–51, 52, 53, 78, 82, 98, 102, 138, 177n–78n, 288–89, 315–16; Soviet repudiation proven counterproductive, 289, 316, 318; and Soviet–U.S. détente, 50, 59–60, 98, 99, 111, 283, 288–89; Taiwan issue, 14, 20, 25, 53, 77, 90, 286, 314–15, 318; trade, 12, 52, 297 (table); U.S., Reagan administration, 20, 77, 317–18; U.S. arms supplies, 23–24, 47, 55, 77, 78, 313–14, 316, 317–18; U.S. "evenhandedness" between China and USSR, 315, 317; U.S. policy choices, 22–27, 306–07, 313–19, 326; U.S. policy modulation, 316–17; U.S. public opinion, 313 and n

Sladkovsky, M. I., 47

Slavinsky, Boris N., 33

Slavs, USSR, and China policy, 109

socialism: abandonment in China charged by Soviets, 44, 94, 105–06; abandonment in USSR charged by China, 94, 181; vs. capitalism, 54, 203; limited appeal of Soviet model, 91

socialist "camp" and community: expectations vs. reality of progress of, 45, 53; failures and decline in Asia, 45, 53, 61; financing of intracommunity trade, 212; recent victories, 50; Soviet charge of Chinese betrayal of, 102–03; Soviet energy exports within, 246 and n; Soviet self-image as leader of, 34–35, 37, 46; trading bloc concept abandoned, 203

Socotra, Soviet military facility on, 289, 292

Sofia, Bulgaria, 1980 meeting of Soviet-bloc countries in, 189

Solomon, Richard H., 22

Somalia, 3, 166, 289

Sonoda, Sunao, 144, 146

South Asia, 87, 324; increased Soviet attention to, 38; Sino–Soviet rivalry in,

73–74, 314; Soviet–American competition in, 80, 84–85; Soviet influence in, 3, 61, 73, 74, 75, 80. *See also* India

South China Sea, 3, 83, 153, 155, 275, 290

Southeast Asia, 71–73, 153–73; Chinese minorities resented, 17, 25, 154, 155, 291; Chinese position in, 19–20, 25, 71–73, 89–90, 153, 154, 155, 158, 160–61, 295, 321–22; increased Soviet attention to, 38, 153; Japanese role in, 8, 42, 156, 173, 257n; Sino–Japanese competition in, 53; Sino–U.S. convergence and divergence of interests, 321–22; Soviet analysis of trends, 40, 47, 51; Soviet goals in, 3 42, 43, 51, 71, 154–55, 257, 295; Soviet goals in conflict with Vietnamese goals, 165–66; Soviet influence and ties in, 3, 42, 71, 72–73, 79–80, 155, 164–65, 291 (*see also* Soviet–Vietnamese relations); Soviet involvement, cost–benefit question, 83–84; Soviet military presence in, 153, 155, 162, 163, 274, 321–22; Soviet-owned banking activities in, 212–13; Soviet policy strategy and tactics in, 155–56; Soviet trade, 204–06 (tables), 206, 207 (table), 208; U.S. military presence in, 4, 154–55, 162, 322; U.S. policy options, 172–73, 275, 306–07, 321–22, 324; U.S. position in, 4, 25, 27, 41, 50, 79, 153, 154–55, 156, 162–63, 309; U.S.–Soviet competition in, 79–80, 83–84, 153–58 passim, 275, 291; U.S.–Soviet trade comparison, 169 (table); Vietnamese strength in, 153, 155, 321; Vietnam's procommunist "empire," 3, 71, 72, 154, 155, 165; Western alliances, 4, 154, 155, 156–58. *See also* ASEAN; Indochina

South Korea, 10–11, 17, 43, 319–20; attitude toward communist neighbors softening, 193; China and, 194, 195, 320; Chinese trade alleged, 192 and n, 320; defense spending, 78, 320; economy of, 12, 45; internal instability, 16–17; international trade, 12, 184; Japan's relations with, 8, 42, 77, 176, 320; raw materials needs of, 278–79; Soviet gestures toward, 69, 81–82, 181n, 187, 188, 193–95, 320; Soviet travel relaxa-

tion toward, 69, 193–94; U.S. and, 4, 6, 11, 25, 49, 77, 321, 327; U.S. arms supplies to, 198–99, 320, 324; U.S. security pact with, 277, 285, 320; U.S. troops in, 11, 41, 76, 176–77, 262n, 278, 309, 320, 321; U.S. troop withdrawal proposal, 4, 9–10, 75, 76, 256, 302, 304; view of Sino–U.S. rapprochement, 25. *See also* Korean peninsula

South Vietnam, 1, 71, 72

Southwest Asia: Soviet power projected into, 33, 153, 291–92, 324; Soviet–U.S. rivalry in, 41, 44. *See also* Persian Gulf; Middle East

South Yakutia Coal Development Cooperation Company, 217–18. *See also* Yakutia

South Yemen: Soviet influence in, 1, 3, 80, 135; Soviet military facilities in, 18, 289, 292, 293; Soviet treaty with, 292

sovereignty and territorial integrity, principle of, 87, 94n, 98n; limitation based on proletarian internationalism, 287

Soviet Academy of Sciences, 55

Soviet alliance system, 61, 63, 92, 97, 292–93, 294, 327; anti-hegemony countercoalition, 288–91. *See also* friendship treaties, Soviet

Soviet–American Trade Agreement of *1972*, 51

Soviet Far East Fleet, 291. *See also* Soviet Pacific Fleet

Soviet–Japanese economic ties and trade, 51, 81, 142–43, 146, 213–23, 263n; actual vs. potential, 42–43; agreements, 70, 142, 215, 216–19 passim, 221; chemicals, 142, 210, 219; coal, 142, 210, 213, 214, 217–18, 247; coastal trade, 214; compensation agreements, 216, 247, 251; complementarity of trade needs, 142, 214; credits granted to USSR, 215–16 and n, 217, 218, 219, 247–48, 325; gas, 70, 218–19, 247–48, 263n; growth expected, 44, 210; intrusion of Japan's China connection on, 142, 142–43 (tables), 225–26, 253, 296, 298–99 (charts), 311; locational factor, 210, 214; negotiations, 147, 215, 221–22; oil, 70, 142, 210, 213, 218, 247, 248, 263n; petrochemicals, 219; problems of, 221–23, 325; products

Soviet–Japanese economic ties (continued) traded, 142, 210, 213–14, 215; Siberian development cooperation, 9, 143, 146–47, 148, 210, 214, 216–19, 247–48, 325; statistics, 142 (table), 202, 203, 204–06 (tables), 297 (table); technology transfer, 216, 219–21; timber, 142, 210, 213–14, 217, 248–49; Trade Treaty of 1957, 142; Tyumen project, 143, 218, 222, 247

Soviet–Japanese relations, 31, 37–38, 50, 69–71, 121–51; accommodation of 1941, 24, 38; anti-hegemony clause issue, 70, 100 and n, 137–38, 144, 145–46, 177n, 225; diplomatic recognition of USSR in 1925; 125; diplomatic relations restored in 1956, 129, 132, 147; early post-World War II relations, 60, 69–70, 129; fishing rights issue, 69, 131, 134, 141–42, 221; good neighbor treaty proposals by Soviets fruitless, 137, 144–45, 147, 311; implications of Sino–Japanese–American entente for, 3, 70, 81, 135, 147, 150, 264; improvement a Soviet goal, 20–21, 42, 52, 53, 55, 70, 87, 132–34, 137, 147, 295; intermittent hard-line strategy of USSR, 268; Japanese internees in Siberia, 130, 131, 261; Japanese "militarism" charged, 35, 49, 78, 81, 261 and n; Japanese military threat potential to USSR, 260–64, 265–66; Japanese sanctions in Afghanistan issue, 8, 51, 150, 263n; Japanese security concerns, 263, 279, 280–81, 311; Korea not a problem, 176; Manchurian encounters, 32, 261; MIG-25 defection incident, 140–41, 221; mutual residual fear based on past enmity, 261 and n; 1955–56 peace treaty negotiations, 129–32, 147, 149; 1956 Hatoyama visit to Moscow, 131–32; 1956 joint declaration, 132, 133; in 1970s, 134–48, 149, 221–22; in 1960s, 132–34, 149; 1973 Tanaka visit to Moscow, 135–37; 1973 joint communiqué, 136, 137, 141; peace treaty obstacles, 55, 131– 40, 144, 147–48, 149; potential "Finlandization" of Japan, 308; Siberian Intervention of Japan (1918–22), 32, 261; Sino–Japanese rapprochement as sore spot in, 3, 42, 48, 69, 70, 98, 100, 135, 136–39,
144, 145–46, 222, 225–26, 263, 264, 289–90, 311; Soviet analysis and rhetoric, 35, 40, 46, 48–49, 52; Soviet "carrot and stick" policy, 81, 264, 295; Soviet military buildup near Japan, 18, 78–79, 146–47, 264, 268, 286, 291, 293, 295, 313; Soviet military maneuvers near Japan, 78, 139, 145, 147; Soviet military threat offset by U.S. presence, 263, 310–13. See also Northern Territories dispute; Soviet–Japanese economic ties and trade

Soviet–Mongolian Friendship and Defense Treaty, 97 and n, 292, 327

Soviet–North Korean relations, 25, 42, 175–93, 228, 319–21; in Afghanistan issue, 189–90, 192; disinterest in Brezhnev's collective security proposal, 287; "dominationism" of USSR, 166, 178, 181, 187, 192–93; independent stance of Kim Il Sung, 176, 179, 185, 187 and n, 189, 192–93, 228, 260; Kim Il Sung distrusted by Soviets, 68, 82, 186–87; limited North Korean dependence, 187, 228, 294–95; mutual aid treaty, 133, 292, 327; in the 1970s, 81–82, 179–86; before 1970, 58, 61, 133, 178–79, 285; North Korea as buffer for USSR, 176, 178; North Korean rebukes to USSR, 181; perceptions of each other, 186–88; port of Najin protocol, 185; port privileges sought by USSR, 274n, 295; recent rapprochement, 69, 191–92; Sino–Soviet rivalry for influence in North Korea, 25, 45, 67–69, 82, 176, 179, 181–82, 184 and n, 187–93, 198, 228, 320; Soviet aid, 178, 179, 201, 228; Soviet arms supplies, 68, 178, 179, 185–86, 198–99, 257, 320, 324; Soviet credit, 183–84, 185, 201, 228; Soviet policy options, 196–97, 294–95; Soviet position on Korean reunification, 11, 69, 81, 177–78, 180, 188, 195, 196, 197; strategic importance of North Korea to USSR, 11, 38, 67, 69, 175, 187, 295, 320–21; trade, 43, 69, 175 and n, 178, 182–85, 183 (table), 201, 202, 204–06 (tables), 206, 207 (table), 208, 209, 226, 228, 296, 297 (table)

Soviet Pacific Fleet, 269–70, 275n, 278; aircraft carrier, 208, 309; air cover insufficient, 270, 274; anti-Chinese orientation of, 97 and n; deployment during Chinese attack on Vietnam, 155, 275, 290; increased strength, 8, 18, 40, 44, 63, 147, 269; inferior to U.S. Seventh Fleet, 269–70, 274–75; inventory of, 269; in Northeast Asian waters, 18, 78, 147, 279; nuclear submarines, 97, 257; port call privileges denied to, by ASEAN nations, 155, 162; in Southeast Asian waters, 153, 162; tonnage, 18, 267, 269; Vietnamese ports used by, 3, 44, 153, 154

Soviet State Committee for Science and Technology, 215, 219

Soviet Trade Unions, 15th Congress of, 98n

Soviet Union: agricultural growth, 118, 232–33; "Asianness" of, 35–37; Asian territory and population, 31, 35, 57; banking, 211–13; centralized administrative structure as obstacle to regional development, 239–40; a conservative, bureaucratic society, 86, 91, 114; demographic trends in labor force, 117; domestic problems, 57, 63, 91, 117–18; Eastern region, industrial output, 232, 233 (table); Eastern region share of total investment, 230–32, 231 (table), 233–34; economic development, 37, 63, 110, 143, 325 (see also Siberia); economic development strategy, 240–44, 252–53; economic growth rate declining, 53, 117; economic problems, 53, 117–18; energy consumption, 245; energy production, 246–47; energy resources, 229, 234, 244–49, 325; energy shortage predicted, 118, 227, 325–26; ethnic minorities issues, 35, 57, 67, 75, 90; European population concurrence on China policy, 109; European population status, 63; geopolitical vulnerability, 24, 31–33, 57, 258, 273; GNP, 117, 118, 213; hard currency debt, 215; hard currency earnings, 210, 246; hard currency needs, 212, 246; historical factors in perception of Asia, 32, 34, 35, 36, 37, 284–85; industrial production, 53, 243 (table); industrial product quality low, 208; internal East–West dichotomy, 2, 35–37, 233; internal trade, East–West, 242–45; leadership age, 54, 115n–16n, 222–23; leadership division

rumored, 107–08; leadership succession, changes expected, 56, 114–17, 295–96; natural resources, 53, 54, 229, 234, 296, 325 (see also Siberia); post-World War II history, 58–59, 129; popular opinions toward China vs. West, 108; racial attitudes toward Asians, 36, 65, 109; its socialism questioned by China, 94, 181; stagnating standard of living, 118–19; unattractive as revolutionary model of development, 4, 86, 91. See also Communist Party of the Soviet Union; Soviet Union, foreign policy and relations of; Soviet Union, military power of

Soviet Union, foreign policy and relations of: Afghanistan venture (see Afghanistan, Soviet invasion of); alliance system, 61, 63, 92, 97, 292–93, 294, 300, 327; Asia experts, 31, 91, 108–09; Asian conditions analysis, 29, 46–56, 108–09; Asian country status questioned by China, 285; Asian perspectives, 29–37, 43–44; behavior of self-fulfilling prophecy, 305; bilateral shipping arrangements, 169–70; China relations (see Sino–Soviet relations); Collective Security System proposal for Asia, 45, 56, 87, 98 and n, 155, 260, 287, 323; containment policy used, 89, 95; Czech occupation of 1968, 287; declaration of 200-mile zone, 141, 144, 150; dominationism toward its allies, 166, 192–93; economic aid, 61, 89, 98, 201, 223; economic influence limited, 2, 42–43, 61, 168–69, 270, 296, 297 (table); "encirclement" fears, 6, 32, 284–85; European policy, 20, 41, 55, 58, 98, 111, 112, 129, 140, 256, 259–60; expansionist policies, 1–3, 13–14, 32, 58–59, 101, 112, 135, 289, 291–92; foreign affairs analysis terminology, 30, 46, 50, 54; foreign affairs research institutes, 30–31; friendship treaties, 1, 2, 260, 292–93, 327; friendship treaties as harbingers of war, 300; global power image rising, 87, 89, 92, 110, 256–57; Indian relations, 3, 38, 44, 45, 73, 80, 84–85, 90, 283, 291 and n, 296; Indonesian relations, 38, 45, 171, 291, 295, 326; influence largely military in nature, 1–3, 101, 256–57,

Soviet Union, foreign policy of (*continued*) 270–71, 296; "inner core" strategy, 58–59, 61; Japanese relations (*see* Northern Territories dispute; Soviet–Japanese economic ties and trade; Soviet–Japanese relations); Korean concerns, 11, 43, 69, 81–82, 175 and n, 176–78, 180, 195–99, 273 (*see also* Soviet–North Korean relations); military aid (*see* arms supplies and military aid); Mongolian relations, 6, 65, 66, 176, 260, 267, 286, 296; multifront problems, 24, 32, 57, 78, 260, 284–85; *1950*s as Soviet golden age in Asia, 61, 285; "*1941* complex," 33; optimism, 52–53; peace treaty initiatives of *1955–56*, 129; policy direction and priorities, 110–12; policy evaluation, 60–63, 85–92 passim, 99–101, 326; policy goals in Asia, 64, 75, 86, 87–89, 95, 291–96; policy issues and options, 284–96, 300; Polish crisis of *1981*, 1–2, 53, 113, 119, 157, 260, 318; political and strategic importance of Asia for USSR, 37–42, 57–58, 256–57; position in Middle East, 3, 33, 41, 260, 284, 291–92; rhetoric of spokesmen, 30, 35, 40, 44–46, 54, 58, 76; security perspectives, 32 and n, 110, 150, 259, 284–85; self-image as leader of "socialist community," 34–35, 37, 46; setbacks, 13, 44–45, 61, 74–75, 85, 289–90, 291, 326; Southeast Asian relations (*see* ASEAN; Indochina: Southeast Asia; Soviet–Vietnamese relations); South Korean relations, 69, 81–82, 181n, 187, 188, 193–95, 320; South Korean travel relaxed, 69, 193–94; status aspirations, 33–34, 135; successes, 44, 61, 74–75; support for Heng Samrin government in Cambodia, 150, 160, 166, 167; territorial expansion as status symbol, 135; territorial issues intransigence of USSR, 81, 121–22, 129, 138, 312; trade, 2, 42–43, 51, 142–43, 156, 169 (table), 201–28, 246–48, 253, 296, 297–99 (tables) (*see also* trade, international); trade switched from political to economic objectives, 202–06; U.S. relations (*see* U.S.–Soviet relations). *See also* triangle, economic, Soviet–Chinese–Japanese;

triangle, strategic, Soviet–American–Chinese

Soviet Union, military power of, 255–82, 284, 299–300; aircraft, 185, 186 and n, 269, 270, 273, 274, 291, 309 (*see also* Backfire bomber); air forces, 13, 267, 278, 293, 309; bases and deployments structure and objectives, 293–94; budgetary constraints expected in future, 118; buildup, 17–18, 40, 44, 61–62, 150, 255–58, 277, 278, 280, 282, 286, 288–89, 293; capabilities and deficiencies enumerated, 271–73; as cause of end of détente, 13, 113, 135; against China, 18, 66, 71, 78, 97, 256, 260, 264, 267–68, 269, 271–72, 276–77, 286–87, 295; against China, qualitative buildup, 97, 267–68, 286; against China, statistics, 97, 267, 286; concept of "defense" in, 301–02; conventional forces, 255–56, 267–70, 299, 300; effect on thinking of Pacific–Asian nations, 13, 75, 78–79, 80; in Europe, 256–57; exaggeration beyond need, 101, 109–10; in Far East, 18, 44, 268–69, 273–74, 286, 291, 318; goal of Soviets debated, 109–10, 300–01; ground forces in Asia, 267–68, 291, 293; in Indian Ocean, 13, 18, 97, 269, 324; Indochina bases, 13, 18, 153, 154, 155, 162, 293, 318; around Japan, 18, 78–79, 146–47, 150, 264, 268, 286, 291, 293, 295; limited-intervention use of, 272–73; logistical problems, 272, 273, 277; maneuvers near Japan, 78, 139, 145, 147; in Northeast Asia, 78–79, 291, 293; nuclear weapons, 18, 40, 66, 109, 258, 268, 270, 278, 293, 299; in Pacific Ocean, 13, 18, 40, 44, 62–63, 78, 147, 150, 269, 293; Red Sea area bases, 18, 289, 292, 293; in Sea of Okhotsk, 21, 40, 268, 274n, 293; in Southeast Asia, 153, 155, 162, 163, 274, 321–22; strategic vs. regional orientation, 258, 266–67; strategy, 293–94, 299–300; use for political goals, 1–3, 4, 13, 33, 39–40, 56, 75–76, 89, 91, 101, 135, 155, 256–57, 270–71; against U.S. forces in Asia, 267, 291, 293; against U.S. land targets, 40, 268, 299n; Vietnam support bases, 13, 18, 42, 44, 51,

71, 79, 98, 153, 155, 162, 274, 275, 290; in "wars of liberation," 271, 277. *See also* ballistic missiles, Soviet; Soviet Pacific Fleet

Soviet–Vietnamese relations, 3, 35, 43, 44, 56, 71, 135, 158–66; commonality of interests, 153–54; cost–benefit question for USSR, 42, 83–84, 90; economic assistance to Hanoi, 159, 163, 164, 201, 226, 276, 321; independence of Hanoi's nationalist communists as brake on, 79, 156, 166; military assistance to Hanoi, 83, 159–60, 163, 276, 290, 321; Moscow in accord on Cambodian invasion, 43, 51, 156, 160, 170, 290; reaction to Brezhnev's collective security proposal, 45, 287; rivalry in Laos and Cambodia, 164–65; significance for containment of China, 42, 71, 83, 153–54, 155; Soviet aloofness in Chinese attack on Vietnam, 42, 51, 72, 94, 155, 157, 171, 259, 290; Soviet fleet deployed during Chinese attack, 155, 275, 290; Soviet loans, 159, 201, 226, 227; Soviet military bases, 13, 18, 42, 44, 51, 71, 79, 98, 153, 155, 162, 274, 275, 293; Soviet use of Vietnamese ports, 153, 154, 166; strains in, 156, 164–65; trade, 159, 164, 201, 202, 204–06 (tables), 206, 208, 209 and n, 226, 227, 296, 297 (table); Vietnamese dependence on Moscow, 72–73, 154, 159–60, 163, 226–27, 321–22

Soviet–Vietnamese Treaty of Friendship and Cooperation, 42, 51, 71, 97 and n, 150, 153–54, 158–59, 227 and n, 274, 292, 327; advantages for Soviets, 155, 163–64, 226, 274; assets and liabilities for Vietnam, 159–60, 163, 227; defense clause, 98n; defense clause not invoked in Chinese attack on Vietnam, 42, 51, 157; directed against China, 156, 158, 160–61; effects for Soviet Union, 153, 157; implications for ASEAN, 161–62; implications for U.S., 162–63; signing of, 290

Soviet–West German treaty of good will (*1970*), 140

Soya Straits, 274, 291

Soyuzvneshtrans, 211

Spandar'ian, V., 215, 222

specialization strategy for development, 241; in Siberia and Far East, 241–44

"spheres of influence" policy, 58, 284

sports events in USSR, admission of South Koreans to, 194

Spratley Islands, 73

Sri Lanka, 74, 87; Soviet arms aid to, 292

SS-N-18 missiles, 40

SS-20 missiles, 18, 97, 109, 270, 291, 308, 324

Stalin, Joseph, 36, 37–38, 54, 116, 232; gloating over Japan's defeat in World War II, 261n; and Korea, 177; Yalta and Potsdam agreements, 125–26, 129, 140, 149

standard of living: Asia, 12; USSR, 118–19

steel, 253; development of industry planned in Soviet Far East, 217, 249; industrial output in Siberia, 242; scrap, Soviet exports of, 213–14; Soviet foreign trade balances, 249; Soviet imports from Japan, 142, 214; Soviet production and consumption, 249

Stevenson Amendment, to Eximbank Act, 51, 216n, 248, 289

strategic parity, U.S.–USSR, 18, 109, 135, 271, 293, 299 and n, 308

strategic superiority: implications of U.S. loss of, 300, 308; as Soviet aim, 110, 299

strategic weapons. *See* nuclear weapons

Strong, Anna Louise, 285n

"struggle" (Soviet term), 54; class, Chinese revision, 103

"subjective trends," 46–47

submarines: Soviet, 269, 279; Soviet missile-carrying, 258, 268, 269, 278; Soviet nuclear, 97, 258; U.S. missile-carrying, 299n, 308

Sudan, 166

sugar, raw, Soviet imports of, 206, 207 (table), 208

Suharto government, Indonesia, 171, 295

Sukarno government, Indonesia, 283

Sumitomo, 215

"superpower" policies, 62–64, 89, 91–92; "deal" proposals by USSR, 284, 323

Suslov, Mikhail, 44

Su Yu, 265n

Suzuki, Zenko, 173

Sweden, 37
synthetics, 208, 214, 219
Syria, Soviet influence in, 3, 185n, 292

Tadzhik SSR, 230; industrial output
    growth, 232, 233 (table)
Taiwan (Republic of China), 4, 38, 47,
    307; action against mainland China pro-
    posed by, 286; defense spending of, 78;
    derecognition by U.S., 75, 302; GNP
    growth, 12; as Sino–American issue, 14,
    20, 25, 53, 74, 77, 90, 314–15, 318;
    Soviet silence on, 83; Soviet vs. U.S.
    trade with, 297 (table); U.S. arms aid to,
    20, 90, 314; U.S. security treaty with,
    285
Taiwan Straits, 83, 315; crisis of 1958,
    286
Tanaka, Kakuei, 135–37, 149
tanks, Chinese, T-59, 185; North Korean,
    185; South Korean M-48, 186; Soviet
    T-54, T-72, 185 and n, T-62, 186, 268
TASS, 139, 177n
technology transfer, 246, 253, 325; Eu-
    rope to USSR, 254; Japan to China,
    223, 266; Japan to USSR, 216, 219–20;
    USSR to China, 222; USSR to Japan,
    220–21; U.S. to China, 317
Teheran Conference of 1943, 125
textiles, Soviet imports of, 209, 214, 219
Thailand, 6, 43, 56, 213; ASEAN mem-
    ber, 10; bilateral shipping arrangements
    with USSR, 169–70; and Cambodian
    issue, 157, 158, 161–62, 166; Chinese
    minority resented, 17; Chinese ties to,
    158, 160, 161, 321–22; communist par-
    ty in, 4, 162; danger of war with Viet-
    nam, 167–68, 322; history of rivalry
    with Vietnam, 161; internal problems
    of, 17; Japanese aid to, 9; Soviet rela-
    tions with, 79, 170–71; Soviet trade
    with, 204–06 (tables), 206, 209; Soviet
    vs. U.S. trade with, 169 (table), 297
    (table); stance toward Vietnam vs.
    China, 20, 73, 158, 161–62, 291; U.S.
    ally, 4, 49, 76–77, 79, 154, 285, 291,
    329; U.S. foreign aid to, 10, 77; U.S.
    policy, 321–22; Vietnamese incursion
    across border (1980), 167, 171
Third World: ASEAN model of free mar-
    ket system, 172; Chinese–Soviet rivalry

in 7, 98, 102, 111, 259, 287; instabilities
    exploited by Soviets, 1–3, 101, 289; re-
    action to Afghanistan invasion, 45; reac-
    tion to Chinese attack on Vietnam, 72;
    Soviet attentions to, 58, 111–12, 113;
    Soviet courting of bourgeois-nationalist
    regimes, 38; Soviet perception of, 46;
    Soviet trade relations with, 169, 178;
    U.S. tensions, 50
Tibet, 67
timber: Siberian resources, 217, 234, 243,
    248; Siberian vs. total USSR output of,
    242, 243 (table); Soviet exports of, 210;
    Soviet exports to China, 223; Soviet ex-
    ports to Japan, 142, 210, 213–14, 217,
    248–49; Soviet–Japanese development
    projects, 217, 248–49
Time magazine, 265
tin, Soviet imports of, 206, 207 (table),
    208, 224
Togo, Fumihiko, 137
Tomsk oblast, gas resources of, 245
trade, international: ASEAN, 12, 27, 43,
    51, 162, 168, 169 (table), 170; China,
    15, 51; China, alleged trade with South
    Korea, 192 and n, 320; China with
    Japan, 12, 50, 70, 100n, 142–43, 143
    (table), 224–25, 296, 297–99 (tables),
    311; China with North Korea, 183–84;
    China with U.S., 12, 52, 297 (table);
    China with USSR, 43, 96, 202, 203–06,
    204–06 (tables), 208, 209, 223–24, 296,
    297 (table); compensation agreements,
    216, 251; financing, Soviet banks, 212;
    of Japan, China gaining as partner
    against USSR, 142, 142–43 (tables),
    224–25, 253, 296, 298–99 (charts), 311;
    Japan's ascendancy, and tensions with
    West, 18–19, 310; Japan with North
    Korea, 184, 228, 320; Japan with USSR
    (see Soviet–Japanese economic ties and
    trade); North Korea, 182–84, 228, 296,
    297 (table); South Korea, 184, 297
    (table); strains in, 307; USSR, 201–28;
    USSR energy exports, 245, 246–47,
    253; USSR lag in, 2, 42–43, 51,
    168–69, 296, 297 (table); USSR trade
    terms, 169, 178, 208, 325; USSR with
    North Korea, 69, 175 and n, 178,
    182–85, 183 (table), 201, 202, 204–06
    (tables), 206, 207 (table), 208, 209, 226,

228, 296, 297 (table); USSR with
OECD, 143, 213; USSR with Third
World, 169, 178; USSR with Vietnam,
159, 164, 201, 202, 204–06 (tables),
206, 208, 209 and n, 226, 227, 296, 297
(table); USSR with Western Europe, 70,
143, 210, 218, 254; U.S. vs. USSR, with
Asian nations, 168, 169 (table), 296, 297
(table); U.S. with Asia, 12, 27; U.S. with
Japan, 18–19, 22, 81, 297 (table); U.S.
with USSR, 51, 215n, 289, 325. *See also*
credit arrangements, international
transport planes, Soviet, 269, 273, 300
Trans-Siberian Landbridge, 211, 216, 250
Trans-Siberian Railroad, 32, 40, 78, 211,
250, 273; possible Chinese interdiction,
318
Treaty for the Exchange of Sakhalin for
the Kurile Islands (*1875*), 124, 125, 127
Treaty of Commerce, Navigation and De-
limination (Russo–Japanese, *1855*), 124
triangle, economic, Soviet–Chinese–Japanese, 9, 142–43, 224–25, 296, 311
triangle, strategic, Soviet–American–Chinese, 59–60, 99 and n, 111–12,
288–89, 313–19, 323
Trident missiles, 40, 308
Troyanovsky, Oleg A., 137
trucks: Soviet exports of, 208; Soviet exports to China, 209, 223; Soviet imports
from Japan, 214, 220; Soviet industry,
220
Truman, Harry S, 126, 285
Tsugaru Straits, 274
Tsushima Straits, 274
Turkey, 9, 292, 312
Turkmen SSR, 230; industrial output
growth, 232, 233 (table)
Turner, Admiral Stansfield, 117n
"two camps" doctrine, 38, 59
Tyumen oil and gas project, 143, 218,
222, 240, 245, 247, 250

UN Conference on the Law of the Sea,
141
UNCTAD (United Nations Conference on
Trade and Development), 10
Union of Soviet Socialist Republics
(USSR). *See* Soviet Union
United Nations, 133, 181, 226; admission
of Red China to, 288; ASEAN united

in, on Cambodia issue, 10, 160;
hegemonism resolution, 65; Soviet anti-
China stance in, 98; Soviet support of
Vietnamese-sponsored Cambodian regime, 51, 160; two-Koreas membership,
193, 199
United States, 53, 57, 59–60; and
Afghanistan, 41, 55, 84, 135, 309, 317;
and ASEAN, 4, 25, 41, 79–80, 84,
154–55, 156, 162, 170, 291, 322;
ASEAN policy options, 172–73, 306;
ASEAN trade, 27, 169 (table); Asian
allies and coalitions, 2–10 passim, 13,
84, 154–55, 156–58, 277, 285, 291,
307, 326–27; Asian balance in favor of,
3–13, 17, 39, 80, 85, 275, 276, 304,
305; balance of power policy, 50, 60,
304–05; and Cambodian issue, 166,
167; Cambodian policy options, 172,
173, 306, 322; China and (*see* Sino–U.S.
relations); containment policy of, 59,
305; conventional military forces, 293,
308, 309; credibility in Asia impaired, 9,
60, 75, 77, 89, 168, 280, 302–04, 308;
credibility restoration, 76–77, 86, 89,
172, 278; defense planning of, 300,
306, 310–28; defense strategy of, 293;
erosion of Middle East influence, 292;
foreign aid by, 59; foreign economic
policy, 307, 327; foreign military sales,
302, 303 (chart) (*see also* arms supplies
and military aid); foreign policy, clarity
of intentions required in, 305–06; foreign policy consensus lacking, 301, 313;
foreign policy evaluated, 60, 62, 63,
85–86, 89, 302; foreign policy issues
and options, 280–82, 284, 296, 300–28;
foreign policy of *1950*s, 285; foreign
policy under Reagan, 60, 113–14,
317–18 (*see also* Reagan administration);
GNP, 213; and India, 74, 80, 84, 306,
328; Indian Ocean buildup, 9, 27, 40,
76, 80, 256, 278; Indochina policy
goals, 321–22, 328; Indonesian relations, 27, 307, 322, 328; Iranian debacle, 50, 55, 56, 63, 80, 84, 302; Japan
and (*see* U.S.–Japanese relations); and
Korea, 176–77, 319–20; Korean cross-
recognition proposed, 195, 197, 198,
199; Korean incidents (Pueblo, EC-121,
murder of officers in DMZ), 187;

United States (*continued*)
  Korean policy options, 197–99, 321,
  324; and Kurile Islands (Northern Territories), 32, 122, 125–28; military presence in Pacific–Asian region, 18,
  39–40, 76, 162, 172, 256, 269–70, 275,
  277–78, 279–80, 293, 304; need for
  military buildup, 302–04, 306, 307–10,
  327; noninvolvement situations in Asia,
  275; North Korea and, 82, 306, 307,
  320, 321, 328; nuclear capability,
  39–40, 293, 299n, 308; nuclear parity
  with USSR, 18, 109, 135, 271, 299, 308;
  and Pakistan, 10, 44, 80, 84, 292; Philippines as ally, 4, 16, 49, 76, 79, 154,
  278, 285, 291, 327; policy options in
  Southeast Asia, 172–73, 275, 306–07,
  322, 324, 328; "politics of strength"
  abandoned, 50; position in Southeast
  Asia, 4, 25, 27, 41, 50, 79–80, 83–84,
  153, 154–55, 156, 291, 309, 322; presence in South Korea, 4, 6, 11, 25, 41,
  76, 176–77, 262n, 277–78, 309, 320,
  321; proposed troop withdrawal from
  South Korea, security concerns, 22, 300,
  304–10, 327; security treaty with South
  Korea, 277, 285, 320, 328; Siberian
  project investments, 51, 218–19,
  247–48, 311n, 325–26; Soviet Union
  and (*see* détente; U.S.–Soviet relations);
  Soviet–Vietnamese treaty implications
  for, 162–63; strategic position in Northeast Asia, 54, 77, 78–79, 262 and n,
  279, 291; and Taiwan, 14, 20, 25, 47,
  90, 285, 286, 302, 307, 314; Taiwan
  derecognition by, 75; temporary strategic withdrawal from Asia reversed, 4,
  9–10, 75–76, 302; tension with Third
  World, 50; Thailand as ally, 4, 49,
  76–77, 79, 154, 285, 291, 328; trade
  with Asian countries, 12, 27, 168, 169
  (table), 296, 297 (table); uncertainty of
  response to invasions of Cambodia and
  Afghanistan, 302, 309–10; Vietnam defeat, 83, 172; Vietnam defeat consequences, 9, 41, 44, 60, 75, 89, 266, 308;
  Vietnam postwar relations, 83, 163,
  173, 225, 306, 307, 328. *See also*
  Sino–Japanese–American entente; triangle, strategic, Soviet–American–
  Chinese

Uruppu, 124, 127, 128
U.S. Department of Defense, 279; one-
  and-one-half-war strategy of, 76
U.S.–Japan Consultative Committee, 8
U.S.–Japanese relations, 21, 55, 326, 327;
  Bonin Islands and Okinawa returned to
  Japan, 121, 134; defense burden issue,
  8, 19, 81, 310–11; defense cooperation,
  262, 304, 310–13, 318; economic relations and rivalry, 18–19, 22, 42, 80–81,
  310; Japan as U.S. ally, 2, 3–4, 6, 8, 13,
  19, 22, 41, 45, 47, 49, 50, 77, 150, 262,
  310 (*see also* U.S. Japan Mutual Security
  Treaty); Lockheed scandal, 139; San
  Francisco Peace Treaty of *1951*,
  126–28, 147; Soviet perception of, 39,
  41, 49, 53, 76, 78, 80–81, 130, 133,
  262–63; trade, 18–19, 22, 81, 297
  (table); U.S. policy alternatives, 310–13;
  U.S. role in Northern Territories dilemma, 125–28, 147; U.S. support for
  Sino–Japanese peace treaty, 48, 145;
  U.S. troops in Japan, 4, 8, 262 and n,
  263, 278
U.S.–Japan Mutual Security Treaty
  (*1951*), 4, 130, 154, 262, 277, 311–12;
  Chinese approval expressed, 190; Japanese internal opposition declining, 8;
  1960 provisions, 145; Soviet perspective
  of, 47, 48; Soviet protests against, 130,
  133
U.S. Seventh Fleet, 18, 269–70, 278, 279,
  291, 304; aircraft carriers, 270, 308,
  309; diversion of units from Pacific to
  Indian Ocean, 256, 270, 278; port call
  privileges granted by ASEAN nations,
  162; superior to Soviet Pacific Fleet,
  269–70, 274–75; tonnage, 18, 269
U.S.–Soviet relations, 75–86, 301–10,
  322–28; accommodation and cooperation, 302, 304–05, 307, 323–26;
  Afghanistan sanctions by U.S., 150,
  263n; arms control negotiations, 26,
  288, 318, 324–25, 328; arms race,
  109–10, 301; balance of power politics,
  50, 60, 287, 304–05; the China factor,
  2–3, 21–26, 33, 34, 46, 50, 51, 77,
  82–83, 98, 111–13, 283, 288, 313–14,
  315–16, 323; clarity of U.S. intentions
  needed, 305–06, 323; cold war, 59,
  283; cold war renewal, 55, 135; cold

war rhetoric of USSR media, 76; condominium, 312, 323, 328; containment
policies, 59, 89, 305; economic relations,
325–26, 328; financing of Siberian development projects, 51, 218–19,
247–48, 263n, 325–26; "great power
deal" proposals by USSR, 284, 323; in
Korea, 176–77, 320–21, 324; 1972
agreement, 66; in Northeast Asia,
78–79, 81, 262–63; nuclear test ban
treaty, 286; and Polish crisis of 1981, 2;
in South Asia, 80, 84–85; Southeast
Asian competition, 43, 79–80, 83–84,
153, 154–55, 156–58, 275, 321–22,
324; Soviet fears and inferiority notions, 32–33; Soviet internal differences
of opinion, 108, 109; Soviet perception
and rhetoric, 34, 35, 40–41, 46, 49–51,
54–55, 76, 305; Soviet status aspirations, 34; trade, 51, 215n, 289, 325;
U.S. as highest priority of USSR, 41,
56; U.S. confrontational stance under
Reagan, 113, 135; U.S. credit to USSR
limited, 216n; U.S. "evenhandedness"
between USSR and China, 315, 317;
U.S. response to Soviet expansionism as
factor in Sino–Soviet relations, 112,
113; U.S. warning against Soviet attack
on China, 286. See also détente; military
strength
USSR State Bank, 212
Ussuri River, border clashes, 222
U.S. Third Fleet, 18
Uzbeks, 57
Uzbek SSR, 230; industrial output
growth, 232, 233 (table)

Vietnam, 17, 25, 51–52, 71, 86–87;
ASEAN membership inquiry by, 226;
ASEAN split perspectives on, 19–20,
73, 79, 158, 161–62, 291; ASEAN suspicions of, 51–52, 73, 79; Cambodian
invasion, 8, 20, 42, 43, 51, 156, 157,
158–59, 160, 166–67, 290, 309; and
China, 5–6, 43, 47, 71–73, 154, 158,
160–61, 226–27, 275, 321–22; Chinese
attack on, 7, 42, 50, 51, 63, 72, 89,
94–95, 155, 157, 159, 275, 290; Chinese economic aid to, 226, 227, 290;
Chinese ethnic and geopolitical rivalry,
5, 7; Chinese ethnics expelled from

(1978), 158, 226–27, 290; CMEA membership, 71, 159, 163, 227 and n; continental shelf oil and gas resources, 227;
danger of war with Thailand, 167–68;
322; dependence on Moscow, 72–73,
154, 159–60, 163, 226–27, 321–22 (see
also Soviet–Vietnamese relations); domination of Cambodia and Laos, 42,
71–72, 84, 87, 164–65, 321–22; economy of, 159, 163, 164, 226–27; encircled
by adversaries, 6; ethnic and geopolitical rivalry with Cambodia, 5; fierce independence of its leaders, 156, 163;
food shortages, 159, 226; former
Sino–Soviet competition in, 71–73, 226;
historical rivalry with Thailand, 161; incursion across Thai border (1980), 167,
171; international trade, 159, 226–27,
297 (table); Japanese sanctions against,
8; militarization of, 159–60; nationalism
of, 79, 156, 161, 166; power potential
of, 27, 155; as proxy for USSR, 42, 56,
300; unification of, 35; U.S. relations
with, 83, 163, 173, 226, 306, 307, 328;
U.S. retreat from, 75, 83, 153, 266
Vietnam War, 71, 72, 83, 276; U.S. loss as
cause of credibility gap, 9, 60, 75, 89
Vilyui Basin, natural gas resources of, 248
Virgin Lands program, Western Siberia
and Kazakhstan, 233, 234–35, 236
Vladimirov, N., 257n
Vladivostok, 18, 67, 153, 175, 216,
273–74, 285, 291, 318
Vostochny, 216
V/STOL aircraft carrier, 270

Warsaw Pact, 61, 283
"wars of liberation," 271, 277
West Asia, 291; Soviet "breakout in the
Arc of Crisis," 292
Western alliance systems, 154–55,
156–58, 277, 291, 326–27; Asian balance favorable to U.S., 3–13, 17,
156–57, 276; of cold war era, 59, 285;
credibility gap, 302; defense needs,
309–10; need for, 307; in Soviet perception, 54–55, 78. See also Sino–Japanese–American entente
West Germany. See Germany, Federal Republic of
wheat, Soviet imports of, 206, 207 (table)

wool, Soviet imports of, 206, 207 (table),
    208, 214
World Bank, 7, 226
World Festival of Youth (Havana, Cuba,
    1978), 181
World Ice Hockey Championship com-
    petition (*1979*), 194
World Shooting Championships (*1978*),
    194
World University Games (Moscow, *1973*),
    194
World War II, 24, 33, 38, 54, 55, 121,
    173, 261; effect of Soviet Eastern re-
    gions' economy, 231–32, 234; territorial
    cessions to USSR, 125–26, 40
World Women's Basketball Tournament
    (*1979*), 194
Wrangel Bay port project, 216

Xinjiang province, China, 67
Xu Xiangquian, 181

Yakutia: coalfield development, 217–18,
    245, 247; natural gas resources and
    project, 219, 245, 248, 253, 311n
Yakutia Gas Exploration Project, 219
Yalta agreement of *1945*, 58, 125–26,
    133, 140, 147
Yalu River, 67
Yankee submarines, 258
"yellow peril," Soviet fear of, 75
Yi Chong Ok, 192
Yoshida, Shigeru, 127–28 and n, 129,
    130
Yoshida Memoirs, 128 and n
Yugoslavia, 7, 65, 100n

Zeya hydropower station, 239n
Zhang Caijian, 265n, 266
Zhdanov, Andrei, 38
Zhou Enlai, 68, 179, 190, 287, 288
Zinoviev, Boris M., 145